LAND & PROPERTY RESEARCH
IN THE UNITED STATES

LAND & PROPERTY RESEARCH
IN THE UNITED STATES

By E. Wade Hone

With Heritage Consulting and Services

Ancestry®

Hone, E. Wade, 1963-
    Land & property research in the United States / by E. Wade Hone.
        p. cm.
    Includes bibliographical references and index.
    ISBN 0-916489-68-X (hardcover)
    1. United States—Genealogy—Handbooks, manuals, etc. 2. Public land
records—United States—Handbooks, manuals, etc. 3. Land tenure—United
States—Handbooks, manuals, etc. I. Title.
CS49.H66 1997
929'.1'072073—dc21   96-52214

© 1997 E. Wade Hone
Published by Ancestry Incorporated
P.O. Box 476
Salt Lake City, Utah 84110-0476

First printing 1997
10 9 8 7 6 5 4 3 2 1

Printed in the United States of America

This book is dedicated to Eva Bernice Davis, my great-grandmother and best friend, and who has been the inspiration for much of what I have accomplished in life.

Contents

Section 2: State-Land States

Section 3: Federal-Land States

Section 4: Individual Lands

Section 5: Special Interest

Foreword

by William Dollarhide

There are at least three reasons why land and property records are vitally important for genealogical and historical research.

1. Written evidence of people's entitlement to land and property goes back in time further than virtually any other type of record a genealogist might use. Extant land records in Denmark, for example, go back to 900 A.D. The earliest tax lists of England, which name even the smallest landholders—The Doomsday Books—date back to the era of the Norman Conquest, 1066 to 1096 A.D. Of all the historical records of interest to genealogists, land records cover the longest span of time in which a researcher may prove that a person lived in a certain place at a certain time.

2. In America, land and property records apply to more people than any other type of written record. It is estimated that by the mid-1800s, as many as ninety percent of all adult white males owned land in the United States. (The figure is estimated to be as high as fifty percent today.) Therefore, before 1850, the lists of landowners that can be extracted from any county's grantee/grantor indexes are the most complete lists of residents that exist for a county. For example, suppose that in 1840 a twenty-two-year-old John Brown, III, owned twenty acres of land, while his forty-four-year-old father, John Brown, Jr., owned 160 acres, and his sixty-seven-year-old grandfather, John Brown, Sr., owned forty acres, and that they all lived together in the same farmhouse. In the 1840 heads-of-households census, only John Brown, Jr., was listed. But in the courthouse, all three landowners' names are recorded in the county's index to deeds. Clearly, a county's deed indexes can be more complete and more useful in determining the names of the residents of a county than even the early census lists.

3. There have been fewer losses of land and property records than any other type of record. The public records of land sales conducted by the U.S. government are practically one-hundred-percent complete from 1787 to today. And at the county level—unlike birth and death records and civil court records, probates, and other typical court records—courthouse-stored land records were the first to be reconstructed or at least partially reconstructed after loss from a fire, flood, or other disaster. Even in American counties where a courthouse burned to the ground, a genealogist may learn that some land records exist there from the time before the fire. Though not legally required to record the deed in earlier times, most people would not buy or sell property without recording the deed for security purposes. Because of this, old deeds were often re-recorded after the courthouse burned. This fact makes land records more complete than other types of county-wide records.

There are many other reasons for the importance of land records as well, because land records affect many other types of records. The second-oldest set of records available to genealogists are marriage records, which go back in time nearly as long as land records. It is no accident of history that land and marriage records are the two most complete written accounts of early people, particularly for European immigrants to America. There has long been a connection between marriage and land entitlements. The Dower Rights system, the English common law dating back to the time of William the Conqueror, gave a widow entitlement to one-third of her deceased husband's estate. This system was continued in America during the colonial period, and the practice was followed well into the nineteenth century. If a wife had dower rights, her given name was often mentioned in a deed. Even though the wife could not own land in her own name, she retained "veto power" over the sale of the land because of her dower or community property rights. (Some communities subscribed to the recording of a dower release more than others.) The marriage record may no longer exist, but the chances are very good that a land record does.

In Spanish areas of the New World, a system was employed in which a woman was entitled to one-half of her husband's estate. Today this system still prevails in Mexico and several U.S. states which continue the Spanish practice of "community property" in estate settlements between a husband and wife. The importance of recording marriages in the Spanish system was even greater than the English system because of the relationship of land entitlements. In the Spanish system, a woman become owner of one-half of her husband's property upon the day of their marriage—another link between marriage and land records.

Insights into other family relationships can also be gained by tracing records relating to a parcel of land. For example, land records can lead a researcher to the knowledge of a wife's maiden name if she received land as an heir of her deceased father. In the colonial period, and in most states well into the nineteenth century, a married woman could not own land in her own name—it passed to her husband. This fact gives a genealogist a possible connection to the wife's father by identifying each parcel of land acquired by her husband. Following the transfer of ownership of land may be just the clue a genealogist needs to identify the wife's father.

A researcher who is reticent about dealing with the federal government and its millions of public land records will find the job is made easier by reviewing the federal land chapters in this book first. It will be a very rewarding experience. The land entry files of the federal land system, the most useful files for genealogists, include the files from cash sales, credit sales, land donations, and homesteads. In some of these records, a lucky researcher may find the most wonderful genealogical treasures imaginable—an original marriage record torn from a family bible, or perhaps an ancestor's original naturalization certificate. But those who never learn how to access the land entry case files will never know if such treasures await.

Researchers often overlook the importance of land records as a source for genealogical research—probably because land records are often tedious and boring to use and the records do not always give quick gratification to a genealogist seeking the names and relationships of ancestors. But significant, often hidden, clues can be found in land and property records. One needs to take the time to become educated about these valuable resources and learn the specific methods required to access them. This book is the answer to that need.

Land and Property Research in the United States is a priceless addition to the research community; it should be in every library in the country. It is a desk reference any researcher can use again and again. Wade Hone has done fine work in showing what researchers are up against, the nature of land and property records, and how to access them. The organization and flow of this book are outstanding; the genealogical significance of each type of record is well explained. With a comprehensive index, a reader can start anywhere in the book without wading through a myriad of information to find the desired topic. Nowhere else will a researcher find the information as conveniently assembled as in this book. For this reason, *Land and Property Research in the United States* is clearly the most comprehensive and useful review of land and property research for genealogists to date. Become familiar with it. Read it from cover to cover. Take it to the library with you. The more you know about land and property records and how to locate them, the more you will learn about your ancestors.

From the Author

Possession of land has been one of the most ancient causes of dispute among human beings. This single concept has molded nearly every aspect of society as we know it. It has produced kings and queens, soldiers and military leaders, peasants and paupers. Almost every occupation known throughout the world has developed from land and its uses. Land also dictated the need for most non-land-related early records. Probate records often resulted from the importance of property, both real and personal. Marriage records recorded the assurance of property transfers to spouse and heirs, and this is the primary reason why marriage records can be found for much earlier periods than other vital records. Most early criminal and civil court records also involved land transactions. All of these aspects indicate that land has truly resulted in more than a modest contribution to historical and genealogical research.

Prior to the Civil War, more than eighty-five percent of all Americans owned or leased land. Therefore, almost every researcher, whether a seasoned professional or weekend hobbyist, has required land records to document the existence, association, or movement of an individual or ancestral family. While many researchers may feel a sense of historical excitement when finding an ancestor in a land deed, many also fail to understand the importance of such a document and how land can be used to make vital links between generations; they are not aware that it can bridge distant origins and help solve even the most difficult genealogical problems.

Land and Property Research in the United States was created to provide a resource through which researchers can quickly determine the types of land records that are available for the times and places in which their ancestors lived; and so that, based upon that determination, they might also gain a better understanding of how to use the records to provide the answers sought after. The illustrations herein are intended to help the researcher visualize the records being discussed; they serve no other purpose and do not impart additional information. Repositories are listed at the end of each applicable chapter, as are references for further reading. As with any address or other time-sensitive material, these are subject to change. A telephone call to directory assistance can quickly correct the information if a discrepancy is found.

I wish to give special thanks to the many individuals who have made this book possible, each contributing in his or her own way—particularly to my wife, Julie, for supporting the endless hours and expenses that have been encountered in the development of such an immense project, and for understanding and accepting that "one more week" really means "three more months"; to my partners in Heritage Consulting and Services, George Ott and Ted Naanes, for their decisions and suggestions to help organize a seemingly endless dream into a more conceivable reality, and for helping me understand the limits of my own expectations; to William Dollarhide and William Thorndale, whose devotion to this subject was an inspiration from the very beginning. Thanks to Jim Gegen, Linda Abbott, Linda Brooks and the entire staff of the Bureau of Land Management, Eastern States Division, in Springfield, Virginia, who have been extremely open and cooperative with their assistance; to Andy Senti of the Denver, Colorado, Office of the Bureau of Land Management for his assistance in gathering information for the maps in appendix B; to Stacey Byas at the Suitland Branch of the National Archives, for her patience and assistance with the many difficult and endless questions; to Greg Bradsher at the National Archives, who has my deepest respect, for helping with questions that he himself was unsure of the answers to but, wanting to learn, diligently sought the necessary information. Thanks to the unique Victoria S. Washington for her sense of humor and her constant direction while researching in the Suitland Branch; to the staff at National Archives II in College Park, Maryland, for their support and patience; to Lou Szucs, whose enthusiasm for the contents of this book was present long before the results, encouraging me to work harder to meet such unprecedented expectations. Thanks to Dwight Radford and his wife, Cindy, for the nights spent sharing our dreams and quests, then through the years encouraging each other to make them a reality; to Arden White for his help with the chapters on Spanish and Mexican possession. Thanks to the staff at the Family History Library of the Church of Jesus Christ of Latter-day Saints, for the sharing of information about unusual and often unavailable sources that helped foster a better understanding of the conflicting information sometimes encountered. Thanks to Thomas Aquinas Burke for the use of the maps reproduced in appendix A. Thanks to Elaine Justesen for her valuable input concerning the grammatical and textual format of this book. Thanks to all those whom I've failed to mention—you were no less important. Lastly, I thank my ancestors for their experiences and the legacy they left.

Change is a natural part of progression in society. While every effort has been made to assure the validity of the information presented, know that addresses will change and that publication information may be altered with the reprinting of any book that is referenced here. Undoubtedly, the contents of this book are not flawless. I not only welcome, but wholeheartedly solicit, comments, observations, and recommendations concerning the subject of land and property. This book is a collection of my own experiences and frustrations, and the results from research of conflicting information found through the years. It is my attempt to better understand the sources, laws, and applications of the many land records that exist. Though I wished to present the many volumes necessary to thoroughly understand each and every aspect of our nation's land and property records, reality suggested a basic overview be written first. This first volume will hopefully allow not only me, but others as well, a chance to build upon and expand the knowledge and understanding of the contributions of land and property to our history, and thus to the lives of us and our ancestors. Through the contents of this book it should be recognized that land and property, when creatively utilized, can provide more answers, more often, than any other single source available.

E. Wade Hone

Section 1:
Pre-U.S. Possessions

An Introduction to Pre-U.S. Possessions

The Spanish, British, French, and Mexican governments each have held vast amounts of land within the present-day boundaries of the United States. Each country had its own system of land distribution and record keeping. Among the more fascinating sources for genealogical research are the land records administered by foreign governments before the United States took possession. While standard documents were created for each individual grant, an abundance of documents detailing family background and present status were also created by each government. These land records are among the least-understood resources for family history research during the pre-Revolutionary War era. Although the types of information vary from one place to another, an understanding of some basic characteristics of land disbursement by each nation can be employed to answer specific questions.

As European powers struggled over the control of territory in the "New World," one country's citizens would be ushered in, displacing the previous settlers and their claims to lands. The British, in 1664, were the first to begin honoring previous land claims as they displaced the Dutch government in Manhattan. A century later, they again promised to recognize existing land claims made by the Spaniards in Florida. Spanish residents were given a limited time to sell their "legitimately titled" property to British subjects or pledge their loyalty to the British crown. In 1783, Spain offered a similar program to the British as the Spaniards regained control, even though the British had failed to recognize many of the earlier Spanish claims as legitimate.

Similar agreements were also exercised between Spain and France. Though more than once the same lands were transferred between the two nations, they remained close allies. Not only did they honor the existing rights of one another's citizens, but they often left many of the existing government administrators in place, and their land grant processes often continued uninterrupted.

Mexico also recorded the claims of Spanish settlers living there before secession from Spain in 1821. The tradition of honoring existing land grants is nothing new to world history, but the quality of records has certainly increased with time.

British records generated by the colonists are particularly valuable for periods before the Revolutionary War. Crown charters and grants were an integral part of each colony and eventual state. The British certainly played the largest role in pre-U.S. possession. Chapter 2, British Possession, is but a brief presentation in contrast to the hundreds of volumes otherwise necessary to analyze and inventory all land records generated by the British administration.

Each chapter in this section, Pre-U.S. Possessions, is designed to provide enough historical background to determine boundary changes and authorities presiding over each area of the present-day United States. Applicable maps and samples from various record sources have also been included. The objectives of this section are to show

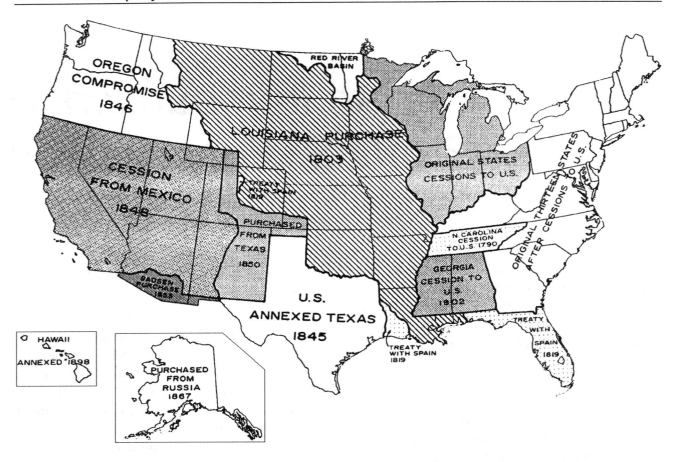

Acquisition of U.S. Territory

how the records were generated and how to access them. Specific guidelines are used to define applicable content. The selection criteria include:

- Major record collections and indexes
- Records covering more than one state, or
- Records covering more than just a portion of a state

- Records applying to a wide spectrum of immigrant or migrant populations

Effort has been made to refer the reader to other sources which will provide additional or more detailed information on the records, repositories, and accessibility for each area.

Spanish Possession

HISTORICAL BACKGROUND

Spain was the first European nation to publicly claim an empire in North America. This empire was once thought to encompass the entire "New World" simply by virtue of discovery. Though the records of Spanish colonization efforts differ from one location to another and over time, the recorded legacy can provide enlightening, educational resources to assist both genealogists and historians.

The earliest Spanish dominions date back to the early 1500s (figure 1-1), when the Franciscans and Jesuits attempted to "Christianize" the Native Americans. Not until the next century, about 1670, were the Spanish possessions first contested by another foreign presence. At that time, British inhabitants began migrating farther south with the founding of a settlement called Charlestown (in present-day South Carolina). At the same time, Spanish settlement efforts encountered difficulty in the west as the Spaniards attempted to colonize Santa Fe and areas along the West Coast.

The size of Spain's New World empire varied greatly during Spain's tenancy. At one time, during the eighteenth century, Spain claimed almost all of the southwestern and central United States, southern portions of Georgia and the Mississippi Territory, and all of present-day Florida. These possessions were additions to their claims on present-day Mexico and many of the Caribbean islands.

Though expeditions worked their way into California and New Mexico as early as the mid-1500s, explorers were continually battling natives and natural elements. Not until the late 1600s were Spanish settlements solidly and successfully established in the west. At that time, Spanish settlements were being established in east Texas, Santa Fe, and throughout the Floridas.

Spain claimed a vast acreage, but successful colonization was slow. The Spaniards tried to recruit settlers from other, allied countries, focusing on strong Catholic nations such as Ireland. The failures of early settlement attempts discouraged many settlers, and enticements were often inadequate. Many of the early colonizers were Catholic priests who were motivated by cause rather than adventure.

Although the Spaniards kept records, most were of their explorations, trading ventures, and religious conversion activities. The earliest group of surviving Spanish land grants was recorded in what is now New Mexico in the 1680s. However, historical evidence of Spanish grants exists for select individuals as early as the 1500s in the Texas gulf and Florida regions.

Most recorded Spanish development did not begin until the 1763–70 period. The French, facing a loss to the British in the French and Indian War, secretly ceded the Louisiana Territory to Spain in 1762; this was a significant recovery of what Spain had considered its rightful domain all along. It held further importance when Spain lost

Figure 1-1. A 1562 map of Spanish holdings in North America as found at National Archives II in College Park, Maryland.

both East and West Florida to the British in 1763. (See figure 1-2.)

The Spanish finally recognized the need for better management of their colonization efforts in order to retain existing possessions. They considered the newly defined borders of the Louisiana Territory an excellent buffer zone between encroaching British and French foes in the east and north, and newly focused areas of growth and trade in Texas and northern Mexico.

In 1783, at the close of the Revolutionary War, both East and West Florida again came under Spanish rule. Most of the grants made by the British in West Florida had never been occupied or improved, simplifying Spain's administrative takeover. East Florida's population had grown considerably, so Spain adopted a policy similar to that of the British by honoring existing legitimate land claims and allowing resale by individual landholders. They were, in fact, more diligent than the British in this regard.

In an attempt to induce population growth and expansion, land grants were given liberally by the Spaniards in all areas, including the Louisiana Territory. Many U.S. citizens, including the famed Daniel Boone, were among the many settlers enticed by generous Spanish offers. Town structures and governments were developed, and selected sites were reserved for Catholic monastery use.

In the Louisiana Territory, Spain often continued the French method of dispersing land in long, narrow river strips. Although land speculation was formally condemned by the Spaniards, incentives for individuals and singular entities spurred large concentrations of Catholic acquisitions in Lower Louisiana. In the Floridas, headright colonization similar to that of early Virginia was used. Under Spanish headrights, an allotment was made for each member of the family, including slaves.

Missions were also successfully expanding along the West Coast, and the area now known as New Mexico was becoming more populated with stable settlers. The Spanish government began a new system of colonization in the west, granting separate farm lands for pueblos and specifically encouraging individual residence on the farms. This provided better maintenance of agriculture and stock, and benefited the existing towns and *presidios*. (A *presidio* was a military settlement that usually included the families of soldiers.) In the Texas region, land was granted according to petitions and was dispersed using the Spanish measurement of leagues.

The Louisiana Territory presented the most problems for Spain. Finally, in 1800, through another secretly arranged treaty, Spain signed over this entire territory to the French. Spain's decision was a result of difficulties encountered in administrating such a large colonization effort, compounded by problems with traders and Native Americans.

Not until 1802 did the United States learn that Spain no longer held authority over the Louisiana Territory. The U.S. government soon began negotiations to secure its own interests there. It succeeded in 1803, obtaining the entire territory through the Louisiana Purchase.

Spanish possession continued only in the Floridas and the southwest (including Texas) after the turn of the nineteenth century. Boundary disputes with the United States in the Mississippi Territory resulted in a second treaty,

signed in 1795, which reduced the Spanish Floridas to almost their present-day size. West Florida continued to include the parishes of Louisiana east of the Mississippi River. These Louisiana parishes were annexed by the United States in 1810, after local rebellions succeeded in ousting the Spanish from power in that region.

The Treaty of 1819 transferred Spain's final possessions in the southeast to the United States. The actual exchange did not take place until Spain officially withdrew from that area for the last time, in 1821 (figure 1-3). That same year, Mexico claimed independence from Spanish control. This succession, including the entire southwest region and Texas, concluded all of Spain's authority in the present-day United States. This transition occurred almost 350 years after Columbus' initial voyage.

Many Americans, from as far north as New Hampshire and Connecticut, are mentioned in a variety of documents from the Spanish era. Loyalists, Catholics, Scots-Irish from the Carolinas, early settlers from southern Georgia, and many others who were persecuted for one reason or another all found haven among the settlements occupied by the Spanish. Though these areas were

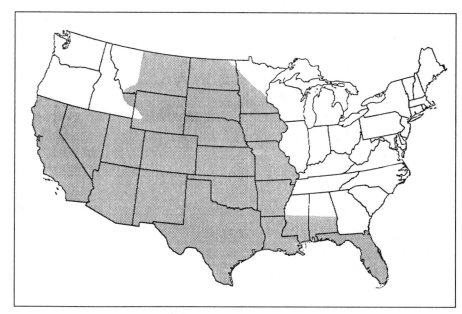

Figure 1-2. Approximate Spanish claims, 1762–1800, in relation to modern state boundaries. East and West Florida were excluded from 1763–83.

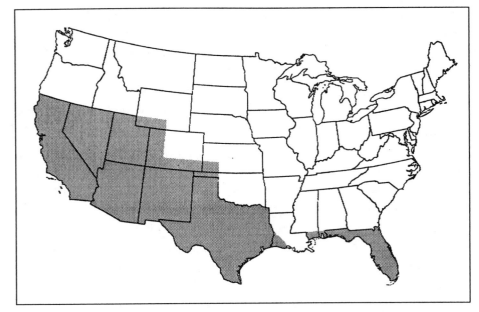

Figure 1-3. Approximate Spanish Claims, 1800–21, in relation to modern state boundaries. Parts of West Florida were annexed in 1810. Though the remainder of the Floridas were sold to the United States in 1819, official possession did not begin until 1821.

controlled by Spain, land records of the Spanish possessions should never be overlooked or discounted when researching inhabitants from America, Spain, Britain, or France.

Many Spanish settlers stayed and continued to prosper long after the United States assumed authority in the former Spanish possessions. These settlers contributed to the prosperity of their communities and left numerous descendants who intermingled with the rest of the American population. Being the first, and almost the last, to lay official claim to American soil, the Spaniards and their descendants have made a significant contribution to the history of land and property in the United States.

THE RECORDS

Very little has been preserved of the individual land grants that were distributed by the Spanish before 1763; the earliest records are mostly of historical value. While captivating in cultural content, they provide little linkage between individuals or other record sources. They do, however, serve as the foundation upon which other records

were later gathered and recorded.

Spanish archives in the east testify mostly of grants given to soldiers before 1763. These grants describe the soldiers' allotments in *peonias* (for foot soldiers) and *caballerias* (for squires or mounted soldiers). A *peonia* was measured as a piece of ground fifty feet by one hundred feet for planting, with extra garden and woodland space, and a small pasture—not much by early American colonial standards. The *caballeria* was one hundred by two hundred feet for planting, plus five times the amount a *peon* (foot soldier) was granted for other amenities. The grant stipulated that a house had to be built and crops cultivated within a period specified by the crown. While this policy of organized development worked in Spain's eastern possessions, the western settlements were more concerned with mere survival.

Thus, property ownership did exist before 1763, and councils were petitioned for land ownership. These councils often permitted occupancy and use of lands, though requests for final deeds were often ignored. In effect, residency was honored as long as occupation and cultivation continued. Actual ownership was bureaucratically retained by the crown. The "Consejo de las Indias" (Council of the Indies) held these powers of land distribution. Unfortunately, only references and innuendos remain, with few organized records for individual documentation.

For the genealogist's purposes, Spanish land records were begun in earnest in 1763. They were recorded in duplicate or triplicate for all transactions. One copy was kept in the recorder's office and one was sent to the "Archivo General de Indias" (Archives of the Indies), based in Seville,

Spain. These records are continually being inventoried, treated for preservation, and microfilmed for easier access by researchers and scholars.

Spanish land records differ slightly from one place to another throughout America. A wide variety of records are available in a number of repositories. Most are only fragments of the complete original collections. Some specific sources, however, warrant particular attention when initially researching ancestry in Spanish territories. General overviews of these sources follow.

Floridas

Memorials are among the earliest preserved records of the Spanish domain. Their use was initiated when Florida's inhabitants suddenly found themselves under British rule in 1763. *Memorials* were petitions to the Spanish government for written evidence of ownership of lots in cities previously under Spanish possession. Spanish citizens were given a brief period by the British to sell their lands and evacuate, or become subjects of the king of England. Regardless, they were required to establish positive proof of ownership. These records also include petitions made to Spain after 1783 to reinforce claims of ownership before or during Britain's occupation. The term *memorial* has also been used to mean "petition" in some histories and record sources.

Most memorial records encompass the years 1790 to 1821 and largely affect the area of East Florida (east of the Apalachicola River). Records created before 1790 mostly involve the city of St. Augustine. Most memorials are in Spanish; some exceptions are found in English. The records provide handwritten or typed indexes for many bundles; they are indexed by the grantee or claimant.

The memorials for the Floridas are housed in the Spanish Land Grant Archives, a name designated for the Spanish collections at the Florida State Archives in Tallahassee. They have also been microfilmed for distribution and are available at the Family History Library of The Church of Jesus Christ of Latter-day Saints in Salt Lake City, Utah, and through its many family history centers. A copy is also stored at the National Archives in Washington, D.C. (Note that these records are sometimes found cataloged under the Board of Commissioners for Private Land Claims, as they were eventually used to settle many private land claims.)

The **Spanish Land Grant Files** are another important early record source for the Floridas. They can provide such information as:

* Date of arrival
* Acreage of land and the improvements thereon
* Name of original grantee
* Name of present claimant
* A vague description of the property location
* Nationality under which the original grant was obtained
* Type of claim (e.g., patent, military grant, etc.)
* Date of instrument
* Surveyor's notes
* Date of presentation

Records *not* found among the Spanish Land Grant Files are the testimonies of witnesses. Testimonies are more often found included with Private Land Claims (see chapter 9, Records Generated by Federal Lands). The Spanish Land Grant Files are currently housed at the Florida State Archives in Tallahassee, and duplicates can be found at the Department of Natural Resources of the State of Florida. (See figure 1-4.)

From the late 1780s to approximately 1815, most Spanish grants were dispersed according to the headright system, providing evidence of family members, ages, and relationships which existed at the time of the original grant.

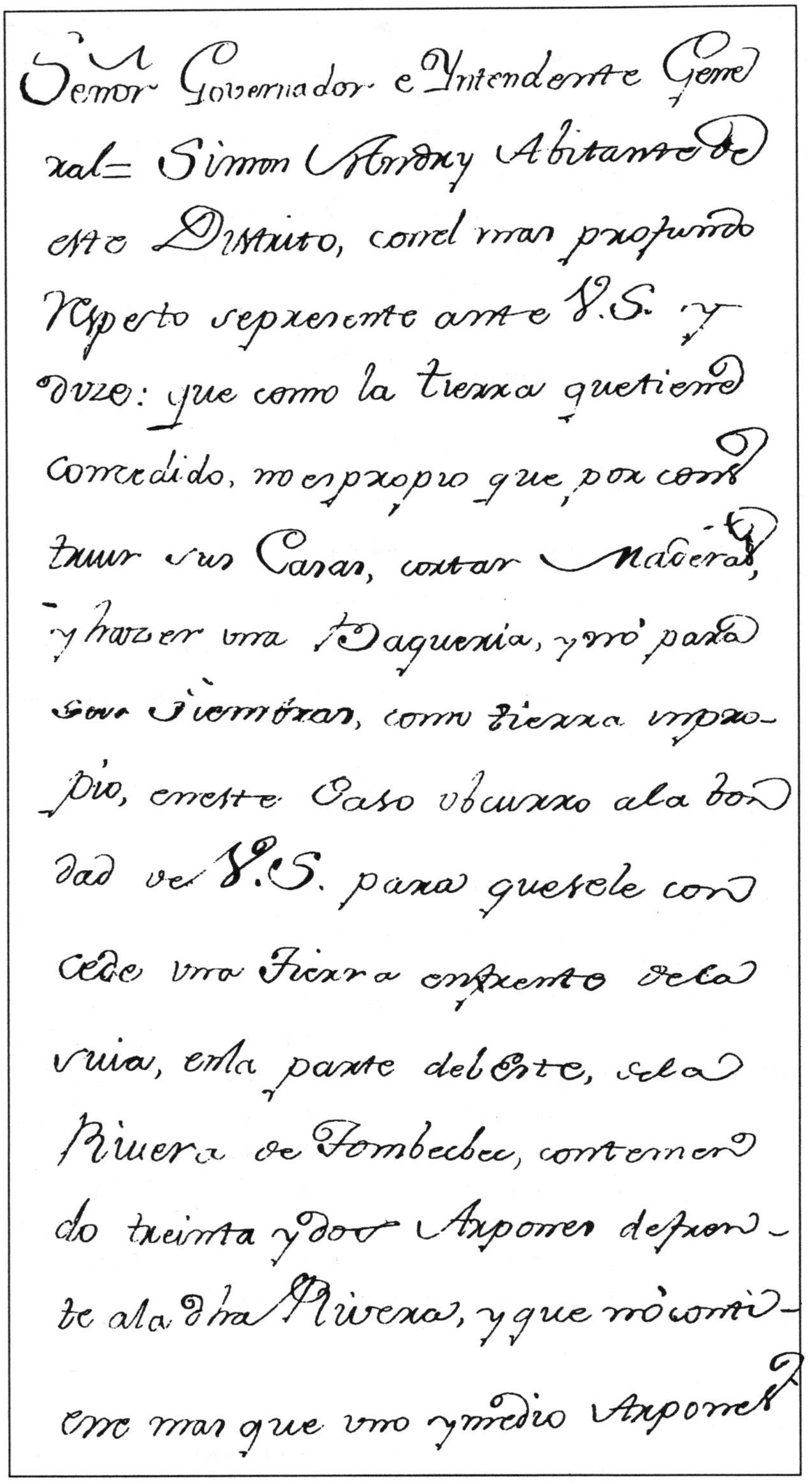
Señor Governador e Yntendente Gene-
ral= Simon Andry Abitante de
esto Distrito, con el mas profundo
respeto representa ante V.S. y
dize: que como la tierra que tiene
concedido, no es propio que, por con-
tener sus Casas, cortar Maderas,
y hazer una Vaqueria, y no para
sus siembras, como tierra impro-
pio, en este caso ocurre a la bon-
dad de V.S. para que se le con-
cede una Tierra enfrente de la
suia, en la parte del Este, de la
Rivera de Tombecbee, conteniendo
do treinta y dos Arpanes de fron-
te a la dha Rivera, y que no conti-
ene mas que uno y medio Arpanes

Figure 1-4. A grant to Simon Andry; from the Spanish Land Grant Files.

Headright grants were used by Spain in the Floridas from the late 1780s to 1815. These headrights were similar to those given by the English in Virginia; they provided lands for families who could pay their own passage and remain self-sufficient after arrival. Upon meeting the appropriate criteria, they would receive title to the land.

The original Spanish headright offered land as follows:

- One hundred acres to the head of household
- Fifty acres for each additional white or "colored" person in the family, regardless of age

Revisions in 1803 produced the following criteria:

- Fifty acres for the head of house
- Twenty-five acres for persons age sixteen and over
- Fifteen acres for persons age eight to sixteen
- No land for those under age eight

These records can serve as a census substitute when land was received under such circumstances because they show the names and ages of the entire household, including slaves. (See figure 1-5.)

The system of headrights did not effectively accomplish the Spanish objective of boosting the Catholic population in the Floridas. As a result, from 1815 on, grants were received only for service to the crown. Grants were awarded for military service, the building and operating of grist mills, raising cattle, or other unusual contributions.

Another set of valuable records for the researcher are portions of the **Spanish Archives of West Florida**. These records were housed in Baton Rouge until the overthrow of the Spanish by local citizens in 1810. In December of

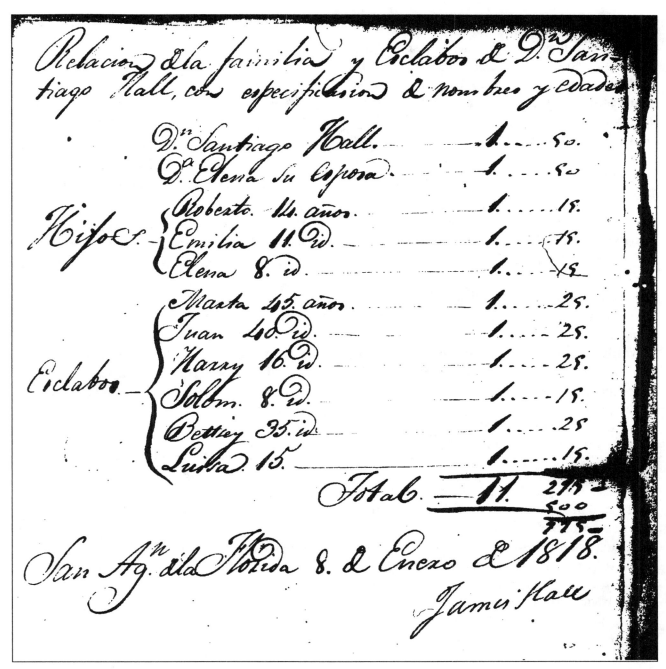

Figure 1-5. Memorial papers from the late 1700s presented in support of a private land claim in 1818. It shows headright acreage granted to Santiago Hall (alias Hames Hall) for his family and slaves.

1810, that area of what is now Louisiana was annexed by the United States. The records cover the years 1782 to 1810 and span eighteen volumes of transcription. They are now housed at the Louisiana State Museum Library in New Orleans. They were microfilmed by the Genealogical Society of Utah in 1963 and are available through the Family History Library. An index has also been published, with an introduction by Stanley Clisby Arthur (see "For Further Reference" at the end of this chapter).

Spanish grants in West Florida differed slightly from East Florida, especially after 1799, when they took on French characteristics from Louisiana. Therefore, a mixture of records inherent to both the Louisiana Territory and the Floridas exist for inhabitants in this area.

Louisiana Territory

Spanish records preserved in the Louisiana Territory began about 1763. Although Spain relinquished control to France in 1800, Spanish administration continued until the United States officially took over on 31 December 1803 through the Louisiana Purchase. Most land records created by the Spanish in this region were never acquired by the United States despite attempts to do so.

After 1770, records in this area were kept in triplicate: one for the office of the notary, one for the governor or intendant, and one for the proprietor. A copy of the notarial records was to be sent to the Archivo General de Indias in Seville, Spain. Many of the records for eighteenth-century Louisiana are now being organized, inventoried, and microfilmed and are becoming more accessible for research. This repository becomes even more important considering the loss of the copies held by the governor or intendants, which were illegally taken to Cuba. Though many records were taken, some remained as the United States began its administration.

Spanish land grants were given to encourage loyalty and inhabitance, unlike the financial trade speculations of the French government. Grants in Louisiana usually involved six to eight arpents of land across a river front, extending back approximately forty arpents in length (an arpent being approximately 0.84 acres). River frontage was critical due to the lack of roads in many areas. Sometimes the grants were distributed in square leagues (three miles square).

No property taxes were charged. After 1795, the Spanish government even gave financial compensation according to the number of family members who were old enough to work. Grant characteristics also included the following:

- Inhabitance and development for three years were required to receive official title to the property

- Signatures were required from the surveyor, a district judge, and two neighbors

- Though age, sex, and color were irrelevant, a distinction was made between free men and slaves. Slaves were not permitted to buy or sell property

- Grants were given to Protestants only if they raised their children as Catholics

- Four-fifths of a land grant was placed in trust for an individual's children and could not be dispersed by the grantee without further litigation

- Dower rights had to be released by a wife before a sale or transfer could be completed. Half of everything acquired during marriage belonged to the wife

After 1797, new settlers in Spanish Louisiana could receive up to two hundred arpents of land (depending on marital status) and fifty arpents for each child. Twenty additional arpents could also be acquired for each slave. A person could not, however, receive more than a total of eight hundred arpents.

By the close of the century, petitions were made and lands were granted on a fluctuating, individual-need basis. The process gradually became more involved, with surveyors keeping copies of the records generated. This allowed for more than one source or repository to include the same information.

The Cabildo Papers, sometimes called **The Spanish Judicial Records**, comprise one of several valuable record sources pertaining to Spanish Louisiana. Similar to notarial records, they contain a wide variety of judicial matters presented before the cabildo, or town council, for the territory of Louisiana between 18 August 1769 and 31 December 1803. Records include petitions for grants, affidavits, inquiries of local officials concerning petitioners, estate settlements, property descriptions, testimonies, and other land-related material. They are intertwined with a myriad of other judicial matters, however, and require sifting to gather desired land-related information.

The Cabildo Papers are now kept in various repositories throughout Louisiana. A portion of them are in the custody of the Louisiana State Museum, though the originals are not generally accessible to researchers. However, this collection has been the focus of extensive restoration and microfilming efforts since the mid-1970s. Other records for the cabildo are located at:

- Loyola University
- St. Martin Parish Library in St. Martinville, Louisiana
- Louisiana State Library
- New Orleans Public Library
- Southern Vital Records Repository in Flora, Mississippi

Some are also found in state archives and libraries in Missouri and Arkansas, as well as the office of Commissioner of State Lands and the Surveyor-General of those states. The Mississippi and Alabama state archives also house Spanish records for their southern regions.

All Cabildo Papers for the city of New Orleans are now on microfilm originating from the New Orleans Public Library. They are also available through the Family History Library. These particular records are minutes of the proceedings of the cabildo. Though often billed as having land transaction content, the records for New Orleans contain very few land matters aside from an occasional lawsuit involving a property dispute. A calendar of the New Orleans records, prepared by Laura L. Porteus, was published in the *Louisiana Historical Quarterly,* volumes 6 through 31.

Papeles de Santo Domingo and the **Papeles Procedentes de Cuba** (Santo Domingo Papers and the Cuban Papers) are available at the Historic New Orleans Collection. The Santo Domingo Papers are also available through the Center for Louisiana Studies, the University of Southern Louisiana, and Loyola University. The Cuban papers can be found, in part, at these same locations. (These records do not denote or represent a complete collection, as many papers from both locations continue to be discovered and inventoried.)

The Louisiana Notarial Archives in New Orleans is another valuable source. Not yet indexed, these records are more difficult to search. They include petitions for grants, mortgages, and other land issues. Tulane University and the Louisiana State University Department of Archives and Manuscripts both house significant collections of manuscripts and books concerning the Spanish period in Louisiana.

Colonial Documents of Avoyelles, dating from 1786, are housed at the State Archives and Records Service in Baton Rouge, Louisiana. Among these papers are records of land grants and sales. A catalog of these documents is available for public purchase; it contains an index. Although the records are from the Spanish period, most are in French, with some translations in English.

Joseph Vidal Papers include land transactions for the earliest part of Joseph Vidal's term as secretary to Manuel Gayoso de Lemos, governor of the district of Natchez, between 1795 and 1821. These records include documents written in Spanish concerning land grants, transfers, and surveys.

The Historic New Orleans Collection, part of the Kemper and Leila Williams Foundation, includes another important group of records for the state of Louisiana. This collection includes the following types of records, dating from 1767 to 1803:

- Colonial land grant petitions
- Grants made by the governors
- Land sales
- Surveys
- Surveyors' certificates

They cover areas of present-day Missouri, Arkansas, Louisiana, and Alabama. This significant collection has been microfilmed and is available through the Louisiana State Archives.

Pintado Papers is a collection of Spanish land grants, surveys, plats, and maps concerning the areas of Missouri, Arkansas, Louisiana, Alabama, and West Florida. Unsuccessfully offered for sale to the federal government in the 1800s by the families of the original surveyors, these records were eventually sold to private citizens. They were later acquired from their respective owners by the Louisiana State University Library. Microfilmed copies of the transcriptions of the Pintado Papers are now available at the following repositories:

- Louisiana State Archives and Records Commission

- Louisiana State University

- P.K. Yonge Library at the University of Florida

- Mississippi Department of Archives and History

- University of West Florida in Gainesville

- Family History Library

For areas of upper Louisiana, which included the present-day states of Arkansas and Missouri, few grants were made. The Arkansas region was primarily regarded as a military outpost during that time. Grants were usually large and were given mostly to military officers stationed there. Most lands were eventually restored to the public domain—forfeited or lost through litigation of private land claims. Grants in Missouri were also "free land grants," charged only for surveys and plats. All of these grants had to be confirmed by the Spanish governor or intendant, and few ever received actual title.

Very few records of individuals were generated or preserved for land grants in Texas before the Mexican administration.

The individual grants given in upper Louisiana continued to use the method of riverfront grants and the measurement of arpents. Lots were initially granted in St. Louis, Cape Girardeau, and St. Genevieve. Many records for the Spanish period in upper Louisiana are now housed at the Missouri State Archives in Jefferson City, and in the office of the Commissioner of State Lands in Little Rock, Arkansas.

Texas

Spain claimed the area of Texas as early as 1498, with the first appearances of Columbus. In 1519, Alvarez de Pineda received the first grant to colonize. Unfortunately, his settlement attempts failed. Though occasional mission efforts were undertaken over the following centuries, it was not until 1690 that another grant was made in this area. This grant was also for a mission, and in 1693 it, too, was abandoned. Nacogdoches, in 1716, became the first successfully settled grant in the Texas region. San Antonio followed as the second in 1718. Columbus' arrival in the New World had predated successful settlement in Texas by more than two hundred years.

Historical records describe a variety of land grants made in Texas during the first half of the eighteenth century, though few were successful. Many of the early grants were made verbally, with no written documents until the "re-proving" of rightful ownership to Mexican authorities. Thus, very few records for individuals were generated or preserved for land grants in Texas prior to the Mexican administration. By 1821, when Mexico officially declared its independence, only three towns were significantly inhabited in Texas: San Antonio, Nacogdoches, and La Bahia (Goliad).

Reproductions of the **Spanish grants for the land between the Nueces and Rio Grande rivers** comprise one set of records available for Texas. The area described was not considered part of Texas during Spanish or Mexican administration. The originals are housed in the Mexican Archives; copies are in the Texas General Land Office.

Spanish Archives is the title of another group of records housed at the Texas General Land Office. These records comprise almost seventy volumes, though they include only about seventy individual patents from the Spanish period. The remaining records of this collection were created during Mexico's possession.

New Mexico Territory

The New Mexico region was the first in the western domain to be successfully developed by Spain. Permanent settlements were established there by the late 1500s. This territory included parts of Colorado and Arizona until the mid-1800s. Land records for this area were well organized and grouped together for easier accountability and access, and have thus been better preserved.

The Spanish Archives of New Mexico is one of the most valuable Spanish collections in New Mexico. These records, originally housed in the office of the Surveyor-General, were taken from the official Spanish Archives in 1854. They have been microfilmed by the New Mexico State Archives and Records Center and are available for research through interlibrary loan. A calendar of these records has also been compiled. It is titled *A Guide to the Microfilm of Papers Relating to New Mexico Land Grants, to the Microfilm Edition of the Land Records of New Mexico, Spanish Archives of New Mexico: Series I, Surveyor General Records, and the Records of the Court of Private Land Claims* (see "For Further Reference" at the end of this chapter).

After the United States took possession of these lands, records concerning Spanish domain continued to be created by the office of the Surveyor-General in New Mexico until 1892. At that time the Court of Private Land Claims was officially established for this purpose, operating from 1892 to 1912. Records from both of these administrations are alphabetized in the calendar described above, listing claim numbers and referencing microfilm rolls for easier access.

Pueblo Grants are the earliest records for this area. They date back to the late 1680s. Though originally written in Spanish, they are usually accompanied by English translations made during the mid-1800s. They describe the property boundaries, neighbors, witnesses, and sometimes heirship. Documents include mostly petitions and replies. They are available through the U.S. Bureau of Land Management in Santa Fe, New Mexico. They have also been microfilmed and are available through the Family History Library.

The Twitchell Archives is another important source for Pueblo Grants. They are microfilmed copies of original land grant records in the Bureau of Land Management in Santa Fe. They show conveyances, grants, estate settlements, suits, and other miscellaneous land issues. This collection also includes records from the office of Surveyor-General for the state of New Mexico; it is more complete than the Pueblo Grants listed above. It is indexed by grantee/grantor. The Twitchell Archives is available at the University of New Mexico and the Family History Library. (See figure 1-6.)

Vigil's Index includes approximately 1,500 Spanish and Mexican land grants, among several other judicial issues, including governors' diaries. It is on microfilm at the Family History Library, the University of New Mexico Library, and the Bureau of Land Management. It has been organized twice: once by grant number and once by year.

California

California was the last of Spain's holdings to be adequately explored and settled. By 1821, as Mexico took over this area, twenty missions, four presidios, twenty-five *ranchos* (a *rancho* consisted of a single grant of more than one thousand acres), and three *pueblos* (a *pueblo* consisted of a single grant of less than one thousand acres) had been permanently established by Spain. The missions and presidios, although subdivided into lots, encompassed very few land grants. Most of the grants for this area were made under Mexican authority after 1821.

Titles to the lands in California were given by the governors and were to be kept in a book of colonization in the government archives. Based upon the history of the area, it could be assumed that these records are now in the Mexican archives. However, records among the Mexican

Anno Domine 1689

In the town of Our Lady of Guadalupe of El Paso of the Rio del Norte, on the twenty-fifth day of the month of September, in the year one thousand six hundred and eighty-nine, His Excellency the Governor and Captain General, Domingo Jironza Petroz de Cruzato, stated, that whereas in the pursuits which was made in ~~Pursuivee~~ of the Queres, the Apostate and the Tiguas Indians and those of the Thanos nation, and after having fought with all the Pueblos of that kingdom, an Indian, of the Pueblo of Zia, named Bartolomé de Ojeda, lending his support everywhere in the battle, being the who most distinguished himself, finding himself wounded by a ball and an arrow, surrendered, and whom, as above stated, I ordered to declare, under oath, how- the Pueblo of San Cristobal [*S^n Xptobal*] is situated, which was disloyal, and which participated in the battles of that kingdom of New Mexico, for they were very rebellious Indians.

Interrogated whether this Pueblo will ever again rebel, as it has been customary with them, and the deponent replied No- that they are now much influenced by fear- that, though they were much emboldened by what had occurred to the Pueblo of Zia the past year, he judges it was an impossibility that they should fail to give in their obedience. Wherefore the Governor and Captain General, Domingo Jironza Petroz de Cruzato granted the boundaries which I here mention- on the

Grant made to San Cristobal [Rubric]

Figure 1-6. A 1689 Spanish pueblo grant to San Cristobal; from the Twitchell Archives Collection for New Mexico.

Spanish Land Grant Measures and Terms*

Caballeria: Land given to horse soldiers—100 by 200 feet for planting, plus extra garden, woodland space, and pasture land.

Cordel: 50 varas.

Criadero de granado mayor: 1/4 of a Sitio de granado mayor.

Dehesa: Common pasture ground.

Ejido: Pueblo commons used for stock, recreation, and land for new settlers. Varied from 16 to 20 suertes to a sitio.

Fanega: 1.59 acres; 6,400 varas square.

Fundo Legal: 1200 varas square; about 250 acres; 1,440,000 square varas.

Labor: 1,000 varas square; 177 1/7 acres.

League: 100 cordeles; 5000 varas; 4,428 acres; a sitio; 3 miles square.

Peonia: Land given to foot soldiers—50 by 100 feet for planting, additional garden, woodland space, and pasture land; 1/5 of a caballeria.

Plaza: Town square or center.

Propio: Part of Royal Lands, rented for a term of 5 years to pay municipal expenses.

Sitio de granado mayor: 5000 varas square; 100 cordeles square; 41 caballerias; 4,428 acres; a sitio.

Sitio de granado menor: 3,333 1/3 varas square.

Solar: House or building lot, varied in size.

Solar de Tierra: Any portion of a Suerte, or less than 1/4 of a caballeria.

Suerte: Agricultural lot, usually 200 by 200 varas.

Suerte de Tierra: 1/4 caballeria; 552 by 276 varas; varied at times.

Vara: 2.78 feet; approximately 33 inches.

* Adapted from Rose Hollenbaugh Avina's *Spanish and Mexican Land Grants in California.*

---

archives relating to grants in the United States are considered nearly nonexistent, according to *Boletin del Archivo General de la Nacion.* Many of the grants are verified only through references in various historical documents or regranted Mexican titles, the original Spanish grant never having been found.

In General

Private Land Claims. One of the most valuable sets of Spanish records was created when the United States began to settle land claims that had occurred before U.S. possession. Many of the individual Spanish land grants were presented to the United States for reconfirmation under a federal program called Private Land Claims (see chapter 9, Records Generated by Federal Lands).

American State Papers: Public Lands, Volume One references almost all Spanish claims

made before 1837. They record a variety of other issues concerning Spanish possession, and are the best single consolidated source for research of the Spanish land grants. This record can also serve as an index to the original Spanish files within the Private Land Claims records. The claimants in these volumes have also been indexed in *Grassroots of America,* by Phillip W. McMullin. This index is generally more reliable and complete than the index found in the *American State Papers.* There are also specific individual indexes to Private Land Claims for many states. They are referenced further in chapter 9.

CONCLUSION

Many of the records concerning Spanish lands which were to be turned over to the United States were taken by the Spaniards to Havana, Cuba. Most of the records for the Spanish in Louisiana and West Florida were taken from Havana to Spain around 1888, though some remained in the Archivo Nacional de Cuba. Retrieval efforts by the United States have been bogged down in the bureaucratic processes of the Spanish, Cuban, and American governments for more than a century. However, the late 1980s and the 1990s have seen tremendous progress in cataloging, organizing, and microfilming efforts by the Archivo General de Indias in Seville, Spain.

Recent efforts by individuals and organizations in Cuba have uncovered portions of records concerning America in such unusual places as church steeples. A large collection of the Cuban Papers for the southeastern part of the United States, housed in Seville, have been microfilmed. They comprise 421 rolls of microfilm and are located at the P.K. Yonge Library of Florida History in Gainesville. Negotiation continues for a more complete inventory and accounting of these records. Reproductions of some archived records from Cuba can be found in the Library of Congress, the Newberry Library, and the Wisconsin State Historical Society.

While much remains hidden and confused concerning record keeping for the Spanish era in America, modern technology is helping to preserve and make available more records for all levels of research. The records created by the Spanish can be extremely helpful in researching the lives and ancestry of the citizens residing within their jurisdiction. Those who did settle on Spanish lands were seldom true Spaniards. Many were enticed from a variety of geographical locations, some from as far north in the Atlantic as Ireland. Therefore, Spanish records should not be overlooked when researching Americans, Mexicans, British, Portuguese, Irish, or other ethnic or culturally varied peoples.

REPOSITORIES

(Organized alphabetically by state postal code.)

Alabama Department of Archives and History
624 Washington Avenue
Montgomery, AL 36130-3601

Arkansas History Commission
1 Capitol Mall
Little Rock, AR 72201

Arizona Department of Library and Archives
1700 West Washington
Phoenix, AZ 85007

Bureau of Land Management
Arizona State Office
3707 North 7th Street
Phoenix, AZ 85011

Bureau of Land Management
California State Office
2800 College Way
Sacramento, CA 95825

California State Archives
Office of Secretary of State
1020 O Street, Room 130
Sacramento, CA 95814

University of California-Berkeley
Bancroft Library
Berkeley, CA 94720

Bureau of Land Management
Colorado State Office
2850 Youngfield Street
Lakewood, CO 80215

National Archives and Records Administration
Textual Reference Branch (NNR1)
Washington, D.C. 20408

Florida State Archives
R.A. Gray Building
500 South Bronough Street
Tallahassee, FL 32399-0250

Division of State Lands
Bureau of Mapping and Survey
3900 Commonwealth Boulevard
Tallahassee, FL 32399-3000

University of Florida
P.K. Yonge Library
Special Collections/Florida History
Gainesville, FL 32611

University of West Florida
John C. Pace Library
Pensacola, FL 32514

St. Augustine Historical Society
271 Charlotte Street
St. Augustine, FL 32084

Louisiana State Archives and Records
Office of the Secretary of State
3851 Essen Lane
P.O. Box 94125
Baton Rouge, LA 70804-9125

Loyola University of New Orleans
Spanish Documents Project
6363 St. Charles Avenue
P.O. Box 198
New Orleans, LA 70118

Southern University
John B. Cade Library
Southern Br. PO
Baton Rouge, LA 70813

New Orleans Public Library
Louisiana Division
219 Loyola Avenue
New Orleans, LA 70140

The Historic New Orleans Collection
Kemper and Leila Williams Foundation
Research Library
533 Royal Street
New Orleans, LA 70130

Tulane University
Howard-Tilton Memorial Library
New Orleans, LA 70118-5682

Louisiana State Museum
Louisiana Historical Center Library
751 Chartres Street
New Orleans, LA 70176

Louisiana Historical Association
Center for Louisiana Studies
The University of Southwestern Louisiana
P.O. Box 40831, USL
Lafayette, LA 70504

Louisiana Notarial Archives
(see Louisiana State Museum)

National Archives and Records Administration
Cartographic Division (NNR2)
8601 Adelphi Road
College Park, MD 20740-6001

Missouri State Archives
600 West Main Street
P.O. Box 778
Jefferson City, MO 65102

Mississippi Archives and Library Division
Mississippi Dept. of Archives and History
P.O. Box 571
Jackson, MS 39205-0571

Center for Southwest Research
University of New Mexico-General Library
Albuquerque, NM 87131-1466

Bureau of Land Management
Dept. of the Interior
P.O. Box 1449
Santa Fe, NM 87501

New Mexico State Library
Southwest Room
325 Don Gaspar Avenue
Santa Fe, NM 87503

New Mexico Records Center and Archives
404 Montezuma Street
Santa Fe, NM 87501

Archivo General de Indias
Avenida de la Constitución, 3
41004 Sevilla, Spain

Texas General Land Office
1700 North Congress Avenue
Austin, TX 78701

Texas State Library
Archives Division
1200 Brazos
Box 12927, Capitol Station
Austin, TX 78711

Family History Library
35 North West Temple
Salt Lake City, UT 84101

Bureau of Land Management
Eastern States Office
7450 Boston Boulevard
Springfield, VA 22153-3121

FOR FURTHER REFERENCE

Almaraz, Felix D., Jr. *The San Antonio Missions and Their System of Land Tenure.* Austin: University of Texas Press, 1989.

American Heritage. *Pictorial Atlas of United States History.* New York: American Heritage Publishing Co., 1966.

Arena, C. Richard. "Land Settlement Policies and Practices in Spanish Louisiana." In *The Spanish in the Mississippi Valley, 1762–1804.* Edited by John F. McDermott. Urbana: University of Illinois Press, 1974.

Atlas of American History. New York: Charles Scribner's Sons, 1984.

Avina, Rose Hollenbaugh. *Spanish and Mexican Land Grants in California.* New York: Arno Press, 1976.

Beck, Warren A., and Ynez D. Haase. *Historical Atlas of California.* Norman: University of Oklahoma Press, 1974. Contains county maps which show the location of individual grants.

Beers, Henry Putney. *French and Spanish Records of Louisiana: A Bibliographical Guide to Archive and Manuscript Sources.* Baton Rouge: Louisiana State University Press, 1989.

_____. *Spanish and Mexican Records of the American Southwest: A Bibliographical Guide to Archive and Manuscript Sources.* Tucson: University of Arizona Press, 1979.

Blackmar, Frank Wilson. *Spanish Institutions of the Southwest.* Reprint. Glorieta, N.M.: Rio Grande Press, 1976.

Bolton, Herbert Eugene. *The Spanish Borderlands: A Chronicle of Old Florida and the Southwest.* New Haven, Conn.: Yale University Press, 1921.

_____. *Guide to Materials for the History of the United States in the Principal Archives of Mexico.* New York: Kraus Reprint, 1965.

Bowden, J.J. *Spanish and Mexican Land Grants in the Chihuahuan Acquisition.* El Paso: Texas Western Press, University of Texas at El Paso, 1971.

Bowman, Jacon N. *California Private Land Grant Records in the National Archives.* Berkeley: University of California Manuscript Collection, 1956.

Boyd, Mark F. *Florida Historical Quarterly* 17: 254-80 (for Spanish mission sites in Florida).

Burns, Francis P. *The Spanish Land Laws of Louisiana.* N.p., n.d.

Casteneda, Carlos E. *A Report on the Spanish Archives in San Antonio, Texas.* San Antonio: Yanaguana Society, 1937.

Catalogo de Documentos del Archivo General de Indias Sobre la Epoca Espanola de Louisiana. New Orleans, La.: Loyola University, 1968.

Cornay, Jeanne. "Spanish and French Land Grants in Southwest Louisiana." *Kinfolks* 17 (4) (1993). Published by the Southwest Louisiana Genealogical Society of Lake Charles, Louisiana.

Crouch, Dora P., et al. *Spanish City Planning in North America.* Cambridge: MIT Press, 1982.

Cumming, William P. *The Southeast in Early Maps.* Princeton, N.J.: Princeton University Press, 1958.

Day, James M., et al. *Maps of Texas, 1527–1900: The Map Collection of the Texas State Archives.* Austin, Tex.: Pemberton Press, 1964.

DeVille, Winston. *Louisiana and Mississippi Lands: A Guide to Spanish Land Grants at the University of Michigan.* Ville Platte, La.: Evangeline Genealogical and Historical Society, 1985.

Diaz, James Albert. *A Guide to the Microfilm of Papers Relating to New Mexico Land Grants.* Santa Fe: University of New Mexico Press, 1960.

Fairbanks, Charles H. *Alabama and the Borderlands: From Pre-history to Statehood.* Tuscaloosa: University of Alabama Press, 1985.

Feldman, Lawrence H. *Anglo-Americans in Spanish Archives.* Baltimore: Genealogical Publishing Co., 1991.

Florida Department of State, Division of Library and Information Services, and Bureau of Archives and Records Management. *Guide to the Records of the Florida State Archives.* Tallahassee: Florida Department of State, 1988.

Hahn, Marilyn Davis. *Old St. Stephens Land Office Records and American State Papers: Public Lands Vol. 1, 1768-1888.* Easley, S.C.: Southern Historical Press, 1983. Extracts are found in this book for a selection of both Spanish and British lands presented at the St. Stephens land office.

Henderson, Ann L., and Gary R. Mormino. *Spanish Pathways in Florida 1492–1992.* Sarasota, Fla.: Pineapple Press, 1991.

Hill, Roscoe R.. *Descriptive Catalog of Documents Relating to the History of the United States in the Papeles Procedentes de Cuba Deposited in the Archivo General de Indies at Seville.* Washington, D.C.: Carnegie Institute of Washington, 1916.

Historical Records Survey, Division of Professional and Service Projects, and the Work Projects Administration. *Spanish Land Grants in Florida.* Tallahassee, Fla.: State Library Board, 1940. An excellent, in-depth discussion of the intricate laws and customs surrounding the Spanish era is in vol. 1, *Unconfirmed Claims.*

Holmes, Jack D.L. *A Guide to Spanish Louisiana 1762–1806.* New Orleans: the author, 1970.

_____. "Genealogical and Historical Sources for Spanish Alabama." *Deep South Genealogical Quarterly* 5 (2) (February 1968).

Houck, Louis. *The Spanish Regime in Missouri.* Chicago: R.R. Donnelley & Sons Co., 1909.

Index to the Archives of Spanish West Florida, 1782–1810. Introduction by Stanley Clisby Arthur. New Orleans: Polyanthos, 1975.

Kirkham, E. Kay. *A Genealogical and Historical Atlas of the United States of America.* Logan, Utah: Everton Publishers, 1976.

Lanning, John Tate. *The Spanish Missions of Georgia.* Chapel Hill: University of North Carolina Press, 1935.

"Louisiana's Spanish Colonial Records." *Kinfolks* 18 (1) (1994). Published by the Southwest Louisiana Genealogical Society of Lake Charles, Louisiana.

Lowery, Woodbury. *The Spanish Settlements Within the Present Limits of the United States: Florida 1562–1574.* New York: Putnam, 1905.

_____. *The Lowery Collection: A Descriptive List of Maps of the Spanish Possessions Within the Present Limits of the United States, 1502–1820.* Edited with notes by Philip Lee Phillips. Washington, D.C.: Government Printing Office, 1912.

Lowrie, Walter. *Early Settlers of Louisiana, Mississippi . . . as Taken from Land Claims in the Mississippi Territory.* Reprint. Easley, S.C.: Southern Historical Press, 1986.

Martin, T.P. *The Confirmation of French and Spanish Land Titles in the Louisiana Purchase.* M.A. thesis, University of California, Berkeley, 1914.

McMullin, Phillip W. *Grassroots of America.* Salt Lake City: Gendex, 1972.

Miller, Gary M. *Spanish and Mexican Land Grants in California: A Summary of Holdings and Guide to Other Sources.* Laguna Niguel, Calif., n.d.

Miller, Thomas Lloyd. *The Public Lands of Texas 1519–1970.* Norman: University of Oklahoma Press, 1972.

Morrow, William W. *Spanish and Mexican Private Land Grants.* San Francisco, 1923. Reprint. New York: Arno Press, 1974.

National Archives and Records Administration. *Special List No. 26: Pre-Federal Maps in the National Archives: An Annotated List.* Compiled by Patrick D. McLaughlin. Washington, D.C.: Government Printing Office, 1971.

_____. *Preliminary Inventory No. 22: Preliminary Inventory of the Land-Entry Papers of the*

General Land Office. Compiled by Harry P. Yoshpe and Philip P. Brower. Washington, D.C.: Government Printing Office, 1949.

Northrop, Marie E. *Spanish-Mexican Families of Early California, 1769–1850.* Burbank: Southern California Genealogical Society, 1984.

Nunis, Doyce B., and Gloria Ricci Lothrop, eds. *A Guide to the History of California.* New York: Greenwood Press, 1989. This includes a directory of historical archives in California.

Potter, Dorothy Williams. *Passports of Southeastern Pioneers, 1770–1823: Indian, Spanish and Other Land Passports for Tennessee, Kentucky, Georgia, Mississippi, Virginia, North and South Carolina.* Baltimore: Genealogical Publishing Co., 1982.

Reeves, Sally K. "Notarial Records of the New Orleans Notarial Archives." *Louisiana Library Association Bulletin* 55 (1) (Summer 1992).

Reynolds, Mathew G. *Spanish and Mexican Land Laws.* St. Louis, 1895.

Ryskamp, George R. "The Archives of Spain." *Heritage Quest* 45 (May-June 1993).

Sadler, Jerry. *History of Texas Land.* Austin, ca. 1970.

Salazar, J. Richard, New Mexico State Records Center and Archives. *Calendar to the Microfilm Edition of the Land Records of New Mexico, Spanish Archives of New Mexico: Series I, Surveyor General Records, and the Records of the Court of Private Land Claims.* Santa Fe, N.M.: National Historical Publications and Records Commission, 1987.

Scott, Florence Johnson. *Royal Land Grants North of the Rio Grande 1777–1821.* Texian Press, 1969.

Shepherd, William R. *Guide to the Materials for the History of the United States in Spanish Archives.* Washington, D.C.: Carnegie Institution of Washington, 1907.

Shumway, Burgess McK. *California Ranchos: Patented Private Land Grants Listed by County.* San Bernardino, Calif.: Borgo Press, 1988.

Snider, Billie Ford, and Janice B. Palmer. *Spanish Plat Book of Land Records of the District of Pensacola, Province of West Florida; British and Spanish Land Grants, 1763–1821.* Pensacola, Fla.: Antique Compiling, 1994.

Sweett, Zelia, and Mary H. Sheppy. *The Spanish Missions of Florida.* St. Augustine, Fla., 1940.

Taylor, Virginia H. *Index to Spanish and Mexican Land Grants in Texas.* Austin, Tex.: Lone Star Press, 1974.

_____. *The Spanish Archives of the General Land Office of Texas.* Austin: Lone Star Press, 1955.

Texas General Land Office, Garry Mauro as Land Commissioner. *Guide to Spanish and Mexican Land Grants in South Texas.* Texas General Land Office, 1988.

Twitchell, Ralph Emerson. *Spanish Archives of New Mexico, I.* Cedar Rapids, Iowa: Torch Press, 1914.

United States Congress. *The American State Papers: Public Lands.* Washington, D.C.: Gales and Seaton, 1832–61.

Westphall, Victor. *Mercedes Reales: Hispanic Land Grants of the Upper Rio Grande Region.* Albuquerque: University of New Mexico Press, ca. 1983.

_____. *The Public Domain in New Mexico, 1854–1891.* Albuquerque: University of New Mexico Press, 1965.

Wehmann, Howard H., and Benjamin L. DeWhitt, comps. *Pre-Federal Records in the National Archives.* Washington, D.C.: National Archives Trust Fund Board, 1989.

White, Joseph M. *A New Collection of Laws, Charters and Local Ordinances on the Governments of Great Britain, France, and Spain, Relating to the Concessions of Land in Their Respective Colonies, Together With the Laws of Mexico and Texas on the Same Subject.* 2 vols. Philadelphia, 1839.

2

British Possession

HISTORICAL BACKGROUND

The British were the last of three major foreign powers to publicly claim lands in America. Their first organized efforts to settle in the present-day United States began in 1585. Led by Sir Walter Raleigh, a party of 108 settlers arrived to establish the settlement of Raleigh (in present-day North Carolina). For the next two hundred years, the British government struggled to contain and administer a land as untamable as the individuals who settled it. The British played a major role in land records created in the states which were at one time its colonies.

From the early 1600s to 1783, the English settled along the East Coast and waged wars on three fronts. One was against France for expansion to the west. A second was against Spain for expansion southward. Wars with these same countries in Europe prevented the British from focusing appropriate attention on "New England," where the third front was against their own colonists in the American Revolution.

Britain's only rightful claim to North America was through the authority of possession, and having inhabitants loyal to England was critical to maintaining that claim. The British solution was to provide charters to large land-speculation companies made up of the wealthier upper-class subjects in England. Not only did they allow each stockholder a specified amount of acreage, they bestowed the necessary authority on companies to distribute grants and titles for all other lands

within their charter to anyone loyal to the crown. Land was essentially given by charter, then sub-granted, sub-leased, or rented to a variety of "lower-class individuals." Each charter was still controlled by the crown, with the company having vested rights to act on its behalf. Governments in the communities established were also under the authority of the crown.

Beginning with Sir Walter Raleigh in 1585, the next twenty-two years saw almost complete annihilation of all British subjects attempting to settle north of the Floridas. English settlement attempts were not considered successful until the founding of Jamestown in 1607. The Virginia Company of London, part of The London Company, is credited with this success; it was among the first of England's charters on the North American continent. They provided one hundred acres for each shareholder in the company. Under a system of headrights, they also provided fifty extra acres to a shareholder for each additional settler brought to the New World. Though they encountered significant losses, the king of England eventually taking over proprietorship, the ventures of The Virginia Company paved the way for Britain's future involvement in America.

The original grant to The London Company in 1606 allotted all lands from the thirty-fourth to the forty-first latitude (northern South Carolina to northern New Jersey), and westward for one hundred miles inland. The Plymouth Company was also granted a charter that year between the

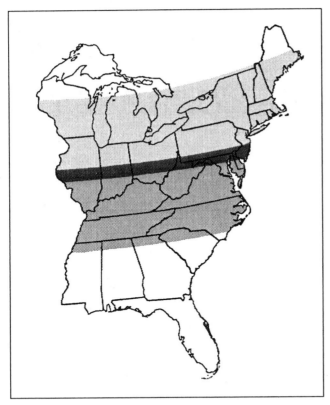

Figure 2-1. The overlapping charter of The London Company (south) and The Plymouth Company (north), 1606.

thirty-eighth and forty-fifth latitudes (mid-Virginia to the northern boundaries of Vermont; see figure 2-1). These overlapping claims were grounds for disputes which lasted nearly two hundred years.

In 1609, both charters were retracted, and new ones were issued. The Virginia Company received a grant similar to that of The London Company, though it extended only to southern Pennsylvania, one degree in latitude south from that of its predecessor. A major difference was the extension of the north boundary at a "west and northwest" angle from the eastern coast to the Pacific Ocean (figure 2-2). It was through this grant that Virginia, nearly two hundred years later, claimed the Northwest Territory and Kentucky. The Plymouth Company never did establish a successful settlement, and its charter was eventually absorbed by the Massachusetts Bay Company.

A charter in 1620 allotted the New England Council full power over the judgements and distribution of land from the fortieth latitude northward to the forty-eighth latitude. By 1622, the council had also distributed two large grants consisting of present-day New Hampshire, Vermont, and Maine.

In 1629, the Massachusetts Bay Company was granted a separate charter in the New England area, though it was revoked in 1684. Reissued in 1691, it defined only present-day Massachusetts. Based upon the earlier charter of 1629, Massachusetts tried to claim portions of western land in Pennsylvania, Michigan, Illinois, and Wisconsin (figure 2-3).

Manhattan Island was first settled by the Dutch in 1624. They immediately began to give out their own grants. The Swedes settled in the Delaware Bay area around 1638. These lands were already claimed by England, which granted them, along with other portions of present-day New

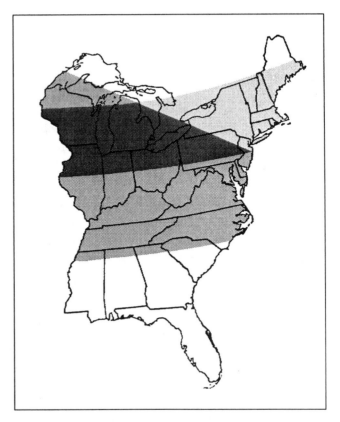

Figure 2-2. 1609 charter to The Virginia Company and overlapping charter of 1620 to The New England Council.

York, Connecticut, Massachusetts, Pennsylvania, and all of present-day New Jersey and Delaware, to the Duke of York in 1664. A variety of boundary disputes quickly resulted from more overlapping grants.

The charter to the Duke of York overlapped the charter of The Virginia Company, which had earlier been given the area as far north as forty degrees latitude. England had already given lands south of forty degrees in a charter to Lord Baltimore in 1632. This area originally included Delaware and New Jersey, which had also been granted to the Duke of York. Lord Baltimore was left mostly with present-day Maryland.

The area of present-day Connecticut was granted in a separate charter in 1662. The western boundary, however, was described as the Pacific Ocean. This charter was the basis for Connecticut to later claim lands in present-day Ohio (the Connecticut Western Reserve and the Firelands).

Rhode Island was settled in 1636—without the authority of a charter but by a deed from the Indians of that area. The deed was not recognized by the British, and the settlers were considered squatters on the property of Massachusetts and Connecticut. They were eventually given their own legitimate charter in 1663.

The British honored prior land claims as early as 1664, when they ousted the Dutch government from Manhattan and granted the charter to the Duke of York. The Dutch claim also included the Swedish settlements in Delaware, which they had taken earlier from the Swedes. The Duke of York deeded the area of present-day New Jersey in 1664, and deeded Delaware to William Penn in 1682. William Penn then granted a separate charter back to Delaware in 1701.

The early grant involving Maine, New Hampshire, and Vermont was separated between two proprietors. One took what is now Vermont and New Hampshire, while the other, Ferdinando Gorges, took the present-day state of Maine. Gorges sold the entire area in 1677 to John Usher. Usher then deeded the lands to the state of Massachusetts. From this deed, Maine remained a part

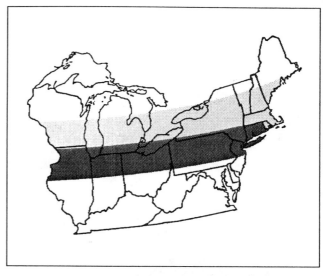

Figure 2-3. Approximate boundaries of the charters to the Massachusetts Bay Company in 1629 (top) and Connecticut in 1662 (bottom).

of Massachusetts until 1820. Vermont's ownership was later disputed between the present-day states of New York and New Hampshire, officially claimed by New York until 1777.

A portion of lands west of the Delaware River were granted to William Penn through another conflicting English charter in 1681. His boundaries extended into western lands previously granted to Connecticut, causing yet another round of boundary disputes. Penn's southern boundary also included parts of the present-day state of Delaware, with the remainder being deeded to him from the Duke of York. A portion of Delaware conflicted with Lord Baltimore's charter, causing years of additional court disputes. The remainder of the southern boundary was eventually settled by Mason and Dixon, surveyors who placed the boundary at 39 degrees, 43.25 minutes, rather than the full 40 degrees latitude originally under warrant.

The Virginia Company saw portions of its borders in the far south granted out in conflicting charters as well. In 1663, the charter for Carolina was given to eight proprietors. This charter was between thirty-one degrees and thirty-six degrees north in latitude, overlapping The Virginia Company by two degrees on its southern border. It

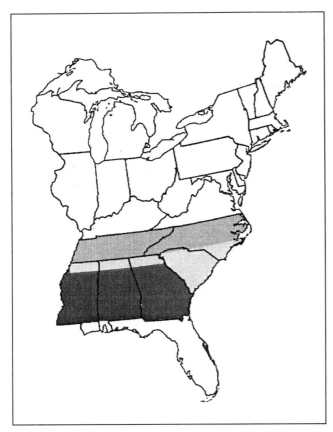

Figure 2-4. Colonial claims for North Carolina, South Carolina, and Georgia.

extended south into the northern Floridas, overlapping areas under active Spanish dominion. In 1729, the British government purchased the rights back and divided the area into North and South Carolina.

In 1732, England granted a separate charter for areas in present-day Georgia, distinguishing it from South Carolina and extending its bounds to the Pacific Ocean. In 1764, the boundaries were altered; it was extended southward only to the thirty-first parallel and westward to the Mississippi River (figure 2-4).

By 1763, the end of the French and Indian War, England had obtained by treaty almost all of France's possessions in Canada, as well as all of the possessions east of the Mississippi, except New Orleans. Through the Treaty of Paris in 1763, England also came into possession of the territories of East and West Florida, acquiring them from Spain. There was an immediate appro-

priation of lands for British citizens. It was essential for the British government to encourage quick settlement and thereby retain a stronger hold on the newly acquired territory.

Though rapid progress was made in colonization during that time, England's tenure in the southern gulf region of East and West Florida was a mere twenty years. The British government promised to recognize any previous Spanish land titles that could be proven to be authentic, though it seldom acknowledged that any were. For Spanish settlers who decided to leave, a period of eighteen months was allowed to dispose of their lands; however, their lands could only be transferred to British subjects. In addition to recognizing previous private land claims, England moved quickly to colonize the remaining lands as thoroughly as possible. Treaties with the Indians were settled by 1765, and British grants were quickly made available in the northwest area of what is now Ohio and the Great Lakes region.

By 1774, individual settlers had caused considerable problems for the British by conducting their own transactions with the Indians, especially in the northwestern regions of British territory. Through the Quebec Act, in 1774, Britain authorized Quebec to govern the treaties and purchases of all Indian lands, refusing to recognize any claims made otherwise. (See figure 2-5.)

Peace was never truly realized by Britain in America. A battle was being fought; more serious than those with Spain or France, it was a battle for the loyalty of England's own subjects in America. Civil unrest soon grew to revolutionary proportions, and war began as the inhabitants officially declared their independence from England on 4 July 1776. The end of the Revolutionary War saw England stripped of all possessions in the present-day United States, except for future claims to a small portion of the Pacific Northwest.

Along the Pacific coast, England had helped to colonize areas near the mouth of the Columbia River. As the United States continued to expand westward, England and the United States both claimed the Oregon Territory, including the present-day states of Washington, Oregon, Idaho, and portions of Montana. By 1846, the United States reached an agreement with England, taking full possession of this area and ending British authority in the United States.

THE RECORDS

As mentioned in "An Introduction to Pre-U.S. Possessions," British records are usually found integrated with their respective colonies/states. The reason is that the people displaced the government—the government did not displace the people. Therefore, following the revolution, pre-existing record sources and the structures for record keeping were absorbed and continued, often by the same individuals, in the new nation: the United States of America.

Individual land titles were not disputed after the independence of the United States, except in cases of questionable loyalty during the war. Larger grants, such as charters, were re-evaluated for public land acquisition. Some states ceded portions of their lands to the federal government for this purpose, especially in the northwest Great Lakes region. The records generated by these cessions caused very few documents regarding individual settlers to be created. Those who were included can be found in *The American State Papers* and *The Territorial Papers*. (For further information on these two sources, see chapter 9, Records Generated by Federal Lands.)

Figure 2-5. British possessions after the Quebec Act of 1774.

Proprietor Records and Crown Grants

Proprietor records and crown grants are among the most valuable resources for land and property issues in British colonial America. Records were kept differently by each proprietorship, which dispersed land within the charter on behalf of the crown. Lands were described in much the same way as any typical land deed, providing witnesses, neighbors, watercourses, and other pertinent identifying information.

Some major colonial collections of proprietor records and crown grants for each state are listed below, as are the locations of the records. Doubtless there are other sources in various state repositories that are not represented here.

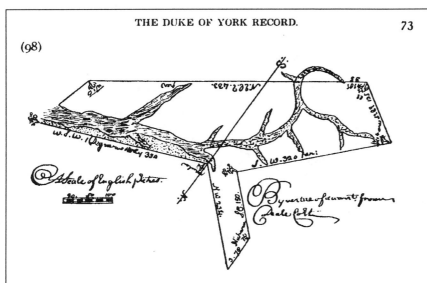

THE DUKE OF YORK RECORD.   73

(98)

By vertue of a warr. from Deale Court.
Laid out for Stephen Whitman a parcell of Land called Whitmans Choise scituated on the West side of Delaware Bay and on the South side of a Creeke called Deale Creeke Beginning at a marked white oake being the bounded tree of Anthony Eenloss standing on a point of woods and a branch on the Marshes of the said Deale Creeke and running from thence west South west One Degree westerly three hundred fifety and fower perches binding on the land of Anthony Eenloss to a bounded popular of the said Anthony Eenloss and John Kipshaven and from thence Northwest two hundred thirty and fower perches binding on the head line of the said John Kipshaven his Land to Patricks Creeke and from thence South Seaventy and eight perches to a bounded Hickarie of the Land the said Stephen Whitman purchased from John Siming and from thence South East binding on the said Land One hundred and fifety perches to a marked black oake & from thence Southwest binding on the said Land to a marked Corner Hickarie—Standing in the woods and from thence South East by East with a line of marked trees One hundred thirty and five perches to a Corner marked black oake standing in the woods and from thence with a line of marked trees North East by East thirty and five perches to a branch and then by several Courses binding on part of the said branch One hundred and twenty perches to the Course aforesaid and from thence Dito, North East by East fower hundred and thirteen perches with a line of marked trees and part binding on a branch to a marked white oake standing on a point of woods and on the marshes of the said Deale Creeke and then North North East to the first bounded white oake Containing and laid out for five hundred acres of Land.
June ye 6th A. 1681.   Cornelis Verhoofe Surveyor.
At a Court held at Deale by the Kings Authority the 14th Feb.

Figure 2-6. A transcription of proprietor records of the Duke of York; from *Original Land Titles in Delaware, Commonly Known as The Duke of York Record.*

Connecticut

Colonial records for Connecticut are housed at the Connecticut State Library. They have been microfilmed for the period 1640 to 1846 and are also available through the Family History Library in Salt Lake City. Missing, however, is the period between 1674 and 1723. Some of this time period can be replaced by research in the Judd Collection, which includes some land transactions among its various other records. It is also housed at the Connecticut State Library and is available on microfilm.

Delaware

Among the best sources for early Delaware land grants are the proprietor records of the Duke of York. These records, which cover the period from 1646 to 1679, have been transcribed and published by order of the General Assembly of the State of Delaware in *Original Land Titles in Delaware; Commonly Known as The Duke of York Record.* The title also suggests the dates above but is misleading; many records are dated after 1680. (See figure 2-6.)

Records generated during Penn's proprietorship, which began in 1682, are housed at the Delaware Hall of Records in Dover and have not yet been microfilmed. They are available for research to those visiting on-site.

Georgia

Georgia's proprietors granted land through normal patent procedures from 1733. Beginning in 1756, they also offered lands through headrights. The original records for both are housed at the Georgia State Archives in Atlanta. They have been microfilmed and are available at the state archives and the Family History Library.

Several abstracts of these early records have been published and are found in most major research libraries and universities around the country. Of particular interest is Marion R. Hemperley's *Georgia Surveyor-General Department: A History and Inventory of Georgia's Land Office.* Several smaller publications also contain indexes and abstracts of the colonial crown land grants for individual parishes in Georgia. See also *Index to the Headright and Bounty Grants of Georgia, 1756–1909,* by Silas Emmett Lucas, Jr.

Maine-Massachusetts

From chapter 8, Research in Land and Tax Records, in *The Source: A Guidebook of American Genealogy:* "Massachusetts granted Maine lands west of the Kennebec as proprietor, while it granted lands east of the river only with crown confirmation." The Maine Land Office does not house any land records created before 1783. Earlier grants can be viewed as having three separate categories: the Massachusetts Bay Colony records, the Plymouth Colony records, and town proprietor records.

The Massachusetts Bay Colony records can be researched through a six-volume series by Nathaniel B. Shurtleff titled *Records of the Governor and Company of the Massachusetts Bay in New England.* The records of the New Plymouth Colony have been microfilmed and are available through the Family History Library and at other major repositories. Copies of all of these records, including the individual town proprietary records, are housed at the Massachusetts state archives. (See figure 2-7.)

Maryland

Land dispersal in Maryland was under the direction of only one proprietor before statehood: Lord Baltimore. Some headrights exist for the earliest grants, though most lands were dis-

tributed by an established land council. All grants, dating from 1634, are held at the Maryland Hall of Records in Annapolis. They have been microfilmed and are available through state interlibrary loan programs and through the Family History Library.

Various published indexes cover most of the patents for the pre-1700 period. An alphabetical card index for all grants exists at the Hall of Records. Some colonial land patents concerning the Calverts are also housed at the Maryland

THE

PROPRIETORS' RECORDS

OF THE

TOWN OF LUNENBURG

MASSACHUSETTS

INCLUDING FITCHBURG AND
A PORTION OF ASHBY

1729—1833

BEING A COMPLETE TRANSCRIPT OF THE PROPRIETORS' RECORDS
AS PRESERVED IN A VOLUME OWNED BY THE TOWN OF
LUNENBURG, AND GIVEN BY WILLIAM CLARK,
ESQ., OF BOSTON, MERCHANT,
MARCH 24, 1730

COMPILED BY

WALTER A. DAVIS, CITY CLERK

FITCHBURG
PUBLISHED BY AUTHORITY OF THE CITY COUNCIL
1897

Figure 2-7. Title page from a published collection of town proprietor's records.

Historical Society in Baltimore, along with other minor collections. The state of Maryland has published extensive inventories for state and county records that can be viewed or purchased from the Hall of Records.

New Hampshire

British-era land grants, distributed from several different sources, are mostly housed in the New Hampshire State Archives. Some, granted by Massachusetts, are housed in the Massachusetts State Archives in Boston. The authority to grant initial lands in New Hampshire involved a complicated web of historical litigation between several states. Records in Vermont, Massachusetts, and New York should all be searched to effectively confirm an ancestor's involvement in this state. The best single source available is the *Provincial and State Papers of New Hampshire,* which has been microfilmed by the Family History Library. It consists of 118 rolls of microfilm, the first twenty-seven of which are alphabetical indexes.

New Jersey

British interests in New Jersey began with the charter to the Duke of York, who quickly re-granted it in two parts to two individual proprietors. Thus, the colony was divided into East and West Jersey. Even after reunification in 1702, lands were still granted from their respective jurisdictions: Perth Amboy for East Jersey and Burlington for West Jersey. Records from both jurisdictions are now housed at the New Jersey State Archives in Trenton. They have been microfilmed and are available through the Family History Library and other major repositories. See John Pomfret's *The New Jersey Proprietors and Their Lands, 1664-1776.*

New York

British grants were distributed through a variety of proprietors and land companies during the colonial era in New York. The general land patents for the state of New York for the period 1664 to 1954 are available at the New York State Ar-

chives, though they have not yet been micro-filmed. Very few colonial land records have been published for easy reference, though many, such as the Holland Land Company records, have been microfilmed. Most are available at the New York State Archives and the Family History Library. Also see chapter 6, Records Generated by State Lands.

North Carolina

Most proprietary grants for North Carolina, including a copy of the Granville Grants, are found in the Office of the Secretary of State in Raleigh. The original Granville Grants are housed in the North Carolina State Archives. The secretary of state has a Master Card File Index to North Carolina Land Grants, 1679 to 1959, which includes the earliest grants. Those created prior to 1729 have been abstracted and indexed in *Province of North Carolina, 1663–1729, Abstracts of Land Patents,* by Margaret M. Hofmann. The original records have not yet been microfilmed for distribution to other repositories. (See figure 2-8.)

Pennsylvania

The Division of Land Records in Harrisburg, Pennsylvania, holds all of the early grants made through the proprietorship of William Penn. They are remarkably structured and organized and have all been microfilmed. Indexes to patents are on microfilm rolls separate from the actual patents. The warrants are arranged alphabetically by county, and applications for warrants are arranged alphabetically by first letter of the surname on a year-by-year basis. See Donna Munger's *Pennsylvania Land Records.*

Rhode Island

All early conveyances of property for Rhode Island are housed at the Rhode Island State Archives in Providence. Some records can also be found in the *Proceedings of the General Assembly, 1646–1851,* which has been microfilmed. These microfilms are available through the Family History Library and the Rhode Island State

Archives. See John R. Bartlett's *Records of the Colony of Rhode Island and Providence Plantations in New England.*

South Carolina

South Carolina has statewide indexes for the colonial (1670–1719) and proprietary (1719–75) periods of land distribution. These indexes have been microfilmed and are available through the Family History Library and the South Carolina State Archives in Columbia. Memorials have also been microfilmed. They are records that trace the entire lineage of a tract of land back to the original patentee. Royal Land Grants from 1695 are also available on microfilm.

Vermont

Vermont's early British grants can be found in the microfilmed collection *New York Land Patents 1688–1786.* It is available through the Secretary of State, Division of State Papers, in Montpelier, Vermont. This office is also called the Vermont State Archives. Other, smaller collections also exist for individual town proprietorships, though they are housed at the Public Records Division, which is at the State Administration Building in Montpelier. All records that have been microfilmed are also available at the Family History Library.

Virginia

British patent records from 1624 are housed at the Virginia State Library in Richmond. They have all been microfilmed and have applicable indexes. Headrights,

purchases, and other methods of obtaining patents are all included together. Records created before 1732 have been abstracted in *Cavaliers and Pioneers* by Nell Marion Nugent. All of these records are available through the Family History Library. Specific proprietary grants are also available for research, such as the Northern Neck Grants and the Lord Fairfax Grants. Most

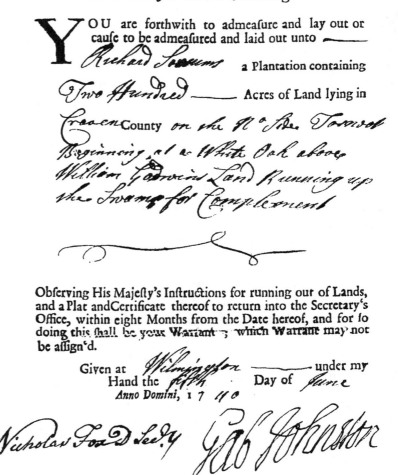

Figure 2-8. A typical early British grant.

are found at the Virginia State Library and the Family History Library.

Summary of Proprietors' Records and Crown Grants

Most of the early British grants have survived in one form or another. Whether as warrants, petitions, patents, surveys, or a combination thereof, some evidence usually remains for those who received land through the crown or one its representative charters or proprietors. Most of these records have been microfilmed and are available through a variety of major repositories, including individual state archives and land offices, as well as through the Family History Library.

These records, when indexed on a statewide basis, can often help define a county of origin for ancestors within the state. Strategically used, they can provide a wealth of information about relatives and associates which will also help link families across the ocean. Many original purchasers were first- or second-generation immigrants.

Loyalist Claims

Loyalist claims comprise another set of records generated through the influence of the British. These records have been the subject of controversy for more than two hundred years. They were created because the United States confiscated property from those considered loyal to Britain during the Revolutionary War. This confiscation actually began before the war started as states passed laws allowing seizure of property from anyone who would not pledge allegiance to the newly forming government.

Actual claims were generated as the British attempted to recompense the losses of loyalists. In 1783, an American Claims Commission was established by the British to oversee the claims, which included personal goods, monies, and agricultural crops, in addition to real estate. A strict deadline was implemented; no claims were to be received after 25 March 1784. Later, limited time extensions were added to this date.

Loyalist claim records have been gathered from a variety of locations in America, England, Canada, and elsewhere. They have been placed together in one significant repository: the Public Record Office in Kew, Surrey, England. Vague indexes to this vast collection are available through the Public Record Office (PRO). However, other authors have published more in-depth references.

One such index, by Clifford S. Dwyer, inventories the first of two series of records in the PRO. Series AO12, a collection of 146 bundles or volumes, is contained on thirty rolls of microfilm and is indexed alphabetically. AO13, a collection of 141 boxes and bundles, is much more extensive and comprises 145 rolls of microfilm. This later collection has been indexed and abstracted for bundles 1 through 35 and 37 by Peter Wilson Coldham, who published them through the National Genealogical Society in 1980. His description of the records housed in Kew is of tremendous value; it should be consulted by anyone interested in Loyalist activities.

Microfilm copies of these records are available through the Library of Congress or through interlibrary loan at most public libraries. They are also available at the Public Archives in Ottawa, Canada, and the Family History Library (figure 2-9.) A related inventory is the *Great Britain Public Record Office Lists and Indexes, Vol. 46,* which describes the documents in AO12 and AO13.

Great Britain Public Record Office Lists and Indexes, Vol. 46 also includes a surname index to other series: T77 and T79. These two series involve records created by the British government concerning land issues in East Florida as the British departed in 1783. They also house special reports on escheated estates in Virginia. (Escheatment refers to lands that were abandoned, forfeited, or were without heirs for further distribution.)

Records were also created by the British in lands that were not relinquished to the United

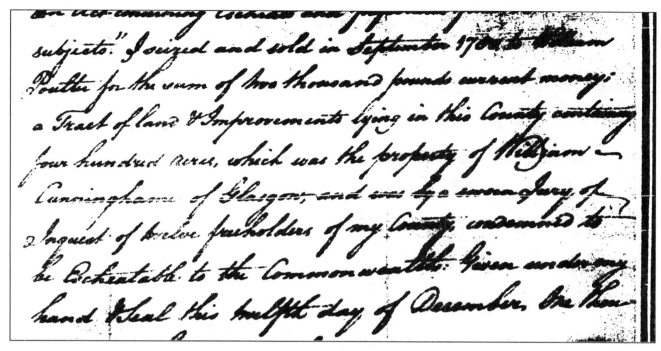

Figure 2-9. Excerpts from testimony concerning a Loyalist claim.

States. In 1783, East and West Florida were transferred from England back into Spanish possession. Even though England supervised this region for a period of only twenty years, an immense amount of land transactions occurred during that time. Between 1765 and 1775 more than 1.5 million acres were dispersed by the British in East Florida alone.

English grants in the Floridas were handled by two different governments: one for East Florida and one for West Florida, with headquarters in St. Augustine and Pensacola, respectively. Much less land was granted in West Florida, where the land was less desirable. Large grants were given there on the basis that one person for every hundred acres would inhabit the grant within ten years.

Headrights

Headrights and other grants were given in both Floridas: one hundred acres for the head of the household and fifty acres for other family members. If a family could prove the need and ability to cultivate more land, up to one thousand acres were additionally granted. Grant widths were usually measured as one-third of the depth, and cultivation and improvements were required on a yearly basis. Records generated by the headright grants include the following:

- Application (wherein the description of the family was given)
- Survey warrants
- Plat records
- Testimonies of witnesses
- The patent or title to the grant

The grants made to the inhabitants of East and West Florida were produced in a single ledger, recording the grantees or recipients separately from the granted land description. It is extremely difficult to match the grantees with the land description, but not impossible. The descriptions add to the genealogical and historical background of the people and places. The description, in fact, is necessary to determine whether the grant falls within the bounds of Louisiana, Mississippi, Alabama, or Florida. All of these states are included in the same volume. This ledger is now available on microfilm through the National Archives and

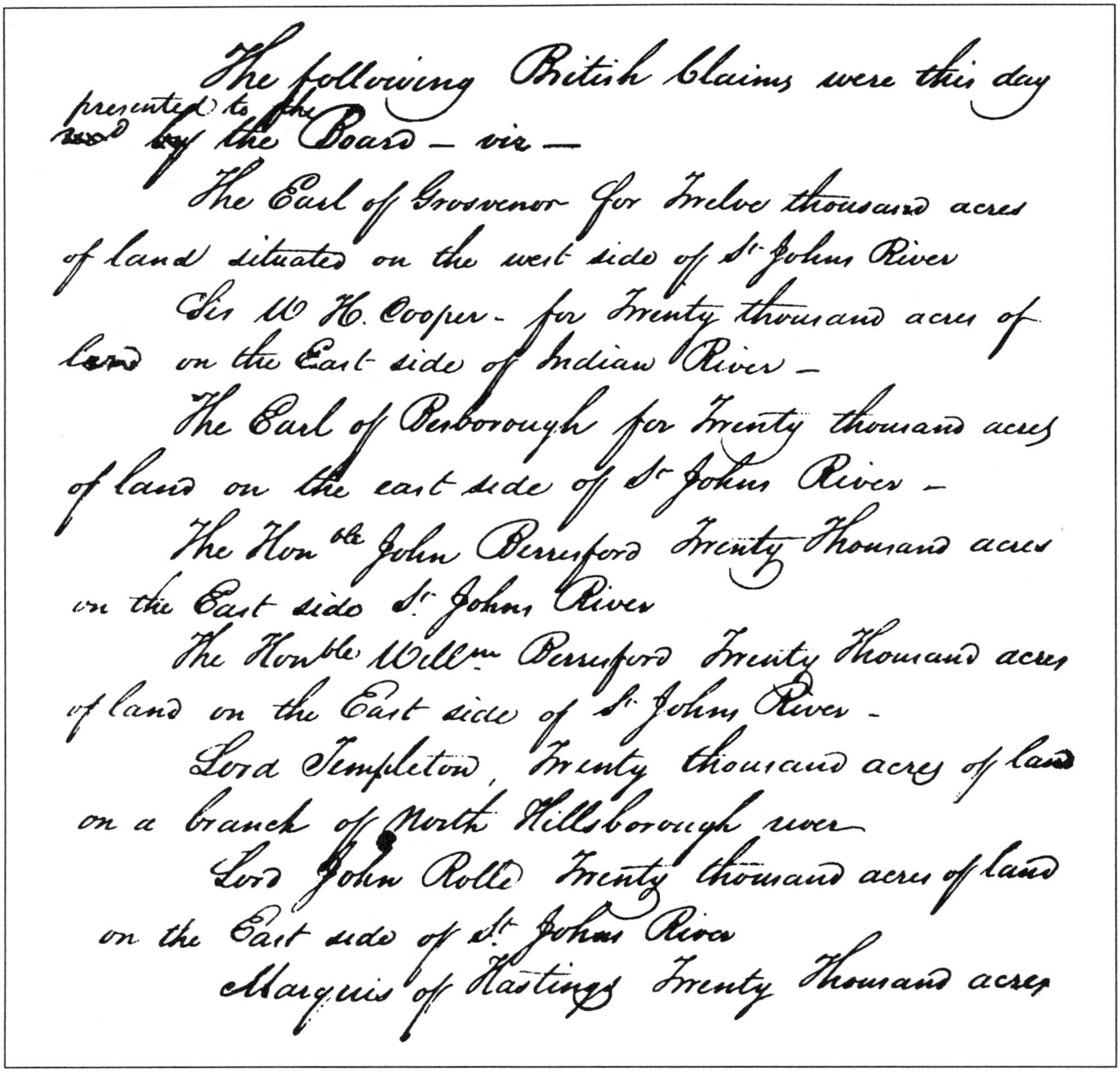

The following British Claims were this day presented to the Board — viz —

The Earl of Grosvenor for Twelve thousand acres of land situated on the west side of St. Johns River

Sir W. H. Cooper - for Twenty thousand acres of land on the East side of Indian River -

The Earl of Peterborough for Twenty thousand acres of land on the east side of St. Johns River -

The Honble John Berresford Twenty Thousand acres on the East side St. Johns River

The Honble Willm Berresford Twenty Thousand acres of land on the East side of St. Johns River -

Lord Templeton, Twenty thousand acres of land on a branch of North Hillsborough river

Lord John Rolle Twenty thousand acres of land on the East side of St. Johns River

Marquis of Hastings Twenty Thousand acres

Figure 2-10. British claims list; recorded in the minutes of the Board of Commissioners for private land claims.

its regional archives. British grants in East Florida can also be found among Spanish memorials. (For more information about memorials, see chapter 1, Spanish Possession.)

Private Land Claims

Private land claims provide another source for British-created land records. When most former British colonies became states, private land claims were not a consideration. The only exceptions were the provinces of East and West Florida. Many British inhabitants from those areas petitioned the United States to keep lands previously acquired under English and Spanish authority. In some cases, an original Spanish claim was confirmed later as an English claim and then eventually reconfirmed as a Spanish claim, with litigation from all three eras presented to the United States for consideration.

Many of the English grants in Florida were never settled by the recipients and generally were not confirmed in later claims processes. Most grants were to wealthier individuals, though some ordinary claims were also included. Smaller claims can be found—mostly in records of the Boards of Commissioners for West Florida. (See figure 2-10.) (For further information about private land claims, see chapter 9, Records Generated by Federal Lands.)

CONCLUSION

For most British-created records, current jurisdictions within each state-land state should be researched. These records are found in state archives, in state land commission offices, historical societies, university libraries, state public libraries, and museums with researchable collections. Dispersed this way, they prohibit complete reference in a single source. Refer to An Introduction to State Lands; chapter 6, Records Generated by State Lands; and to chapter 11, Records Generated by Individual Lands. In addition, see "For Further Reference" at the end of this chapter.

REPOSITORIES

(Organized alphabetically by state postal code.)

Public Record Office
Ruskin Avenue
Kew, Surrey TW9 4DU
England

National Archives of Canada
395 Wellington Street
Ottawa, Ontario K1A 0M8
Canada

North Carolina State Archives
Division of Archives and History
State Library Building
109 East Jones Street
Raleigh, NC 27601-2807

The New England Historical and Genealogical Society
99-101 Newbury Street
Boston, MA 02116

National Archives and Records Administration
Textual Reference Branch (NNR1)
Washington, D.C. 20408

National Archives and Records Administration
Cartographic Division (NNR2)
8601 Adelphi Road
College Park, MD 20740-6001

Florida State Archives
R.A. Gray Building
500 South Bronough St.
Tallahassee, FL 32399-0250

University of Florida
P.K. Yonge Library
Special Collections/Florida History
Gainesville, FL 32611

University of West Florida
John C. Pace Library
Pensacola, FL 32514

Library of Congress
Local History and Genealogy Reading Room
Humanities and Social Sciences Division
Thomas Jefferson Building LJ20
10 First Street, S.E.
Washington, D.C. 20540-5554

Family History Library
35 North West Temple
Salt Lake City, UT 84101

College of William and Mary
Institute of Early American History and Culture
Earl Gregg Swem Library Building
P.O. Box 8781
Williamsburg, VA 23187-8781

National Genealogical Society
4527 Seventeenth Street North
Arlington, VA 22207

FOR FURTHER REFERENCE

Akagi, Roy Hidemichi. *The Town Proprietors of the New England Colonies: A Study of Their Development, Organization, Activities and Controversies, 1620–1770.* Gloucester, Mass.: Peter Smith, 1963.

Allen, Robert S. *Loyalist Literature: An Annotated Bibliographic Guide to the Writings on the Loyalists of the American Revolution.* Toronto, Ontario: Dundurn Press, 1982.

Andrews, Charles M. *The Colonial Period of American History.* 4 vols. New Haven, Conn.: Yale University Press, 1934–38.

Bartlett, John R. *Records of the Colony of Rhode Island and Providence Plantations in New England.* Providence: Rhode Island General Assembly, 1857–65.

Bond, Beverley Waugh. *The Quit-Rent System in the American Colonies.* New Haven, Conn.: Yale University Press, 1919.

Boyd, Julian P., and Robert J. Taylor. *The Susquehannah Company Papers.* Wilkes-Barre, Pa.: Wyoming Historical and Genealogical Society, 1930.

Clark, Murtie June. *Loyalists in the Southern Campaign of the Revolutionary War.* Baltimore: Genealogical Publishing Co., 1981.

Clawson, Marion. *The Land System of the United States: An Introduction to the History and Practice of Land Use and Land Tenure.* Lincoln: University of Nebraska, 1968.

Coldham, Peter Wilson. *American Loyalist Claims, Vol. I, Abstracted from the Public Record Office Audit Office Series 13, Bundles 1–35 and 37.* Washington, D.C.: National Genealogical Society, 1980.

Cunningham, John T. *The East of Jersey: A History of the General Board of Proprietors of the Eastern Division of New Jersey.* Newark: New Jersey Historical Society, 1992.

De Ville, Winston. *English Land Grants in West Florida: A Register for the States of Alabama, Mississippi, and Parts of Florida and Louisiana, 1766–1776.* Ville Platte, La.: the author, 1986. This lists only those receiving grants, and not the description of the actual grant, though it can be very useful in determining existence and can even serve as a census substitute.

Ditz, Toby L. *Property and Kinship: Inheritance in Early Connecticut, 1750–1820.* Princeton, N.J.: Princeton University Press, 1986.

Dwyer, Clifford S. *Index to Series I of American Loyalist's Claims.* DeFuniak Springs, Fla.: Ram Publishing, 1985.

———. *Index to Series II of American Loyalist's Claims.* DeFuniak Springs, Fla.: Ram Publishing, 1985.

Esker, Katie-Prince Ward. *South Carolina Memorials: Registration of Land Grants.* 2 vols. Cottonport, La.: Polyanthos, 1973–77.

Fernow, B. *Documents Relating to the History of the Dutch and Swedish Settlements on the Delaware River.* Albany, N.Y.: Argus, 1877.

Fraser, Alexander. *United Empire Loyalists Inquiry into the Losses and Services in Consequence of Their Loyalty. Evidence in the Canadian Claims.* Toronto, Ontario: The King's Printer, 1905.

Gates, Paul W., et al. *History of Public Land Law Development.* Washington, D.C.: Government Printing Office, 1968.

General Assembly of the State of Delaware. *Original Land Titles in Delaware; Commonly Known as The Duke of York Record.* Wilmington: Delaware General Assembly, 1903.

Georgia Department of Archives and History. *A Preliminary Guide to Eighteenth Century Records Held by the Georgia Department of Archives and History.* Atlanta: Georgia Department of Archives and History, 1976.

Gold, Robert L. *Borderland Empires in Transition: The Triple Nation Transfer of Florida.* Carbondale and Edwardsville: Southern Illinois University Press, 1969.

Gould, Clarence P. *The Land System in Maryland, 1720–1765.* Baltimore: Johns Hopkins Press, 1913.

Greenwood, Val D. *The Researcher's Guide to American Genealogy, 2nd Edition.* Baltimore: Genealogical Publishing Co., 1990.

Hannah, Samuel D. *Permissive Uses of the Common Lands of Proprietary Plantations.* Yarmouthport, Mass.: C.W. Swift, 1927.

Hemperley, Marion R. *Georgia Surveyor-General Department: A History and Inventory of Georgia's Land Office.* Atlanta: State Printing Office, 1982.

Historical Records Survey, Division of Professional and Service Projects, and Work Projects Administration. *Spanish Land Grants in Florida.* Tallahassee, Fla.: State Library Board, 1940. Includes information on the British Land Grants in East and West Florida.

Hofmann, Margaret M. "Land Grants" in *North Carolina Research: Genealogy and Local History.* Raleigh: North Carolina Genealogical Society, 1980.

_____. *Province of North Carolina, 1663–1729: Abstracts of Land Patents.* Weldon, N.C.: Roanoke News, 1979.

Kershaw, Gordon E. *The Kennebec Proprietors, 1749–1775.* Portland: Maine Historical Society, 1975.

Kim, Sung Bok. *Landlord and Tenant in Colonial New York: Manorial Society, 1664–1775.* Chapel Hill: University of North Carolina Press, 1978.

Lowrie, Walter. *Early Settlers of Louisiana, Mississippi . . . as Taken from Land Claims in the Louisiana, Mississippi . . . Territory.* Reprint. Easley, S.C.: Southern Historical Press, 1986.

Lucas, Silas Emmett, Jr. *Index to the Headright and Bounty Grants of Georgia, 1756–1909.* Vidalia, Ga.: Georgia Genealogical Reprints, 1970.

Mershon, Stephen Lyon. *English Crown Grants: The Foundation of Colonial Land Titles Under English Common Law.* New York: Law and History Club, 1918.

Morgan, Lawrence N. *Land Tenure in Proprietary North Carolina.* James Sprunt Historical Publications. Vol. 12, no. 2. Chapel Hill: University of North Carolina, 1912.

Munger, Donna Bingham. *Pennsylvania Land Records: A History and Guide for Research.* Wilmington, Del.: Scholarly Resources, 1991.

New York State Archives. *Public Records Relating to Land in New York State.* Albany: New York State Archives, 1979.

Nugent, Nell Marion. *Cavaliers and Pioneers: A Calendar of Virginia Land Grants.* 5 vols. Richmond: Virginia State Library, 1934.

Palmer, Gregory, ed. *A Bibliography of Loyalist Source Material in the United States, Canada, and Great Britain.* Westport and London: Meckler Publishing and the American Antiquarian Society, 1982.

Petersen, Mary A. "British West Florida: Abstracts of Land Petitions." *Louisiana Genealogical Register* 18 (4) (December 1971)–20 (1) (March 1973).

Pomfret, John E. *The New Jersey Proprietors and Their Lands, 1664–1776.* Princeton, N.J.: D. Van Nostrand, 1964.

Powell, William Stevens. *The Proprietors of Carolina.* Raleigh, N.C.: State Department of Archives and History, 1968.

Pruitt, Albert Bruce. *Colonial Petitions for Land Resurveys, Some Land Warrants 1753–1774, Caveats of Land Warrants 1767–1773 in North Carolina.* Whitakers, N.C.: the author, 1993.

_____. *Abstracts of Confiscated Loyalists Land and Property in North Carolina.* Rocky Mount, N.C.: the author, 1989.

"Research in Land and Tax Records." In *The Source: A Guidebook of American Genealogy.* Rev. ed. Salt Lake City: Ancestry, 1997.

Russ, William A. *How Pennsylvania Acquired its Present Boundaries.* University Park: Pennsylvania Historical Association, 1966.

Sale, Edith Dabney Tunis. *Manors of Virginia in Colonial Times.* Philadelphia: J.B. Lippincott Co., 1909.

Salley, A.S., Jr. *Warrants for Land in South Carolina, 1672–1711*. Columbia: University of South Carolina Press, 1973.

Sears, Joan N. *The First One Hundred Years of Town Planning in Georgia*. Atlanta: Cherokee Publishing Co., 1979.

Sergeant, Thomas. *View of the Land Laws of Pennsylvania*. Laughlin: Southwest Pennsylvania Genealogical Services, 1992.

Shurtleff, Nathaniel B. *Records of the Governor and Company of the Massachusetts Bay in New England*. Boston: Order of the Legislature, 1853–54.

_____. *Records of the Colony of New Plymouth in the New England*. Boston: Order of the Legislature, 1855–61.

Skordas, Gustaf. *The Early Settlers of Maryland; An Index to Names of Immigrants Compiled from Records of Land Patents, 1633–1680*. Baltimore: Genealogical Publishing Co., 1968.

Sullivan, James. *History of Land Titles in Massachusetts*. Boston: I. Thomas and E.T. Andrews, 1801.

United States Congress. *The American State Papers: Public Lands*. Washington, D.C.: Gales and Seaton, 1832–61.

Weinberg, Allen, and Thomas E. Slattery. *Warrants and Surveys of the Province of Pennsylvania, Including the Three Lower Counties, 1759*. Philadelphia: Philadelphia Department of Records, 1965.

Wehmann, Howard H., and Benjamin L. DeWhitt, comps. *Pre-Federal Records in the National Archives*. Washington, D.C.: National Archives Trust Fund Board, 1989.

Winsor, Justin. *The Cartographic History of the North-Eastern Boundary Controversy Between the United States and Great Britain*. Cambridge, Mass.: J. Wilson and Son, 1887.

Woodward, Florence May. *The Town Proprietors in Vermont: New England Town Proprietorship in Decline*. New York: Columbia University Press, 1936.

Worthington, Dorothy. *Rhode Island Land Evidences, Vol. 1, 1648–1696*. Providence: Rhode Island Historical Society, 1921.

3
French Possession

HISTORICAL BACKGROUND

The French first attempted to establish settlements in North America in 1534, exploring areas in present-day Canada. Their claims were vast, but French inhabitance was insufficient to maintain large amounts of unexplored lands. By 1763, French possessions in the present-day United States had ceased to exist. Though the years of France's tenure in America were limited, French influence is still recognized today in architecture, culture, and land organization.

The sixteenth century was an active yet frustrating era for the French. By 1540, they had begun to explore the Gulf of St. Lawrence and the island of Montreal. In 1541, a settlement named Charlesbourg was established on the present-day site of the city of Quebec. Further to the south, a group of persecuted Huguenots founded a colony in Carolina, so named by them, in 1562. Though their settlement soon failed, the name was retained by the British and applied to the whole country from the Savannah River to the southern boundary of Virginia. By 1570, the French were also building forts in the southern Gulf Coast region of La Florida. However, the Spanish were quick to eliminate these Florida settlements as soon as each was built, in efforts to maintain their own claims.

Other settlements came and went. France eventually followed the example of the British, granting charters to companies or individuals. In 1603 a grant was made to De Monts. This grant began at the latitude of present-day Philadelphia and extended northward to one degree north of Montreal. In addition to the land grant, he received a monopoly on the fur trade and religious freedom for Huguenot immigrants. Through this same charter, in 1605, the first permanent French settlement in North America was established. Called Port Royal, it encompassed present-day Nova Scotia. The entire surrounding area was given the name Acadia. Not until 1608 did France establish another permanent settlement, in Quebec, founded by Samuel de Champlain.

The French focused more on the fur trade than on exploration and colonization. The first documented voyage from the Great Lakes region down the Mississippi River and into Arkansas did not take place until 1673. In 1682, Sieur de La Salle made another Mississippi voyage, this time completing the journey south to the Gulf of Mexico. He quietly claimed the entire vast central region for France, calling it Louisiana for King Louis XIV. Through this claim, the French began to generate more consistent records of their presence in North America.

In 1699, the first successful French settlement in lower Louisiana was established through a charter to an enterprising explorer named Iberville. Several other settlements followed, though all were sheltered under the cloaks of fortresses, housing mostly fur traders and soldiers. No individual grants were made.

By 1712, under a charter granted to Antoine Crozat, Louisiana included four small settlement fortresses: Mobile, Biloxi, Dauphine Island, and Ship Island. Within the next five years two more were added: Rosalie at Natchez, and "Natchitoches." By 1717, the French population in Louisiana had increased to seven hundred French citizens, though a weary Crozat petitioned the French government to be released from his contract.

France reassigned the charter in 1717 to The Mississippi Company, also called The Company of the West. The company was headed by John Law, a renowned financier, and the contract was for a period of twenty-five years. The Mississippi Company's first accomplishment was the founding of New Orleans in 1718 by Bienville, Iberville's younger brother. During its term, which ended by forfeiture in 1731, The Company of the West succeeded in attracting more than seven thousand new settlers to Louisiana. By that time, France's claims through the central United States had also extended eastward into the Indian territories that England claimed as her own, generating new conflicts between the two powers. In the southern gulf region, the French had also established settlements as far east as the mouth of the Alabama River.

France's concentration on financial gain through trade and precious minerals met with bitter disappointment. Settlement efforts had been largely unsuccessful as well, due to forced emigration and attempts to populate areas with former prisoners and undesirables from the homeland. Aside from fortresses and a few unsuccessful land companies, very few land records were generated.

France, disillusioned and weakened by the French and Indian War with England, secretly ceded the Louisiana Territory to Spain in 1762; this was done to ensure that England did not eventually gain possession. In 1763, at the conclusion of the war, France lost its remaining possessions in Canada to the British. The French continued to settle in the Louisiana Territory under the Spanish government, even holding positions in the Spanish administration. They remained close allies with Spain. In 1800, the Spanish became weary of struggling to contain and efficiently administer a territory as large as Louisiana, so they secretly ceded the territory of Louisiana back to France; this was done in hopes that the territory would not fall into the hands of the Americans.

The Louisiana Territory, though once again claimed by the French, existed mostly under the preexisting Spanish administration for another three years. In 1803, Napoleon, needing revenue to finance France's exhausting European war with Britain, sold the Louisiana Territory to the United States.

The Louisiana Territory, even when sold to the United States, was loosely defined in boundaries (see figure 3-1). It took almost two decades to resolve subsequent disputes and to establish a precise definition of bounds. However, if not for the French, the world's geography today might be much different. It can be surmised that by exploring and occupying the vast continental interior of America, the French forestalled attempts by the more active Spanish and English to solidly occupy this area. This prevented either of the two from restricting the influence of, or militarily advancing against, the newly formed government of the United States.

THE RECORDS

Though France held a vast amount of territory (figure 3-2), some of the richest on earth, its settlements were closely grouped and isolated in purpose. Records were generated mostly on an ecclesiastical or economic basis. The commanding officers of fortress-style colonies documented daily happenings and created census-like lists of inhabitants. However, a concerted effort to organize, distribute, and record land transactions was among the least of French concerns.

Settlements were established with private grants to selected individuals or companies, but lands in the upper Louisiana Territory were never actually sold by any French or Spanish authorities. Because the French government had vested authority only in the charters, the earliest documentations were the concern of the proprietary grantee, not the government. Carelessness and indifference to

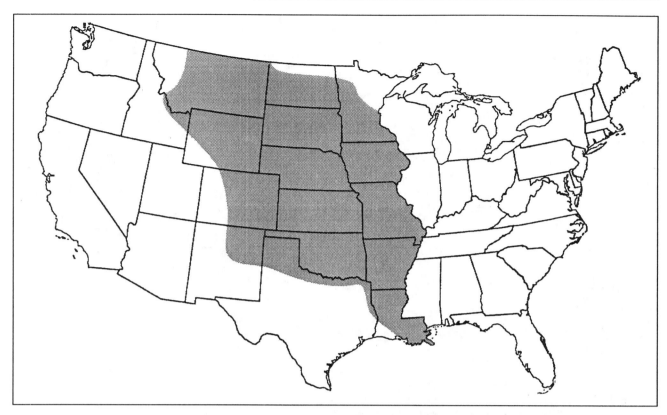

Figure 3-1. Approximate boundaries of the Louisiana Purchase in relation to present-day states.

the aspect of organized growth by the proprietors resulted in only vague references to land for the earliest time periods.

Though many different records exist from the French regime, most are ecclesiastical records or records created by the industry of trade (e.g., shipping logs, sailors' accounts and advances, contracts, passenger lists, muster rolls). While the French records are not as thorough as Spanish records, they do provide some critical clues for researchers. Some noteworthy collections are described below.

The Superior Council Records comprise one of the more important collections regarding the French occupation of Louisiana Territory. These records include a wide variety of documents, such as marriage contracts, criminal and civil suits, and maritime litigation. Also included are land suits, inventories of property, leases, mortgages, and notaries' certificates for land transactions. Though extensive in source coverage, this collection pertains mostly to present-day Louisiana, where the

majority of French settlement occurred. Most of the records are in French. (See figure 3-3.)

The Superior Council Records are now housed in the Old United States Mint in New Orleans. Preserved along with several other historical collections, the records at this repository are under the authority of the Louisiana Historical Center, a branch of the Louisiana State Museum. They have been microfilmed and are available through Tulane University, the Louisiana State Museum, and the Family History Library.

Various indexes and calendars are available for the Superior Council Records, each having varying degrees of accuracy and completeness. One is a calendar which has been published by the *Louisiana Historical Quarterly,* a publication which is itself indexed for quick reference. The "Black Books," housed in the Louisiana State Museum Library, provide an alphabetical index to records and include a brief description of each document involved. These books are incomplete, and they contain errors in both transcription and reference.

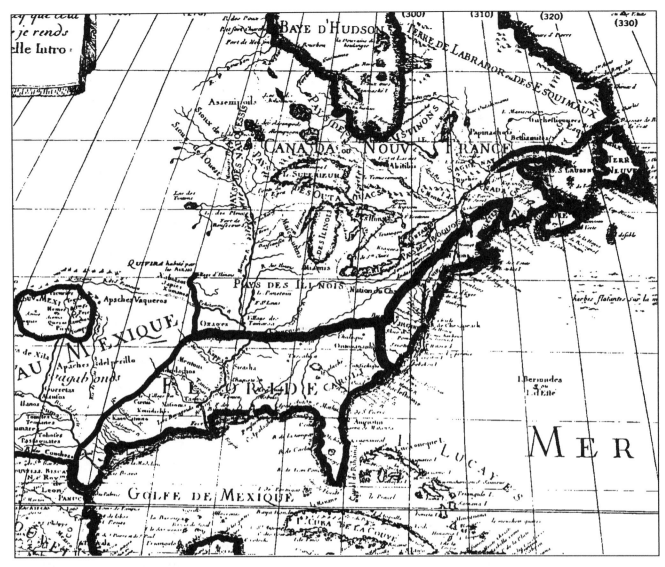

Figure 3-2. Early map (ca. 1700) which depicts the immense size of the French claim in America in comparison with the British possessions and the two Spanish claims of Florida and New Mexico.

Notarial Records. Eventually, French land records were kept by notaries. Such records are noted to have been in existence as early as 1702, though many were carried off by both Confederate and Union soldiers during the Civil War. Most remaining notarial records from the French period are now at the Louisiana State Museum in New Orleans.

Some smaller but significant collections are described below.

• **The Land Grants of French Louisiana, 1753–1769** are in the Howard-Tilton Memorial Library at Tulane University. They contain 110 items concerning land grants, petitions, and surveys for Louisiana during French occupancy.

• **Land District at Opelousas** includes abstracts of French patents and surveys from 1757. They are mingled with Spanish records dating to 1802.

• **French Land Grants in Mobile** is a volume of manuscripts found in the library at the University of Alabama. This volume also contains Spanish land grants for West Florida.

• **The Cabildo Papers,** described in chapter 1, Spanish Possession, should also be referenced. Though they mostly document the Spanish era,

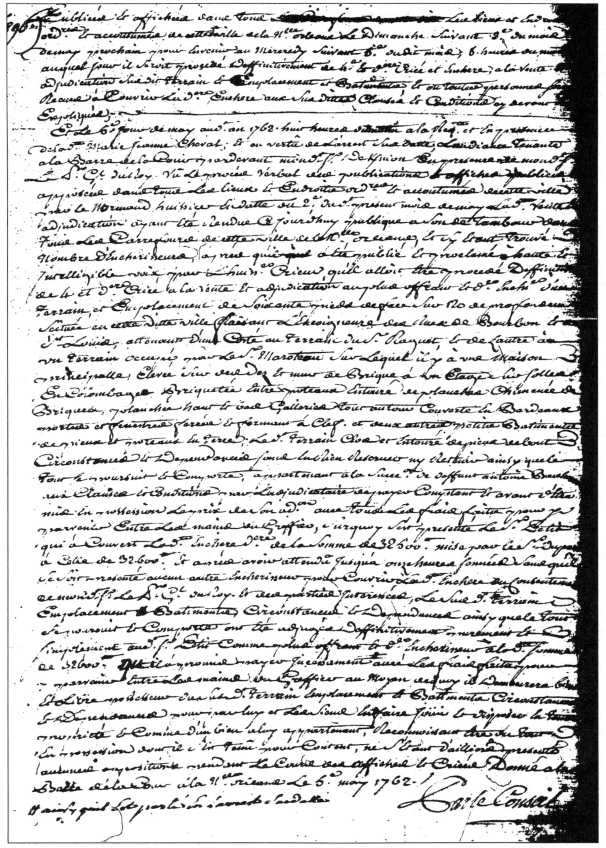

Figure 3-3. A 1762 deed, written in French, for property involving the now-famous Bourbon Street in New Orleans; from the Superior Council Records.

these records also include many documents created by the French.

- **Memorial Records.** French records can often be found among other Spanish documents as well, mostly in memorials. They were created when French grants were reconfirmed as Spain took possession of the Louisiana Territory in 1763. (See chapter 1, Spanish Possession.)

- **Private Land Claims.** Many French documents were presented for the first time in an attempt to reconfirm grants as the United States took possession of the Louisiana Territory in 1803. These papers are included with the records of various boards of land commissioners and surveyor-general offices. Many are housed at the National Archives, including records for Louisiana, Arkansas, and Missouri. (See figure 3-4.) (For further reference, see chapter 9, Records Generated by Federal Lands.)

CONCLUSION

Few records assembled by the French in North America ever reached France. Those that did were mostly settlement administrative minutes, maritime records, and records concerning the trade agreements for the Louisiana Territory. Many others were lost at sea. Most of those that involve land issues were kept in Louisiana. Ironically, the greatest threat to the survival of these records was not the French, Spanish, or British, but rather American actions during the Civil War. Many records were carried away or fell into the hands of those for whom proper preservation and protection were of low priority.

Fortunately, through the foresight of organizations such as the Louisiana State Museum and the Louisiana Historical Society, as well as major university libraries throughout the United States, many records have been purchased, collected, and preserved on microfilm. Many smaller collections are identified in Henry Putney Beers' *French and Spanish Records of Louisiana*. Also see "For Further Reference" at the end of this chapter.

REPOSITORIES

(Organized alphabetically by state postal code.)

Alabama Department of Archives and History
624 Washington Avenue
Montgomery, AL 36130-3601

Arkansas History Commission
1 Capitol Mall
Little Rock, AR 72201

National Archives and Records Administration
Textual Reference Branch (NNR1)
Washington, D.C. 20408

Archives Nationales
11, Rue des Quatre-Fils
75141 Paris 3e
France

Bibliotheque Nationale
58 Rue de Richelieu
75084 Paris Cedex 02
France

Commission Nationale de Genealogie Archives
9 Place Royale
Quebec, Quebec G1K 4G3
Canada

Illinois State Archives Division
Office of the Secretary of State
Archives Building
Capitol Complex
Springfield, IL 62756

Newberry Public Library
60 West Walton Street
Chicago, IL 60610

Southern University
John B. Cade Library
Southern Br. PO
Baton Rouge, LA 70813

Louisiana Notarial Archives
(see Louisiana State Museum)

New Orleans Public Library
Louisiana Division
219 Loyola Avenue
New Orleans, LA 70140

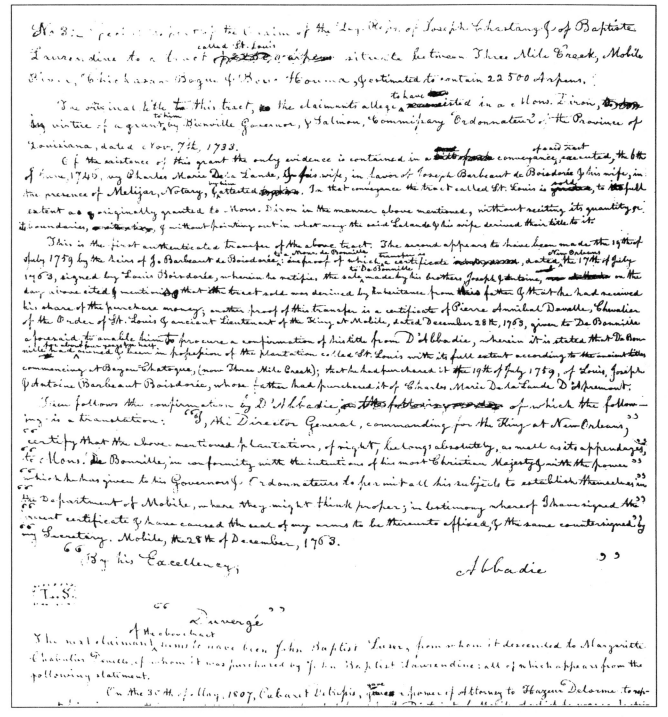

Figure 3-4. A French document presented during private land claims processes. It describes title transfers from 1733–63. Document from St. Stephen's Land Office, Alabama.

Loyola University of New Orleans
Spanish Documents Project
6363 St. Charles Avenue
P.O. Box 198
New Orleans, LA 70118

Louisiana State Archives and Records
Office of the Secretary of State
3851 Essen Lane
P.O. Box 94125
Baton Rouge, LA 70804-9125

Louisiana State Museum
Louisiana Historical Center Library
751 Chartres Street
New Orleans, LA 70176

Louisiana Historical Association
Center for Louisiana Studies
The University of Southwestern Louisiana
P.O. Box 40831, USL
Lafayette, LA 70504

The Historic New Orleans Collection
Kemper and Leila Williams Foundation
Research Library
533 Royal Street
New Orleans, LA 70130

Tulane University
Howard-Tilton Memorial Library
New Orleans, LA 70118-5682

National Archives and Records Administration
Cartographic Division (NNR2)
8601 Adelphi Road
College Park, MD 20740-6001

Missouri State Archives
600 West Main Street
P.O. Box 778
Jefferson City, MO 65102

Mississippi Archives and Library Division
Mississippi Dept. of Archives and History
P.O. Box 571
Jackson, MS 39205-0571

Family History Library
35 North West Temple
Salt Lake City, UT 84101

FOR FURTHER REFERENCE

American Heritage. *Pictorial Atlas of United States History.* New York: American Heritage Publishing Co., 1966.

Beers, Henry Putney. *French and Spanish Records of Louisiana: A Bibliographical Guide to Archive and Manuscript Sources.* Baton Rouge: Louisiana State University Press, 1989.

Conrad, Glenn R., and Carl A. Brasseaux. *A Selected Bibliography of Scholarly Literature on Colonial Louisiana and New France.* Lafayette: Center for Louisiana Studies, 1982.

Cornay, Jeanne. "Spanish and French Land Grants in Southwest Louisiana." *Kinfolks* 17 (4) (1993).

Cox, Isaac J., ed. *The West Florida Controversy, 1798–1813.* Baltimore: Johns Hopkins University Press, 1918.

Giraud, Marcel. *A History of French Louisiana.* Translated by Brian Pearce. Baton Rouge: Louisiana State University Press, 1974.

Hill, Roscoe R. *Descriptive Catalog of Documents Relating to the History of the United States in the Papeles Procedentes de Cuba Deposited in the Archivo General de Indies at Seville.* Washington, D.C.: Carnegie Institute of Washington, 1916.

Kirkham, E. Kay. *A Genealogical and Historical Atlas of the United States of America.* Logan, Utah: Everton Publishers, 1976.

Leland, Waldo G. *Guide to Materials for American History in the Libraries and Archives of France.* Washington, D.C.: Carnegie Institute, 1932.

"Louisiana's Spanish Colonial Records." *Kinfolks* 18 (1) (1994).

Lowrie, Walter. *Early Settlers of Louisiana, Mississippi . . . as Taken from Land Claims in the Mississippi Territory.* Reprint. Easley, S.C.: Southern Historical Press, 1986.

Martin, T.P. *The Confirmation of French and Spanish Land Titles in the Louisiana Purchase.* M.A. thesis, University of California, Berkeley, 1914.

McMullin, Phillip W. *Grassroots of America.* Salt Lake City: Gendex, 1972.

Oudard, Georges. *Four Cents an Acre.* New York: Brewer and Warren, 1931.

Pitot, James. *Observations on the Colony of Louisiana from 1796–1802.* Baton Rouge: Louisiana State University Press, 1979.

Reeves, Sally K. "Notarial Records of the New Orleans Notarial Archives." *Louisiana Library Association Bulletin* 55 (1) (Summer 1992).

Rowland, Dunbar, and A.G. Sanders, eds. *Mississippi Provincial Archives, French Dominion.* Revised and edited by Patricia Kay Galloway. 5+ vols. Baton Rouge: Louisiana State University Press, 1984.

Stenberg, Richard. "The Boundaries of the Louisiana Purchase." *The Hispanic American Historical Review* 3 (1898).

United States Congress. *The American State Papers: Public Lands.* Washington, D.C.: Gales and Seaton, 1832–61.

Wallace, Joseph. *The History of Illinois and Louisiana Under the French Rule.* Cincinnati: Robert Clarke and Co., 1893.

Wehmann, Howard H., and Benjamin DeWhitt, comps. *A Guide to Pre-Federal Records in the National Archives.* Washington, D.C.: National Archives Trust Fund Board, 1989.

Wilson, Lyle E. *Louisiana in French Diplomacy: 1759–1804.* Norman: University of Oklahoma Press, 1974.

White, Joseph M. *A New Collection of Laws, Charters and Local Ordinances on the Governments of Great Britain, France, and Spain, Relating to the Concessions of Land in Their Respective Colonies, Together with the Laws of Mexico and Texas on the Same Subject.* 2 vols. Philadelphia, 1839.

4

Mexican Possession

HISTORICAL BACKGROUND

At one time, Mexico's northern reaches included almost one quarter of the present-day United States. While Spain had been successful in exploring these northern borderlands, it was the Mexicans who stimulated massive colonization and economic stability. In 1821, while Spain was withdrawing from the Floridas, Mexico officially gained its independence from Spain and began its own administration of the southwest, including Texas. It was under Mexican influence that California and Texas truly flourished. Mexico's rule lasted twenty-seven years, until 1848, and most early ancestors in these regions can be shown as being of Mexican descent—generally Indians and Mestizos (mixed bloods).

In September of 1821, as Mexico separated from Spain, provinces were created for purposes of administration. These provinces were California: Province of the West; New Mexico: Province of the North; and Texas: Province of the East. California included much of Arizona. New Mexico encompassed the present-day states of New Mexico, Nevada, Colorado, and Utah. Texas included portions of Oklahoma, Kansas, and Wyoming. (See figure 4-1.)

Under an act of 18 August 1824, Mexico began a liberal attempt to solicit settlers and promote more widespread colonization in Texas. A ban on American settlers was removed, and tariffs were lifted on emigration for those who arrived within the following four years. However, restrictions were placed on settlement within twenty leagues of any foreign nation's boundaries and on settlement within ten leagues of any gulf shoreline without government permission. The act was followed by a more specific Empresario Act in 1825. *Empresarios* were colonizers, such as Stephen F. Austin, who received large grants in order to form entire communities.

In an act of 1828, Mexico ordered direct colonization of California and New Mexico. This act allowed grants to be made by the respective governors of each territory. They could grant to empresarios, families, or individuals, whether of Mexican descent or foreigners, though cultivation and residency were required. Similar to the Spanish grants, these grants were requested through petitions. Land was usually portioned out within each grant, giving separate specified acreages for cultivation, cattle breeding, and other necessities.

On 29 January 1829, Mexico passed legislation providing debt relief for those who colonized under the Empresario Act of 1825. These lands could not be sold for debt acquired prior to their settlement there, and no such suit could be brought for a period of twelve years. This included all suits from former countries of origin.

On 6 April 1830, Mexico finally passed laws designed to halt American emigration to Texas. There was concern of a revolution as the Mexican government suddenly realized that the American population was growing too rapidly. Ironically, it was the passage of laws in response to these con-

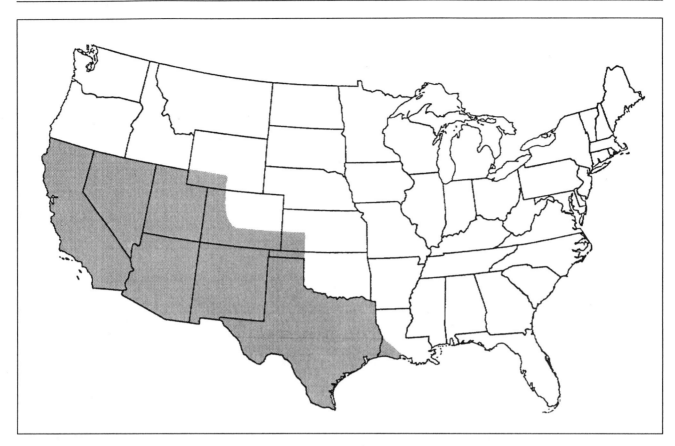

Figure 4-1. Approximate area under Mexican administration after Mexico's separation from Spain in 1821.

cerns that, over the next five years, produced the very revolution the laws were designed to prevent.

By 1835, more than 30,000 Americans lived in Mexican-administrated Texas. Those who came to settle without the assistance of an empresario were to receive one additional *labor* (approximately 177 acres) than those settling under the direction of an empresario. According to the Texas General Land Office, most American settlers there came from Alabama, Arkansas, Kentucky, Louisiana, Missouri, and Tennessee. Most were Protestant, in spite of the adherence to Catholicism being required for land ownership and citizenship in Mexico.

As Texas gained its independence, the newly formed republic recognized only those grants made before November of 1835, the date Mexican administration officially ceased in Texas. The original declaration also included portions of New Mexico that were in conflict with later treaties between the United States and Mexico. The bound-

ary dispute was settled in 1850, defining the present-day borders of New Mexico and Colorado. (See figure 4-2.)

Internal revolutions in Mexico increased dramatically over the following years. In 1845, the Republic of Texas was annexed by the United States. Mexico had warned that this annexation would be considered a declaration of war. However, it was the boundary dispute over Texas' western border that actually ignited the Mexican War. This war lasted from 1845 to 1848. At its conclusion, the Treaty of Guadalupe Hidalgo transferred the northern borderlands of California and the New Mexico Territory to American administration.

There was further dispute over the actual southern boundaries of the United States after the Mexican War. In 1854, these disputes were settled with the Gadsden Purchase, by which the United States acquired the most southern parts of present-day New Mexico and Arizona. This purchase secured the present-day continental United States from all foreign possession.

Mexican possession within the present-day United States lasted less than three decades. During that time, however, the Mexicans contributed as much to settlement and land development as the Spanish and French had in more than three hundred years. Their records are the basis for researching not only their own colonization, but much of Spain's colonization efforts as well.

THE RECORDS

More than 26 million acres were granted by Spain and Mexico in Texas; approximately two-thirds of them were distributed by Mexico. More grants were given in any two years of Mexican authority than during the entire administration of Spain. Grants were largely in the form of *ranchos* (any grant over one thousand acres was considered a *rancho*) and were given mostly in the regions of

California and Texas. For those distributed in New Mexico, refer to chapter 1, Spanish Possessions.

Texas

Grants similar to headrights were given by the Mexican government in Texas and, after 1834, in California. Grants included property, as well as cultivation tools and even livestock in some circumstances. Petitions, proof of stipulations met, final title to the property, and plat maps of the land involved were all to have been recorded and reported to the supreme government on a quarterly basis. This requirement was generally disregarded, and few grantees ever followed through to obtain official title as long as rightful inhabitance was not questioned.

Most records refer to empresario grants in Texas. Empresarios were colonizers who received large grants in order to form entire communities. Their own personal grants were based upon the number

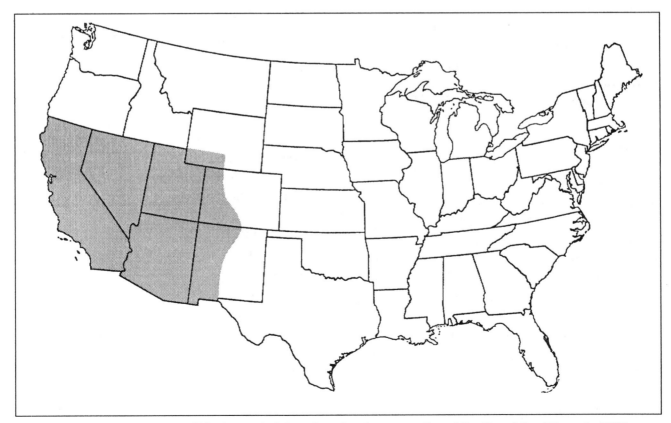

Figure 4-2. Approximate area of Mexican administration after the separation of the Republic of Texas in 1836.

of productive settlers introduced to the area. The first act, in 1823, was called the Imperial Colonization Act. Stephen Austin was the only person to receive a grant under this act. Under a new act in 1825, empresarios in Coahuila and Texas were to receive five leagues and five labors (23,025 acres) of land for each one hundred families brought to the area. For a list of empresario grants, see George J. Nixon's "Genealogical and Historical Sources in the Spanish and Mexican Southwest" in *The Source: A Guidebook of American Genealogy* (first edition).

In order to receive an empresario grant, the petitioner needed to provide at least twelve families for initial settlement. A number of additional settlers had to follow within the first six years. Designated cultivation and improvements had to be performed on the lands within a specified time period or the empresario grant was voided. For his own administration, the empresario received 230.25 acres for each family successfully settled (up to eight hundred families).

Each family that settled under the empresario grant was to receive one labor of farm land (approximately 177 acres) and twenty-four labors (4,251 acres) of grazing land. A single man received one-fourth of a league (a league being three miles square)—the remainder if and when he married. He received an additional one-fourth of a league if he married a woman of Mexican descent.

Under empresario grants, colonists paid $2 for stamped paper, $15 to the local land commissioner, $10 to the clerk, $30 to the Mexican government (due after four years), and $60 to the empresario. For 4,428 acres, this totalled $117, or about $0.38 per acre. Meanwhile, the United States, under the Act of 1820, was requiring cash to be paid up front, for a minimum of eighty acres at $1.25 per acre. The incentives for American emigration to Texas were obvious. The empresarios oversaw the property application and distribution process, though the land commissioner was to record titles. One copy, a *testimonio,* was given to the grantees, while the original, the *protocol,* was kept by the commissioner. At times, the empresario also acted as commissioner.

As Texas gained independence from Mexico, one of its first congressional acts required all land transactions from the acquired territory to be submitted to the newly formed General Land Office, which was in Houston at that time. This requirement did not include the area between the Nueces and Rio Grande rivers, as that area was not acquired until after the Mexican War, in 1848. The records from this area were later copied from the archives in Mexico and are now housed in the Texas General Land Office with the other land records.

The Spanish Archives of the Texas General Land Office are contained in sixty-nine volumes. Four volumes involve grants to missions and five volumes involve grants to empresarios. The remainder contain individual grants. These records are not in alphabetical or chronological order. They have, however, been indexed by Virginia H. Taylor in *Index to Spanish and Mexican Land Grants in Texas.* This index lists the names of the grantees, the date of title, amount of land, the colony (if under an empresario; otherwise, the name of the land commissioner), and the present-day county/state in which the grant was made. This index takes into account both completed and incomplete grants made in the area.

California

There is a collection from the Surveyor-General's Office in the state of California titled **"Spanish Archives."** The records are housed in the California State Archives, and concern Mexican administration of lands from 1833 to 1845. Grants, petitions, survey plat maps, testimonies, and general correspondence are among the types of records included.

This collection is available in two formats. One is the original Spanish version, and the other is an English translation. Both versions have been microfilmed and are available through the Family History Library and the California State Archives in Sacramento. Included are indexes that are organized once by grantee and once by the name of the grant/property. (See figure 4-3.)

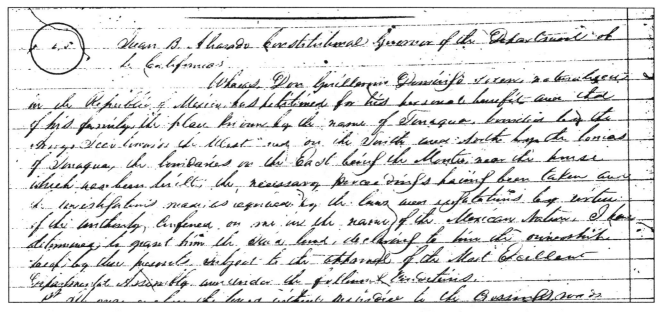

Figure 4-3. An English translation of a Mexican land grant; found among the Spanish Archives at the California State Archives in Sacramento.

References to most Mexican grants are found among the **Private Land Claims** papers. Boards of commissioners and specially appointed U.S. courts adjudicated these claims. Most of these records for the state of California have been microfilmed and are available through the California State Archives and through the Family History Library. (See figure 4-4.) (For further reference, see "Private Land Claims" in chapter 9, Records Generated by Federal Lands.)

CONCLUSION

Only 588 grants were made by Spanish and Mexican authorities between 1769 and 1846; they comprise almost 9 million acres of confirmed claims and more than 3 million acres of unconfirmed claims. It is said that more than two-thirds of these grants can be attributed solely to Mexican dispensation. Mexican land records are more organized and consistent than those of their Spanish predecessors. Though limited in number, they provide information about thousands of individuals who were witnesses, neighbors, relatives, and acquaintances. Mexican land records help researchers uncover information that would otherwise be lost, about a people who struggled to improve and develop the southwestern region of what is now known as the United States.

REPOSITORIES

National Archives and Records Administration
Textual Reference Branch (NNR1)
Washington, D.C. 20408

National Archives and Records Administration
Cartographic Division (NNR2)
College Park, MD 20740

Bureau of Land Management
Dept. of the Interior
P.O. Box 1449
Santa Fe, NM 87501

Bureau of Land Management
California State Office
2800 College Way
Sacramento, CA 95825

New Mexico Records Center and Archives
404 Montezuma Street
Santa Fe, NM 87501

California State Archives
Office of Secretary of State
1020 O Street, Room 130
Sacramento, CA 95814

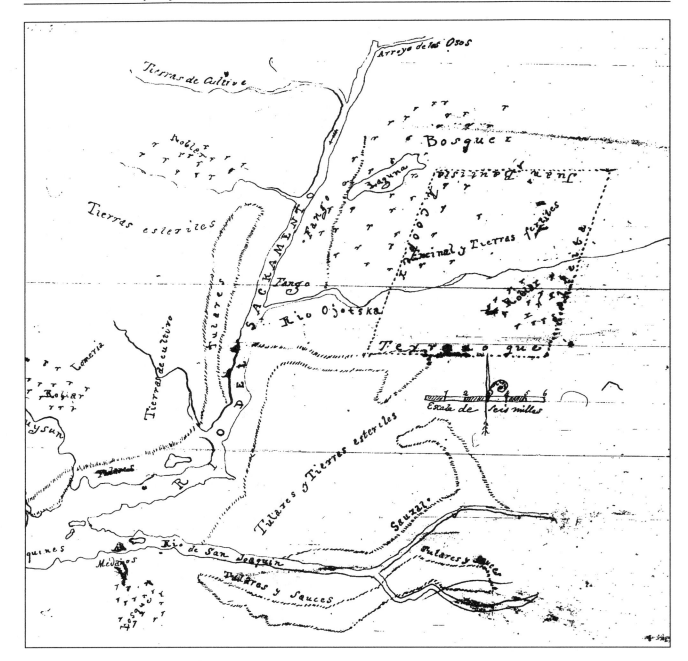

Figure 4-4. A Mexican survey plat map.

University of California-Berkeley
Bancroft Library
Berkeley, CA 94720

New Mexico State Library
Southwest Room
325 Don Gaspar Avenue
Santa Fe, NM 87503

Texas General Land Office
1700 North Congress Ave.
Austin, TX 78701

Family History Library
35 North West Temple
Salt Lake City, UT 84101

Archivo General de la Nación
Antiguo Palacio de Lecumberri
Col. Penitenciaría
Mexico City, Mexico

Center for Southwest Research
University of New Mexico-General Library
Albuquerque, NM 87131-1466

FOR FURTHER REFERENCE

American Heritage. *Pictorial Atlas of United States History.* New York: American Heritage Publishing Co., 1966.

Avina, Rose Hollenbaugh. *Spanish and Mexican Land Grants in California.* New York: Arno Press, 1976.

Beck, Warren A., and Ynez D. Haase. *Historical Atlas of California.* Norman: University of Oklahoma Press, 1974. Contains county maps which show the locations of individual grants.

Beers, Henry Putney. *Spanish and Mexican Records of the American Southwest: A Bibliographical Guide to Archive and Manuscript Sources.* Tucson: University of Arizona Press, 1979.

Blackmar, Frank Wilson. *Spanish Institutions of the Southwest.* Reprint. Glorieta, New Mexico: Rio Grande Press, 1976.

Bolton, Herbert Eugene. *The Spanish Borderlands: A Chronicle of Old Florida and the Southwest.* New Haven, Conn.: Yale University Press, 1921.

_____. *Guide to Materials for the History of the United States in the Principal Archives of Mexico.* New York: Kraus Reprint, 1965.

Bowden, J.J. *Spanish and Mexican Land Grants in the Chihuahuan Acquisition.* El Paso: Texas Western Press, University of Texas at El Paso, 1971.

California State Library. *Index to Spanish Archives on File in the State Library, XIV—Spanish Archives Collected in Monterey in 1851, by Order of the Legislature.* San Francisco: Whitton, Towne and Co. Excelsior Steam Presses, 1857.

Cowan, Robert Granniss. *Ranchos of California, A List of Spanish Concessions, 1775–1822, and Mexican Grants, 1822–1846.* Fresno, Calif.: Academy Library Guild, 1956.

Evans, Edward G. "A Guide to Pre-1850 Manuscripts in the United States Relating to Mexico and the Southwestern United States." *Ethnohistory* 17 (Winter-Spring 1970).

Greenleaf, Richard E., and Michael C. Meyer. *Research in Mexican History: Topics, Methodology, Sources, and a Practical Guide to Field Research.* Lincoln: University of Nebraska Press, 1973.

Hutchinson, Cecil A. *Frontier Settlement in Mexican California: Hijar Padres Colony and Its Origins, 1769–1835.* New Haven, Conn.: Yale University Press, 1969.

McMullin, Phillip W. *Grassroots of America.* Salt Lake City: Gendex, 1972.

Miller, Gary M. *Spanish and Mexican Land Grants in California: A Summary of Holdings and Guide to Other Sources.* Laguna Niguel, Calif., n.d.

Miller, Thomas Lloyd. *The Public Lands of Texas 1519–1970.* Norman: University of Oklahoma Press, 1972. An excellent publication.

Morrow, William W. *Spanish and Mexican Private Land Grants.* San Francisco, 1923. Reprint. New York: Arno Press, 1974.

Nixon, George J. "Genealogical and Historical Sources in the Spanish and Mexican Southwest." In *The Source: A Guidebook of American Genealogy.* 1st ed. Salt Lake City: Ancestry, 1984.

Nogales, Luis G. *The Mexican-American: A Selected and Annotated Bibliography.* Stanford, Calif.: Stanford University Press, 1971.

Reynolds, Mathew G. *Spanish and Mexican Land Laws.* St. Louis, Mo., 1895.

Salazar, J. Richard, and New Mexico State Records Center and Archives. *Calendar to the Microfilm Edition of the Land Records of New Mexico, Spanish Archives of New Mexico: Series I, Surveyor General Records, and the Records of the Court of Private Land Claims.* Santa Fe, N.M.: National Historical Publications and Records Commission, 1987.

Shumway, Burgess McK. *California Ranchos: Patented Private Land Grants Listed by County.* San Bernardino, Calif.: Borgo Press, 1988.

Taylor, Virginia H. *Index to Spanish and Mexican Land Grants in Texas.* Reprint. Austin, Tex.: Lone Star Press, 1974.

Texas General Land Office, Garry Mauro as Land Commissioner. *Guide to Spanish and Mexican Land Grants in South Texas.* Texas General Land Office, 1988.

United States Congress. *The American State Papers: Public Lands.* Washington, D.C.: Gales and Seaton, 1832–61.

Westphall, Victor. *Mercedes Reales: Hispanic Land Grants of the Upper Rio Grande Region.* Albuquerque: University of New Mexico Press, ca. 1983.

_____. *The Public Domain in New Mexico, 1854–1891.* Albuquerque: University of New Mexico Press, 1965.

Woods, Richard D. *Reference Materials on Mexican Americans: An Annotated Bibliography.* Metuchen, N.J.: Scarecrow Press, 1976.

White, Joseph M. *A New Collection of Laws, Charters, and Local Ordinances on the Governments of Great Britain, France, and Spain, relating to the concessions of land in their respective colonies, together with the laws of Mexico and Texas on the same subject.* 2 vols. Philadelphia, 1839.

Section 2:
State-Land States

An Introduction to State Lands

Lands initially controlled and dispersed by the state government are called state lands. State lands were labeled such only for the first transaction. Subsequent transactions were considered to be "individual," or private lands. State-land states are the following:

Connecticut	New York
Delaware	North Carolina
Georgia	Pennsylvania
Hawaii	Rhode Island
Kentucky	South Carolina
Maine	Tennessee
Maryland	Texas
Massachusetts	Vermont
New Hampshire	Virginia
New Jersey	West Virginia

Most land systems used by state-land states originated under the administration of foreign governments. Texas was administered by the Mexican government. Until 1848, Hawaiian lands were allocated by the high chiefs of the islands. The remaining state-land states were under English authority until the Revolutionary War. Each government dictated the administrative structures still in use today.

Very little changed as the individual states took possession at the conclusion of the Revolutionary War. The same inhabitants usually held title both before and after the war. Much of the state-land domain was in the private or individual sector long before the states took over the responsibility of distribution. Therefore, the categories of *Pre-U.S. Possession, State-Land States,* and *Individual Lands* together provide a more complete history of state-land states.

At the conclusion of the Revolutionary War, the territorial claims of various states differed drastically from the state boundaries of today. By 1802, however, all of the states had ceded lands outside of their present-day boundaries to the government of the United States. Most of this ceded land was used to create new federal-land states.

The records of state-land states do not vary as widely as those of the federal government. Most are distinctive for each individual state. There are, however, some predominant characteristics that pertain to state-land states in general.

The exceptions were Virginia and North Carolina. Kentucky and Tennessee were ceded by Virginia and North Carolina, respectively, to the United States, though they are still defined as state-land states. Virginia and North Carolina each retained enough ceded lands as might be necessary to fill their own state bounty-land warrants issued for service during the Revolutionary War. The size of the retained territories was so great, however, that the entire geographical areas of both states were classified as state land.

The types of records produced by state-land states do not vary as widely as those of the federal government. Most records are distinctive for each individual state. There are, however, some predominant characteristics that pertain to state-land states in general. It is these characteristics that are discussed in the following chapters.

Non-colonial records issued by state-land states include bounty lands, homesteads, and direct sales, as well as a mixture of other miscellaneous sources. Costs for lands were never uniform, but simply the market price supported by each individual area.

Qualifications were strategically chosen to meet settlement and development requisites and the mandates of local economics.

Though the records generated by state-land states are not as detailed as their federal counterparts, the records can all be used for a variety of genealogical purposes. They help determine migration information such as dates of arrival and dates of departure, associations, military service, lengths of residence, and various other clues, depending on the creativity of the researcher. They also help add significant historical background to the research of ancestors. The following chapters in this section discuss, in more detail, the land organization, the patent process, and the various record sources created by state-land states.

5

Organization of State Lands

COMMON SURVEY METHODS

The term **metes and bounds** refers to "measurements and markers." The indiscriminate method of metes and bounds has been used by most state-land states since the earliest of land grants on this continent. This method of survey was so thoroughly imbedded in the organization of each state that it was impossible, even in the earliest days of American government, to convert states to a more manageable system of township, range, and section.

Surveys for metes and bounds began at a designated marker and, using a series of straight lines, proceeded from point to point. The lines surrounded the boundaries of a piece of property, circumventing all encountered obstacles, man-made and natural. The shape was ultimately defined by topography and neighboring properties, and rarely closed perfectly where it began. Often, the land descriptions relied upon creeks and other natural boundaries to close the final line of the survey.

Today, very little has changed. Updated equipment and more permanent markers are the only differences from surveys of old. Pre-twentieth-century markers were generally local features, such as tree stumps, blazed trees, rocks, and even watercourses or seeps. All were constantly being altered by both man and nature. Boundary disputes were commonplace, and processioning became customary among neighbors. Processioning involved two or more neighbors periodically walking the bounds of their adjoining properties to confirm markers and boundaries. Sometimes surveyors, tax collectors, or other officials would also be present.

When surveying a tract of land, a compass was used for direction. **Directions** were recorded as degrees on the compass in east, west, north, south, or a combined bearing thereof. **Distances** for each direction were measured in a variety of units. Chains and links were common, as were rods, poles, and perches, depending on the time period and place involved. Only one form of measurement was introduced in a single deed. Surveyors also created a plat, or picture, of the property description (figure 5-1). This was used to calculate the actual acreage included and physically illustrate the measurements, markers, and neighbors for future reference.

Descriptions within the system of metes and bounds can be confusing. Directions and measurements can be written in a variety of formats, all describing the same line. For example, a line running northeast twenty-two degrees for a length of forty-five chains might be listed in any one of the following ways:

- . . . NE22, 45 chains

- . . . 22 degrees northeast, 45 chains

- . . . north 22 degrees east, 45 chains

Sometimes, when chains, rods, or poles have been mentioned in earlier parts of the description, the measurement method will not be repeated. Only the amount will appear:

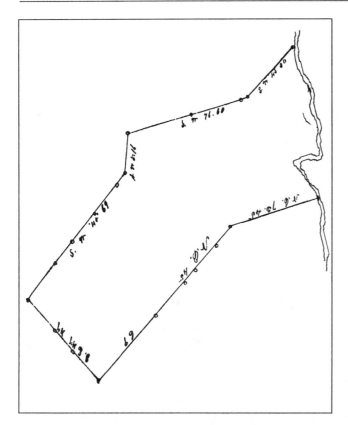

Figure 5-1. A typical metes and bounds diagram.

• . . . northeast 22, 45

Each segment of the description should be viewed as having three parts. Regardless of how the numbers and words are arranged, the meanings for these three parts will always be the same:

1. A **direction**, usually a combination of north, south, east, or west.

2. A compass direction in **degrees**, always between 0 and 90.

3. A **distance**, measured in chains, poles, or other units.

Forms of land measurement, such as rods or chains, vary in different geographical regions. At times, they even vary within the same county. However, they are always consistent within the same land transaction. Sometimes these measurements are irrelevant to the issues of genealogical research. They become necessary, however, when problems can be solved only through the platting

of metes and bounds (drawing a picture of the property description).

Metes and bounds were used consistently throughout the southern state-land states. Many of the northern states used their own forms or variations of this system, as did Texas and Hawaii. Some of the most important variations to be considered by researchers are listed below.

OTHER METHODS

Delaware

A division of land called a "hundred" was introduced early in Delaware. Originating in England, the hundred in America eventually became a division within a borough. Though this division had been almost extinct since the mid-1600s, except in the state of Delaware, it was seriously considered as the measurement for the federal land system in the early 1780s. Hundreds can also be found in Virginia and Maryland, though mostly prior to 1635. Numerous definitions of the hundred have been concocted over the years. Some believe the area consisted of subsistence for one hundred families. Others believe it was made up of one hundred acres. For further reference, see Barbara Jean Evans' *A to Zax.*

More factually, the hundred was a territorial measurement—similar to a town—and taxes were levied according to its jurisdictions. Justices of the peace and government representatives were also apportioned according to the hundred. Though no longer an important governmental jurisdiction, the hundred still serves as a breakdown of measurement within counties in Delaware. When researching tax lists and land records, hundreds can help segregate individuals more specifically within the county's borders.

Georgia

Georgia was unique in that its colonial lands were extremely well organized into square or rectangular districts within the bounds of early counties. These districts were often used in land descriptions. They can be used to further segregate or group individuals, similar to graphing township, range, and section.(See chapter 10, Strategies for Federal Land Records, and chapter 7, Strategies for State Land Records.)

Hawaii

Hawaiian lands were dispersed in methods that resemble metes and bounds. The lands were allocated from the royal family for use only. Actual ownership was rarely found until after 1848. At that time, the Royal Land Commission began a system of distributing permanent ownership of lands to the island government. The government then granted lands to common individuals.

Maine

Traditionally, Maine was part of the lands controlled by Massachusetts. After gaining statehood and a separate identity in 1820, Massachusetts continued to control the disbursement of one-half of all state lands in Maine. The state of Maine controlled the other half. In 1853, Maine purchased the remaining "Massachusetts lands" within its borders. Between 1820 and 1853, lands in Maine can be found granted by both states.

New England

The New England states frequently issued grants under town charters for eventual distribution in lots by town proprietors. These townships were generally six miles square, and were used as a model for the nation's federal land system. Town charters were created during the colonial era. Their impact carried on long afterward as towns often continued to govern the distribution of unclaimed lands within their jurisdiction. For this reason, some New England states have their records filed by town. Land deeds can also be found in probate districts, since land transactions were occasionally filed with the probate court.

Various Measurement Conversions for State-Land States*

1 chain =	100 links
	4 rods/poles/perches
	0.10 furlongs
	1/80th mile
	22 yards
	66 feet
	23.76 varas
1 link =	7.92 inches
1 furlong =	10 chains
	1006 links
	40 rods/poles/perches
	1/8th mile
	237 varas
	664 feet
1 rod/	0.25 chains
pole/perch =	0.025 furlongs
	0.003125 miles
	0.594 varas
	16.5 feet
1 mile =	80 chains
	1,760 yards
	5,280 feet
	320 rods/poles/perches
	8 furlongs
	1,901 varas
1 league =	5,000 varas square
	13,889 feet square
	4,428.4 acres
1 labor =	1,000 varas square
	2,788 feet square
	177.136 acres
1 acre =	160 rods square
	10 square chains
	5,645.4 square varas
	75.13 varas square
	43,560 square feet
	4,840 square yards
1 arpent =	0.84 acres
	36,590 square feet
	4,066 square yards

* All measurements are approximate.

Pennsylvania and New York

Some areas of New York and Pennsylvania used a combination of townships and metes and bounds (figure 5-2). A large tract may have been patented by individuals or land companies under the traditional system of metes and bounds, then subdivided into town lots and sections similar to New England townships. While sizes of lots were somewhat uniform, lot numbering was rarely consistent from town to town. Numbering was usually done at the discretion of the original proprietors. Manors also played an important role in the subleasing of patented lands in New York, Pennsylvania, and Maryland. (For more information on manors, see chapter 11, Records Generated by Individual Lands.)

South Carolina

Before 1799, South Carolina was organized into nine old districts. These were often referred to in colonial and early state land grants. These district boundaries did not evolve into new districts like most counties throughout the country. Rather, they were abolished in 1799, with twenty-four new districts imposed in their place. At times, both the old and new districts are referred to in a single document. In 1868, these districts officially became known as counties.

Tennessee

Organized mostly in traditional metes and bounds, Tennessee was also surveyed into rectangular townships and lots in areas west of the Tennessee River. Originally ceded to the United States as federal land, North Carolina reserved the right to distribute bounty land warrants in Tennessee. Initially, this distribution was to occupy the eastern two-thirds of the state, and plans were made to survey the western one-third (still occupied by the Chickasaw Indians until 1818) into township, range, and section. However, bounty land and other distributions eventually exceeded the central and eastern regions, spilling over into the western area as well.

No land office was ever officially opened for western Tennessee, and no meridian was ever established. Many of these western lands, however, were prematurely organized in methods similar to the federal land system of township, range, and section.

Texas

Texas was acquired by the United States well after the federal land system was initiated. It retained the right to govern the distribution and recording of all lands within its borders. Many land transactions in Texas use the Spanish system of leagues and labors. (See chapter 1, Spanish Possession, for further information on Spanish measurements.) A few places in Texas used the French method of surveying long, narrow strips of land that extended inland from the riverbanks. (See chapter 3, French Possession, for further reference to French systems of measurement.) Portions of western Texas, particularly the oil field country, are laid out in blocks similar to the federal survey system.

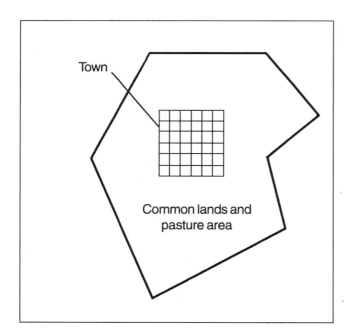

Figure 5-2. A metes and bounds grant or charter subdivided into townships.

Virginia

Virginia was organized as most southern states were: in metes and bounds. Uniquely, though, Virginia was able to retain its system of metes and bounds for use in the Virginia Military Tract in the federal-land state of Ohio. The recipients of bounty lands for this tract often chose their own locations, rarely adjoining another settler's property. This created "scrap" land in between, which was often undesirable or too small to justify acquisition by anyone other than adjacent property holders.

Virginia cities are politically and administratively independent of the county or counties in which they are geographically situated. This policy created what is known as "independent cities." Each independent city was responsible for its own set of records. See the next heading for more information about these anomalies of Virginia and other states.

Independent Cities

Another organizational system found in state-land states, particularly in Virginia, is the **independent city.** These cities are separate from the governmental jurisdictions of the county in which they are located. They keep their own records and administer their own political affairs. There were thirty-seven independent cities in the United States before 1900:

Alexandria	Lynchburg
Baltimore*	Martinsville
Bristol	Newport News
Buena Vista	Norfolk
Charlottesville	Norton
Chesapeake	Petersburg
Clifton Forge	Portsmouth
Colonial Heights	Radford
Covington	Richmond
Danville	Roanoke
Fairfax	St. Louis*
Falls Church	South Boston
Fort Monroe	Staunton
Franklin	Suffolk
Fredericksburg	Virginia Beach
Galax	Waynesboro
Hampton	Williamsburg
Harrisonburg	Winchester
Hopewell	

Thirty-five of these independent cities are located in Virginia. The two exceptions are Baltimore, Maryland, and St. Louis in the federal-land state of Missouri. Others have since been added to the list, including Denver, Colorado; Jacksonville, Florida; Indianapolis, Indiana; and Los Angeles, California.

Independent cities also dispersed state lands. These documents will be found among the cities' own records, and not the records of county governments. They are usually included among the grantee/grantor lists for their respective cities. For a better understanding of the structure and purpose of independent cities, see Carol McGinnis' *Virginia Genealogy Sources and Resources.*

CONCLUSION

State-land states are unique, even from each other. They each developed their own system of organizing and dispersing lands within their jurisdictions. They were, in essence, developing as one country or culture would from another. Researching and understanding more of their peculiarities can open avenues for continuing research and reveal clues that otherwise might not be found. Records created by state-land states and how to access them are discussed in chapter 6, Records Generated by State Lands.

FOR FURTHER REFERENCE

Akagi, Roy Hidemichi. *The Town Proprietors of the New England Colonies; A Study of Their Development, Organization, Activities and Controversies, 1620–1770.* Philadelphia: Press of the University of Pennsylvania, 1924.

Cadle, Farris W. *Georgia Land Surveying History and Law.* Athens: University of Georgia Press, 1991.

Carter, Fran. *Searching American Land and Deed Records.* Orting, Wash.: Heritage Quest, 1991.

Chinen, Jon J. *The Great Mahele: Hawaii's Land Division of 1848.* Honolulu: University of Hawaii Press, 1958.

Egleston, Melville. *The Land System of the New England Colonies.* Baltimore: Johns Hopkins University, 1886.

Eichholz, Alice, ed. *Ancestry's Redbook: American State, County and Town Sources.* Rev. ed. Salt Lake City: Ancestry, 1992.

Evans, Barbara Jean. *A to Zax: A Comprehensive Dictionary for Genealogists and Historians.* Alexandria, Va.: the author, 1995.

Gould, Clarence P. *The Land System in Maryland, 1720–1765.* Baltimore: Johns Hopkins Press, 1913.

Hofmann, Margaret M. "Land Grants." In *North Carolina Research: Genealogy and Local History.* Raleigh: North Carolina Genealogical Society, 1980.

Hughes, Sarah S. *Surveyors and Statesmen: Land Measuring in Colonial Virginia.* Richmond: The Virginia Association of Surveyors, 1979.

Lawson, Charles E. *Surveying Your Land: A Common-Sense Guide to Surveys, Deeds, and Title Searches.* Woodstock, Vt.: The Countryman Press, 1990.

Leary, Helen F.M., and Maurice R. Stirewalt, eds. *North Carolina Research: Genealogy and Local History.* Raleigh: North Carolina Genealogical Society, 1980.

Marschner, Francis J. *Boundaries and Records in the Territory of Early Settlement from Canada to Florida.* Washington, D.C.: Agricultural Research Service, U.S. Department of Agriculture, 1960.

McEntyre, John G. *Land Survey Systems.* New York: John Wiley and Sons, 1978.

McGinnis, Carol. *Virginia Genealogy: Sources and Resources.* Baltimore: Genealogical Publishing Co., 1993.

McKitrick, Reuben. *The Public Land System of Texas.* Madison: University of Wisconsin, 1918.

McLendon, Samuel Guyton. *History of the Public Domain of Georgia.* Spartanburg, S.C.: Reprint Co., 1974.

Powell, Sumner Chilton. *Puritan Village: The Formation of a New England Town.* Middletown, Mass.: Wesleyan University Press, 1963.

Sears, Joan N. *The First One Hundred Years of Town Planning in Georgia.* Atlanta, Ga.: Cherokee Publishing Co., 1979.

Szucs, Loretto Dennis, and Sandra Luebking, eds. "Research in Land and Tax Records." In *The Source: A Guidebook of American Genealogy.* Rev. ed. Salt Lake City: Ancestry, 1997.

Wattles, Wm. C. *Land Survey Descriptions.* Los Angeles: Title Insurance and Trust Company, 1970.

6

Records Generated by State Lands

When the Revolutionary War ended and colonies officially became states, each state retained the rights and responsibilities of dispersing property within its own boundaries. Distribution often continued in the same manner as before the war. Usually, the same types of records were generated as had been created during the colonial era. Later, as Texas was annexed, it also reserved the rights to control land distribution within its own territory. Hawaii did the same.

States' claims were much smaller after the war, in contrast with their colonial acreage under British authority. Most ceded their property outside of present-day boundaries to the federal government between 1782 and 1800. These cessions introduced the federal land system, but quickly limited unclaimed acreage available in each state. Once reduced, state boundaries were not permitted to increase in size. Some states, such as Virginia, retained the right to continue granting certain lands within their cessions to their own residents, specifically for bounty-land purposes. States also granted lands for a variety of other reasons—mostly to generate revenue for the state and to encourage settlement. Regardless of the purposes, each patent issued was the end result of an application process. This process is described below.

LAND ACQUISITION PROCESS

Whenever land has been distributed by governments at any level, it has been in the form of a **grant.** The term does not imply that the need for payment was forfeited. Rather, lands were provided for an agreed set of terms and/or sum of money by the initial title holder. Title to that land was in the form of a patent. It was the process of obtaining the patent which helped create some of the most beneficial records of early settlers in state-land states. Because state land acquisition generated a series of records, each state usually has at least one or more of the records that have survived. Refer also to section 1, Pre-U.S. Possession, and section 4, Individual Lands.

State-land transactions in the southern states were usually performed by the county registrar of deeds. Many New England states recorded their transactions through the town clerk's office. Each state had unique circumstances and requirements for land dispersal, and their records varied. Most states, however, followed basic procedures that generated specific record sources. (For a listing of authorities that record land transactions for each state, see page 184.)

Typical procedures began with an **application,** or entry, for land. This was made through the land office—usually in the county recorder's office, town hall, or similar agency. The application process described the conditions of the property, provided proof of prior vacancy, assessed the quality, or "rate," of the land, and its intended use. It also described improvements already underway, provided the date of initial or intended inhabitance, contained a copy of published intention to patent, and a variety of other types of information, depending on the laws of each state at the time.

A successful application resulted in a **warrant** for survey. The warrant was an authorization for surveyors to mark, plat (draw), and record a formal description for official title. Sometimes, the property had already been surveyed for a forfeited or relinquished claim. In these instances, the warrant was used to obtain and *accept* the previous survey. (It should be noted that an application and issuance of a warrant did not guarantee a complete or successful patent. A person may have received a warrant, then moved on, never finishing the patent process.) Most states' warrants have been preserved.

A patent is only the final receipt, or title, for a piece of property. There is an entire process prior to patent that creates other, more informative records about our ancestors.

The **survey** was next recorded in the appropriate land office. Surveys often show bordering properties, including neighbors' names. They usually include a description of the property, detailing markers and distances around the perimeter. Natural features, such as streams, rivers, and swamps, were usually recorded, as were man-made obstacles, such as railroads and roadways. Surveys have survived for most states, but they are not always organized and accessible. Sometimes only surveyors' notes remain, with no copy of an actual drawing.

Upon the return of the survey, the **patent** was prepared. The patent is the official title to the property and indicates completion of the land acquisition process. The term "patent" indicates the first sale of a piece of property. Once a patent is issued, the property becomes part of the "private" or individual sector of land ownership and is subsequently sold in the form of a "deed." (See section 4 on federal lands.)

Patents are the most commonly preserved records of state land acquisition. Many states have indexed their patents for easy reference. A patent,

however, is only the final receipt for a piece of property. There is an entire process prior to patent; records from that process can yield even more detailed information about one's ancestors.

While copies of state patents and related records may have been duplicated and separated from other land records, they are usually also recorded in the deed books of each county or town. This allows access through the grantee/grantor index, with the grantor being listed as "State of ____," (e.g., State of Tennessee, or Tennessee, State of). Many states have also produced their own indexes to early land grants. Some of the most important collections and indexes are reviewed below.

COMMON RECORDS

Unlike federal-land states, each state-land state was responsible for its own records, management, and organization. Each state must be addressed individually, a process that would take numerous volumes to fully discuss. Therefore, what follows is a brief presentation of the most accessible and helpful records for each state-land state. It does not necessarily represent all major collections. Often, the records from statehood eras are combined with colonial collections. (Refer also to section 1, Pre-U.S. Possession.) For additional publication information on materials described below, see "For Further Reference" at the end of this chapter.

Also refer to the discussion of each state under "Military Bounty Lands," below.

Connecticut

Most of Connecticut's state lands were distributed before the Revolutionary War. Afterward, town proprietorships continued to govern the disbursement of state lands remaining in their jurisdiction. Copies of the town records, and other early land records distributed directly by the state, are kept at the Connecticut State Library in Hartford. Many records created up to the 1900s have been microfilmed, along with grantee/grantor indexes for each town. These microfilms are also available at the Family History Library.

The grantee/grantor indexes are the best source for determining an ancestor's involvement in Connecticut state land grants. Unfortunately, the town must first be identified; there are no statewide indexes specifically for land grants. The *Judd Collection* contains some early state grants, although they are not complete. It has been indexed and microfilmed and is available through the Connecticut State Library and the Family History Library. For information on other, more recent lands granted by the state, contact the Commissioner at the Department of Environmental Protection, or the Connecticut State Library.

Delaware

Most Delaware lands were dispersed to individuals prior to statehood. They are referenced in more detail in chapter 2, British Possession. Copies of all land records are located at the Hall of Records in Dover. Few land records have been microfilmed, though all records are available for research to those visiting on site at the Hall of Records. The Hall of Records in Annapolis, Maryland, also contains information concerning some Delaware lands. See *Delaware's Fugitive Records: An Inventory of the Official Land Grant Records Relating to the Present State of Delaware*, by Edward F. Heite.

Georgia

Georgia has earned the distinction of distributing headright grants more recently than any other state—as late as 1862. Headrights were distributed in the eastern third of the state. They were used to encourage settlement there and, unfortunately, to encourage further displacement of the Native Americans still occupying that area. All grants, headrights, warrants, and surveys distributed by the state of Georgia up to 1939 have been microfilmed. The original records are housed at the Georgia State Archives in Atlanta. Microfilm copies are available through the state archives and through the Family History Library. (See figure 6-1.)

An excellent source for reference to these records is the *Index to the Headright and Bounty Grants of Georgia, 1756–1909,* by Rev. Silas Emmett Lucas, Jr. This book also includes some excellent historical data about bounty-land distributions for the state of Georgia. Another, titled *Index of the Georgia Land Office Records from 1767–1908,* has been produced and microfilmed by the Georgia Department of State. It encompasses twelve rolls of microfilm which are also available at the Family History Library and the Georgia State Archives.

Georgia also distributed lands through a lottery system. Drawings were held in 1805, 1807, 1820, 1821, 1827, and 1832. Residency requirements should be carefully studied for each lottery. Lottery applicants were required to be resident for several years prior to application. The application, in turn, usually preceded the drawing by several years. Various publications index and record the results of the Georgia land lotteries. They usually list only those who successfully drew lots. Only the 1805 publication documents all eligible participants. (See "For Further Reference" at the end of this chapter, under Davis, Houstun, Lucas, Smith, and Wood.)

Hawaii

Hawaii is unique in that its lands were not initially distributed by a government *per se,* but through the royal families of the islands. The lands remained the property of the king, and individuals were allotted only the use of such lands. It was not until 1848 that a land commission was established to oversee the transition of actual land titles to the common citizen.

The Board of Commissioners to Quiet Land Titles processed most claims between 1848 and 1852. These claims, and others since, are now housed in the Bureau of Conveyances in Honolulu. An index is available; it is titled *Indices of Awards Made by The Board of Commissioners to Quiet Land Titles in the Hawaiian Islands.* It was assembled by the Office of the Commissioner of Public Lands. Many records are now available on microfilm at the Hawaii State Archives and the Family History Library.

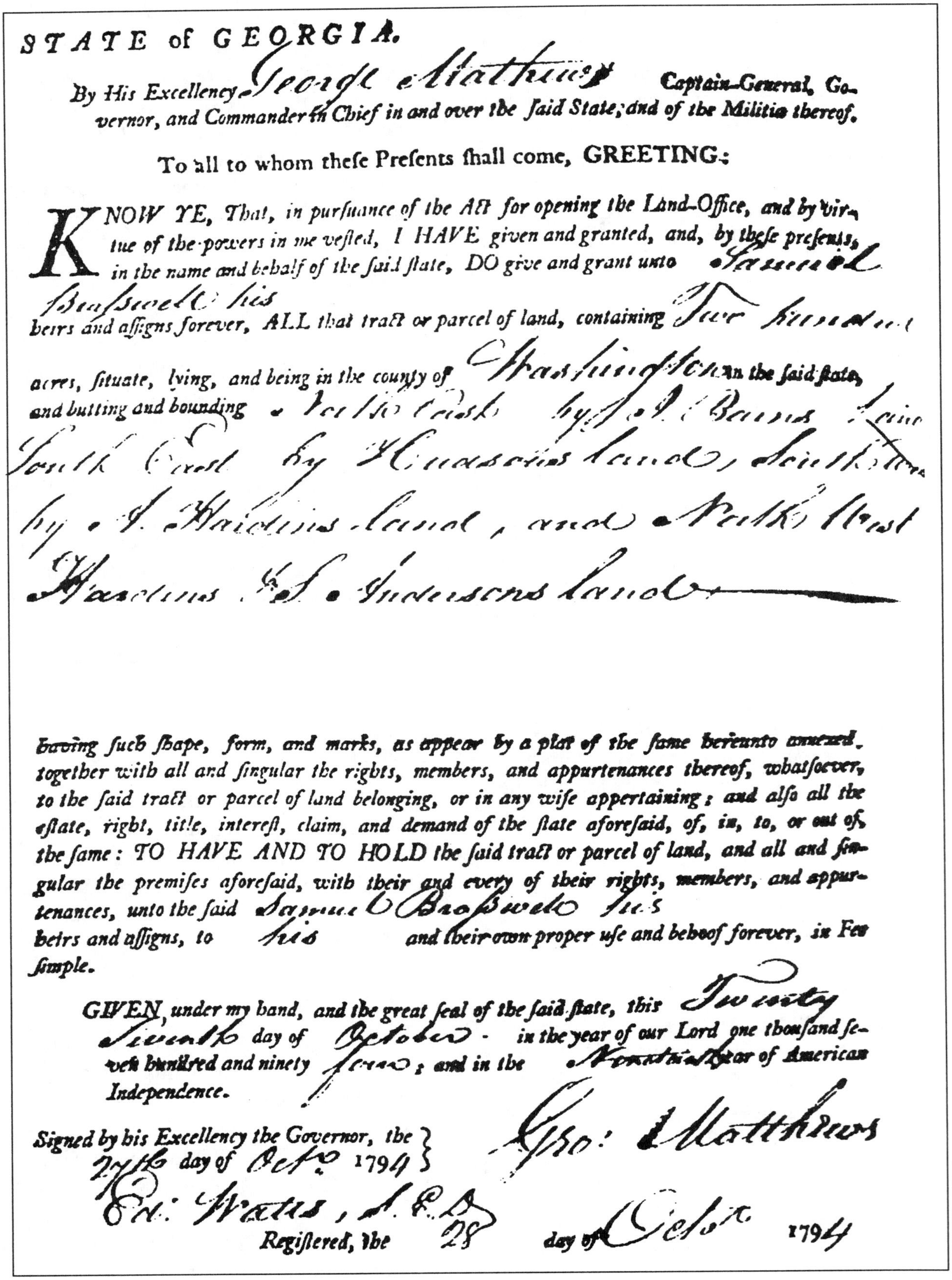

STATE of *GEORGIA.*

By His Excellency *George Matthews* Captain-General, Go-
vernor, and Commander in Chief in and over the said State; and of the Militia thereof.

To all to whom these Presents shall come, GREETING.:

KNOW YE, That, in pursuance of the Act for opening the Land-Office, and by virtue of the powers in me vested, I HAVE given and granted, and, by these presents,
in the name and behalf of the said state, DO give and grant unto *Samuel*
Braswell his
heirs and assigns forever, ALL that tract or parcel of land, containing *Two hundred*
acres, situate, lying, and being in the county of *Washington* in the said state,
and butting and bounding *North East by J A Burns line*
South East by Hudsons land, South West
by A Haidans land, and North West
Haidans & S Andersons land

having such shape, form, and marks, as appear by a plat of the same hereunto annexed,
together with all and singular the rights, members, and appurtenances thereof, whatsoever,
to the said tract or parcel of land belonging, or in any wise appertaining : and also all the
estate, right, title, interest, claim, and demand of the state aforesaid, of, in, to, or out of,
the same : TO HAVE AND TO HOLD the said tract or parcel of land, and all and singular the premises aforesaid, with their and every of their rights, members, and appurtenances, unto the said *Samuel Braswell his*
heirs and assigns, to *his* and their own proper use and behoof forever, in Fee
simple.

GIVEN, under my hand, and the great seal of the said state, this *Twenty*
Seventh day of *October* - in the year of our Lord one thousand se-
ven hundred and ninety *four* : and in the *Nineteenth* year of American
Independence.

Signed by his Excellency the Governor, the
27th day of Octo 1794

Geo: Matthews

Jno: Watts, S. E. D.
Registered, the 28 day of Octor 1794

Figure 6-1. A typical patent given by the state of Georgia, dated 1794.

Kentucky

After Kentucky's statehood, lands were distributed by both Kentucky and Virginia. Virginia, however, distributed lands in Kentucky only in the form of military bounty warrants. The right for this distribution was retained when Virginia ceded the lands of Kentucky to the United States at the end of the Revolutionary War. (Bounty lands are discussed later in this chapter.)

Original grants given by the state of Kentucky are now housed in the Secretary of State's Office at the Capitol Building in Frankfort. This is where the Kentucky Land Office is located. An index has been compiled by Willard Rouse Jillson; it is titled *The Kentucky Land Grants: A Systematic Index to All of the Land Grants Recorded in the State Land Office at Frankfort, Kentucky, 1782–1924.* The book is divided into eight different geographical categories of land grants, all filed in the Kentucky Land Office. The original records and the index are available on microfilm at the repositories listed below. Some microfilm versions only include records up to the 1850s and 1860s.

In addition to the Kentucky State Land Office, warrants were also issued by county courts. A complete collection of these records, up to 1948, has been microfilmed. These, and most records mentioned above, are available through the Family History Library, The Kentucky Department for Libraries and Archives, and the Filson Club Library. (See "Repositories" at the end of the chapter.)

Maine

Maine lands were initially owned and controlled by Massachusetts. Massachusetts continued to dispense lands in Maine until the mid-1820s, mostly in the form of military bounty warrants. This was done by the Committee for the Sale of Eastern Lands, whose records have been microfilmed. They are available through the Family History Library and the Maine State Archives. When Maine attained statehood in 1820, Massachusetts reserved the right to dispense half of the remaining state lands in that area. In 1853, Maine purchased all remaining land rights from Massachusetts. (See "Massachusetts," below, for further information about distributions made by that state.)

The Maine Land Office in Portland distributed all state lands under Maine's jurisdiction after 1824. Their records are available on microfilm through the Maine State Archives in Augusta, and the Family History Library. Records of both Maine and Massachusetts grants in the state of Maine from 1832 to 1853 are available on microfilm at the Massachusetts State Archives and the Family History Library.

Maryland

Currently, Maryland has one of the most organized and simplified collections of colonial and state records in existence. All patents for the state are grouped in a large card index at the Hall of Records in Annapolis. The index is organized alphabetically by both name of person and name of tract. It has not been microfilmed, nor is it available through any other repository. However, Peter Coldham is in the process of producing a series of books based upon this card index at the Hall of Records which will eventually cover statehood periods of time. They begin in 1680, where Gust Skordas left off in *Early Settlers of Maryland.*

Statewide patent, warrant, or survey indexes can often help distinguish a family's county origins.

The actual patents for the state of Maryland are available on microfilm up to 1852. Individual indexes are included with most volumes. These microfilms are available at the Hall of Records in Annapolis and the Family History Library. Some records created after 1852 have also been microfilmed. The films, and the original records for the same time period, are housed only at the Hall of Records. Another valuable source for Maryland is a collection of plat maps for state land patents. They, too, are available only at the Hall of Records. Inventory books with further information are available for purchase there as well. (See figure 6-2.)

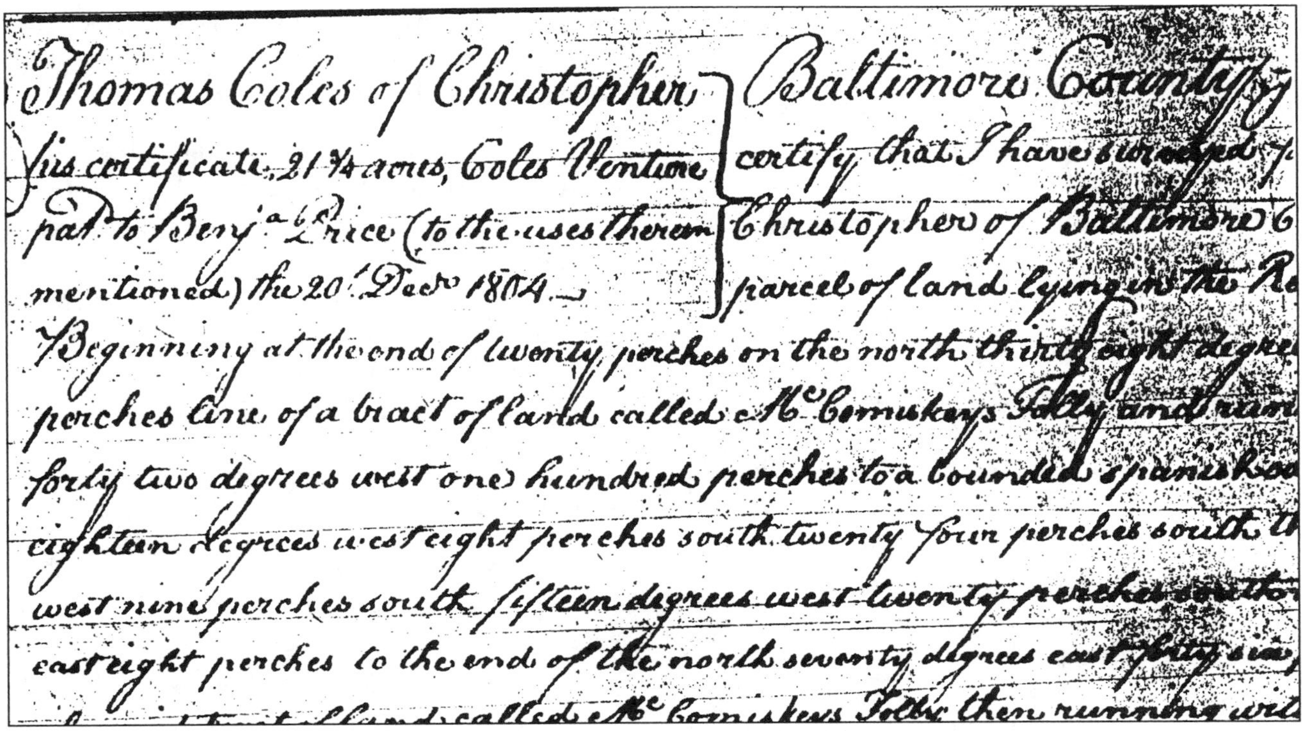
Thomas Coles of Christopher } Baltimore County
his certificate, 21 1/4 acres, Coles Venture } certify that I have surveyed
pat. to Benj.a Price (to the uses therein } Christopher of Baltimore C
mentioned) the 20th Decr 1804. } parcel of land lying in the R
Beginning at the end of twenty perches on the north thirty eight degrees
perches line of a tract of land called McComuskeys Folly and run
forty two degrees west one hundred perches to a bounded Spanish oak
eighteen degrees west eight perches south twenty four perches south
west nine perches south fifteen degrees west twenty perches south
east eight perches to the end of the north seventy degrees east forty six

Figure 6-2. A Maryland patent. Note that the property is referred to as "Coles Venture." Such names, in addition to the description, were given for all Maryland properties.

Massachusetts

Most lands in present-day Massachusetts were distributed before the Revolutionary War. After statehood, lands were generally distributed through town governments. Some distribution of state grants was performed by districts within the counties. Each district had its own courthouse for grant and deed registration.

Massachusetts also granted lands in present-day Maine. When Maine acquired statehood, Massachusetts reserved the right to disperse one-half of the public lands remaining in Maine. This disbursement continued until Maine purchased the remaining Massachusetts lands in 1853. Original grants made by both states in the boundaries of present-day Maine are available on microfilm at the Maine State Archives in Augusta and at the Family History Library. These and all Massachusetts-related records are also housed at the Archives of the Commonwealth (also called the Massachusetts State Archives) in Boston. For information on other, more recent land grants, contact the State Director of Environmental Affairs, located in Boston. Most known statewide indexes are for colonial periods only. For lands distributed afterward, town grantee/grantor indexes are often the most helpful.

New Hampshire

In New Hampshire, few, if any, state lands remained after the Revolutionary War. Any disbursements after that time were made through the county recorder's office and are included in the county grantee/grantor deed indexes. Microfilm copies of the original records and indexes, up to the mid-1800s, are found at the New England Historic Genealogical Society, New Hampshire Division of Records Management and Archives, and the Family History Library. For more recent records, contact the individual county recorder's office.

New Jersey

Most New Jersey lands were distributed before the Revolutionary War. The east and west divisions of the state continued to make small proprietary well into the twentieth century (see chapter 5, Organization of State Lands). Lands were distributed by the Council of Proprietors of West New Jersey, located in Burlington, and the East Jersey Board of Proprietors, in Perth Amboy. These offices have been in existence since colonial times. For further information, consult *The New Jersey Proprietors and their Lands* by John E. Pomfret. Few state-land records beyond the colonial era have been microfilmed and made available through other repositories.

New York

Land grants given by the state of New York are all housed in one repository: the New York State Archives in Albany. Though some collections of grants are being microfilmed for easier access, few have been published or abstracted for the post-colonial period. One important collection is the New York Land Grant Application Files, which date from 1803 to the present. Patents from 1664 to 1954 are also available. These records are kept at the New York State Archives and have not yet been microfilmed. A more detailed reference to these records can be found in *Public Records Relating to Land in New York State*, a publication produced by the New York State Archives.

Proprietary and land company records also play a large part in the distribution of state lands in New York. Companies such as the Holland Land Company have extensive record collections that have been microfilmed. The Holland Land Company records are available for research through the Family History Library, the Erie County Historical Society, the Daniel E. Reed Library in Fredonia, New York, and the New York State Archives.

North Carolina

Land grants in the state of North Carolina were mostly handled by the County Recorder's Office. These records can be found referenced in the grantee/grantor indexes of each county. A master index of all land grants for the state has also been compiled; it is titled *Master Card File Index to*

North Carolina Land Grants 1679–1959. This index is available in the North Carolina Land Grant Office in Raleigh, a division of the Secretary of State. A similar land grant index is also available on microfilm at the Family History Library. It involves warrants from the 1600s through the 1800s, and it is structured alphabetically by county. The original warrants, as of 1996, are also being microfilmed (alphabetically by county).

Pennsylvania

Pennsylvania has one of the most complete collections of each phase of the patent process. The Division of Land Records serves as the official land office for Pennsylvania. The Bureau of Archives and History oversees this division, and it houses the land records generated during colonial and state periods.

Applications for warrants exist from 1784 to the present. They are helpful when determining settlement date versus filing date. The actual warrants are available from 1779 to the present. They are filed alphabetically by the first letter of the surname within each county. A master index of warrants is also available on a county basis for the entire state, from 1733 to the present. Surveys exist for most warrants, but they are not as complete or organized. The patents for the entire state are complete from 1781. All of these records, with the exception of the surveys, have been microfilmed and are available through the Pennsylvania State Archives and the Family History Library. For further details, refer to Donna Bingham Munger's *Pennsylvania Land Records: A History and Guide for Research.* It is considered one of the best land reference books available.

South Carolina

Original land grants for the state of South Carolina are housed in the Office of the Surveyor-General. They have been microfilmed from 1784 to 1882 and are available at the South Carolina Department of Archives and History in Columbia and the Family History Library. Indexes for state grants begin

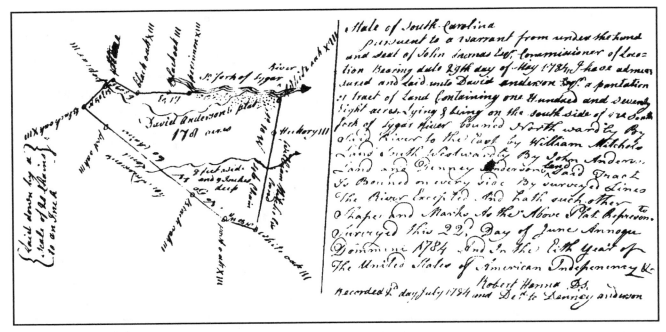

Figure 6-3. From the survey plat maps of South Carolina. Plat maps usually include a map and deed description, as shown here. Sometimes neighbors' names are also included on the map.

in 1790. A consolidated index, in the form of a computer printout, is also available at the Department of Archives and History. It includes patents and other early land distributions for the entire state during colonial and state periods. It is also available at the Family History Library on microfilm.

Another important collection for South Carolina is the Surveyor-General Land Plats. The original plats, from 1713 to 1861, are available on twenty-eight rolls of microfilm, including an index from 1688 to 1872. Microfilmed copies are available at the South Carolina Department of Archives and History and the Family History Library. (See figure 6-3.)

Tennessee

Tennessee did not begin administering its own lands until ten years after statehood. At that time, it began overseeing lands only in the eastern two-thirds of the state. The western third was still reserved for eventual federal land administration. Even though North Carolina had ceded political control to the United States at the end of the Revolutionary War, it retained rights for the distribution of lands in order to fill bounty-land warrants. North

Carolina continued dispersing lands jointly with the state of Tennessee from 1806 through the 1820s. Eventually, these disbursements occupied enough land to justify categorizing the entire state as a state-land state. The original intent had been to create another state like Ohio—a federal-land state with bounty distributions in the format of state-land states.

The records of land grants given by both North Carolina and Tennessee are now kept at the Tennessee State Library and Archives. Copies of the grants made by North Carolina are also kept in the North Carolina Division of Archives and History in Raleigh. All of the land grants through 1927 are in a consolidated card index. The index has been microfilmed and is available through several larger repositories, including the Tennessee State Library and Archives in Nashville and the Family History Library. The actual grants are also available on microfilm at these same locations; they encompass over 230 rolls. (See figure 6-4.)

Texas

It is estimated by the Texas General Land Office that Texas has distributed more than 150 million acres of state land since 1836. This includes republic and statehood periods. Texas distributed land in many forms, including headrights, for the first six years (1836 to 1842). All land grants for Texas, regardless of their nature, are housed at the General Land Office of Texas in Austin.

Many grants made during statehood are also found in county deed books, which are referenced through the grantee/grantor indexes. A statewide index is provided at the General Land Office in Austin; unfortunately, it has not been microfilmed. Searches can be ordered from the land office for a minimal fee. Wendy Elliott, in the Texas chapter of *Ancestry's Red Book*, also mentions a published index titled *Abstract of All Original Texas Land Titles Comprising Grants and Locations to August 31, 1941*, by Giles Bascom.

Vermont

Lands came under Vermont jurisdiction only after official separation from New York and New Hampshire in 1777. All state lands from that time were granted through town proprietorships only. The towns would then disperse initial titles of land in the form of town lots. The records of these grants can be found in the deed books of each individual town clerk's office; they can be accessed through grantee/grantor indexes.

The Vermont Public Records Division in Montpelier has microfilm copies of all transactions through the mid-nineteenth century and is continuously microfilming to the present. Many of the transactions already microfilmed are available at the Family History Library. The only indexes available are the grantee/grantor indexes for each town. No statewide index has yet been compiled.

Virginia

State land grants for Virginia are housed at the Virginia State Land

Office in Richmond. Records up to 1921 have been microfilmed and are available at the Virginia State Library and Archives and the Family History Library. They are indexed according to county; a separate, statewide index is available for 1825 to 1858. Survey plats also exist for the entire state as recently as 1963. They have been microfilmed up to 1878 and include an index to 1914. These microfilms are available at the repositories mentioned above.

There is also a card file index at the Virginia Land Office. It indexes all land grants and miscellaneous land records through Grant Book 126 (around 1980). This card file index has yet to be microfilmed. Copies of all grants issued from 1779 are also contained in 161 bound books housed at the Virginia Land Office. These books are chronologically organized and are included in the card file index just mentioned. For additional information, refer to *Virginia Land Office Inventory*, compiled by Daphne S. Gentry and revised by John S. Salmon. (See figure 6-5.)

West Virginia

Land grants in present-day West Virginia are available on microfilm to 1912. They are organized on a county basis to 1864 and are duplicates of those found in the Virginia Land Office. Grants created

```
Grantee    Gains, David

Grant No.  1569

No. Acres  200           Map No.

Date of Grant   August 31, 1809

County     Franklin

Book       4      Page 370      MT. DIST.
```

Figure 6-4. Reproduction of an index card from the Tennessee land grants.

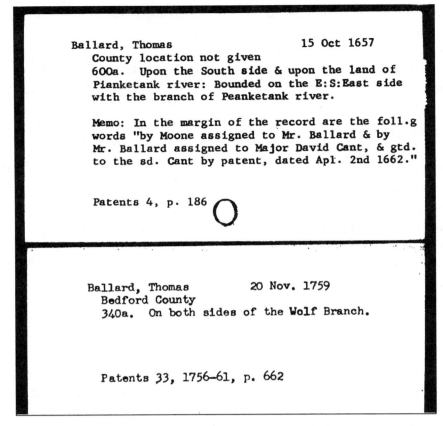

Figure 6-5. From Virginia's statewide card file index. It shows county of residence, acreage, watercourse, and date, and references the patent book and page number.

since statehood in 1863 are grouped for present-day West Virginia only. The originals are kept in the Office of State Auditor at the State Capitol Building in Charleston. Microfilm copies are available at the Archives and History Library in Charleston and through the Family History Library.

MILITARY BOUNTY LANDS

In addition to federal bounty-land warrants (discussed in chapter 9, Records Generated by Federal Lands), several states produced their own bounty-land warrants. Those that did so include:

Georgia	North Carolina
Maryland	Pennsylvania
Massachusetts	South Carolina
New York	Virginia

Each state provided different acreages and established different prerequisites, depending on its needs and circumstances. Only Massachusetts forbade servicemen to receive bounty lands from both the federal and state governments. Elsewhere, even if federal bounty lands had been received, state lands could also be applied for. A brief overview of each state's bounty-land collections follows.

Connecticut

Though not bounty lands in the truest sense, certain Connecticut lands are discussed here as military-related land compensations. At the conclusion of the Revolutionary War, Connecticut continued to claim Ohio lands north of the forty-first parallel and westward from the state line to the present-day counties of Sandusky and Seneca. These lands were known as the "Connecticut Western Reserve." From this reserve, Connecticut set aside 500,000 acres to be used to compensate for the losses experienced by residents of specific towns during the Revolutionary War. This acreage is most often referred to as the "Firelands."

The towns of Danbury, East Haven, Fairfield, Greenwich, Groton, New Haven, New London, Norwalk, and Ridgefield were almost completely destroyed by the British and Tories in 1781. Their destruction affected more than 1,800 individuals and families, termed "sufferers," who were awarded lands in the Firelands area of Ohio. A corporation was established by the sufferers to manage and oversee the allotted lands. Lands were then distributed to individual claimants by lottery. Draws in the lottery were determined by the extent of losses in each claim.

Revolutionary War Bounty Land Acreage

	Private	Officer	Ensign	Lieut.	Captain
United States	100	100	150	200	300
Georgia	230–287	345	460	460	575–690
Maryland	50	200	200	200	200
Massachusetts	100	100	100	100	100
New York	500	500	1,000	1,000	1,500
North Carolina	640	1,000	2,560	2,560	3,840
Pennsylvania	200	250	300	400	500
South Carolina	100	100	100	100	100
Virginia	100–300	200–400	2,666	2,666	4,000
	Major	**Lt. Col.**	**Colonel**	**Brig. Gen.**	**General**
United States	400	450	500	850	1,100
Georgia	920	1,035	1,150	1,955	—
Maryland	200	200	200	200	200
Massachusetts	100	100	100	100	100
New York	2,000	2,250	2,500	4,250	5,500
North Carolina	4,800	5,760	7,200	12,000	25,000
Pennsylvania	600	800	1,000	1,500	2,000
South Carolina	100	100	100	100	100
Virginia	5333	6000	6,667	10,000	15,000

The Ohio counties involved are Erie, Huron, Ashland (Ruggles Township only), and Ottawa (Danbury Township only). For organization and structure of these lands, see chapter 8, Organization of Federal Lands.

The records generated by the distribution of lands to the Connecticut sufferers are often found in deed books. This is because the corporation had first title, then it distributed lands to the individuals. The best reference for sufferers and their origins is Clifford Neal Smith's *Federal Land Series, Volume One*. This volume lists many Connecticut claimants and the towns from which they originated. It also references the sources from which the material was taken. *Federal Land Series* can be found in most major libraries, including the Family History Library.

Georgia

Many of Georgia's bounty lands are included in the form of extra lottery draws. Extra draws were given not only for service in the Revolution, but for residence in the state during the war as well. For further information about the lotteries, see "Georgia" under "Common Records," above.

Aside from lottery draws, bounty lands were distributed in various areas around the state. Some areas were more concentrated with bounty lands than others. Robert Davis, Jr., indicates in the Georgia chapter of *Ancestry's Red Book* that most of present-day Greene County was reserved for bounty lands. Surviving original bounty certificates are housed at the Georgia Department of Archives and History. They are indexed in Lucas' *Index to the Headright and Bounty Grants of Georgia, 1756–1909*. Another good reference is Alex M. Hitz's compilation *Authentic List of All Land Lottery Grants Made to Veterans of the Revolutionary War by the State of Georgia*. Also see Marion Hemperley's *Military Certificates of Georgia, 1776–1800*, which includes a list of more than two thousand bounty-land recipients.

Maryland

Maryland's bounty lands were given in the western arm of the state in the counties of Allegany and Garrett. Few bounty-land warrants were actually issued by the state. Most servicemen preferred the options provided by federal bounty warrants. Bounty lands were distributed in fifty-acre rectangular sections, even though the remainder of the state was surveyed in metes and bounds. Most recipients can be found in Bettie Carothers' *Maryland Soldiers Entitled to Lands West of Fort Cumberland*. A similar list can be found in volume one of the *History of Western Maryland*, by J. Thomas Scharf. These lists show name, rank, regiment, and lot number(s) assigned. Privates received one lot each, while officers received four. The original records are housed in the Maryland Hall of Records in Annapolis.

Massachusetts

Massachusetts issued bounty-land warrants redeemable in the present-day state of Maine. There was no specified district in which these warrants had to be used, though most are found among the land records of the southern counties of York and Cumberland. Only those enlistees of Massachusetts regiments who did not qualify for a federal warrant could receive a state warrant.

The bounty-land records issued by Massachusetts are housed at the Massachusetts State Archives. Copies are available at the Maine State Land Office and are included in a collection microfilmed by the Family History Library. This collection, called *Revolutionary War Veteran's Land Records*, includes applications, declarations, and miscellaneous related land documents, on thirteen rolls of microfilm. The microfilmed version is also available through the Maine State Library, which now encompasses the Maine State Land Office.

Reference is made in James C. Neagles' *U.S. Military Records* to a notebook at the Massachusetts State Archives titled "Pensions." Within this notebook, further reference is made to issued bounty lands and their locations. This notebook also refers to *Two-Hundred-Acre Grants to Soldiers of the Massachusetts Continental Army*, though no publication data is given. A copy of this book is available at the Massachusetts State Archives. See also Charles J. House's *Names of Soldiers of the American Revolution who Applied for State Bounty under Resolves of March 17, 1835, March 24, 1836 and March 20, 1836*.

New York

New York distributed bounty lands in the form of lottery drawings, giving five-hundred-acre tracts to servicemen of the rank of private. Surveys were made in the form of six-hundred-acre rectangular tracts. This is in contrast with the metes and bounds used by most of the state. (See figure 6-6.)

Many of the original bounty-land warrants were destroyed by fire in 1911. The best resource for searching bounty lands is an index found at the New York State Archives titled *Index to Abstracts of Land Patents for Lands in the Military Tract, 1764–1797*. This indexes an eight-volume set of abstracts of the same title, also found at the State Archives. The collection and index are also available on microfilm at the Family History Library. Records of awarded bounty lands can also be researched using *The Balloting Book, and Other Documents Relating to Military Bounty Lands in the State of New York*. This was produced by the New York State Legislature, which also produced *A List of the Names of Persons to Whom Military Patents Have Issued Out of the Secretary's Office, and to Whom Delivered*. The latter was published in 1793, however, and does not include patents issued afterward.

North Carolina

North Carolina's bounty-land warrants were redeemable in the present-day state of Tennessee. This area was considered part of North Carolina until after the revolution. Warrants were given only to those who enlisted for two or more years. The Tennessee State Archives in Nashville houses all existing grants given by North Carolina for military service in the Revolutionary War. The records are included in a master card file index at the same location. The records and the index have also been microfilmed and are available at the Family History Library.

North Carolina first began issuing bounty-land warrants in the North Carolina Military Reservation in central Tennessee, though lands were issued in the eastern region as well. Records of North Carolina's distributions are also housed at the North Carolina Division of Archives and History in Raleigh. See Helen Leary's *North Carolina Genealogy* and George M. Battey's *The Tennessee Bee-hives; or Early (1778–1791) North Carolina Land Grants in the Volunteer State, Being an Index with Some 3100 Names of Revolutionary Soldiers and Settlers Who Participated in the Distribution of More Than 5,000,000 Acres of Land*.

Pennsylvania

Pennsylvania issued bounty depreciation certificates. In compensation for the decreased economic value of military pay slips, depreciation certificates allowed bounty-land purchases at a reduced price. These certificates were issued in addition to regular bounty-land warrants, which provided free land as a bonus for military service. Bounty warrants and depreciation certificates were redeemed for settlement in "the donation lands." Donation (or bounty) lands were located on the far western side of the state. They began at the northern bounds of Allegheny County and continued northward to the state line.

The Pennsylvania State Archives houses a collection called the *Return of Pennsylvania Line Entitled to Donation Lands*. A second collection there is titled *Return of Officers and Soldiers to Whom Patents Were Not Issued*. It details warrants that did not proceed to patent. Most other records are held at the Bureau of Land Records in Harrisburg.

A list of bounty-land claimants can also be found in *Pennsylvania Archives, 3rd Series, Volumes Three* and *Seven*. The entire publication spans 138 volumes in nine series; however, only these

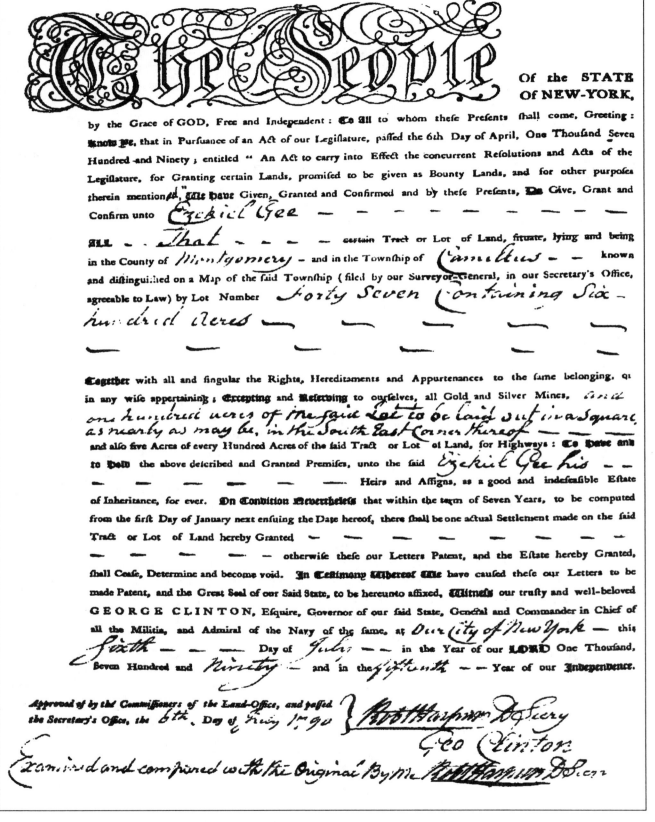

Figure 6-6. A New York bounty-land patent.

two are directed at the subject of bounty lands. They have been microfiched and are available through the Pennsylvania State Archives, the Library of Congress, and the Family History Library. Refer also to *Donation of Military Tracts of Land Granted the Soldiers of the Pennsylvania Line* by the Surveyor General's Office of Pennsylvania.

South Carolina

In South Carolina, an extremely small tract of land was reserved for bounty-land warrants. Most servicemen participated in federal bounty lands. The receipt of bounty lands can best be documented through the statewide consolidated index, which includes bounty lands with other state and colonial distributions. This index is in the form of a computer printout, and it has been microfilmed. The microfilm is available at the Department of Archives and History in Columbia, South Carolina, and at the Family History Library. The original records are housed only at the Department of Archives and History. See also "Bounty Grants and Revolutionary Soldiers" in *South Carolina Historical Magazine,* volume 7.

Virginia

Virginia generated more bounty-land records for its residents than any other state. At the conclusion of the Revolutionary War, Virginia ceded immense claims to the federal land system. However, they reserved the right to disperse bounty lands for their servicemen in the states of Kentucky and Ohio.

In Ohio, Virginia's activities were initially restricted to the Virginia Military District. Warrants for these lands were only given to those who served in the Continental Line from Virginia. Those who served in state militia units were required to redeem their warrants in the Kentucky District. During the 1830s, those who received warrants for the district in Ohio were eventually allowed to exchange their unused warrants for scrip. This scrip could then be redeemed in any one of the three newer districts that had been created for federal bounty warrants of the War of 1812: Indi-

ana, Illinois, or Missouri. By 1842, the warrants for Ohio could be exchanged for scrip redeemable at any federal land office.

The records generated contain a variety of information. Some contain only a name and a date. Others contain regiment, rank, duration of service, place of enlistment, and other critical information. Many of the early recipients are indexed in *A Roll of the Officers in the Virginia Line of the Revolutionary Army, Who Have Received Land Bounty in the States of Ohio and Kentucky* by Allen Latham. A more complete listing is found in Joan E. Brookes-Smith's *Master Index, Virginia Surveys and Grants, 1774–1791.* This publication documents only the bounty-land grants given in Kentucky. For further reference to those distributed in Ohio, refer to chapter 9, Records Generated by Federal Lands.

CONCLUSION

State-land grants were issued for a variety of reasons, and they generated a variety of documents. Though some records of many states have been destroyed or lost, at least portions of the process usually survived. These records help segregate and associate groups of settlers, which aids in further identifying possible ancestors. Records that were generated through basic patent processes, as well as through military bounty lands, have been discussed. Indexes and the most widely used collections have been identified for quick reference.

Below are the repositories in which many of these records can be found. Note that any address or other time-sensitive information is frequently subject to change. A telephone call, through directory assistance, can quickly correct the information if a problem is encountered. Following the list of repositories, a more detailed reference is available for a variety of publications that can be consulted when researching state-distributed lands. (See figure 6-7.)

Figure 6-7. Approximate federal and state military bounty-land areas within each state.

REPOSITORIES

Connecticut

Connecticut State Library
State Archives
231 Capitol Avenue
Hartford, CT 06106

Connecticut Historical Society
1 Elizabeth Street
Hartford, CT 06105

Department of Environmental Protection
165 Capitol Avenue
Hartford, CT 06106

Delaware

Delaware State Archives
Hall of Records
Dover, DE 19901

Secretary
Department of Natural Resources
P.O. Box 1401
Dover, DE 19903

Georgia

Georgia Surveyor-General Dept.
Department of Archives and History
330 Capitol Avenue, S.E.
Atlanta, GA 30334

Commissioner
Department of Natural Resources
205 Butler Street, S.E.
Suite 1252
Atlanta, GA 30334

Hawaii

Land Management Section
Department of Land and Natural Resources
1151 Punchbowl Street
Honolulu, HI 96813

Hawaii State Archives
Iolani Palace Grounds
478 South King Street
Honolulu, HI 96813

Kentucky

The Kentucky Land Office
Capitol Building
Frankfort, KY 40602

Kentucky Department for Libraries and Archives
Public Records Division
300 Coffee Tree Road
Frankfort, KY 40601

Filson Club Library
1310 South Third Street
Louisville, KY 40205

Commissioner
Department of Natural Resources
Capitol Plaza Tower
Frankfort, KY 40601

Maine

Maine Land Office
State House Station 84
Augusta, ME 04333

Maine State Archives
State House Station 84
Augusta, ME 04333

Commissioner
Department of Conservation
State House Station 22
Augusta, ME 04333

Maryland

Maryland State Archives
Hall of Records
350 Rowe Boulevard
Annapolis, MD 21401
or
P.O. Box 828
Annapolis, MD 21404

Secretary
Department of Natural Resources
Tawes State Office Building
Annapolis, MD 21401

Massachusetts

Massachusetts State Archives
220 Morrissey Boulevard
Boston, MA 02125

New England Historic Genealogical Society
101 Newbury Street
Boston, MA 02116-3087

Director
Environmental Affairs
100 Cambridge Street
Boston, MA 02202

New Hampshire

New Hampshire Division of Records
Management and Archives
71 South Fruit Street
Concord, NH 03301

New Hampshire State Library
20 Park Street
Concord, NH 03301

Commissioner
Dept. of Resources and Economic Development
105 Loudon Road, Box 856
Concord, NH 03301

New Jersey

Department of State
Division of Archives and Records Management
State Library Building
185 West State Street, CN 307
Trenton, NJ 08625-0307

Assistant Commissioner
Department of Environmental Protection
410 East State Street, CN 402
Trenton, NJ 08625

New York

New York State Archives
Cultural Education Center, 11th Floor
Empire State Plaza
Albany, NY 12230

Commissioner
Department of Environmental Conservation
50 Wolf Road
Albany, NY 12233

North Carolina

North Carolina Land Office
Secretary of State
Administration Building
Raleigh, NC 27603

North Carolina Division of Archives and History
109 East Jones Street
Raleigh, NC 27611

Pennsylvania

Bureau of Archives and History
William Penn Memorial Building
3rd and Forster Streets
P.O. Box 1026
Harrisburg, PA 17108-1026

Secretary
Department of Environmental Resources
P.O. Box 2063
Harrisburg, PA 17120

Rhode Island

Rhode Island State Archives
337 Westminster Street
Providence, RI 02903

Director
Department of Environmental Management
83 Park Street
Providence, RI 02903

South Carolina

South Carolina Dept. of Archives and History
1430 Senate Street
P.O. Box 11669, Capitol Station
Columbia, SC 29211-1669

Director
Division of Energy, Agriculture, and Natural Resources
1205 Pendelton Street
Columbia, SC 29201

Tennessee

Tennessee State Library and Archives
403 Seventh Avenue, North
Nashville, TN 37243-0312

Commissioner
Department of Conservation
701 Broadway
Nashville, TN 37203

Texas

Texas General Land Office
1700 North Congress Avenue
Austin, TX 78701

Texas State Library
State Archives and Library Building
Capitol Station
P.O. Box 12927
Austin, TX 78711-2927

Vermont

Division of State Papers
Office of Secretary of State
109 State Street
Montpelier, VT 05609

Vermont State Archives
Redstone Building
26 Terrace Street
Montpelier, VT 05609

Secretary
Agency of Natural Resources
103 S. Main Street
Waterbury, VT 05676

Virginia

Virginia State Library and Archives
11th Street at Capitol Square
Richmond, VA 23219-3491

Director
Department of Conservation and Historic
 Resources
1101 Washington Building
Richmond, VA 23219

West Virginia

State Auditor
Capitol Building
West Wing 231
Charleston, WV 25305

Archives and History Library
Division of Culture and History
Cultural Center, Capitol Complex
Charleston, WV 25305

Department of Natural Resources
Capitol Complex
Bldg. 3, Room 669
1900 Kanawha Blvd.
Charleston, WV 25305

FOR FURTHER REFERENCE

Bogart, Walter Thompson, Ph.D. *The Vermont Lease Lands.* Montpelier: Vermont Historical Society, 1950.

Blesser, Carol K. R. *The Promised Land: The History of the South Carolina Land Commission, 1869–1890.* Columbia: University of South Carolina Press, 1969.

Boyd, Julian P., and Robert J. Taylor. *The Susquehannah Company Papers.* Wilkes-Barre, Pa.: Wyoming Historical and Genealogical Society; and Ithaca, N.Y.: Cornell University Press, 1930-71.

Brewer, John M., and Lewis Mayer. *The Laws and Rules of the Land Office of Maryland.* Baltimore: Kelly, Piet, 1871.

Brookes-Smith, Joan E. *Master Index, Virginia Surveys and Grants, 1774–1791.* Frankfort: Kentucky Historical Society, 1976.

Burgner, Goldene Fillers. *North Carolina Land Grants in Tennessee, 1778–1791.* Easley, S.C.: Southern Historical Press, 1981. This is a revised edition of the title listed under Betty Cartwright.

Carothers, Bettie. *Maryland Soldiers Entitled to Lands West of Fort Cumberland.* Lutherville, Md.: the author, 1973.

Cartwright, Betty, and Lillian Johnson Gardiner. *North Carolina Land Grants in Tennessee, 1778–1791.* Memphis, Tenn.: the authors, 1958.

Chinen, Jon J. *Original Land Titles in Hawaii.* The author, 1961.

Clement, John. *Extracts From Minutes of the Council of Proprietors of the Western Division of the State of New Jersey, From 1687–1859.* Philadelphia, n.d.

Cunningham, John T. *The East of Jersey: A History of the General Board of Proprietors of the Eastern Division of New Jersey.* Newark: New Jersey Historical Society, 1992.

Davis, Robert S. *The 1830 Land Lottery of Georgia and Other Missing Names of Winners in the Georgia Land Lotteries.* Greenville, S.C.: Southern Historical Press, 1991.

Davis, Robert Scott, and Silas Emmett Lucas. *The Georgia Land Lottery Papers, 1805–1914.* Easley, S.C.: Southern Historical Press, 1979.

Davis, Robert Scott. *A Researcher's Library of Georgia History, Genealogy, and Record Sources.* Easley, S.C.: Southern Historical Press, 1987.

Deming, Dorothy. *The Settlement of the Connecticut Towns.* New Haven, Conn.: Tercentenary Commission, 1953.

Ditz, Toby L. *Property and Kinship: Inheritance in Early Connecticut, 1750–1820.* Princeton, N.J.: Princeton University Press, 1986.

Draine, Tony, and John Skinner. *Revolutionary War Bounty Land Grants in South Carolina.* Columbia, S.C.: Congaree Publications, 1986.

Duffin, James M. *Guide to the Mortgages of the General Loan Office of the Province of Pennsylvania, 1724–1756.* Philadelphia: Genealogical Society of Pennsylvania, 1995.

Eakle, Arlene, and Vincent L. Jones. *Solving American Pedigrees: American Property Records—Land and Tax Records.* Salt Lake City: Genealogical Institute, 1973.

Egleston, Melville. *The Land System of the New England Colonies.* Baltimore: Johns Hopkins University, 1986.

Fowler, Robert L. *History of the Law of Real Property in New York.* New York: Baker Voorhis, 1895.

Gates, Paul W., et al. *History of Public Land Law Development.* Washington, D.C.: Government Printing Office, 1968.

Gentry, Daphne S., comp. *Virginia Land Office Inventory.* Richmond: Virginia State Library and Archives, 1981.

Hatcher, Harlan. *The Western Reserve: The Story of New Connecticut in Ohio.* Indianapolis: The Bobbs-Merrill Company, 1949.

Heite, Edward F. *Delaware's Fugitive Records: An Inventory of the Official Land Grant Records Relating to the Present State of Delaware.* Dover: Delaware Division of Historical and Cultural Affairs, 1980.

Hemperley, Marion R. *Military Certificates of Georgia, 1776–1800.* Atlanta, Ga.: State Printing Office, 1983.

Hemperley, Marion R. *Georgia Surveyor-General Department: A History and Inventory of Georgia's Land Office.* Atlanta, Ga.: State Printing Office, 1982.

Hibbard, Benjamin Horace. *A History of Public Land Policies.* New York: MacMillan, 1924.

Hitz, Alex M. *Authentic List of All Land Lottery Grants Made to Veterans of the Revolutionary War by the State of Georgia.* N.p., 1955.

_____. *Georgia Bounty Land Grants.* Savannah: Georgia Historical Society, 1954.

Hopkins, William Lindsay. *Virginia Revolutionary War Land Grant Claims, 1783–1850 (Rejected Claims).* Richmond, Va.: Gen-N-Dex, 1988.

Horwitz, Robert H. *Public Land Policy in Hawaii: A Historical Analysis.* Honolulu: University of Hawaii, 1969.

House, Charles J. *Names of Soldiers of the American Revolution Who Applied for the State Bounty under Resolves of March 17, 1835, March 24, 1836 and March 20, 1836, as Appears of Record in Land Office.* Augusta, Maine: Order of the Governor and Executive Council, 1893.

Houston, Martha Lou. *Reprint of Official Register of Land Lottery of Georgia, 1827.* Columbus, Ga.: the author, 1929.

Jillson, Willard Rouse, Sc.D. *The Kentucky Land Grants.* Baltimore: Genealogical Publishing Co., 1971.

Jones, Vincent L., and Arlene H. Eakle. *Genealogical Research: American Jurisdictions and Sources.* N.p., 1965.

Kentucky Historical Society. *Index for Old Kentucky Grants Microfilmed by Kentucky Historical Society.* Frankfort: Kentucky Historical Society, 1975.

Latham, Allen. *A Roll of the Officers in the Virginia Line of the Revolutionary Army Who Have Received Land Bounty in the States of Ohio and Kentucky.* N.p, n.d.

Leary, Helen, and Maurice R. Stirewalt, eds. *North Carolina Research: Genealogy and Local History*. Raleigh: North Carolina Genealogical Society, 1980.

Lucas, Silas Emmett, Jr. *Index to the Headright and Bounty Grants of Georgia, 1756–1909*. Vidalia: Georgia Genealogical Reprints, 1970. Also author of several publications concerning the Georgia Land Lotteries.

McGinnis, Carol. *Virginia Genealogy Sources and Resources*. Baltimore: Genealogical Publishing Co., n.d. Contains excellent information on independent cities.

McLendon, Samuel Guyton. *History of the Public Domain of Georgia*. Spartanburg, S.C.: Reprint Co., 1974.

Munger, Donna Bingham. *Pennsylvania Land Records: A History and Guide for Research*. Wilmington, Del.: Scholarly Resources, 1991.

Neagles, James C. *U.S. Military Records: A Guide to Federal and State Sources*. Salt Lake City: Ancestry, 1994.

New York State Archives. *Public Records Relating to Land in New York State*. Albany: New York State Archives, 1979.

Oberly, James W. *Sixty Million Acres: American Veterans and the Public Lands Before the Civil War*. Kent, Ohio: Kent State University Press, 1990. Considered one of the most informative books on military bounty lands.

Office of the Commissioner of Public Lands of the Territory of Hawaii. *Indices of Awards Made by the Board of Commissioners to Quiet Land Titles in the Hawaiian Islands*. Honolulu: Office of the Commissioner of Public Lands of the Territory of Hawaii, 1929.

Pomfret, John E. *The New Jersey Proprietors and their Lands*. Princeton, N.J.: D. Van Nostrand Co., 1964.

Pruitt, Albert Bruce. *Glasgow Land Fraud Papers, 1783–1800: North Carolina Revolutionary War Bounty Land in Tennessee*. The author, 1993.

Rice, Shirley Hollis. *The Hidden Revolutionary War Land Grants in the Tennessee Military Reservation*. Lawrenceburg, Tenn.: Family Tree Press, 1992.

Rose, Robert S. "The Military Tract of Central N.Y." M.A. thesis, Syracuse University, 1935.

Scharf, J. Thomas. *History of Western Maryland*. Philadelphia: Louis H. Everts, 1882.

Scott, Kenneth, and Roseanne Conway. *New York Alien Residents 1825–1848*. Baltimore: Genealogical Publishing Co., 1978.

Sears, Joan N. *The First One Hundred Years of Town Planning in Georgia*. Atlanta, Ga.: Cherokee Publishing Co., 1979.

Sergeant, Thomas. *View of the Land Laws of Pennsylvania*. Laughlin: Southwest Pennsylvania Genealogical Services, 1992.

Skordas, Gust. *The Early Settlers of Maryland: An Index to Names of Immigrants Compiled From Records of Land Patents, 1633–1680*. Baltimore: Genealogical Publishing Co., 1968.

Smith, Clifford Neal. *Federal Land Series: A Calendar of Archival Materials on the Land Patents Issued by the United States Government, with Subject, Tract, and Name Indexes*. Chicago: American Library Association, 1972-.

Southerland, James F., comp. *Early Kentucky Landholders, 1787–1811*. Baltimore: Genealogical Publishing Co., 1986.

Sullivan, James. *History of Land Titles in Massachusetts*. Boston: I. Thomas and E. T. Andrews, 1801.

Swathers, George Henry. *The History of Land Titles in Western North Carolina*. Asheville, N.C.: Miller Printing, 1938.

Taylor, Philip Fall, comp. *A Calendar of the Warrants for Land in Kentucky, Granted for Service in the French and Indian War*. Baltimore: Genealogical Publishing Co., 1967.

Texas General Land Office. *Abstracts of All Original Texas Land Titles*. Austin: General Land Office, 1941–42.

Wilson, Samuel S. *Catalogue of Revolutionary Soldiers and Sailors of the Commonwealth of Virginia to Whom Land Bounty Warrants Were Granted*. Baltimore: Southern Book Co., 1953.

Whitney, Henry D. *The Land Laws of Tennessee.* Chattanooga, Tenn.: J.M. Deardorff and Sons, 1891.

Winner, John E. "The Depreciation and Donation Lands." In *Western Pennsylvania Historical Magazine* (1925).

Wood, Virginia S., and Ralph V. Wood. *1805 Land Lottery of Georgia.* Cambridge, Mass.: Greenwood Press, 1964. This includes all eligible participants.

Woodward, Florence May. *The Town Proprietors in Vermont: New England Town Proprietorship in Decline.* New York: Columbia University Press, 1936.

Strategies for State Land Records

PLATTING METES AND BOUNDS

A seldom-used strategy concerning land records is the platting of metes and bounds. Platting—drawing the property description—can sometimes be tedious and difficult. However, it can offer as much additional understanding as the difference between only reading a manual and actually seeing an assembled model. For a more detailed description of metes and bounds, see chapter 5, Organization of State Lands.

Methods of platting are as various as the deeds they represent. Many methods, however, tend to place more burden than benefit on those who are using them. Mathematics can play an important role in many of these methods. The most important thing about platting is learning what is valuable and what is not. It must also be determined whether platting will answer the questions at hand.

The purposes for platting are numerous. Most genealogical searches have one of two purposes: either to segregate or associate. Platting can assist in both, especially when dealing with common surnames such as Williams or Davis. There are many other occasions in which platting will help to confirm answers to otherwise ambiguous hypotheses. Imagination and creativity are the only restrictions. Some of the most common applications are mentioned below. They are classic examples of when platting can be beneficial.

Platting Can Be Used To:

- Prove that two people with slightly different names are actually one and the same.

- Distinguish lands that were bought from lands possibly inherited (for later comparison).

- Segregate people having the same last and/or first names.

- Precisely group individuals on an exact piece of property within the same county.

- Determine if someone sold more property than bought. This raises questions of inheritance or acquisition through marriage.

- Define common neighbors of different individuals who are not mentioned in their own deeds as specifically bordering each other.

- In addition to providing many other types of answers, platting can simply be an aid to understanding an ancestor's past.

Example 1

Josiah Wilson and his wife, Jane, were noted in the 1850 census in Missouri. They had several children, one born as early as 1838 and one born as late as 1849, all in the state of Tennessee. They were obviously new arrivals to the state of Missouri.

Living a few households away were Elias Wilson, Levi Wilson, Jr., Jacob Wilson, and others who also had had children born recently in Tennessee. They were all grouped together in a defined area, and they all dealt in land transactions with one another. First impressions from age analysis would place them as brothers or cousins. Their ages did not prevent them from being brothers within the same family.

Research in the 1840 census index for the state of Tennessee showed that the same families appeared together in one county. The extracted data from this census showed a Levi Wilson, Sr., old enough to have been their father. The earlier censuses showed him to have had ten males consistently in the household and four females. Questions immediately arise about whether they were all actually family, or whether there were farmhands living with Levi. There were enough males later identified through the 1850 census to have accounted for most of them as family.

Further research in the probate records uncovered a will for Levi Wilson, Sr. He very proudly described thirteen children by name. Several times within the will he stated, ". . . all 13 of my children, to wit: . . ." He described Elias, Jeremy, Levi, Jr., Jacob, and a total of nine boys. Josiah was not mentioned. Four daughters were also mentioned: Mary Kendrick, Ann Bartholomew, Sarah Toliver, and Jane Wilson. All of the children would have been over age forty, and likely married.

Where did Josiah fit into the family? Though Wilson is a common surname in the United States, these were the only families with that surname in the county. Surely Josiah was related; yet everyone had been accounted for within the family of Levi, Sr. Ordinarily, his absence from the will would not have been sufficient evidence to dismiss him from this family. However, the terminology was explicit throughout the will. The precise names and the number of children were mentioned several times.

A study of the land records showed Levi Wilson's children dealing with one another, and occasionally even with Josiah. They each received a portion of land from their father, except for Josiah. Josiah bought his land from a neighbor.

It was noted through research of the land deeds that Josiah sold more land than he bought. He received no grants from the state of Tennessee that would account for this excess. One method for answering this puzzle was to plat the metes and bounds of the various property descriptions.

Through platting, the property that Josiah bought was more easily distinguished and compared with the properties of the heirs of Levi, Sr. It was noted through platting that Josiah and his wife, Jane, sold not only the lands that Josiah had purchased, but also the neighboring property that Levi Wilson willed to his daughter, Jane Wilson (see the accompanying drawing).

Two thoughts immediately occur: 1) All of Levi's daughters were old enough to have been married, yet Jane was still listed with the surname of Wilson in Levi's will. 2) Josiah Wilson and his wife, Jane, sold the land that Josiah had bought and the land that Jane Wilson had inherited. The result was the hypothesis that Jane and Josiah were cousins who had married. This theory was later supported through additional research. Josiah was the nephew of Levi. It would have been carelessly easy to assume a more direct relationship to Levi if in-depth studies through platting had not been made. (See figures 7-1 and 7-2.)

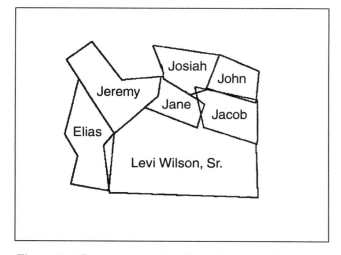

Figure 7-1. Property was distributed by Levi, Sr., to all except the ancestral Josiah, who bought his own land.

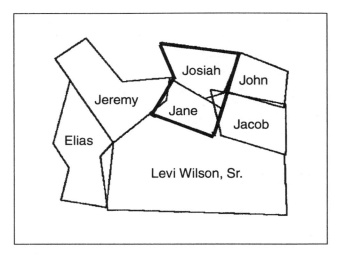

Figure 7-2. Josiah Wilson and his wife, Jane, sold property that included the inheritance of Jane Wilson from Levi, Sr. (Josiah Wilson had married Jane Wilson).

Example 2

William Geslett, a resident of southern Virginia, was believed to belong to a family in a northern county of that state. Because of the uncommon surname, this hypothesis seemed practical, though no records had been found to prove a relationship. Another family, consisting of several children with the same last name, lived in the same northern county. Research suggested that Thomas Geslett was the most likely of two candidates to have been the ancestral William's father. He left a will dividing his estate into seven nearly equal parts: one portion for his wife and one for each of six children. However, no names were mentioned.

Deeds were researched in the county where Thomas had resided, and several transactions between Thomas and four of his children were found. They were specifically identified as his children in the deeds. Nothing, however, could be found about the other two children. They did not sell their inheritance during the next seventy-five years.

Research in the southern county where William had lived revealed that he had sold more land than he had bought. Close inspection of the deeds described property in the north which he had inherited from his father nearly twenty years earlier. Again, no names were mentioned.

Platting of the metes and bounds in both counties showed this property to have been one of the two missing parts from the divisions in the will of Thomas Geslett. This adequately linked William across several counties and proved the necessary relationships, even though the names of father and son never appeared together in the same document.

Platting Process

Though technology has produced many excellent computer programs for platting metes and bounds, there is still a need to learn manual methods of platting. The following is presented as one of the most practical and simple manual methods. By following this exercise step by step, a better understanding of platting can be realized. This same understanding can then be applied to other property descriptions.

You will need:

- a protractor
- a ruler (metric is best)
- lined or graph paper
- a deed description (provided here)

(See figure 7-3.)

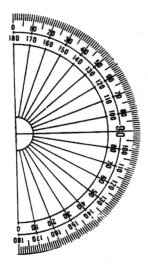

Figure 7-3. Protractor and ruler.

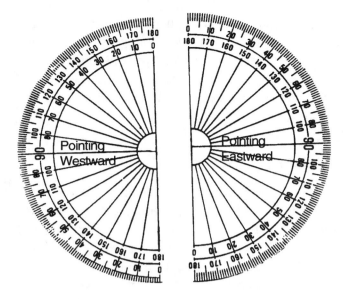

Figure 7-4. The protractor should never appear other than in one of these two orientations.

Use graph paper to keep the protractor's baseline running north and south at all times. Otherwise, the type of paper used makes no difference. Once north is established on your paper, your protractor should always appear in one of the two orientations shown in figure 7-4. The curve of the protractor will indicate east or west.

There are only three items to consider when platting metes and bounds: direction, degrees, and distance of measurement. Rarely are **directions** exactly north, south, east, or west. They are almost always combinations thereof (e.g., *northwest*). **Degrees** indicate, more precisely, the directions to be taken (e.g., *22 degrees* northwest). Measurements are the **distance** of each line (e.g., 22 degrees northwest, *42 chains*).

Keep in mind that there will never be a measurement greater than ninety degrees, so ignore higher rows of numbers on the protractor.

PREPARATION

Visualize, and perhaps mark directly on the protractor, locations as shown in figure 7-5.

Note that either way the protractor faces, the applicable directions are labeled right side up. For example, if platting a northwest direction, the pro-

tractor should be turned until NW appears right side up. That is the quadrant that will be used, using only the numbers 1 through 90. The protractor is now ready for platting.

Metes and bounds are most easily platted from the middle of the page on a small scale (size). Copies can then be made to enlarge the drawing to the desired scale. If the plat is made too large in the beginning, there may not be enough space and lines may run off the paper. A good scale for measurements is to allow one chain, rod, pole, or perch to equal one millimeter. Links and other, smaller measurements are of little consequence. They need only be considered when drawing an official or legal document.

Consider the following land description:

. . . beginning at the great white oak, on the banks of Simpson Creek, thence southwest 45 degrees 30 chains to the felled maple, thence south 76 degrees west 60 chains to the marked oak. From the marked oak, along the bounds of Jeremiah Wilson's line S.W. 5 degrees 16 to the big rock, thence 40 degrees southwest 69 chains to the corner where Jones and Smith's bounds meet. From the said corner, thence in a southeast direction 47 degrees 47 chains to a designated marker, thence 45 degrees

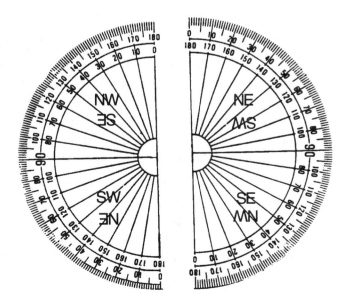

Figure 7-5. Directions to be marked on the protractor.

northeast 69 chains, thence north 72 degrees east 45 chains to the creek aforesaid, Simpson Creek.

Step One

A description which at first appears complicated actually contains only seven drawn lines. Separating what is important and what is not important will make platting much easier and less intimidating. The first step is to extract the important information. In doing so, only the following information is found to be of value for platting: direction, degree, and distance.

- Southwest 45 degrees 30 chains
- South 76 degrees west 60 chains
- S.W. 5 degrees 16
- 40 degrees southwest 69 chains
- Southeast 47 degrees 47 chains
- 45 degrees northeast 69 chains
- North 72 degrees east 45 chains

Of the seven simple statements above, note the various configurations of information. Regardless of the order in which they are listed, the meaning remains the same for each of the three considered aspects: direction, degrees, and distance. For example, "south 76 degrees west 60 chains" still has a direction of southwest, despite the fact that the words "south" and "west" are separated. Whenever a distance is not given, such as in "S.W. 5 degrees 16," the "16" is assumed to be the same form of measurement as the previous distance; in this case, "chains." With a complicated deed reduced to seven simple measurements, the platting process is well under way.

Step Two

Arrange an 8 ½- by 11-inch sheet of paper in a "landscape" position (horizontal). Place a dot in the upper right hand corner to be used as a beginning point. As more deeds are platted, an intuition for placing the beginning point on a sheet of paper will develop. (See figure 7-6.)

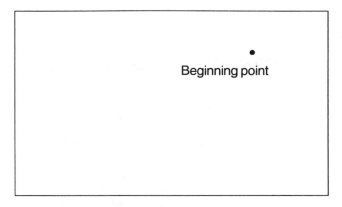

Figure 7-6. Step two.

Step Three

Place the center of the protractor's baseline on the dot with "SW" right side up (because the first measurement is in a southwest direction). Be sure to use the baseline drawn on the protractor, not the edge of the protractor. They usually differ.

Use only the row of numbers that include 0 to 90 degrees. In the portion labeled SW, measure 45 degrees and make a mark. Placing the ruler's edge across the beginning mark and the mark at 45 degrees, measure a distance of 30 chains (30 millimeters). Draw a line that exact distance. (See figure 7-7.)

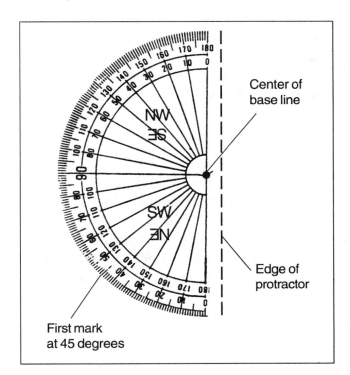

Figure 7-7. Step three.

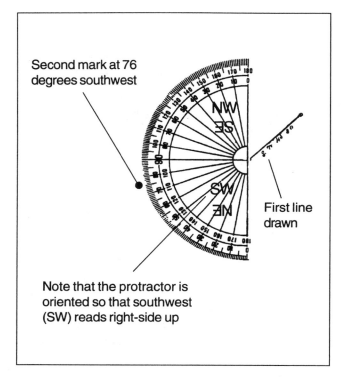

Figure 7-8. Step four.

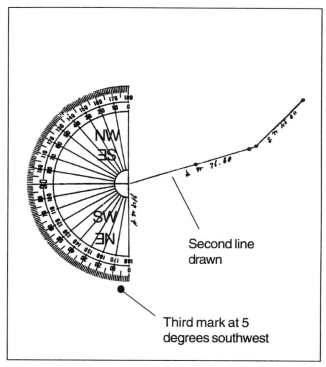

Figure 7-9. Step five.

Step Four

Move the center of the protractor's baseline to the end of the line just drawn. Keep the baseline running north and south. The second measurement also involves a southwest direction, so measure from the bottom of the protractor again for the second line. Measure 76 degrees and make a new mark. Beginning at the end of the previous line, measure 60 chains (60 millimeters or 6 centimeters) in the direction of the new mark. (See figure 7-8.)

Step Five

The third line is also in a southwest direction, so the protractor should continue to face westward. Placing the center of the baseline where the previous line ended, measure only 5 degrees this time. Make a mark, and use the ruler to draw a straight line for 16 chains (16 millimeters). (See figure 7-9.)

Step Six

Sliding the protractor down, match the center of the baseline with the end of the last line drawn.

Measure according to the fourth item in the deed description, marking 40 degrees southwest. Then, using the ruler, measure and draw a line exactly 69 chains (69 millimeters) in the direction of the newest mark. (See figure 7-10.)

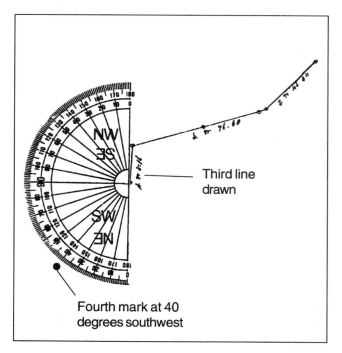

Figure 7-10. Step six.

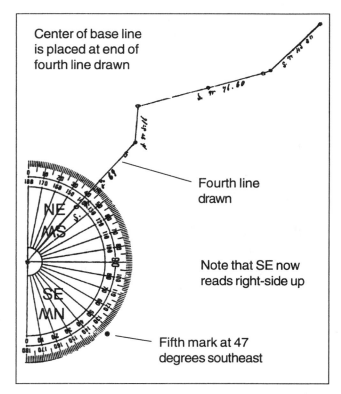

Figure 7-11. Step seven.

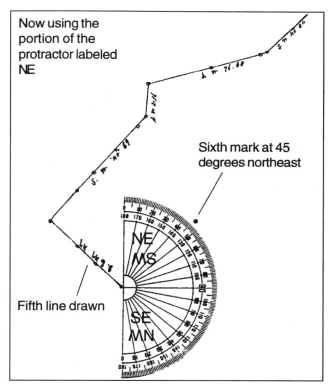

Figure 7-12. Step eight.

Step Seven

Now, for the first time in this deed, the directions change. The fifth line contains the direction southeast, rather than southwest. The protractor then needs to be placed so that "SE" is right side up, but still with the baseline running north and south. Placing the protractor as shown, mark 47 degrees. Remember, use only the row of numbers containing 0 to 90 degrees. Then, using a ruler, finish by measuring a line 47 chains (47 millimeters) in length toward the newest mark. (See figure 7-11.)

Step Eight

The process continues to repeat itself. Placing the center of the protractor's baseline at the end of the last line drawn, measure and mark 45 degrees from the northeast (NE) portion of the protractor. Using the ruler, draw a line for a distance of 69 chains (69 millimeters). With this line, the plat will begin to take shape. (See figure 7-12.)

Step Nine

The final piece of information states another northeast direction of 72 degrees. Placing the center of the protractor's baseline at the end of the last line drawn, measure and mark 72 degrees. With the ruler, measure a distance of 45 chains (45 millimeters) and draw the line (figure 7-13). Notice that the lines in the deed description do not meet where they began. While it is normal for plats not to completely close, the gap for this deed is extreme. A closer look at the deed description shows the last line to go "to the creek aforesaid, Simpson Creek." This presents the tenth and final step.

Step Ten

As mentioned previously, creeks and other boundaries, both natural and man-made, play an important role in many plat maps. In these circumstances, the creek must be imagined and platted along the last boundary line. Its precision is not critical to the objectives of platting for genealogists and similar researchers. Critical, however, is the placement of neighbors and the comparison of lands bought

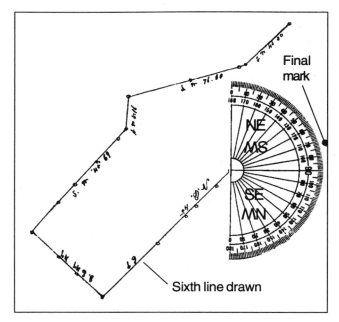

Figure 7-13. Step nine.

versus lands sold. Finish the platting exercise by drawing the creek between the beginning and ending plat lines. (See figure 7-14.)

The steps followed here will work for almost any circumstance encountered in deed descriptions. Platting allows for a more visual understanding of ancestors, their neighbors, associates, and relatives. For these purposes, perfection is not nec-

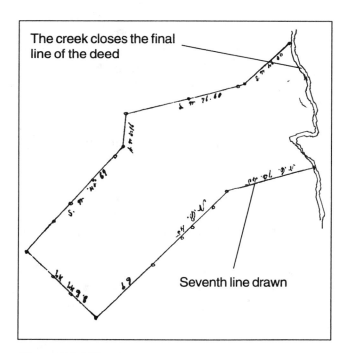

Figure 7-14. Step ten.

essary. Patience, however, is needed. With patience and persistence, platting metes and bounds can be a strategy which helps uncover answers previously hidden in other types of research.

OTHER STRATEGIES FOR STATE LANDS

Ingenuity will always determine the frequency of successful answers in land and property research. Give attention to the laws of each different state, and the specific qualification requirements for each different state land program. The following list illustrates some of the aspects that need particular attention when researching land records for state lands. Some of these apply to federal and individual lands as well.

- Legal age in the state. This alludes to a minimum and maximum age for an individual at the time the record was created (e.g., is the person in the deed really a father with the same name, because the ancestor would have been too young?).

- Special tax exemptions for state land purchases can explain why an ancestor may have been absent from tax lists for as many as ten years.

- Signatures, when not marked with an "X," can help identify different people with the same name. The fact that one could spell well and another could not may also help segregate individuals with common names.

- Military bounty lands can lead to service and pension records. Even if a person received federal bounty lands, he could also apply for state compensations as well (except in Massachusetts). Each offered a different set of qualifications and procedures that generated a variety of record sources. State military bounty lands were more apt to be settled on by the recipient than federal bounty lands.

- Remember that the date of patent is not the date of application. An ancestor may prove to have been in a location for several years earlier than originally thought if both documents are researched.

- Always look for multiple grants. The earlier grants may have generated more information.

- A land grant can serve as a census substitute for censuses that were lost or destroyed. Most early inhabitants held land. Land records were not restricted to a decennial year, as are censuses, but were generated each and every day. Thus, they can also fill in the years between censuses.

- Observe the prerequisites of residence (for example, a person had to reside in Georgia before 26 June 1800 to apply in 1803 for the 1807 lottery. A draw in that lottery indicates residence before June of 1800).

- When indexes are available, search all entries for a designated surname, not just the ancestor. Compare others and their lands with the ancestor's land description. Persons of the same names receiving grants in the same areas might indicate a relationship.

- Did an ancestor appear in a new region while supposedly still living at an earlier residence? This could indicate that the earlier residence belongs to someone other than the ancestor. The settlement requirements for each state can help determine if he could have lived elsewhere while receiving a grant.

There obviously are other strategies that are just as useful. Each circumstance creates a need for using land records in different ways. Again, ingenuity is the only restriction.

Locating places listed in many of the early colonial and state land records can also be frustrating.

A variety of resources are available to help determine more about an abstract location. These resources are referred to further in chapter 10, Strategies for Federal Lands.

FOR FURTHER REFERENCE

Elliott, Wendy L. *Using Land Records to Solve Research Problems.* Bountiful, Utah: American Genealogical Lending Library, 1987.

Greenwood, Val. *The Researcher's Guide to American Genealogy.* Baltimore: Genealogical Publishing Co., 1990.

"How to Plat a Deed." *Eswau Huppeday* (Bulletin of the Broad River Genealogical Society) 1 (1) (February 1981).

Lawson, Charles E. *Surveying Your Land: A Common-Sense Guide to Surveys, Deeds, and Title Searches.* Woodstock, Vt.: The Countryman Press, 1990.

Leary, Helen F.M., and Maurice R. Stirewalt, eds. *North Carolina Research, Genealogy and Local History.* Raleigh: North Carolina Genealogical Society, 1980.

Miller, James W., Jr. "Platting Land Grants and Deeds." *The North Carolina Genealogical Society Journal* 16 (2) (May 1990).

Read, Helen Hunt. *Property Deeds for Genealogy.* Toledo, Ohio: the author, 1985.

Szucs, Loretto Dennis, and Sandra Hargreaves Luebking, eds. *The Source: A Guidebook of American Genealogy.* Rev. ed. Salt Lake City: Ancestry, 1997.

Section 3:
Federal-Land States

An Introduction to Federal Lands

Lands that were initially controlled and dispersed by the United States government are called federal lands. Thirty states, listed below, contain such lands:

Alabama	Mississippi
Alaska	Missouri
Arizona	Montana
Arkansas	Nebraska
California	Nevada
Colorado	New Mexico
Florida	North Dakota
Idaho	Ohio
Illinois	Oklahoma
Indiana	Oregon
Iowa	South Dakota
Kansas	Utah
Louisiana	Washington
Michigan	Wisconsin
Minnesota	Wyoming

U.S. government control over the distribution of federal lands resulted in a unique system of organization. The federal government's bureaucratic processes resulted in some of the best genealogical records of America's past.

Public lands were first introduced in 1785. They were dispersed by the government to accomplish three objectives: to raise revenues to help compensate for the depletions of the Revolutionary War, to grant lands in lieu of financial rewards to soldiers, and to both accommodate and encourage western migration. Through a system of surveys and meridians, the lands were tracked and dispersed to individual property owners.

The types of land claims on public domain (federal lands) vary widely. They encompass the largest group of records ever produced for a single subject prior to the twentieth century. They include records generated for pre-U.S. settlement, preemption rights, cash and credit entries, homesteading, military bounty lands, mining claims, agricultural and timber management, and a complex web of accompanying documents.

Land office activity began as early as 1797, when western lands were sold from an office in New York City. Philadelphia followed in 1800. By 1805, land offices were opened in Ohio and the Mississippi Territories. Most offices were heavily burdened during the first years of their existence as they attempted to assess and honor grants made by previous governments. Spain, Britain, and France had given out numerous land grants. Each had to be carefully assessed and recognized according to the treaties with each nation. Records generated by this process are generally referred to as "private land claims."

As private claims were settled, lands were opened for general purchase. Lands were first auctioned off, then made available for both cash and credit. Records of the first twenty years mostly show purchases at $2 per acre. As the credit system began to fail, however, land was broken into smaller sizes with more affordable prices. "Tax-free" incentives were also offered, for as long as the first five years of ownership, to help offset the financial limits faced by many. These measures quickly increased the flow of settlers into a virtual flood.

Those who purchased federal lands usually completed a structured application process. This began by filing claims with the registrar. Once the claim or application requirements were met, a warrant to survey the specified tract of land was issued. After completion of the registration, payment, surveys, and necessary proofs and testimonies, a final certificate would be issued for the patent. At that time the papers would be gathered into case files and sent to the General Land Office. The overall process, though bothersome to those who dealt with the bureaucracy, created a wealth of information about the early inhabitants of the United States. The case files can show origins, relationships with family and friends, naturalization information, and a variety of other clues.

Because the records were created through land districts and offices, understanding their existence and boundaries can be of great importance. Districts and offices vary in the length of their terms, depending on the acreage within the district and the settlement circumstances of each area. Though the land office might change within the bounds of the district, the district boundaries themselves seldom changed unless new ones were created or old ones terminated. When less than 100,000 acres remained to be sold, the district could be dissolved and was usually combined with another nearby district. Alabama, for example, had a total of eight land districts in the mid-nineteenth century. By 1906, however, it had only one, the Montgomery district. By 1927 it, too, was discontinued and merged with the Eastern States Office of the Bureau of Land Management.

Federal lands, land offices and their jurisdictions, and the records created by the patent process all help to determine time periods, places of origin, relationships, and associations. Each helps to add historical background to the research of our ancestors. The chapters in this section discuss, in more detail, the land organization, the patent process, and the various record sources created by the federal land system. Access to many of these records and how to use them strategically is also discussed.

8

Organization of Federal Lands

MERIDIANS

Meridians provide a means of measuring distances and locating positions on the earth's surface. This measurement technique has been in existence for almost two hundred years. Before any of the federal land districts in the United States were opened for land transactions, a survey was made of the area and meridians were established. (See figure 8-1.) Every other process in the organization and distribution of federal lands depends upon the survey of the meridian.

A **meridian** is an imaginary line running directly north and south, from pole to pole. East and west measurements within the meridian are then counted from this line. Placed twenty-four miles to the east and west of each meridian line are additional lines called **guide meridians**. To help complete the meridian grid, there is a horizontal line that runs east and west, intersecting the meridian line at a right angle. This horizontal line is identified as the **base line**. It is the line from which north and south descriptions begin their measurements.

Whenever a parcel of land is researched in search of an individual, the meridian for that location must be identified. Once the meridian is known, any land description can be quickly and precisely located.

Whenever the surveying of new lands from existing meridians became difficult or cumbersome, or as geography demanded, a new meridian was created; however, new meridians were sometimes created before existing meridians reached their capacity. In other instances, acquisitions of new territory sometimes led to the creation of a new meridian.

The curvature of the earth causes the meridian lines to converge on one another toward the poles (figure 8-2). As the meridian lines grow closer together, the sizes of tracts, townships and sections grow smaller. The more northerly townships and sections need to be realigned to compensate for this convergence factor. Correction lines have been created to help solve this problem, and sections that border the west side of a township contain lands that are not perfectly square.

The meridian locations can be determined through the use of most commercial atlases. Rand McNally's *Commercial Atlas and Marketing Guide* can be found in most libraries. It shows not only the names of the meridians, but also the townships and ranges discussed later in this chapter. This information is extremely useful when studying township plat maps and other records that are organized by meridian rather than land office or county.

Only the federal-land states base their land organization system on meridians. Meridians have also been used in parts of Canada and Australia. Many meridians serve more than one state. The various meridians and the states which they completely or partially cover are shown in "Meridians Used Within Each State" on page 105.

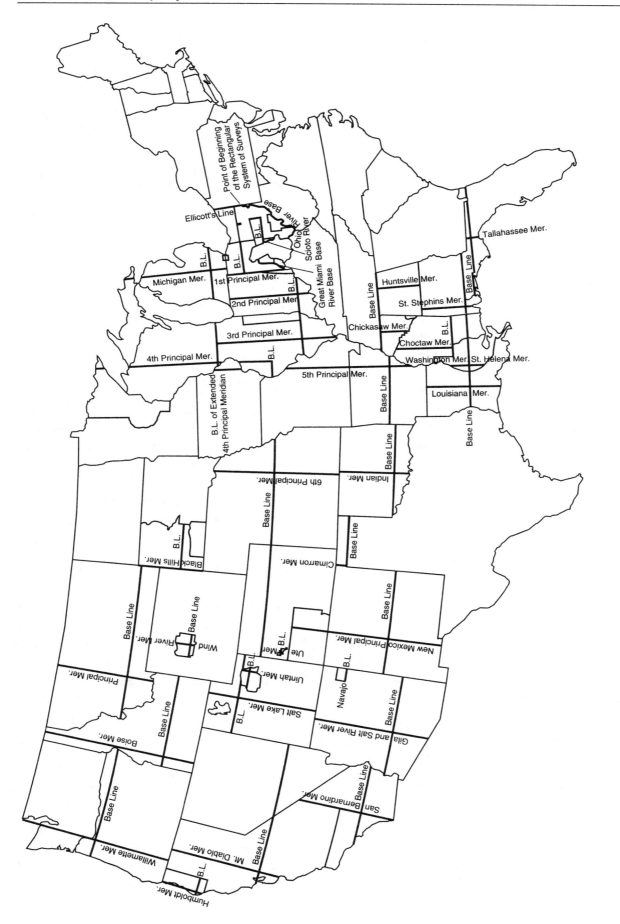

Figure 8-1. The principal meridians and base lines of the United States.

Meridians Used Within Each State

Alabama
St. Stephens
Huntsville
Tallahassee

Alaska
Copper River
Fairbanks
Kateel River
Seward
Uniat

Arizona
Gila and Salt River
Navajo

Arkansas
Fifth Principal

California
Humboldt
Mount Diablo
San Bernardino

Colorado
New Mexico Principal
Sixth Principal
Ute

Florida
Tallahassee

Idaho
Boise

Illinois
Fourth Principal
Second Principal
Third Principal

Indiana
First Principal
Second Principal

Iowa
Fifth Principal

Kansas
Sixth Principal

Louisiana
Louisiana
St. Helena

Michigan
Michigan

Minnesota
Fourth Principal
Fifth Principal

Mississippi
Chickasaw
Choctaw
Huntsville
St. Stephens
Washington

Missouri
Fifth Principal

Montana
Principal

Nebraska
Sixth Principal

Nevada
Mount Diablo

New Mexico
New Mexico Principal

North Dakota
Fifth Principal

Ohio
First Principal

Oklahoma
Cimarron
Indian

Oregon
Willamette

South Dakota
Black Hills
Fifth Principal
Sixth Principal

Utah
Salt Lake
Uintah

Washington
Willamette

Wisconsin
Fourth Principal

Wyoming
Sixth Principal
Wind River

TRACTS

Each of the meridian regions of the United States is divided into **tracts.** Each tract is approximately twenty-four miles square. Each tract is then subdivided into sixteen townships, each about six miles square. A meridian should contain a maximum measurement of eight square tracts.

The term "tract" has two definitions: 1) it can refer to a specific parcel, or "tract," of land (tract books refer to these individual parcels, and deeds sometimes use this term), and 2) it can refer to a portion of a meridian as described above (these tracts are seldom referred to in land descriptions and play only a minor role in the overall land system).

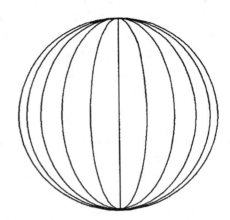

Figure 8-2. Square land measurements must take into account the varying widths of meridians on a sphere.

	T3N R2W				T3N R3E
Base Line			T1N R1E		
T2S R3W					
			T3S R2E		

Figure 8-3. Meridian and congressional township grid. Each square depicts a congressional township. Township directions are always north or south, and range directions are always east or west.

TOWNSHIPS/RANGES

The term **township** refers to a six-mile-square piece of land within the meridian. **Ranges** are imaginary lines running north-south, set six miles apart—the width of a township. When measuring lands within the meridian, the *township*, or tier, directive of the land description always indicates a count in a north-south direction from the base line. The *range* directive, in turn, indicates an east-west count of township within that same meridian. A description of T3N R2W, for example, would count three townships to the north of the base line and two ranges (township widths) to the west of the meridian (figure 8-3).

Congressional townships are those townships that are part of the meridian grid system. Land descriptions found in deeds and patents for federal lands will generally use the congressional township by describing specific township, range, and section. They do, at times, also refer to civil townships.

Civil townships may cover, in whole or in part, several of the congressional townships and may even include more than one major city. Civil townships are often described in census headings or land records and usually are defined by a name

(for example, Silver Springs Township). They are the most common of the township terms, though the congressional townships define a more precise locality within the meridian grid.

Both definitions are valuable. An understanding of the difference between a civil and congressional township is vital to fully utilize the various records encountered.

SECTIONS

A **section** is a piece of land one mile square containing approximately six hundred and forty acres. Within standard congressional townships there are a total of thirty-six sections (figure 8-4). They provide a more precise means of describing the lands found within a township.

Standard sections are numbered throughout a township, starting in the northeast corner and counting westward. As numbering reaches the confines of the township it drops down one section and reverses direction. It is important to note this numbering of the sections within the township. Land descriptions that appear to be far apart according to number may actually border one another. For example, the south half of section one will be directly adjacent to the northern half of section

6	5	4	3	2	1
7	8	9	10	11	12
18	17	16	15	14	13
19	20	21	22	23	24
30	29	28	27	26	25
31	32	33	34	35	36

Figure 8-4. Sectional numbering.

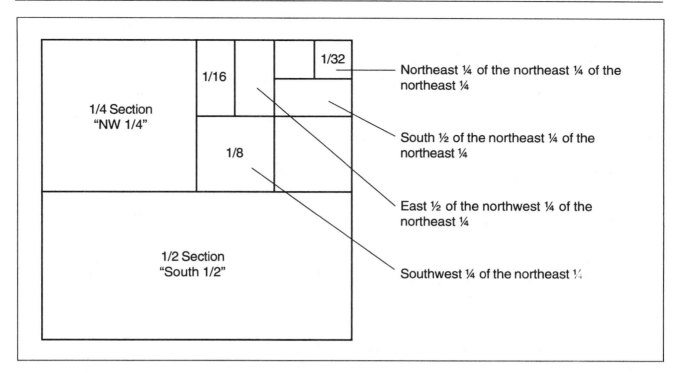

Figure 8-5. Sectional breakdown.

twelve. Section five borders the north part of section eight, and section thirty-two is on the southern border of section twenty-nine.

The shapes and acreage of sections along the western boundary of a township are altered according to the meridian lines as convergence becomes greater toward the north pole. Therefore, these sections do not always contain the full six hundred and forty acres normally allocated.

Sections are subdivided into a variety of sizes, though they are always mostly square or rectangular in shape (figure 8-5). They can be divided into halves, fourths, eighths, sixteenths, and even thirty-seconds. The divisions can easily describe a piece of land within a piece of land, and they leave no confusion as to the precise boundaries that are being discussed. The simplest method of tracking a fractional section is to begin at the end of the description and work backward to the beginning.

Townships have not always been broken into the traditional thirty-six sections. In the first stages of the nation's land system there were various shapes and sizes of townships. These rare configurations are found mostly in present-day Ohio. Be-

ginning with the Land Ordinance of 1785, townships were first numbered in the southeast corner, moving north through a total of six sections, then starting back at the south end for each subsequent column, for a total of thirty-six sections. This system was used for the Seven Ranges Survey, the survey Between the Miami Rivers, and the survey for Symmes (Miami) Purchase.

Before the Act of 18 May 1796 set the standard for all future surveys, two other unorthodox numbering systems were also used. One was for the Firelands and Connecticut Western Reserve. The other encompassed the U.S. Congressional Military District. Both are found only in the state of Ohio.

The Connecticut Western Reserve and the Firelands were surveyed with only four distinct sections in each township. Numbering began in the southeast corner, proceeded to the northeast corner, then went to the northwest and the southwest corners, respectively.

3	2
4	1

The townships found within the Congressional Military District were also surveyed in four sections. Note that these sections were numbered differently, however. They began at the northeast corner, proceeded to the northwest corner, then down to the southwest then southeast corners.

2	1
3	4

Surveys for private land claims in Louisiana present the last major deviation from the standard survey system. Traditional methods of land distribution among the French allotted each settler equal riverfront property with acreage extending back at right angles from the general course of the river or stream. These long rectangular strips of land were usually surveyed at five arpents wide and forty arpents deep (approximately 0.18 miles wide and 1.5 miles deep). They were numbered consecutively from an established landmark. (See figure 8-6.)

A final rule applies to townships which are imperfect due to the terrain. When swamps, lakes, and other obstructions exist, the remaining section is broken up randomly into individual "lots." These lots may have a variety of shapes and sizes, and no specific rules were established for numbering.

TOWNSITES

Private land claims and townsites posed problems for surveyors because they had to skirt around these existing claims. In 1812, surveyors were directed to begin work on eleven cities, including St. Louis. Townsites were not given any standard of uniformity, however, and complied mostly with local needs and previous deed structures. Though miscellaneous legislation had informally addressed the issues of town lots and cities, this concern was never given proper attention until 1844.

The Act of 23 May 1844 allowed for a town council or corporation to claim up to 320 acres as a townsite. Such a claim preempted rights within that town for new settlers and previous occupants. The entry had to be made before lands were put up for public sale, and were sold at minimum price. Prior to this act each individual was required to purchase these lands at public auctions and sales, competing against the highest bid.

By the 1860s, legislation began requiring townsites to be surveyed into urban or suburban locations, designating lots and blocks which were in turn surveyed for individual disbursement. These inner township surveys were eventually placed under the jurisdiction and financial responsibility of the town rather than the U.S. government.

A town was still identified with township, range, and section, though the lots within could be divided in a variety of ways. Organization de-

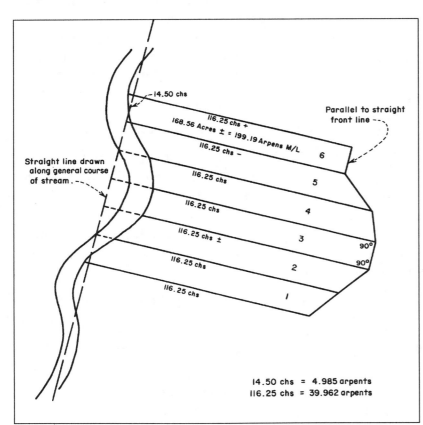

Figure 8-6. The system of surveying private land claim tracts previously distributed by the French.

pended on the community's desires and needs. Towns were actually subdivided lands that had been claimed by an individual or corporation; the individual or corporation had claimed the townsite according to the standard land tract description.

CONCLUSION

In spite of the many obstacles encountered in surveying U.S. federal land, the rectangular system of organizing and distributing land involved some of the most successful pieces of legislation drafted during the post-colonial era. In state-land states, the indiscriminate system of metes and bounds continues to haunt surveyors and title companies even today. The rectangular system, however, is a foundation upon which many other records rely for order and efficiency.

FOR FURTHER REFERENCE

Andriot, Jay, comp. *Township Atlas of the United States*. McLean, Va.: Documents Index, 1991.

Bartlett, Richard A. *Great Surveys of the American West*. Norman: University of Oklahoma Press, 1966.

Carstensen, Vernon, ed. *The Public Lands: Studies in the History of the Public Domain*. Madison: University of Wisconsin Press, 1968.

Cazier, Lola. *Surveys and Surveyors of the Public Domain, 1785–1975*. Washington, D.C.: Department of the Interior, Bureau of Land Management, 1976.

Clawson, Marion. *The Land System of the United States: An Introduction to the History and Practice of Land Use and Land Tenure*. Lincoln: University of Nebraska, 1968.

Eakle, Arlene. *Solving American Pedigrees: American Property Records, Land and Tax Records*. Salt Lake City: Genealogical Institute, 1973.

Ferguson, Thomas E. *Ohio Lands; A Short History*. Columbus: Ohio Auditor of State, 1987.

Gates, Paul W. *History of Public Land Law Development*. Washington, D.C.: Government Printing Office, 1968.

Hibbard, Benjamin Horrace. *A History of the Public Land Policies*. New York: The MacMillan Co., 1924.

Johnson, Hildegard Binder. *Order Upon the Land: The U.S. Rectangular Survey and the Upper Mississippi Country*. New York: Oxford University Press, 1976.

Pattison, William D. *Beginnings of the American Rectangular Land Survey System, 1784–1800*. Columbus: The Ohio Historical Society, 1957.

Rohrbough, Malcolm J. *The Land Office Business: The Settlement and Administration of American Public Lands, 1789–1837*. New York: Oxford University Press, 1968.

Robbins, Roy M. *Our Landed Heritage: The Public Domain, 1776–1936*. Princeton, N.J.: Princeton University Press, 1942.

Stewart, Lowell O. *Public Land Surveys—History, Instructions, Methods*. Ames, Iowa: Collegiate Press, 1935.

Thompson, Don W. *Men and Meridians, Vol. 1, Prior to 1867 & Vol. 2, 1867–1917*. Ottawa, Ontario: Queen's Printer and Controller of Stationery, 1966–67.

Thrower, Norman J.W. *Original Surveys and Land Sub-Division*. Chicago: Rand McNally and Co., 1966.

Treat, Payson Jackson. *The National Land System, 1785–1820*. New York: E.B. Treat and Co., 1910.

9

Records Generated by Federal Lands

Millions of individuals who lived during the busiest phases of the public domain era, 1790 to 1930, went through at least portions of the processes listed in this chapter. Strict regulations generated more information about the claimants of federal land than those of state land. Each stage of the federal patent process created a new record source about the claimant, even if only to place him in a particular place at a specific time.

As with any genealogical resource, the records vary greatly in content. While some files contain exact birthplaces and birth dates, others may contain only a name, location of land, and purchase price. The possible clues contained in federal land records are often limited only by the creativity of the researcher. Various circumstances, such as a person having been of foreign birth, may have created additional record sources. Some land acts may indicate simultaneous or subsequent involvement in other land records. Understanding the records and their laws will ensure more productive research.

Land records can be difficult to understand and access. Land-entry case files, which house the history of the patent process for most federal land transactions, have received very little publicity. Information on the patent itself, the most commonly requested record, can be discouraging for those who realize it contains only the information originally required to order the document. Anyone finding an ancestor who received land through a government source needs to seriously consider the vast amounts of history and biography that could

be waiting among the records created and deposited in the land-entry case files.

LAND ACQUISITION PROCESS

Though requirements differed from act to act, there were certain basic elements involved in almost every public land transaction. When a desired tract or parcel of land was located in the public domain, an individual first needed to make an **application,** or entry, for that particular segment of land (figure 9-1). This step could have been accomplished through several different methods, depending on the area and the time period involved. Sometimes payment itself was considered adequate for successful application.

Auctions were usually held when an area first opened for public sale. The land would be sold to the highest bidder, though at a minimum price of two dollars per acre. Later that minimum was reduced to $1.25 per acre. Soon afterward, land offices opened for business to a waiting crowd of anxious settlers who applied on a "first come, first served" basis for each segment of land.

One of the most helpful requirements for eligibility in many federal land purchases was the need for the applicant to have been a native-born citizen, or have at least *declared an intention to become a citizen of the United States.* This applied to most federal land purchases, except for military bounty-land warrants, where service was the primary criterion, and some preemption and private

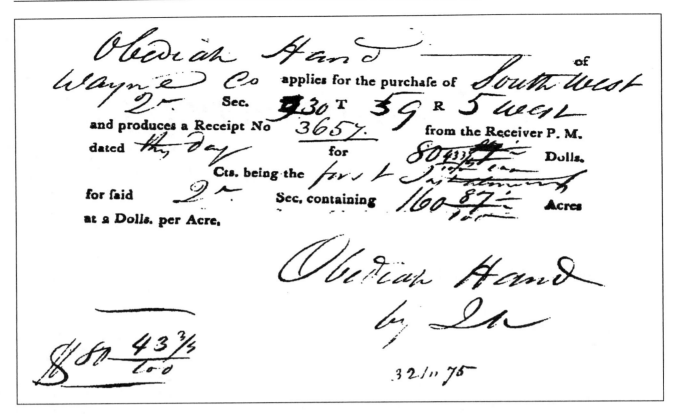

Figure 9-1. A land application. Some applications have little information aside from the property description and name. This one from an Alabama file fails to mention the date.

land claims. Though this requirement could not be monitored with the efficiency originally intended, conformity increased as time went by.

Once the application was completed, cash was paid, or appropriate arrangements made for credit, and a **receipt** was issued. This receipt may be all that is found in many of the earliest case files. Next, a **warrant for survey** was issued for the specified land entry. This was to insure that organization and uniformity existed, and to eliminate overlap and controversy between neighbors and/or government. Though not always successful, a visible boundary was defined for those involved.

The warrant was given to, and usually carried out by, one of the few approved surveyors. Though monitoring their activity was not a priority, some areas, such as the Washington Land Office in the Mississippi Territory, actually enacted special bonds for the surveyors. These bonds required oaths of commitment and loyalty as well as financial penalties for nonconformance. Eventually, the need to

quickly expedite a multitude of claims saw less and less regulation of surveyors.

Upon completion, the **survey** was recorded in township plat books. These books usually encompassed an entire township on each page. They also noted physical characteristics of the land, such as swamps, rivers, and lakes. Surveys also helped illustrate neighborhood ownership.

The information was then filed in a **tract book** by the registrar. This paperwork, together with all other records created by the applicable acts of Congress, was then transferred to the General Land Office. Testimonies, declarations of intent, affidavits, receipt copies, bounty-land warrants, and even proof of citizenship and naturalization can be found in these collections, called **land-entry case files.** Specific birth dates, birthplaces, military ranks, and enlistment information can also be found, depending on the types of lands acquired. Genealogical information can be found in the case files that would never surface in the records kept on location.

Case files also exist for those whose land claims were rejected, revoked, contested, or cancelled for some other reason. The information in those files is often more graphic in historical content than the files for those that were readily accepted. Even if there was no final certificate issued, there should still be a case file of each application for federal land.

As these files were being transferred to the General Land Office, a **final certificate** for the patent was issued to the applicant. This certificate was proof of patent approval, and served as evidence that all of the previously required steps had been fulfilled. It was similar to a coupon, redeemable for the patent, which could only be given out by the General Land Office. These **patents** were often sent to the local land office, where the patentees could more easily exchange their final certificates and take the precaution of registering the certificates with the local courthouse for legal reference and protection (figure 9-2). Though many final certificates were never exchanged, a land-entry case file was still created.

Tract Books

Tract books serve as an index to the multitude of case files currently held at the National Archives in Washington, D.C. Organized according to land description rather than the name of the claimant, they include a complete series of applicants for all federal lands, including land forfeitures, rejections, and cancellations.

Tract books are grouped by land office, according to the legal description of township, range, and section. They give a genealogy, of sorts, for each piece of land during federal ownership. Names of purchasers are included, whether rejected, relinquished, or finalized. Many tract books offer categories for the following information:

- Name of claimant
- Section description and acreage
- Township, range, and section number
- Price per acre and total purchase price

- Payments made and balance due
- Date of entry
- Final certificate number

In some areas the patent number is also included. The grouping of individuals within the same township, range, and section is beneficial when studying the neighbors, associates, and relatives that may have followed the ancestral family from place to place. Various indexes for federal land disbursements, some of which have been published for genealogical reference, usually include only those who successfully obtained patents. Most will not provide access to case files for almost 2 million individuals who did not complete the process. The tract books include the names of everyone attempting to acquire federal land, and usually provide enough information to allow access to their land-entry case files. (See figure 9-3.)

A rejected, relinquished, or otherwise cancelled claim will nonetheless have a land-entry case file. These files, especially when contested, can provide more detailed information than those which were readily accepted. Seldom included in indexes, they can be found by researching the tract books for the vicinity in which your ancestor lived.

The tract books are complete for the entire federal land system with the exceptions of Missouri and Alaska, whose tracts books have been lost. The originals are housed in two different locations. The Eastern States Office of the Bureau of Land Management holds those involving the states of Florida, Alabama, Mississippi, Louisiana, Arkansas, Iowa, Minnesota, Wisconsin, Illinois, Indiana, Michigan, and Ohio. The National Archives hold the original tract books for the remaining federal-land states. Duplicate copies were made as the records were created, and many state offices of the Bureau of Land Management have a second copy for their own jurisdiction.

The tract books from both the National Archives and the Bureau of Land Management-East-

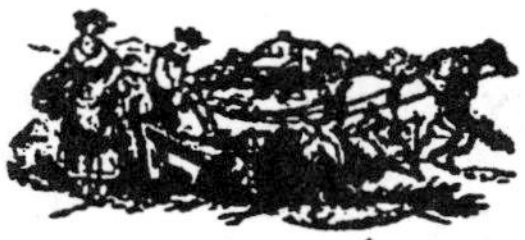

The United States of America,

TO ALL TO WHOM THESE PRESENTS SHALL COME, GREETING:

Homestead Certificate No. 6198
Application 12137

Whereas there has been deposited in the GENERAL LAND OFFICE of the United States a CERTIFICATE of the Register of the Land Office at Camden Arkansas whereby it appears that, pursuant to the Act of Congress approved 20th May, 1862, "To secure Homesteads to actual settlers on the public domain," and the acts supplemental thereto, the claim of William C. Clinton has been established and duly consummated in conformity to law for the West half of the South West quarter of Section seven in Township seven South of Range thirty West, and the North East quarter of the South East quarter and the South East quarter of the North East quarter of Section twelve, in Township seven South of Range thirty one West of the Fifth Principal Meridian in Arkansas, containing one hundred and fifty seven acres and sixty hundredths of an acre -

according to the Official Plat of the Survey of the said Land returned to the GENERAL LAND OFFICE by the SURVEYOR GENERAL.

Now know ye, That there is therefore granted by the UNITED STATES unto the said William C. Clinton the tract of Land above described: TO HAVE AND TO HOLD the said tract of Land, with the appurtenances thereof, unto the said William C. Clinton and to his heirs and assigns forever.

In testimony whereof I, Benjamin Harrison President of the United States of America, have caused these letters to be made Patent, and the Seal of the General Land Office to be hereunto affixed.

Given under my hand, at the City of Washington, the seventh day of March, in the year of Our Lord one thousand eight hundred and ninety two, and of the Independence of the United States the one hundred and sixteenth.

[L. S.]

By the President: Benjamin Harrison

By E Macfarland Ass. Sec'y.

J.R. Conwell, Recorder of the General Land Office. ad interim

Figure 9-2. A patent that shows the name, land description, and date. The process leading to such a final document can provide much more information, all of it contained in the land-entry case file.

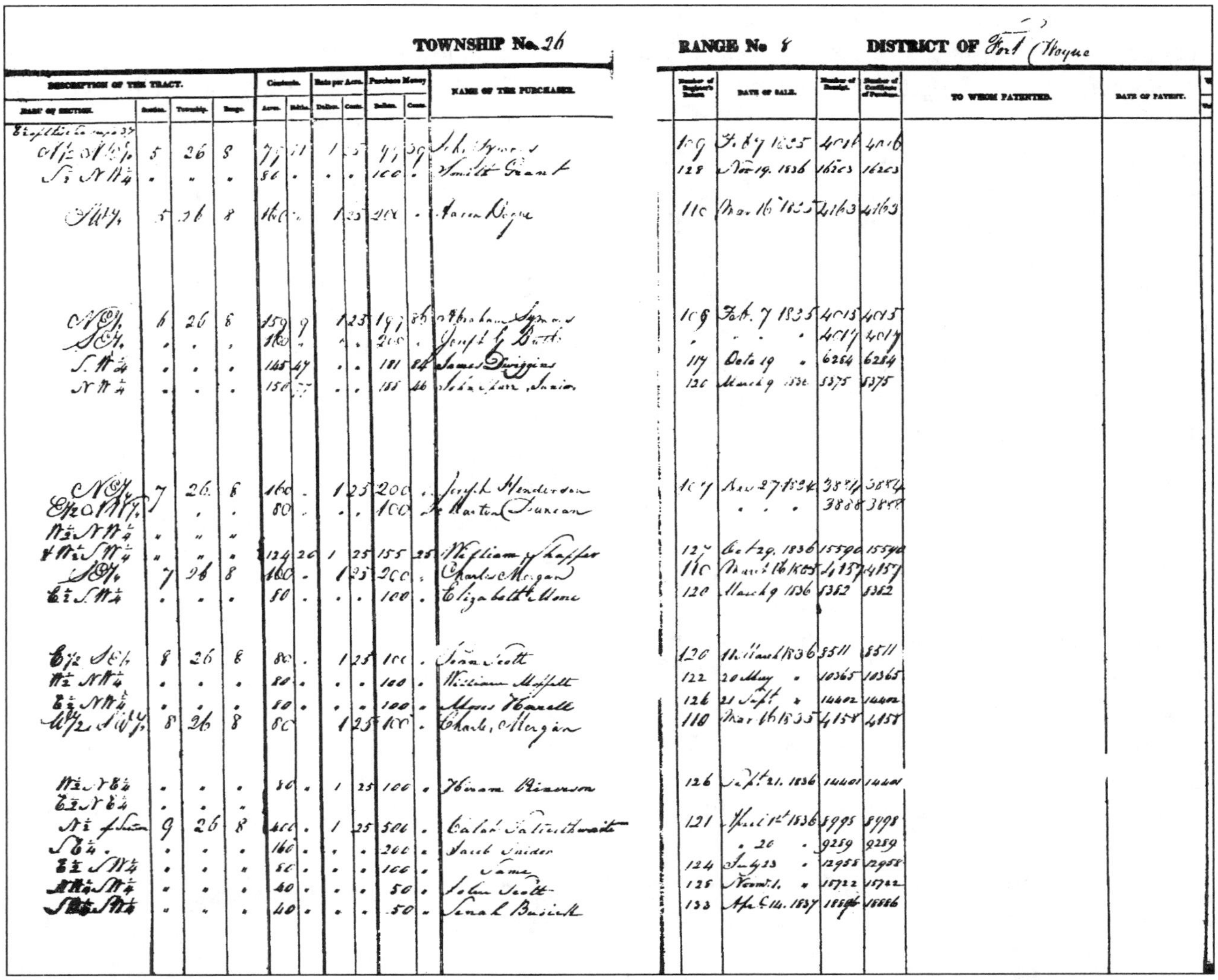

Figure 9-3. A tract book page from the Fort Wayne Land Office, Fort Wayne, Indiana. The heading denotes the organization according to township and range, while the page entries are for sections within the description.

ern States Office have all been microfilmed. They are available through the National Archives, the Family History Library, and their respective branch libraries around the world. They can also be found in various state archives, historical societies, and university libraries.

A special **tract book guide** is included in this book as appendix A. Specified tract book coordinates are listed for each county in every federal-land state. The northern, southern, eastern, and western township and range boundary for each county is listed, as is the name of the meridian involved.

MILITARY BOUNTY LANDS

Bounty warrants were the earliest distributions of federal land. The federal government proceeded with bounties after witnessing the success of such programs in state-land states both during and after the colonial era. Military bounties had been given by foreign countries for centuries, for a variety of purposes. They were usually offered in lieu of monetary compensation for loyalty and service during times of military conflict. At times, bounty lands have been given in advance to entice enlistments for anticipated conflicts. (See figures 9-4 through 9-8.)

A variety of acts by the Continental Congress accommodated the needs of Revolutionary War participants even before there were lands to give. The Congressional Act of 16 September 1776 offered those who enlisted in the Continental Army a parcel ranging from one hundred to five hundred acres, depending on the rank achieved. Acts in 1780 offered as much as 1,100 acres for major generals. In the event there were no lands won, the government was to buy lands from each of the individual states. Maryland's fear of not being able to provide land eventually led to the creation of the public domain. The public land policy was initiated by having landed states cede portions of their western claims to the government.

Virginia played a critical role in both state-land states and federal-land states. Providing the bulk of the fighting force during the revolution, Virginia's bounties were originally to be redeemed in the district between the Green, Ohio, and Mississippi rivers in present-day Kentucky. However, amounts given out by the end of the war totaled more than this district could accommodate. Virginia then re-served, from its cessions to the government, the tract of land in present-day Ohio known as the Virginia Military Tract. Only those from Virginia who had served in the Continental Army were permitted to settle there, however; state regiments were required to utilize the Kentucky district.

The Virginia Military Tract was located between the Scioto and Little Miami rivers, and produced state lands in a federally governed state. The United States retained ownership, but allowed first rights to Virginians selecting lands in exchange for bounty warrants. The U.S. government also allowed the tract to retain the organizational system of metes and bounds for the warrants redeemed. It was just one of several similar incidents which make Ohio one of the most confusing—yet extremely rewarding—states in which to perform land record research.

Bounty lands were given by both state and federal governments. State bounties were mostly redeemed within the state's jurisdictions. Federal lands, however, were to be redeemed only in designated federal-land states and districts. The first

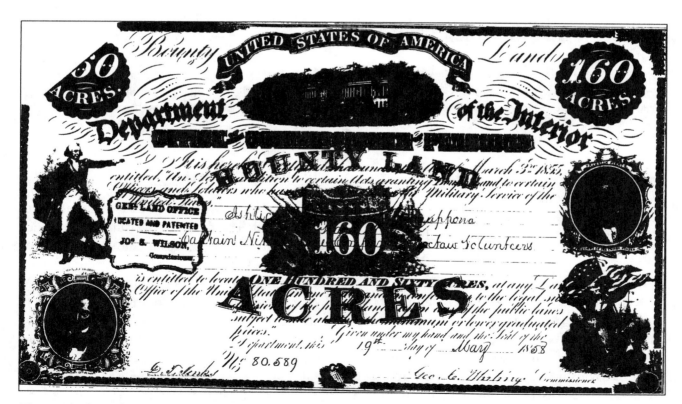

Figure 9-4. One of the last bounty-land warrants to be issued; it is dated 1858. Exciting clues are often written on the back, detailing heirs who were, more often than not, the eventual applicants and recipients.

land ordinance was established in 1785, followed soon after by the Northwest Ordinance of 1787. This allotted lands to the Ohio Land Company and others, who could use exchanged bounty-land warrants as partial payment for their large speculation purchases. It also opened up lands for the first federal bounty warrants.

The ordinances were essentially unsuccessful, due to improper management and failure to financially meet intended acreage purchases. Additional attempts were made by designating two tracts to be used exclusively for bounty-land warrants, one in Ohio and one in Illinois. Indian trouble prevented success in either of these areas.

While a few warrants were accepted in the Seven Ranges portion of Ohio, it was not until the Act of 1 June 1796 that Congress successfully established the Congressional Military Tract in Ohio. These lands were divided into five-mile-square townships rather than the conventional six, and claimants were required to purchase a minimum of a quarter-township, or four thousand acres. Since federal bounty warrants were usually no more than 160 acres, the recipient would either have to group with several other claimants and form a corporate entity, or personally pay for the balance of acreage in cash or credit. This led to an immense amount of land speculation, based upon purchases of bounty-land warrants. The four-thousand-acre stipulation had essentially deprived veterans of any value from their warrants. In 1800, lots as small as 100 acres were offered, but that was seventeen years after many warrants had actually been issued.

Bounty lands were again issued under the Acts of 1803 and 1806. These warrants were the first to contain the specific description of land directly on the warrant. Later, under the Acts of the 1830s, warrants from these two acts could be exchanged for scrip.

The War of 1812 again brought the need for enticed enlistments. The Revolutionary War was still fresh in the memories of everyone, and the new war had resulted in a British embargo which created hardships for all. Congress responded by creating three new military districts for the exclu-sive use of new enlistees: one in the Michigan territory, one in Illinois, and one in Louisiana (present-day Arkansas). Six million acres were allotted for this purpose, and claimants were required to pre-select the district they preferred. A lottery was then held to determine the precise parcel of land, which could not be assigned or mortgaged until the patent had been issued.

Many bounty lands were redeemed by heirs of the qualifying veteran, especially under scrip acts and acts in 1852 and 1855.

The Michigan Tract was later abandoned due to lands being misrepresented as "undesirable" by early explorers. The necessary acreage was reallocated in the Missouri Territory, with additional acreage also allotted in the Illinois and Arkansas tracts. One hundred sixty acres and $16 cash were given to each man who would enlist for five years or the duration of the war.

Ensuing acts began to distinguish between types of warrants for officers and enlisted men for the War of 1812. Previously, there was no distinction for service in that war. The right to apply for entitled warrants that had not been previously obtained was extended in 1835, and again in 1842 and 1854. In 1842, the restrictions on location were lifted from U.S. bounty warrants issued for the War of 1812. They could be redeemed on any public land open for cash entry.

The Act of 30 May 1830 acknowledged the shortage of lands to fulfill all Revolutionary bounty warrants issued for the Virginia Military Tract. Congress allowed unused warrants to be exchanged for Revolutionary War scrip. This scrip could then be redeemed at land offices for public land in other areas of Ohio, as well as Indiana and Illinois. Scrip in the amount of 310,000 acres was initially authorized for this act. By 1836, distribution had risen to almost a million and a half acres.

The Act of 2 March 1833 removed restrictions on location for all Revolutionary bounty warrants. They were then to be accepted at any public land office. The warrants or scrip could not be redeemed,

Figure 9-5. A typical bounty-land warrant. Many warrants were redeemed by second- and third-generation heirs.

however, until after the initial auction of lands had been held for any given area. Redemption was also restricted from Indian Trust lands and could not be used in areas later considered "homestead only." Preemptions filed by others were also recognized before scrip purchases. These records are more fully described later in this chapter.

The threat of war with Mexico in 1847 caused Congress to again consider the issue of bounty land as an incentive for enlistment. More-careful attention was given to preventing assignment of the property to speculators and induce settlement by the actual recipient. Changes in the public land system reduced the smallest tract purchasable from 160 to a mere forty acres. This was a tremendous reduction from the four-thousand-acre tracts required for initial Revolutionary War warrants.

A 160-acre warrant was given for those who served at least one year, and forty-acre warrants were given to those serving less time. The warrants could be used on any lands open for private entry, except lands that were subject to preemption. Those who qualified for warrants were also given the option of receiving either $100, or $25 in government scrip. This scrip could be used as cash for any payment due the government, for any purpose, including taxes. Nearly 81,000 warrants were issued for 160-acre tracts and nearly eight thousand warrants were issued for forty-acre tracts. Attempts at making these warrants unassignable were futile. Almost from the beginning, they were found in the hands of speculators on the open market. This was to be the last conflict for which bounty lands were given, though bounty-land litigation continued into the twentieth century.

An act in 1850 was a catchall which provided land for those who had served in any war previous to 1790 and had not already received a warrant. This act included those who had fought in various Indian conflicts. Soldiers who had served nine months were to have 160 acres, and those with at least four months of service were to receive eighty acres. Even men who had served as little as one month received forty acres. This opened up bounty lands to many who were previously ineligible. The ban against preemption was also lifted, as long as the preemption settler was the owner of the warrant or the preemption settler's permission was received.

Through the Act of 31 August 1852, Congress required any outstanding Virginia warrants to be exchanged for scrip. At this time, Virginia ceded all remaining unused lands in the Virginia Military Tract to the United States. Bounty lands, by that time, were mostly being given to heirs of servicemen who never received or redeemed their own warrants. Because of this, these records sometimes document two or three generations of family in the bounty-land case file.

Another act in 1852 removed all unassignable clauses and extended the time for bounty land privileges to militiamen who were called into service after 1812. By 1855, the time of service had been reduced to only fourteen days. Persons who had marched or traveled 1,200 miles but had not served fourteen days were also eligible. Native Americans who had served were included for the first time as well. All those who had previously received warrants for less than 160 acres were now permitted to receive additional warrants for the difference. This brought about second applications by many, and required more information than their initial applications.

Though warrants themselves exist, a much broader group of records may also exist in the case file.

In the four acts from 1847 to 1855, authorization was issued for 552,494 warrants totaling more than 34 million acres. In 1858, the issuance of bounty-land warrants ceased, and the right to locate lands from them concluded in 1863. In 1872, Congress itself ceded the remainder of the Congressional Military Tract to the state of Ohio for the Ohio Agricultural and Mechanical College. This officially completed the legislation involving military bounty lands.

The acts involving military bounty land were numerous. Between 11 February 1800 and 8 February 1854, Congress adopted over twenty measures extending the time for veterans of the Revo-

List of Land Warrants, *the Property of* Thomas McKean Thompson *presented by* Jacob D Hart *for the purpose of being registered under the Acts of Congress, of* 1st *June,* 1796, *and the* 2d *March,* 1799. *Dated this* 21st *Day of* August 1799

NUMBER Expressed in each Warrant.	NAME Expressed in each Warrant.	Number of Acres.	NUMBER Expressed in each Warrant.	NAME Expressed in each Warrant.	Number of Acres.
1041	William Tillen	500.	6448	Martin Smith	100.
1523	George Monroe	400.	5533	Benjamin Clarke	100.
1153	James Jones	400	5561	Benjamin Cole	100.
1725	John Patton	400.	10,830	William McGlauhy	100.
1160	Peter Jacquett	300.	13,108	Robert Ferrel	100.
1471	William McKennan	300.	13,242	John Hanson	100.
39	Thomas Anderson	200.	10,743	James Davis	100
227	Caleb P. Bennett	200.	8,345	Thomas Gibson	100.
405	James Campbell	200.	12,000	Charles Crawford	100.
10,766	John Fopless	100	10,826	Samuel Ireland	100.
	Acres	3,000			1000

Figure 9-6. Found among *The Lists of Federal Revolutionary Bounty Land Warrants Presented for Registry,* this list illustrates the four-thousand-acre minimum purchase that caused individuals to sell to speculators rather than face the remaining financial requirements.

lutionary War and the War of 1812 to apply and enter military bounty-land warrants. Warrants were given for the Revolutionary War, the War of 1812, the Mexican War, and various Indian conflicts. Though warrants themselves often exist, a much broader group of records were likely created in the case file, depending on the act under which the warrant was obtained.

For bounty-land warrants, the application process began with the Pension Bureau. The Pension Bureau was divided into two parts prior to 1849: the War Department and the Navy Department. Applications during that time will be found separated between the two, according to their respective jurisdictions. After 1849, they were combined under the authority of the Department of the Interior. Once the application was reviewed and the documentation was found to be satisfactory, the Pension Bureau would prepare and issue a warrant. This warrant would then be presented to the appropriate land office for official registration and recording of the tract that was chosen or allotted.

All federal military bounty-land records are housed at the National Archives in Washington, D.C. Since the Pension Bureau handled the application, and the General Land Office fulfilled the warrant, records were created by two completely different government agencies. Applications for federal bounty-land warrants were assigned to the Veterans Administration, Record Group 15. Warrants and related paperwork are among documents in Record Group 49, assigned to the Bureau of Land Management. Some of the more prominent collections for each are listed below.

Record Group 15, Federal Bounty-Land Applications

Records Relating to Pension and Bounty-Land Claims, 1773–1942. This collection consists of several different groups of records. Military conflicts from the Revolutionary War to 1917 are covered, and include both pensions and bounty lands. Case files for the Revolutionary War include bounty-land applications filed after 1800. Files for the War of 1812 contain bounty-land applications filed from 1812. The Mexican War files begin in 1847. A miscellaneous group of records contains case files for bounty-land applications between 1812 and 1855.

Among other records in this collection are registers of bounty-land claims and warrants issued from 1800 to 1912. This seems to be in conflict with the many references made to bounty-land privileges concluding in 1863. Litigation, however, continued to produce records long after 1863. There are also duplicate bounty-land warrants and scrip certificates from 1803 to 1897.

A tragic loss prevents the earliest records from being as complete as desired: More than 14,000 applications for bounty warrants issued between 1789 and 1800 were destroyed by fire. An ancestor may have filed an application, but may not appear in any of the surviving application records. There is a card abstract of basic information for those applicants whose records were destroyed, but the critical data appeared on the applications themselves. These cards are interfiled with the applications and pensions for all other claimants.

The total collection occupies 2,811 rolls of microfilm, and includes indexes for many of the

groups of records. The records are organized into two distinct series: claims concerning the Revolutionary War, and claims for the wars thereafter, through the Mexican War.

The Bounty-Land Pension and Warrant Application File serves as an index to many of the files in the first series, the Revolutionary War. These records make up more than eighty percent of the 2,811 rolls just mentioned. They are organized alphabetically, and are available on microfilm at regional archives of the National Archives and at the Family History Library. However, they are incomplete for applicants involved in the last congressional acts concerning bounty lands.

Several formal indexes and abstracts have also been compiled for the Revolutionary War series. The National Genealogical Society has produced "Special Publication 40," titled *Index of Revolutionary War Pension Applications in the National Archives* (also called "Hoyt's Index"). Perhaps the most prominent and widely used index is Virgil D. White's *Genealogical Abstracts of Revolutionary War Pension Files.* This index covers only those original records designated as "selected." There may be additional information found under the applicant's "non-selected" records. The last volume by White is a cross-referenced index that allows searches to be made for names appearing in other individual's pensions. An ancestor may not have received a pension or bounty-land warrant, but may have been a critical witness to a relative's application.

Copies of the original records can be obtained by writing to the National Archives. They will provide NATF Form 80, free of charge. A separate form needs to be used for each search requested. The present address is:

> Reference Branch (NNR1)
> National Archives
> Washington, D.C. 20408

This search does not encompass all pension or bounty-land acts, though it does cover a majority. If the search is successful, a cost for photocopying will be determined and returned to the inquiring individual. Upon receipt of the payment, the copies will be mailed out.

The second series, those for post-Revolutionary War claims, is also filed in alphabetical order by the veteran's surname. When a spouse was applying, the veterans's name was still used for filing purposes. This series no longer includes War of 1812 applications; they have been placed in their respective pension files, whether accepted or rejected. This second series is very broad, so fewer resources are available for cross-referencing, and there are no indexes aside from the alphabetical structure of the files. There is no patentee index to help discern warrants assigned to a third party.

There is a *Card Index for Remarried Widows.* This is often helpful in tracking spouses who may have applied for bounty lands after the original qualified veteran passed away. This index involves applicants for military conflicts after the Revolutionary War, extending to World War I.

The applications contained in the second series, and those for the War of 1812, can also be requested using the NATF Form 80 previously mentioned. Most records are also available for public research at the National Archives. Some, however, are restricted to staff-only searches. All microfilm copies are available for purchase and rental, including those mentioned in Record Group 49.

Record Group 49, Federal Bounty-Land Records

Included in this category are several collections pertaining to state bounty-land warrants and surveys for the state of Virginia. Because they involved federal bounty lands in the federal-land state of Ohio, they have been included here as well. For further information concerning Virginia bounty-land records, see chapter 6, Records Generated by State Lands. The records of group 49 are housed at the National Archives in downtown Washington, D.C. Most records are grouped according to congressional act. The categories are as follows:

Warrants Issued under Act of 9 July 1788. Portions of this collection were destroyed during the War of 1812. The remainder have been microfilmed by the National Archives with acts in 1803 and 1806, titled *U.S. Revolutionary War Bounty Land Warrants Used in the U.S. Military District of Ohio, and Related Papers (Acts of 1788, 1803, 1806).* These films are also available at the Family History Library.

Virginia Military Warrants Surrendered to the Federal Government. These warrants were exchanged for bounty lands outside of the Virginia Military District in Ohio. Warrants not found here, and the actual application files, are located in the Virginia State Archives in Richmond.

Lists of Revolutionary Bounty-Land Warrants Presented for Registry. These warrants were presented under the acts of 1 June 1796 and 2 March 1799, for claims in the United States Military Reserve in Ohio. There is also an index for this collection. (These records, as of 1996, included non-land-related material such as muster rolls, payrolls, and powers of attorney for various Virginia soldiers. Rank, regiment, promotions, reasons for dismissal, and other information is identified in these records, kept in box number 114 in this collection.)

Treasury Certificates were for bounty lands of persons engaged in military action during the Revolutionary War, but not specifically assigned to any state unit or line. They were issued by the Board of Treasury, and essentially served as bounty warrants. They were subject to the same rules and regulations as bounty warrants, but originated from and returned to a different source.

Warrants Issued under Acts of 3 March 1803 and 15 April 1806. Warrants under these acts could be exchanged for scrip. In these instances, the originals will be found under the scrip acts listed below. Those under the Act of 1806 describe exact rank and regiment instead of referencing only "soldier." (Reference *Warrants Issued Under Act of July 9th, 1788.* The warrants exchanged for scrip are cross-referenced on the microfilm described there.)

Revolutionary Warrants. These warrants were originally issued under the acts of 1803 and 1806.

They were actually redeemed under later acts which extended the time for which application for bounty-land warrants could be made.

Virginia Resolution Warrants. These warrants were issued in addition to the amount of acreage originally designated for Virginia's distribution. More soldiers applied than expected, and additional legislation was required to continue issuance of bounty lands.

Virginia Military Warrants—Kendrick Cases. Warrants and related papers filed through Eleazer P. Kendrick, a surveyor for the Virginia Military District in Ohio. Many are field notes, with little information.

Exchange Certificates. The warrants in these files were issued for service in the War of 1812. They were exchanged for certificates allowing the claimant to locate his warrant in a district other than the one originally chosen before the lottery drawings were held. These exchanges were according to the Act of 22 May 1826, for issued lands found to be unfit for cultivation.

Papers Relating to Revolutionary Bounty-Land Scrip. These records provide additional coverage of the applicants of the Scrip Act of 31 August 1852. Often, additional information on heirs and their various residences can be found in these records.

Double Bounty-Land Warrants Issued Under Act of 6 May 1812. These warrants were issued for 320 acres instead of 160 acres, according to the added enticements for enlistment at that time. These records are duplicates of those under the same act listed below, but are in book form rather than file packets.

Figure 9-7. Although this warrant gives little information about William Cook, the case file papers showed that, like many, his heirs applied for the warrant. The papers prove that Cook served in the Connecticut Line, died in Orange County, New York (a copy of his will was included), that his widow remarried and moved to Saratoga, and they describe the tract that was eventually located in Ohio by his heirs.

Warrants Issued Under Acts of 24 December 1811, 11 January 1812, 6 May 1812, and 27 July 1842. One-hundred-sixty-acre warrants. Some double bounty-land warrants under 6 May 1812.

Warrants Issued Under Act of 11 February 1847. There are two groups: forty-acre warrants and 160-acre warrants.

Warrants Issued Under Act of 28 September 1850. There are three groups: forty-acre, eighty-acre, and 160-acre warrants.

Warrants Issued Under Act of 22 March 1852. There are three groups: forty-acre, eighty-acre, and 160-acre warrants.

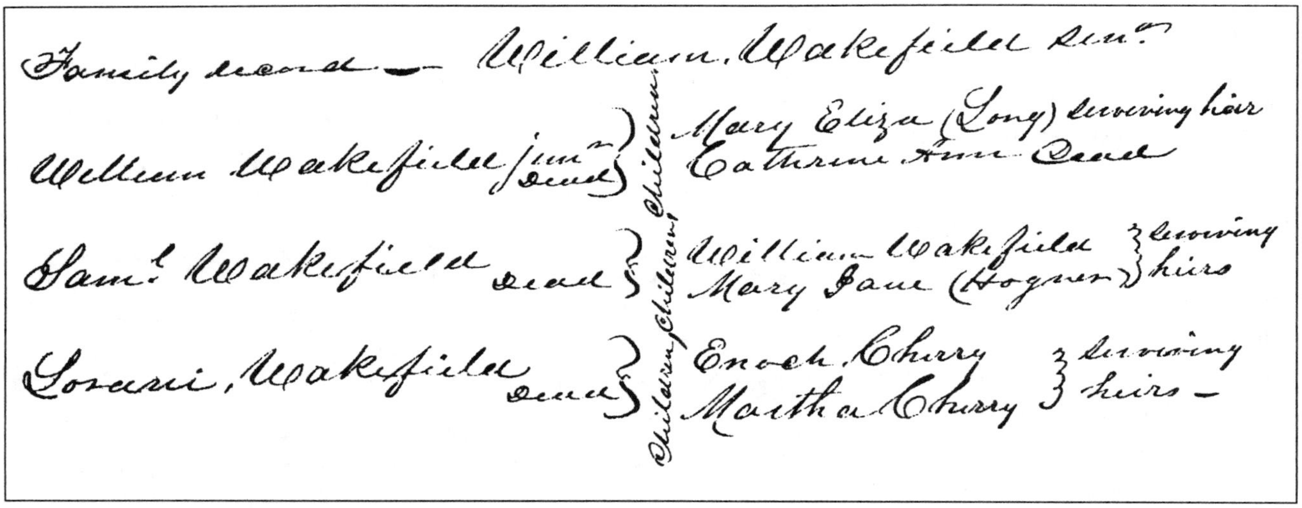
Family record — William Wakefield Senr

William Wakefield Junr (Decd) } Mary Eliza (Long) surviving heir; Catharine Ann Decd

Saml Wakefield Decd } William Wakefield, Mary Jane (Hogner) } surviving heirs

Lorain Wakefield Decd } Enoch Cherry, Martha Cherry } surviving heirs —

Children Children Children

Figure 9-8. Another example of "no genealogical information" found among bounty-land papers. This example shows three generations, beginning with William Wakefield, Sr.

Applications for Military Bounty-Land Scrip. These files contain applications to exchange Virginia military warrants for federal scrip certificates that could be used in any land office. They are separated according to the following acts:

- Acts of 30 May 1830 and 13 July 1832
- Act of 2 March 1833
- Act of 3 March 1835
- Act of 31 August 1852

Warrants Issued Under Act of 3 March 1855. There are seven groups: ten-acre, forty-acre, sixty-acre, eighty-acre, 100-acre, 120-acre, and 160-acre warrants.

Few of the records listed above are available on microfilm. Those that are may sometimes be titled differently, depending on the cataloging procedures at different repositories. Most of these records are available only at the National Archives. Various publications and indexes have been produced to simplify access and help identify an ancestor who was involved.

A Register of Warrants, 1789–1805, Surrendered for Land in the Military District of Ohio is available on microfilm at the Family History Library and the National Archives. Another index, the *Register of Army Land Warrants per Acts of 1796, 1799, 1803, and 1806,* is available through the same repositories. Also available at these locations is another, later register, titled *Register of Military Land Warrants Presented at the Treasury for Locating and Patenting, 1804–1835.* This finding aid is also valuable for many War of 1812 warrants.

The Ohio State Auditor's Office in Columbus, Ohio, among its manuscript collections, houses *A List of Virginia Military Warrants, Located in Ohio and Kentucky and Issued to the Virginia Soldiers, (Their Heirs or Assignees) of the Revolutionary War, With the Names of Warrantees, Surveyees and Patentees.* The collection dates to 1842 only. This same office houses other miscellaneous military bounty-land records for both the Virginia Military Tract and the U.S. Military District.

The Bureau of Land Management-Eastern States Office, in Springfield, Virginia, has a *Register of Army Land Warrants per Acts of June 1, 1796 and March 2, 1799,* as well as a thirty-volume set of records titled *Abstracts of Military Warrants, Act of March 3, 1855, 160-Acre Warrants.* This office also maintains a collection called *Alphabetical Index of Virginia Military Land Warrants Granted for Services in the Continental Line,* and a variety of other collections.

War of 1812 Bounty-Land Warrants, 1815–1858, encompasses 105 volumes. They were microfilmed by the National Archives in 1971 on sixteen rolls of microfilm, including one roll of indexes for the states of Missouri and Arkansas, and a partial index for Illinois (surnames *C* through *D*). They also include one roll of unindexed warrants that are structured chronologically. These microfilms are also available through the Family History Library. The state of Illinois has produced a statewide index to land patents which includes military bounty warrants for that state. It can be used in place of the missing surname letters in the index mentioned above. This index is now available on microfiche at the Family History Library. Another quality work, though not as complete for bounty-land warrants, is Virgil D. White's *Index to War of 1812 Pension Files.*

The Ohio Historical Society has an *Index for Federal Land Entries, circa 1802–1849.* This index has been microfilmed and is available through the Family History Library and the Ohio State Auditor's Office. It does not include the Connecticut Western Reserve, the Firelands, or Symmes Purchase. Military bounty lands are included.

Bounty-land recipients for the Mexican War can be identified using Virgil D. White's *Index to Mexican War Pension Files.* They can also be accessed through the veteran's records in Record Group 15, available at the National Archives. They are included in an alphabetical arrangement of bounty-land warrant applications under the acts of 1847 to 1855.

Selected application abstracts have also been indexed in *Genealogical Abstracts, Revolutionary War Veterans, Scrip Act of 1852.* This act allowed Virginia warrants to be exchanged for scrip, redeemable in any federal land office. They were compiled for publication by Margie G. Brown, and include most pertinent relationships revealed in the records. However, additional important information can also be found in the original files. The first twelve years of bounty warrants are also covered in Ronald Vern Jackson's *Ohio Military Land Warrants, 1789–1801.*

One of the most valuable sources for identifying bounty-land recipients is *Federal Land Series,* by Clifford Neal Smith. In volume two, many of the earliest bounty-land warrants are found, complete with abstracted information from the original files. Volume four is divided into two parts, and includes information about the warrants for the Virginia Military District. Though all the intended volumes for this project were never finished, those that were completed provide a tremendous service for researchers.

Conclusion of this segment on bounty-land warrants would not be complete without the mention of three other major contributions to bounty-land research: the *History of Public Land Law Development,* by Paul W. Gates, et al.; *The Bounty Lands of the American Revolution in Ohio,* by William Thomas Hutchinson; and perhaps the most in-depth study of bounty lands yet, James W. Oberly's *Sixty Million Acres, American Veterans and Public Lands before the Civil War.* Other sources, though no less significant, are listed at the end of this chapter under "For Further Reference."

Military bounty lands played a critical role in shaping government policies and the economic structure of the United States. Assignment of warrants became big business. Brokerage firms were even established solely for the purpose of bounty warrants. Though applicants may have assigned their warrants, they still needed to apply and qualify for that warrant.

In summary, applications for bounty-land warrants were sent to the Secretary of War, the Commissioner of Pensions, or the Secretary of the Interior. Applications were segregated according to army and navy. These records are now grouped together for easier access. Once accepted, the warrants were redeemed through the Treasury Department before 1849, then to the Department of the Interior, Bureau of Land Management.

Except for Ohio, it is surprising to note that more Revolutionary War bounty lands were redeemed in Iowa than any other state, by a two-to-one ratio over second-place Wisconsin. Also leading the list were Minnesota, Kansas, Michigan, Nebraska, Illinois, and Missouri. For further information about bounty-land records, see *Guide to*

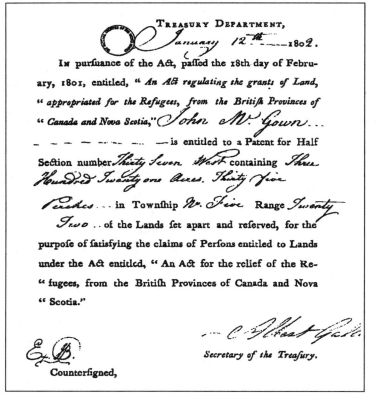

Figure 9-9. A Canadian refugee warrant issued to John McGown.

Genealogical Research in the National Archives, published by the National Archives Trust Fund Board.

CANADIAN REFUGEE WARRANTS

Canadian refugee warrants are a seldom-used source that can provide critical clues for researchers. They were first issued under the Act of 7 April 1798, and again under the Act of 18 February 1801. Ranges sixteen through twenty-two in the Ohio River Survey were subdivided into half-sections for disbursement among refugees. The "refugees" aided Americans during the Revolutionary War, and were primarily from Nova Scotia and Quebec. The coordinates for land distribution encompassed at least portions of Fairfield, Franklin, Licking, and Perry counties in Ohio.

Most refugees had been residing in Massachusetts, Maine, New York, and Connecticut, though many had gone back to Canada by 1800. Applica-

tions for claims under this act can show residences before the war, residences in the New England area after the war, and residences in Ohio after the claim was honored. It should be noted that not everyone applied for or responded to this offer. Many individuals were not even aware they were eligible for land until military debit logs were finally used to determine disbursement. Several claimants stated they had learned of their allotment only through reading the newspaper.

Warrants were given for a variety of assistance, based on the individual value of each circumstance. Claims were originally presented to the United States for monetary reimbursement (i.e., $10,000 in food and sundries given to a specific regiment). These claims were compensated with land, the only commodity readily available to the government at that time.

Each individual was granted half-section lots through a lottery-type drawing, according to the value being claimed. Therefore, a person qualifying for more than one lot would not necessarily draw multiple lots next to each other. Some received as many as six or seven half-sections.

Just as with other Revolutionary War warrants, many who received refugee warrants sold them to land speculators. Some were elderly and hadn't the desire or ability to relocate. These were sentiments shared by many early bounty recipients in America. Among the papers are inquiries as to the value of their draws—lands they often never saw. Powers of attorney are the most important documents, showing residences and other helpful information about the claimant. (See figures 9-9 and 9-10.)

Canadian refugee warrants are available at the National Archives in downtown Washington, D.C. They are also indexed in Clifford Neal Smith's *Federal Land Series, Volume One,* available at most major libraries.

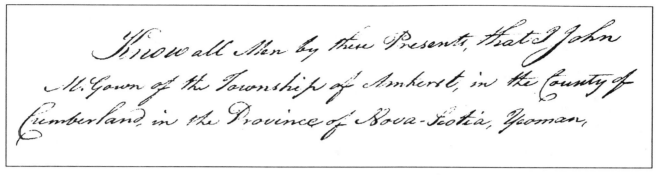

Figure 9-10. "Beyond the warrant"; papers in the case file provide much more information about the claimant. (Compare with the warrant in figure 9-9.)

CANADIAN VOLUNTEER WARRANTS

Canadian volunteer warrants are more informative than refugee warrants. They were issued according to the Act of 5 March 1816, for volunteer service during the War of 1812. Most warrants were issued to individuals residing in Niagara or Genessee counties in New York, where the majority of the volunteer regiments were formed. The warrants were to be redeemed in the Vincennes Land District in the Indiana Territory.

Volunteer warrants show powers of attorney, assignments, miscellaneous correspondence, tract location, and county of residence in New York at the time the warrant was issued. They also identify rank and specific corps or regiment. Included in the files is an alphabetical list of names showing rank, regiment, warrant number, and date of warrant. This allows for further research in military sources such as service records.

Canadian volunteer warrant records identify the assignee, as well as who located the tract. Many of these warrants were assigned to land speculators. Many, in fact, were bought by Joseph Richardson of Ontario County, New York, a bounty-land broker. A total of 283 warrants were issued under this program for Canadian volunteers. The original records are located at the National Archives, and have not yet been microfilmed. (See figure 9-11.)

CASH ENTRY

The Land Ordinance of 1785 directed that surveying begin in the Northwest Territory. As soon as the first seven ranges in Ohio were completed, the surveys were to be returned to the treasury. These lands were earmarked for the raising of funds needed to compensate losses incurred during the war. One-seventh of the ranges were allotted for use as military bounty lands. The remaining ranges were to be divided among each of the states for immediate auction, selling for no less than $1 per acre. This was the general price of land among the colonies before the war. This began the cash-entry system for federal lands.

The first patent issued was in New York City, to John Martin. He purchased one section for $640. Soon, the Ohio Company succeeded in obtaining a contract to purchase 1.5 million acres for resale purposes at about 67 cents per acre. They later forfeited much of this area because they were unsuccessful in enticing the necessary settlers. The United States government was equally unsuccessful, receiving only a fragment of the necessary revenue during its own endeavors. The land was sold in whole townships in every other township, and by section in the remaining townships. A section, or 640 acres, was the minimum purchase.

The Land Law of 1796 reduced minimum purchases to a quarter-township for half of the townships, and full townships for the remainder. The price increased to $2 per acre, but a year was given for full payment. The first lands under this pro-

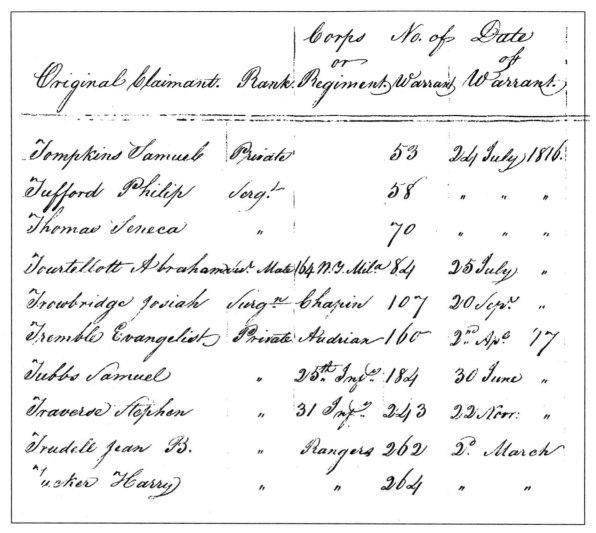

Figure 9-11. From "List of Canadian Volunteer Warrants Issued by War Department as of March 1st, 1820." This list includes name, rank, regiment, warrant number, and date of warrant. Such information can help access military service records.

gram were sold at public auction in 1798. The auctions were held in Pittsburgh and Philadelphia, and sold only fifty thousand acres.

In response, the Land Law of 1800 reduced the minimum purchase even further, to 320 acres for those sections previously at 640-acre minimums. Credit was also introduced, allowing four years for the full balance to be paid. Eight percent was deducted if the full amount was paid at the time of auction. Prices continued to fluctuate over the years—an attempt to meet the needs and desires of the settlers, yet still raise needed funds.

Cash entries will often contain only a receipt in the case file. While seemingly uninformative, these receipts can provide property descriptions for lands that have not been identified through deed sales. This allows follow-up research on those who possessed the property when there was no recording of an official deed. This often leads to relatives and other associates, and to other record sources. (See figure 9-12.)

Cash-entry records are organized by land office at the National Archives. The tract books can be used to determine if your ancestor was involved, and the applicable land-entry case file can then be ordered. The case files have not been microfilmed.

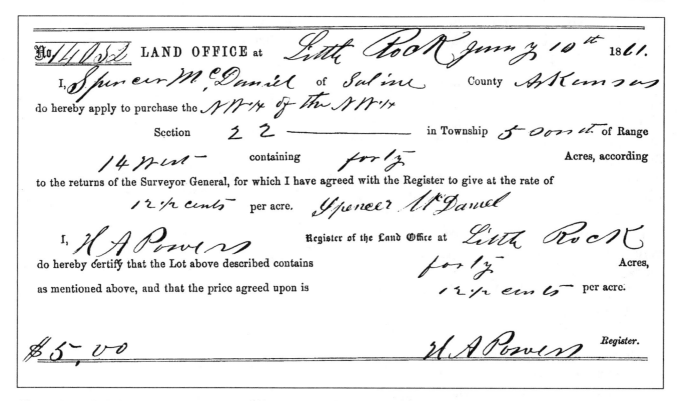

Figure 9-12. A typical cash entry receipt; from the Little Rock Land Office in Arkansas.

There are no indexes, except those that have been published by independent authors or societies for a specific land office and time period. The largest collection of these publications is found at the Family History Library.

CREDIT SALES

The Land Law of 1800 introduced credit sales to the federal land system. It gave purchasers four years to pay the full balance on their newly acquired lands. By 1802, more than 750,000 acres were sold as a result. This was a significant amount when compared with total lands sold through previous acts. Those delinquent with final payment were to completely forfeit their lands to the United States, together with any payments already made. Forfeited lands were then auctioned to anyone willing to pay the outstanding balance.

Acts in 1806 and 1809 provided time extensions for repayment on credit purchases. The Act of 1806 pertained to those who had bought land in 1800 and 1801, and who were still residing on the land at the time of the extension. In 1809, Con-

gress extended the same benefits to those who had purchased before 1804, giving them an additional two years to comply. Interest payments, however, had to be kept current.

Further extensions were granted in 1812 and in almost every subsequent year until 1820. People were eager to settle, hopeful for prosperity, but were constantly subdued by reality. After the economic crash of 1819, the treasury was owed almost 23 million dollars for land ventures alone. This brought about swift and direct measures as the new Land Law of 1820 abolished the nation's twenty-year experiment with credit. Cash payment was thereafter required in full at the time of purchase. To compensate, the price per acre was reduced to $1.25. Entries made before this act are referred to as "credit-prior" entries, while those made after are called "credit-under" entries.

Though sales slowed significantly, the abolishment of credit eventually helped stabilize the economic failures caused by land distribution. An act in 1821 provided for the dismissal of all interest due from those who had already bought on credit.

It also allowed debtors to relinquish a portion of their lands and have their previous payments apply only to what was kept.

Those who had made one-fourth of their payments were granted eight additional years to complete the remainder. Those who had paid one-half were granted six years, and those who had paid three-fourths were granted four additional years. If payments were made on time, all future interest was also waived. As a final incentive, those who made final payments by 30 September 1822 were to have a reduction of thirty-seven and one-half percent on the amount due. Even further relief acts were initiated in 1822 and 1823, and again in 1826 and 1828. As a result, the land debt subsided considerably by the end of 1825, dropping from 23 million to approximately 6 million dollars.

Though no new credit was issued after 1820, it was not until eleven different relief measures were applied over the next twelve years that the end of the credit era was finally recognized. Government credit was never issued again in the nineteenth century.

Credit sales are similar to cash entries, with the amount of information varying only according to the amounts and frequency of payments. The name, property description, price per acre, and interest payments were recorded. The county of residence can also be found on these documents, and can be helpful if the settler was residing elsewhere during the purchase period. Many of those who forfeited their lands through nonpayment of credit purchases eventually tried to file preemption claims, leading to another valuable source of information.

Credit entries are a part of the land-entry case files housed in the National Archives, and can be accessed through the same processes described for cash entries. They are not on microfilm and not available through any other repository. The tract books are the only index.

PRIVATE LAND CLAIMS

The term "private land claim" indicates an application to the United States government for re-owner-ship of lands that were originally acquired by the claimant while living under the administration of a foreign government. It does not include lands won during the Revolutionary War, except for portions of the Northwest Territory. It otherwise refers to the lands originally distributed by the governments of Spain, Britain, France, and Mexico (figure 9-13). These claims often contain the verification of title or settlement through several generations of previous ownership. Sometimes they outline a pedigree, from grandfather to father to son, over a period of more than half a century. Creatively used, they can provide excellent clues to migrations and family structures.

Private land claims were recognized as early as 1784, after the close of the Revolutionary War. Legislation began to take into consideration the plight of the French and Canadian inhabitants of Detroit, Vincennes, Kaskaskia, Cahokia, Fort Wayne, and Green Bay. Litigation of private land claims continued well into the twentieth century, as titles in Florida and Louisiana continued to be disputed as recently as 1960. More recent claims often contain the most information. Several generations passed away between the original and present-day claimant, with owners and relationships often provided back to the original patentee.

The process of filing a private land claim was as involved then as one would expect today. Boards of commissioners were set up to assess and adjudicate the hundreds of thousands of claims being presented. Administration was not perfect, and fraud was prevalent in some areas. However, these boards weeded out many of the fraudulent claims, and controlled the consistency of the disbursement of newly acquired lands in both size and circumstance.

No other act or group of acts for a specific land issue has ever generated as many headaches and as much paperwork as the private land claims process. It involved extraction of materials from foreign-government records and repositories, and the testimonies of numerous witnesses. A concerted effort was made to know and understand the land laws of previous governments. The process involved assessing the size and needs of house-

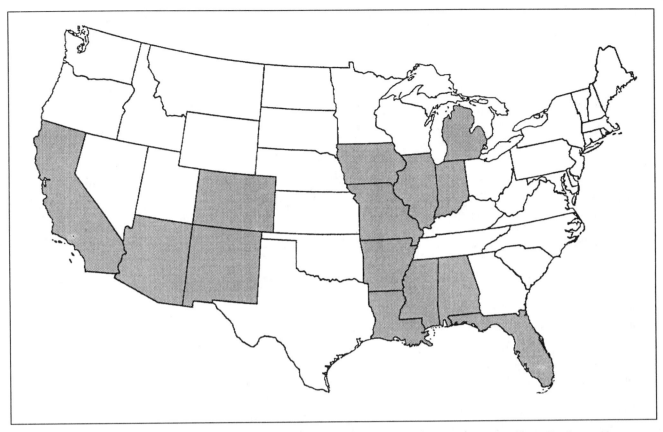

Figure 9-13. The most significant private land claim records were created by the fourteen states indicated here, although they sometimes involved small portions of other states.

holds, then blending this information—and more—into the land-disposal system newly created and implemented by the United States.

The types of documents included in private land claims differ from case to case, time to time, and place to place. The more a claim was contested, the more information the case file contains. Case files for private land claims can include the following:

- Copies of surveys by both foreign and American officials

- Descriptions of improvements made and lengths of residence on the property in question

- Evidence of title transfers through multiple generations

- Descriptions of heirs for each generation involved

- Evidence of previous origins and loyalty

- Political affiliation

- Testimonies from witnesses and claimant

- Family structures

- Time periods and places of migration

Sizes of private land claims range from small town lots to single claims of almost 1.5 million acres. These claims took precedence over the existing federal system of township, range, and section. Many of the private land claims had been originally granted under the survey method of metes and bounds. Thus, the awards given to claimants by the boards of commissioners created odd fractions in the remaining land, which were more difficult to disperse through other programs. (See figure 9-14.)

Applications for private land claims often took on a personal and political flavor, especially in California and Florida. Since many who were on the boards of commissioners also held political offices, claimants often testified as to which political party they loyally subscribed (figure 9-15).

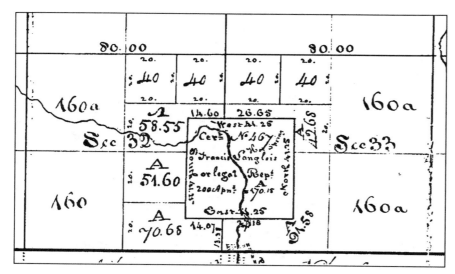

Figure 9-14. A survey that shows public lands circumventing a preexisting private land claim.

A tremendous number of so-called "Americans" can be found among the multitude of private land claims. Catholic persecution, land speculation, and the enticements of individual settlement were driving forces for emigration from America to areas under foreign administration. Ancestors from New England to the Carolinas and across to the West Coast can all be found among the papers created by private land claims. Ultimately, 34 million acres in nineteen states were distributed in answer to private land claims legislation.

When contested by another individual, the claimants would go to extreme lengths to portray that individual as having extremely low character due to contrasting political views.

Over 125 private land claims cases were contested all the way to the Supreme Court by 1860. Not all were settled in the courts, however. In one incident, the son of a federal judge was killed by a U.S. senator in an argument over the validity of certain Spanish land grants.

Testimonies and applications of the claimant can be helpful to researchers. Information provided by witnesses and comments by the commission are also of historical and genealogical value. In fact, testimonies of witnesses can sometimes be more informative about the claimant than the claimant's own testimony. (See figure 9-16.)

Private land claims were usually adjudicated from two sources: congressional branches such as the Senate and House of Representatives, and specially appointed federal and state boards of commissioners. Congress was generally consulted only as a source of appeal for decisions made by the boards of commissioners.

State boards were generally used to validate claims under 3,500 acres, though in special circumstances that limitation was raised. They were usually headed by the Office of the Surveyor-General for the state or territory involved. The federal boards would oversee the larger claims—those at risk of defrauding the most from the public land system. Both boards generated a tremendous amount of history and genealogy. They gathered records from previous governments and from indi-

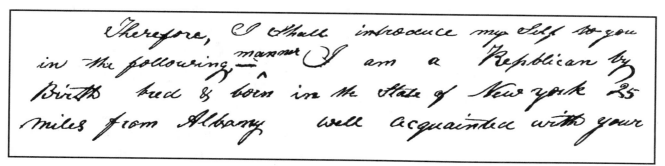

Figure 9-15. Private land claims often took the form of personal pleas to governing officials that declared birthplace and political affiliation. This claim from Spanish Florida supports the supposition that many American-born citizens were in Spanish-occupied regions.

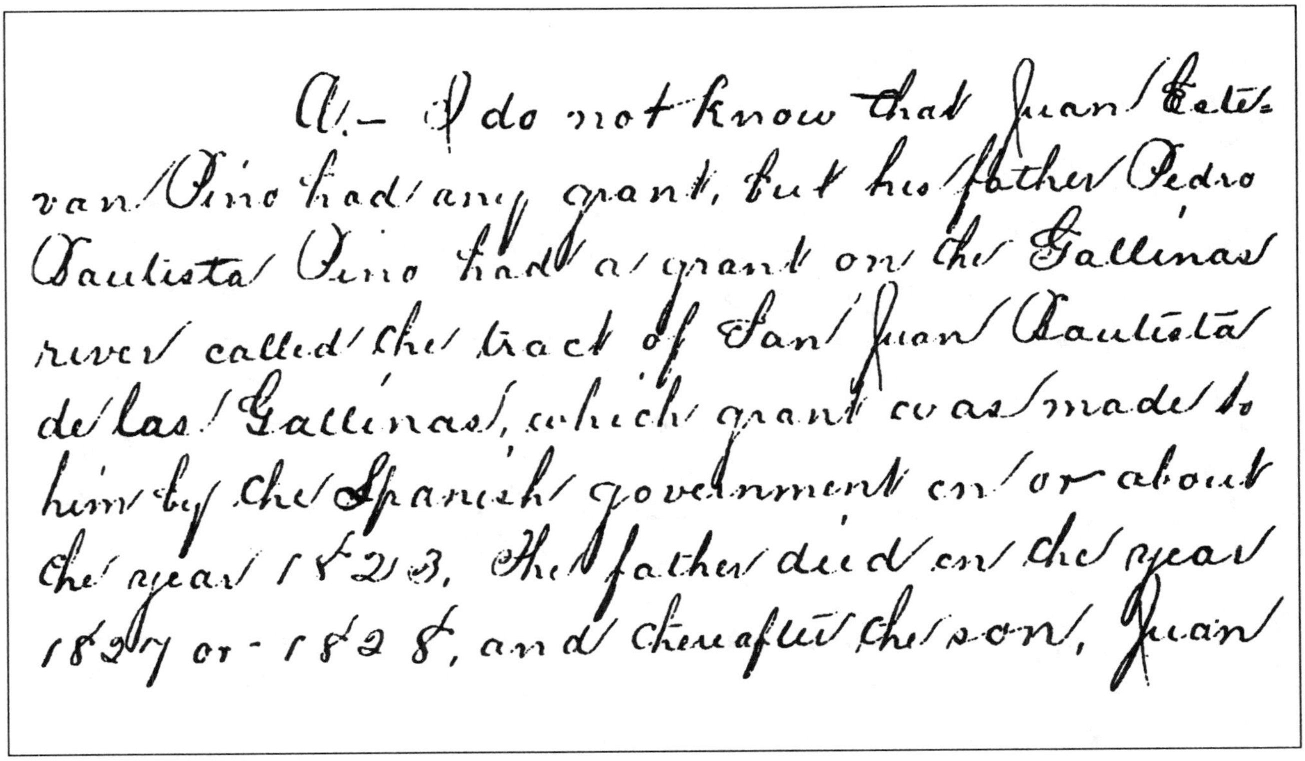

A.- I do not know that Juan Este-
van Pino had any grant, but his father Pedro
Bautista Pino had a grant on the Gallinas
river called the tract of San Juan Bautista
de las Gallinas, which grant was made to
him by the Spanish government in or about
the year 1823. The father died in the year
1827 or 1828, and thereafter the son, Juan

Figure 9-16. Witness's testimony regarding Juan Estevan Piño.

viduals, and created their own set of records in the process. Sometimes similar records can also be found among the collections of foreign administrations. These records are further described in section 1, Pre-U.S. Possessions.

The claims involving the state boards can be found in state archives, state libraries, Surveyor-General offices, major university repositories, and in the National Archives. They are usually organized according to the administrating entity. Records generated by the federal boards are now housed at the National Archives. They are separated according to state. Within each state, they are filed alphabetically according to the first letter of the claimant's surname. The only exception is the state of Indiana. It is not in alphabetical order, but rather is organized according to file number.

Documents found in private land claims were created at different times for different purposes, and have thus been kept in different groups of files in the past. Records for federal boards are now gathered in one file, keeping all pertinent material together in one location for easier access. These records are part of Record Group 49, for the Bureau of Land Management.

Private land claims for Florida, New Mexico/Colorado, and California are among the richest in historical and genealogical content. Those in California often evolved from mining claims being disputed by several parties. More litigation was generated for California than for almost any other two areas combined. California and New Mexico entries usually contain large, detailed maps of the property and surroundings. Louisiana, Mississippi, Alabama, Missouri, and Arkansas are mostly uniform and typical in content and procedures. (See figure 9-17.)

Michigan and Wisconsin are combined, as are New Mexico and Colorado. Claims for Michigan were still being litigated in the early 1900s. Many owners held no official deeds of title transfer. To get a perfected title, efforts were made to trace the property back to the original title holder, who often held the land before it was acquired by the United States. Though several generations of title transfers are documented in these papers, there is very

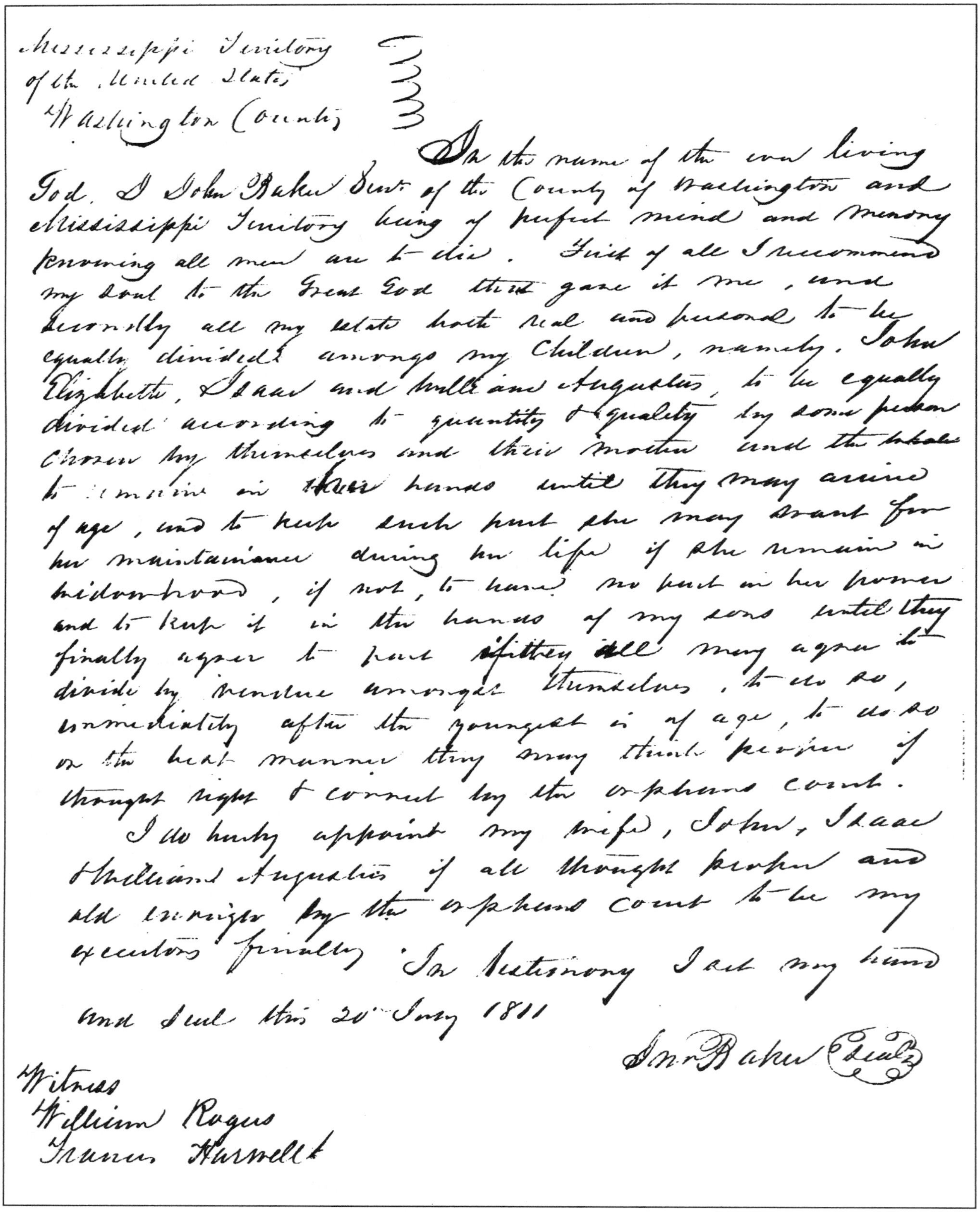

Figure 9-17. The 1811 will of John Baker. It proved that heirs were still waiting for patent on four hundred acres previously received by their father from the Spanish government. Located in the private land claims in Alabama, it is a significant find, especially because wills from this time period and place may never have been recorded elsewhere.

little detail about each generation, and very few claims in this region were held by consecutive generations of the same family.

Many private land claims in Illinois were processed on preprinted forms, with only the blanks filled in. This eliminated many of the impromptu testimonials which are found in many of the other states. Most claims provide only the name of the claimant, or state "heirs of" without providing the names of the heirs. Testimonies are mostly from neighbors, not the original claimant.

Private land claims in Indiana often mention the one-hundred-acre military tracts of the Vincennes Land District issued to early French inhabitants of that area. No actual patents were ever issued for these early French grants, though anyone needing to perfect a patent could appropriately apply.

There are many recorded circumstances of Spanish and British claims contending for the same piece of property. In these instances, the land awaited final judicial decisions on actual ownership. Conflicting claims can often be the most genealogically beneficial because of the processes and evidence presented. Testimonies were vividly descriptive of people, places, and times. However, as could be expected, many claims and patents were found to be fraudulent and many did not meet the requirements stipulated in the treaties. These cases and others were rejected, but should not be overlooked. Records were still created, and may provide clues to authentic relationships and associations during that time.

Case files housed in the General Land Office have been arranged alphabetically at the National Archives. Searches are more productive when indexes are first used to insure that a private land claim file actually exists. Indexes for private land claims for the General Land Office (Record Group 49) have been assembled for many of the states, including the non-alphabetical state of Indiana. Fern Ainsworth has produced several of them, including *Private Land Claims: Illinois, Indiana, Michigan and Wisconsin; Private Land Claims: Mississippi and Missouri;* and *Private Land Claims: Alabama, Arkansas, Florida.*

All of the claims presented to federal boards or other acting federal agencies, such as district courts or district land offices, were reported to Congress. These claims, prior to 1837, are included in *American State Papers: Public Lands*. This collection encompasses eight volumes. Their contents are as follows:

Volume One: 1790–1809

Volume Two: 1809–1815

Volume Three: 1815–1824

Volume Four: 1824–1828

Volume Five: 1827–1829

Volume Six: 1829–1834

Volume Seven: 1834–1835

Volume Eight: 1835–1837

Each volume has an individual index for the name of the claimant. These indexes are not complete, however. For a more precise index, see Phillip W. McMullin's *Grassroots of America*. Few original volumes remain in existence, though they can be found at various larger repositories, including the National Archives. They are also available on microfilm at the Family History Library.

Congressional indexes include the House of Representatives' *Digested Summary and Alphabetical List of Private Land Claims . . . Presented to the House of Representatives from the First to the Thirty-First Congress,* covering approximately 1793 to 1852. A similar publication, titled *List of Private Claims Brought Before the Senate of the United States,* includes the period from 1815 to 1881. Records of congressional reports from both the House and the Senate concerning private land claims from 1826 to 1876 have been abstracted in a two-volume series called *Reports of the Committees on Private Land Claims of the Senate and House of Representatives.* T.M. McKee's *House Index to Committee Reports* includes an index for these reports. Original records of the House of

Representatives are held at the National Archives in Record Group 233. Those for the Senate are in Record Group 46. See also *Guide to the Records of the United States Senate at the National Archives,* by Robert W. Coren, et al.

The Court of Private Land Claims for the Adjudication of Spanish and Mexican Land Titles in Colorado, New Mexico, Arizona, Nevada, Utah and Wyoming has been microfilmed. It includes indexes, and is available through the Bureau of Land Management in Santa Fe, New Mexico, the Family History Library, the National Archives, and the University of New Mexico.

Similar records for the state of California are available at the California State Archives in Sacramento. They include the following sets of records, which have all been microfilmed:

- *Index by County to Private Land Grant Cases, U.S. District Court, Northern District of California*

- *Index to Private Land Grant Cases, U.S. District Court, Northern District of California, 1853–1910*

- *Private Land Grant Cases, U.S. Circuit Court of the Northern District of California, 1852–1910*

- *Index to Private Land Grant Cases, U.S. District Court, Southern District of California*

These records are available through the National Archives, the California State Archives, the Family History Library, and their branch facilities.

SURVEYOR-GENERAL SCRIP

The Act of 4 July 1836 provided for scrip to be issued by the Surveyor-General of Missouri. This scrip was issued in lieu of private land claims, when lands had been sold before claim confirmation by the Board of Commissioners. Scrip provided a selection of land in place of the original claim, since the original claim could not be honored. At times, claim conflicts were not discovered until the surveys were taken. Surveyor-general scrip was issued under the direction of the Board

of Land Commissioners in Missouri, and was to be located elsewhere within the boundaries of that state. This scrip is discussed here in conjunction with private land claims, and further reference should be made to that segment in this chapter.

A later act, dated 2 June 1858, allowed scrip to be used at any public land office in the United States, for any public lands open for cash entry, at a price not exceeding $1.25 per acre. The price restriction protected the choicest of lands from being immediately ravaged without generating the intended revenue. All entries included a non-mineral affidavit. Most entries under the act of 1858 were not completed until 1900–1910, by heirs of the original claimant. This created even more family information.

Surveyor-general scrip is housed at the National Archives. It is not indexed, but includes only 232 individual packets, each with the name and case number on the outside jacket. Currently, this collection has not been microfilmed.

SUPREME COURT SCRIP

Similar to the surveyor-general scrip for Missouri, there were instances when the United States granted lands predating private land claims, or found conflicting claims due to preemption acts. At times, both claims were found to be legitimate. These and similar circumstances brought about the need for the Supreme Court to issue scrip for one of the parties involved. This scrip could be used for other lands at any federal land office, except in those states designated as "homestead-only" states (Alabama, Arkansas, Florida, Louisiana, and Mississippi). The congressional acts producing this scrip were implemented in 1860, 1867, and 1872.

Records created as a result of Supreme Court scrip contain the same information as the type of claim it was issued for. If it was issued for a private land claim, then testimonies and litigation were the same as for any other private land claim. If the scrip was issued in lieu of a conflict in homesteading, the same records were generated as with any other homestead claim.

Records specific to Supreme Court scrip are applications, assignments, certificates of location, and patents. As with other scrip, many bearers assigned their lands to someone else. However, this did not prevent a series of documents from being created about the claimant. The original scrip holder was still the applicant and qualifier.

Supreme Court scrip includes 852 files, numerous in comparison with the amount of records created by surveyor-general scrip. It is located at the National Archives, and has not been microfilmed or indexed. It is not available at any other repository.

PREEMPTION

From the time federal land became a distinct and important source of revenue for the United States, the government had to deal with squatters. Squatters were people who took up residence and improved lands for which they had not applied nor paid for through any of the methods provided by legislation. The land-tenure system adopted by the United States could not recognize squatters as legitimate while supporting cash-entry guidelines.

Genuine efforts were made during the earliest days of the federal land system to prevent squatters from taking up residence on federal lands. At times, military force was even used to evict those found squatting in the Northwest Territory. Stiff penalties included fines and imprisonment for violators. Finally, an act of Congress in 1807 provided for preemption rights. Though harsher penalties were initiated for future violators, existing squatters were allowed to claim up to 320 acres of land if they registered with the local land office. When the land was eventually sold to someone else, the squatter had to promise to leave peacefully. Those who did not register their claims were duly charged, fined as much as $100, and received a six-month jail term. Otherwise, no fees were required. No titles were ever given to the squatters—only permission for temporary inhabitance. This policy encouraged future violations by recognizing those who had violated federal land policy in the past.

Public outcry was heard for decades, from literally every corner of the federal domain. Improvements to property could not be casually dismissed by the squatter when asked to leave lands that finally had been purchased by another claimant. As the sale of public lands drew more and more publicity, squatters became more concerned about land speculators and companies purchasing large tracts that would encompass their claims. This fear brought about petitions for an opportunity to receive first rights to purchase the claim and secure their invested labor and improvements at an agreed price. Preemption legislation was eventually passed, allowing the claimant first rights, but only when matching the bid price.

Preemption differs from private land claims. Those who filed for preemption were filing for first rights of purchase, rather than claiming and proving existing ownership.

As soon as preemption was recognized as a viable alternative, the issue of price became the focus of frustration. Obviously the land speculators and the rich would get the finest when lands were made available only to the highest bidder. The term "modest price" became the center of debate over the following decades.

A total of twenty-four different acts were passed before 1820, each granting various types of preemption privileges under specific conditions. Most offered a purchase price of $2 per acre for lands not sold through auction. Those who lost their lands by forfeiture to the credit system usually retained residence as squatters, and found that preemption acts applied specifically to their plight. Through preemption, they were allowed to have first rights to purchase the lands they had developed and cultivated.

It was not until 1830 that the first broad-scale preemption act was passed. This act allowed every settler who had been residing on and cultivating his property before and during 1829 to file for preemption rights for up to 160 acres at $1.25 an acre. Filing could be done up to one year following the enactment without bidding on the property. Both entry and payment were required before auction sales of the particular tract to keep others from bidding on the land. Assignment of the property declared the entry null and void unless the patent had been issued before assignment.

Settlement in advance of surveys continued. For each instance in which trespasses were forgiven and preemption rights were granted, new circumstances would evolve. The Preemption Act of 1838 allowed the right of preemption to each settler who was over twenty-one years of age, head of a family, and residing on public lands. An act in 1841 also permitted widows or a single man over the age of twenty-one to participate. None of the acts applied to Indian lands.

Heirs also applied for preemptions, though the residence requirements made it more difficult than with bounty lands or homesteads. Preemptions by heirs mostly took place when credit entries of parents had been forfeited. They would then exercise preemption rights on the same property.

Preemption records (figures 18 through 20) are housed at the National Archives. They have not been microfilmed at present. Since there is no

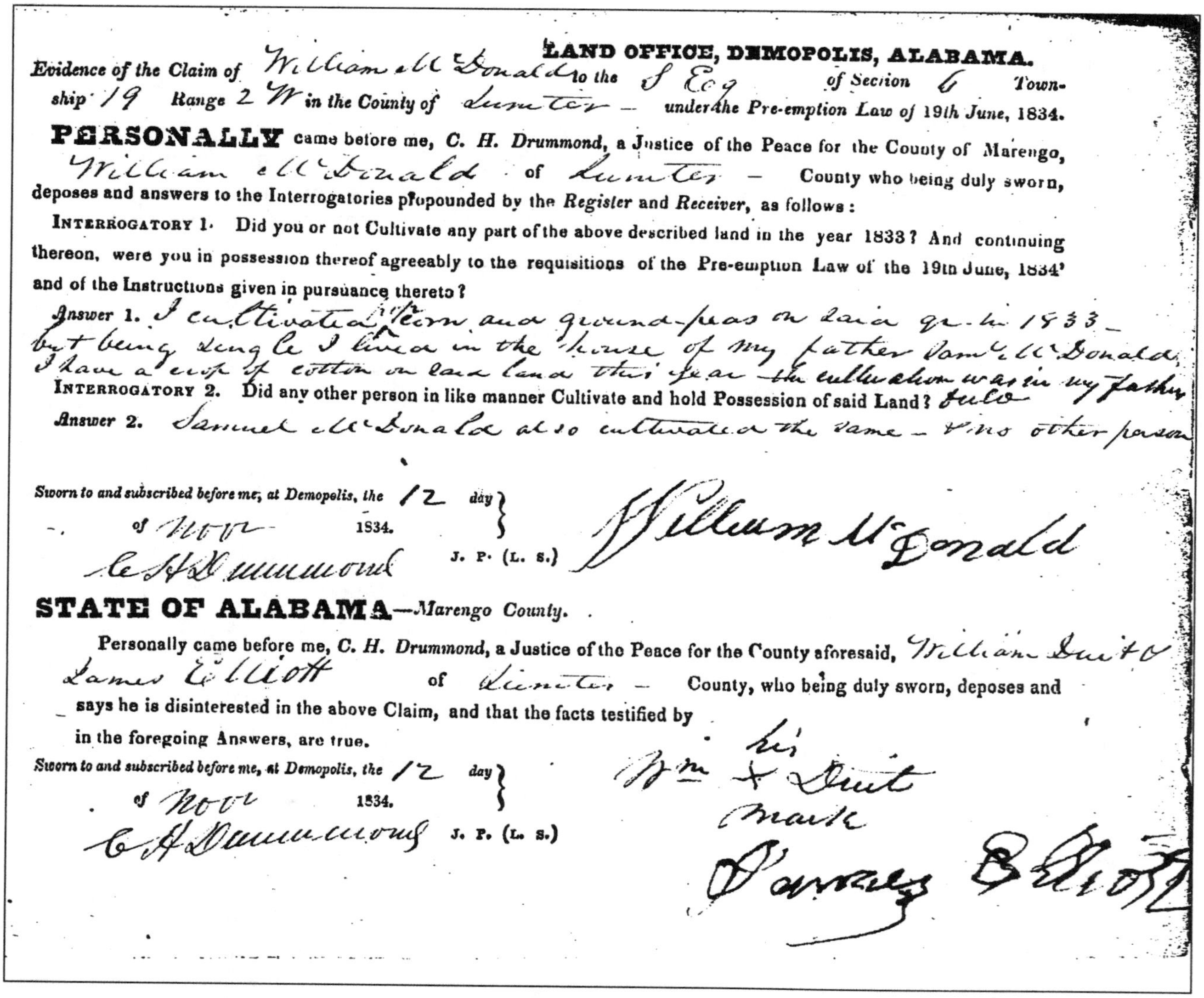

LAND OFFICE, DEMOPOLIS, ALABAMA.

Evidence of the Claim of William McDonald *to the* S Eq *of Section* 6 *Township* 19 *Range* 2 W *in the County of* Sumter — *under the Pre-emption Law of 19th June, 1834.*

PERSONALLY came before me, *C. H. Drummond*, a Justice of the Peace for the County of Marengo, William McDonald of Sumter — County who being duly sworn, deposes and answers to the Interrogatories propounded by the *Register* and *Receiver*, as follows:

INTERROGATORY 1. Did you or not Cultivate any part of the above described land in the year 1833? And continuing thereon, were you in possession thereof agreeably to the requisitions of the Pre-emption Law of the 19th June, 1834' and of the Instructions given in pursuance thereto?

Answer 1. I cultivated corn and ground-peas on said qr. in 1833 — but being single I lived in the house of my father Saml McDonald, I have a crop of cotton on said land this year the cultivation was in my father

INTERROGATORY 2. Did any other person in like manner Cultivate and hold Possession of said Land? Into

Answer 2. Samuel McDonald also cultivated the same — & no other person

Sworn to and subscribed before me, at Demopolis, the 12 *day of* Nov 1834.

C H Drummond J. P. (L. S.)

William McDonald

STATE OF ALABAMA—*Marengo County.*

Personally came before me, *C. H. Drummond*, a Justice of the Peace for the County aforesaid, William Swift & James Elliott of Sumter — County, who being duly sworn, deposes and says he is disinterested in the above Claim, and that the facts testified by in the foregoing Answers, are true.

Sworn to and subscribed before me, at Demopolis, the 12 *day of* Nov 1834.

C H Drummond J. P. (L. S.)

Wm his + mark Swift

James Elliott

Figure 9-18. A typical preemption record from the Demopolis Land Office in Alabama. This example notes that William McDonald was the son of Samuel McDonald—critical information if the family moved there after 1830 and the father died before 1840. They would be missed in the 1830 and 1840 censuses and would not likely be found in any other land records if preemption was needed.

In Virtue of a licence from the Clerk
of Amite County. I have this day celebra-
ted the Rites of Matrimony Between
Philip Quigly. and Mary McCoy.
Given under my hand the 24th
day of February. 1820.
J Jones J.P.

Figure 9-19. A marriage affidavit used to illustrate the relationship between Phillip Quigly, the claimant, and Mary McCoy, heir of Alexander McCoy. It was through the rights of Alexander McCoy, a forfeited land claimant under the credit act, that preemption was being filed by Phillip Quigly for the land which Alexander had improved and lived upon until his death, and on which Phillip and Mary were currently living. This document, and more, was found in the case file.

N°. 135 LAND OFFICE WEST OF PEARL RIVER,

JANUARY 1, 1807.

IT IS HEREBY CERTIFIED, That Isaac Johnson of Wilkinson County did on the twenty fourth day of December 1806, enter with the Register of the Land Office west of Pearl River, a Certificate from the Board of Commissioners, stating, that he is entitled, by pre-emption, to a lot or tract of land on the waters of Thompson's creek containing twelve hundred and fifty —— acres, at two dollars per acre, amounting in the whole, for said lot or tract, to Two thousand five hundred —— dollars, of which there has been paid on account agreeably to law, to the receiver of public monies, the sum of six hundred and twenty five dollars —— being one fourth part of the purchase money of said tract of land.——NOW THEREFORE BE IT KNOWN, That if the remaining balance, being eighteen hundred and seventy five dollars —— cents, shall be paid to the said receiver of public monies for the district west of Pearl river, or to the Treasurer of the United States, at or before the dates following, that is to say: Six hundred and twenty five — dollars —— cents thereof, on or before the first day of January 1809; Six hundred and twenty five dollars —— cents thereof, on or before the first day of January 1810; and Six hundred and twenty five dollars —— cents thereof, on or before the first day of January 1811; then the said Isaac Johnson, —— or his assignee, or other legal representative, shall be entitled to receive a Patent for the lot or tract of land above described.

Tho H Williams,
Register of the Land Office.

Figure 9-20. A preemption record dated 1806. The land was paid for on credit; the record shows one-quarter payment made up front with three equal annual installments thereafter.

index, tract books must be used to determine if an ancestor ever received preemption land. The tract book information can then be used to order the land-entry case file. The records are organized according to land office and patent number or final certificate number.

HOMESTEAD RECORDS

The Homestead Law was a series of enactments beginning with the Act of 20 May 1862. Its purpose was to distribute public lands to those who were without. The only compensation required, aside from filing fees, was in the form of residence, cultivation, and improvement. Extensive immigration initially created the need for homestead legislation. The Civil War also brought about the need to encourage settlement in less-developed areas by individuals loyal to the Union. With the passage of the initial law, people could begin filing homestead claims as early as 1 January 1863. (See figures 9-21 through 9-26.)

The Homestead Law enabled an estimated 783,000 citizens, or intended citizens, to become patented land holders. However, almost 2 million entries were made, indicating approximately sixty percent cancellation for one reason or another. Since files were created for each entry, whether cancelled or not, they encompass one of the largest collections of land records in history. Claims were mostly made between 1863 and 1917, though the law was not completely abolished until 1976. Together, military bounty lands, private land claims, railroad grants, and timber grants amounted to approximately 221 million acres. Grants to various states totaled approximately 225 million acres. Approximately 285 million acres (almost one-eighth of the entire United States) were actually dispersed through homestead claims.

The initial Homestead Law provided for as much as 160 acres of federal land to be allotted to heads of households, widows, single persons over the age of twenty-one, and anyone "who has never borne arms against the United States government or given aid and comfort to its enemies." The law was intended for those who were landless or who owned less than 160 acres (a quarter-section). A single woman could apply, just as a single man could. Her rights were not forfeited upon marriage, though a husband and wife could not both hold separate unfinished claims. While a married wife had no right to a claim separate from her husband, a deserted wife did qualify. If a single man and a single woman obtained patents before marriage, the marriage did not dissolve either claim.

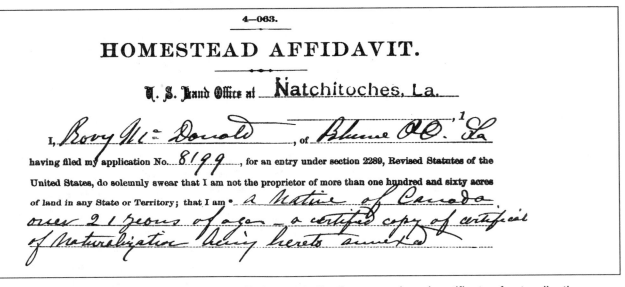

Figure 9-21. A homestead affidavit from a cancelled entry, indicating an enclosed certificate of naturalization. Although not as informative as some, the certificate (shown in figure 9-22) provides helpful clues about the date and port of the applicant's arrival. This case file is from the Natchitoches land office in Louisiana.

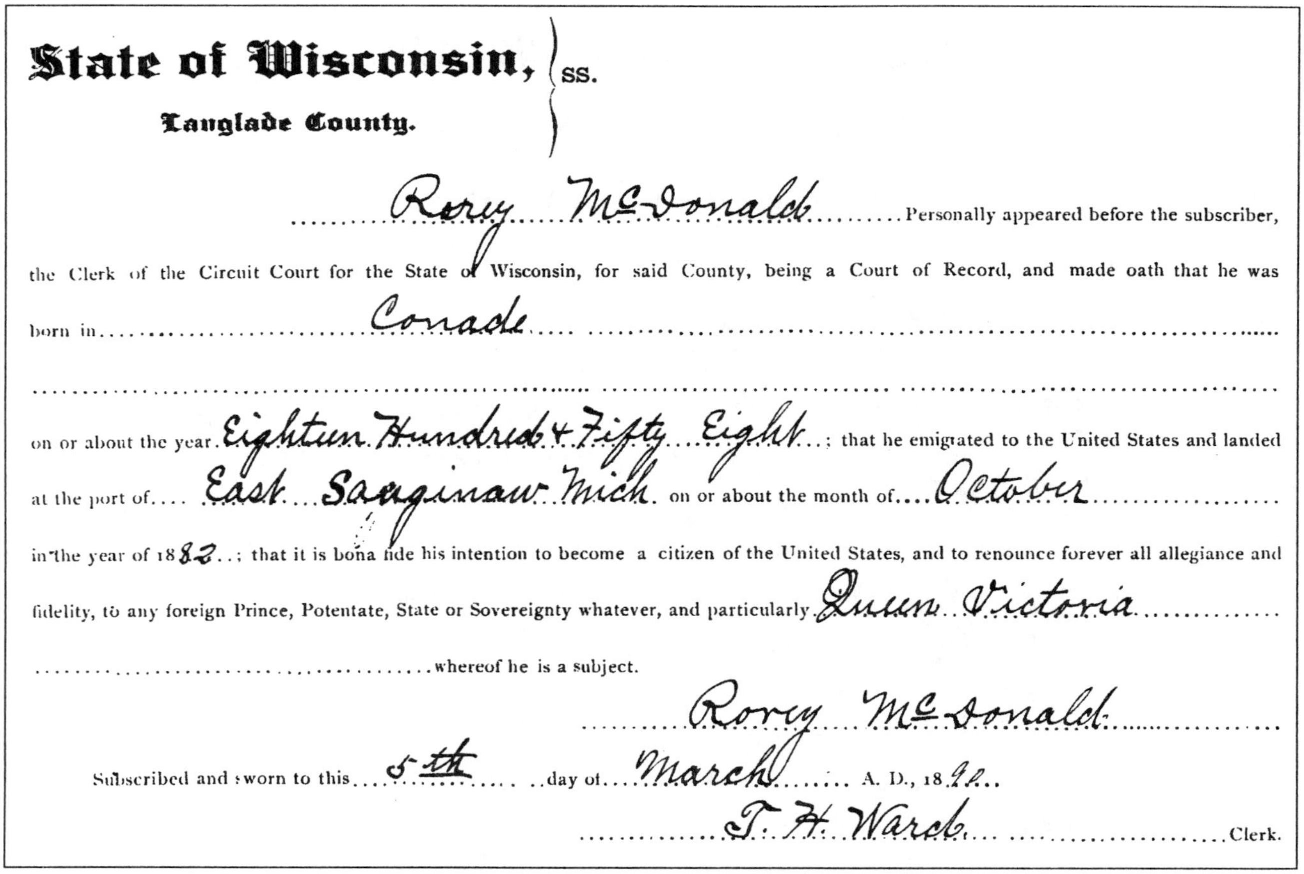

State of Wisconsin, } ss.
Langlade County.

Rory McDonald Personally appeared before the subscriber, the Clerk of the Circuit Court for the State of Wisconsin, for said County, being a Court of Record, and made oath that he was born in Conade

on or about the year Eightun Hundred & Fifty Eight; that he emigrated to the United States and landed at the port of East Saaginaw Mich on or about the month of October in the year of 1882; that it is bona fide his intention to become a citizen of the United States, and to renounce forever all allegiance and fidelity, to any foreign Prince, Potentate, State or Sovereignty whatever, and particularly Queen Victoria whereof he is a subject.

Rory McDonald

Subscribed and sworn to this 5th day of March A. D., 1892.

T. H. Ward Clerk.

Figure 9-22. A certificate of naturalization from Langlade County, Wisconsin, presented at the Natchitoches Land Office in Louisiana. The claim was forfeited and was among the cancelled entries. This type of file can presently be found only by searching the tract books, because no patent was ever issued.

The law required that homesteaded property be consistently resided upon, built upon, and cultivated over a five-year period. A widow, however, could enter a separate claim from that of her deceased husband, and was only required to reside upon the claim filed in her own name. The applicant could not be the owner of any other property totaling 160 acres or more, and qualified only for the difference in those amounts. For example, if a person owned forty acres, he could then apply only for an additional 120 acres under the Homestead Act. If he owned none, he could apply for the entire 160 acres.

The enlarged Homestead Act of 1909 increased the total acreage receivable to 320 acres. This applied to public lands that could not be easily irrigated, encouraging development in the Midwest plains and the Southwest. If an entry had already been filed under the original Homestead Act for 160 acres, or a portion thereof, a person could file for additional acreage under the new act for up to a combined total of 320 acres.

Lands acquired under the Homestead Act were exempt from repossession for any debts incurred before the issue of the patent. This allowed many families to get a fresh start in a new location. Soldiers and sailors were permitted to deduct active military duty, up to four years, from their residency requirements. This program replaced military bounty land as an incentive for enlistment. The families of servicemen could file for a homestead in their behalf and reside on the property during the said service, completing much of the requirements while the serviceman was away.

As with many federal land purchases, the entry had to be made by a citizen, or an immigrant who had filed a declaration to become a citizen. This

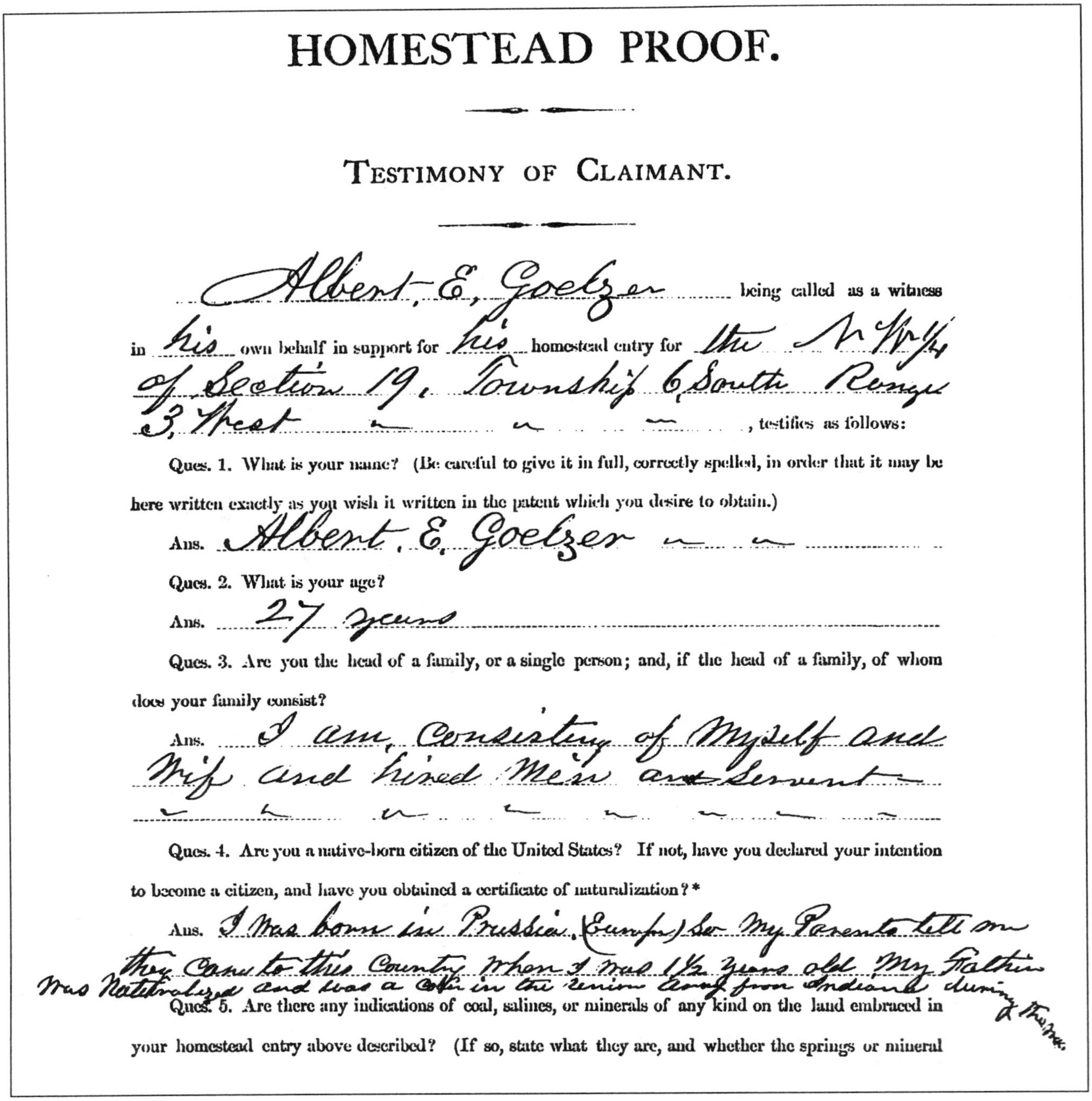

HOMESTEAD PROOF.

TESTIMONY OF CLAIMANT.

Albert, E, Goelzer .... being called as a witness in *his* own behalf in support for *his* homestead entry for *the N W ¼ of Section 19, Township 6 South Range 3, West* ...., testifies as follows:

Ques. 1. What is your name? (Be careful to give it in full, correctly spelled, in order that it may be here written exactly as you wish it written in the patent which you desire to obtain.)

Ans. *Albert, E, Goelzer*

Ques. 2. What is your age?

Ans. *27 years*

Ques. 3. Are you the head of a family, or a single person; and, if the head of a family, of whom does your family consist?

Ans. *I am, Consisting of Myself and Wife and hired Men and Servent*

Ques. 4. Are you a native-born citizen of the United States? If not, have you declared your intention to become a citizen, and have you obtained a certificate of naturalization?*

Ans. *I was born in Prussia (Europe) So My Parents tell me they Came to this Country When I was 1½ years old My Father was Naturalized and was a Coln in the Union Army from Indiana during*

Ques. 5. Are there any indications of coal, salines, or minerals of any kind on the land embraced in your homestead entry above described? (If so, state what they are, and whether the springs or mineral

Figure 9-23. The proof was among many papers ordinarily found in a land-entry case file for a homestead. It states: "I was born in Prussia (Europe), so my parents tell me. They came to this country when I was 1 1/2 years old. My father was naturalized and was a Coln. in the Union Army from Indiana during the war."

was difficult to enforce, although diligent attempts were made. Sometimes information about origins was vague, and sometimes it was very detailed.

Unlike most other types of land acquisition, there were few prerequisites for homesteaders. Most of their qualifications were fulfilled during the application process, rather than before. When

people located a desired piece of land, they filed a claim for the property chosen. This was done in person through the local land office or directly at the General Land Office in Washington, D.C. The people filing the claims took oath that they were over the age of twenty-one or married and head of a family. They also testified concerning their citi-

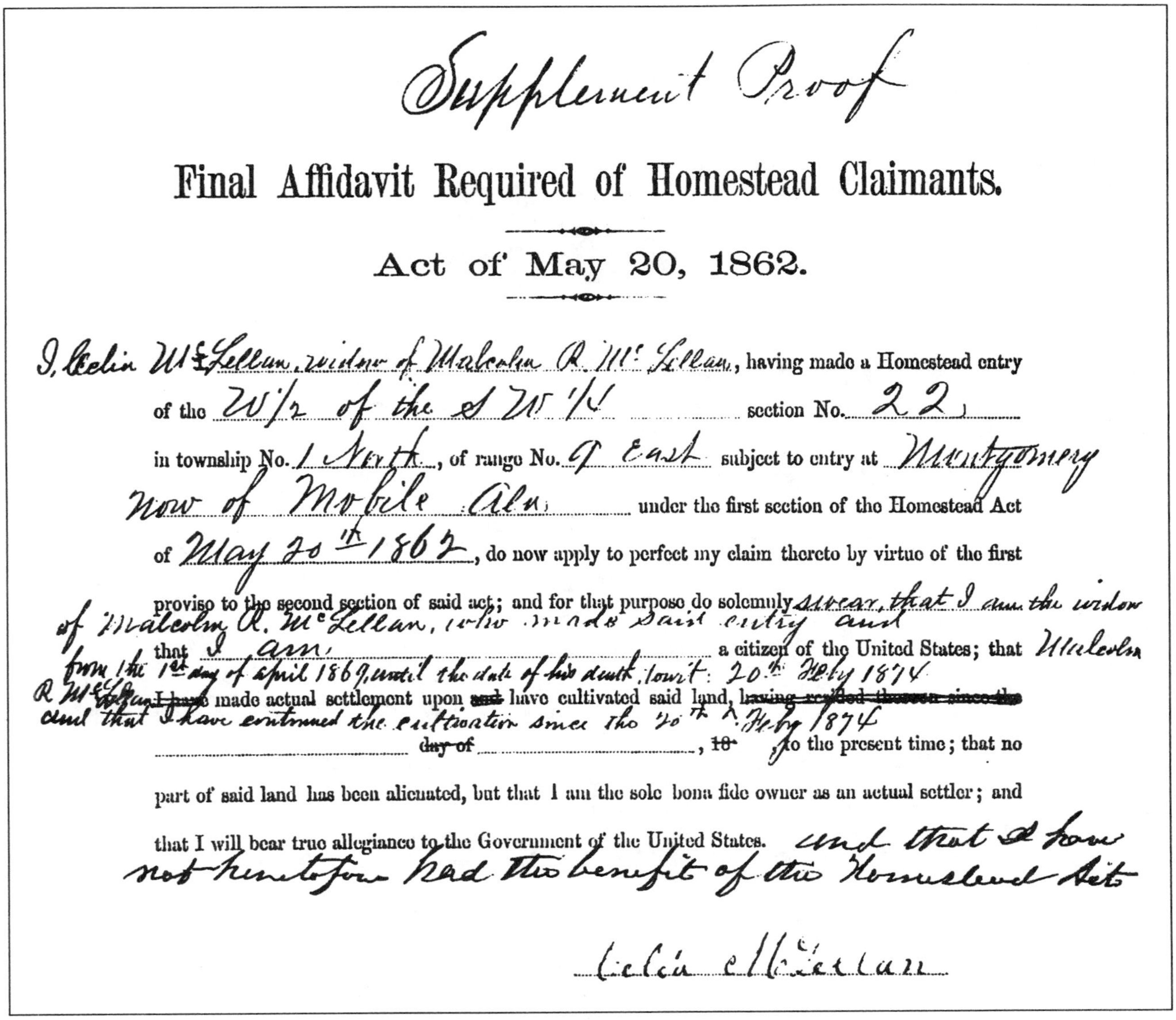

Supplement Proof

Final Affidavit Required of Homestead Claimants.

Act of May 20, 1862.

I, Celia McClellan, widow of Malcolm R. McLellan, having made a Homestead entry of the W ½ of the S W ¼ section No. 22 in township No. 1 North, of range No. 9 East subject to entry at Montgomery now of Mobile Ala, under the first section of the Homestead Act of May 20th 1862, do now apply to perfect my claim thereto by virtue of the first proviso to the second section of said act; and for that purpose do solemnly swear, that I am the widow of Malcolm R. McLellan, who made said entry and that I am, a citizen of the United States; that Malcolm R. McLellan from the 1st day of April 1869, until the date of his death, to wit: 20th Feby 1874 made actual settlement upon and have cultivated said land, having resided thereon since the and that I have continued the cultivation since the 20th A Feby 1874 day of , 18 to the present time; that no part of said land has been alienated, but that I am the sole bona fide owner as an actual settler; and that I will bear true allegiance to the Government of the United States. and that I have not heretofore had the benefit of the Homestead Act

Celia McClellan

Figure 9-24. "Supplement Proof" in a homestead file, proving widow's continuance of a claim by her late husband, whose date of death—"to wit: 20 February 1874"—was also recorded.

zenship. If they were naturalized, or had declared their intention to become a citizen, they also testified as to when and where this process had taken place.

Fees for a full 160 acres totaled $18 by the time the process was complete. Four dollars had to be paid for commission, and $10 was required for entry fees when the entry was first made. The final $4 was due when the final certificate was issued. These fees were for administrative costs, not for the property itself.

A duplicate receipt was issued at the time of initial payment, as proof that the claim had been filed. The person was then required to begin inhabiting the premises within the following six months or risk forfeiture of the claim. During five years of residency, the claimant could only be absent from the property for a total of six months during any given year, and could not maintain an actual residence elsewhere. In 1912, the residency requirement was shortened from five years to three years.

The final application for the certificate of patent had to be made within two years after the completion of the residency requirements, or the claim was no longer valid. If a homesteader died, his widow—or, if already a widower, his heirs—would

No. 27.

TO ALL WHOM IT MAY CONCERN.

know ye, *That* ___John A. Ulumn___ *a*
___Private___ *of Captain* ___John W Fruse___
Company, ___H___ (___,) First___ *Regiment of* ___Maine Cavalry___
VOLUNTEERS, who was enrolled on the ___15___ *day of* ___January___
one thousand eight hundred and ___Sixty four___ *to serve* ___Three___ *years or*
during the war, is hereby **DISCHARGED** *from the service of the United States, this* ___20___
day of ___June___ *186 5 , at* ___near Petersburg Va___ *, by reason of*
___Order from War Dept dated June 5 1865___
(No objection to his being re-enlisted is known to exist.*)
Said ___Pvt John A Ulumn___ *was born in* ___Litchfield___
in the State of ___Maine___ *, is* ___eighteen___ *years of age*
___5___ *feet* ___5½___ *inches high,* ___Light___ *complexion,* ___Blue___ *eyes,*
___Light___ *hair, and by occupation, when enrolled, a* ___Farmer___
Given *at* ___Camp near Petersburg Va___ *, this* ___20th___ *day of*
___June___ *186 5 .*

☞ *This sentence will be erased should there be anything*
in the conduct or physical condition of the soldier }
rendering him unfit for the army.

___John W Fruse___
Printed and For Sale by John F. Sheiry, Claim Blank Printer,
413-415 Ninth Street, N. W., Washington, D. C.
___Capt. Comdy Co A___

___A J Bellows___
___1st Lt. 14th U S Inf.___
___a.c.m.   Dept of Va,___
Commanding the Reg't.

Figure 9-25. A soldier's declaratory statement indicating qualification for a reduction of one and one-half years from the five-year term for a homestead. In this document, from the Harrison Land Office in Arkansas, even the birthplace was recorded.

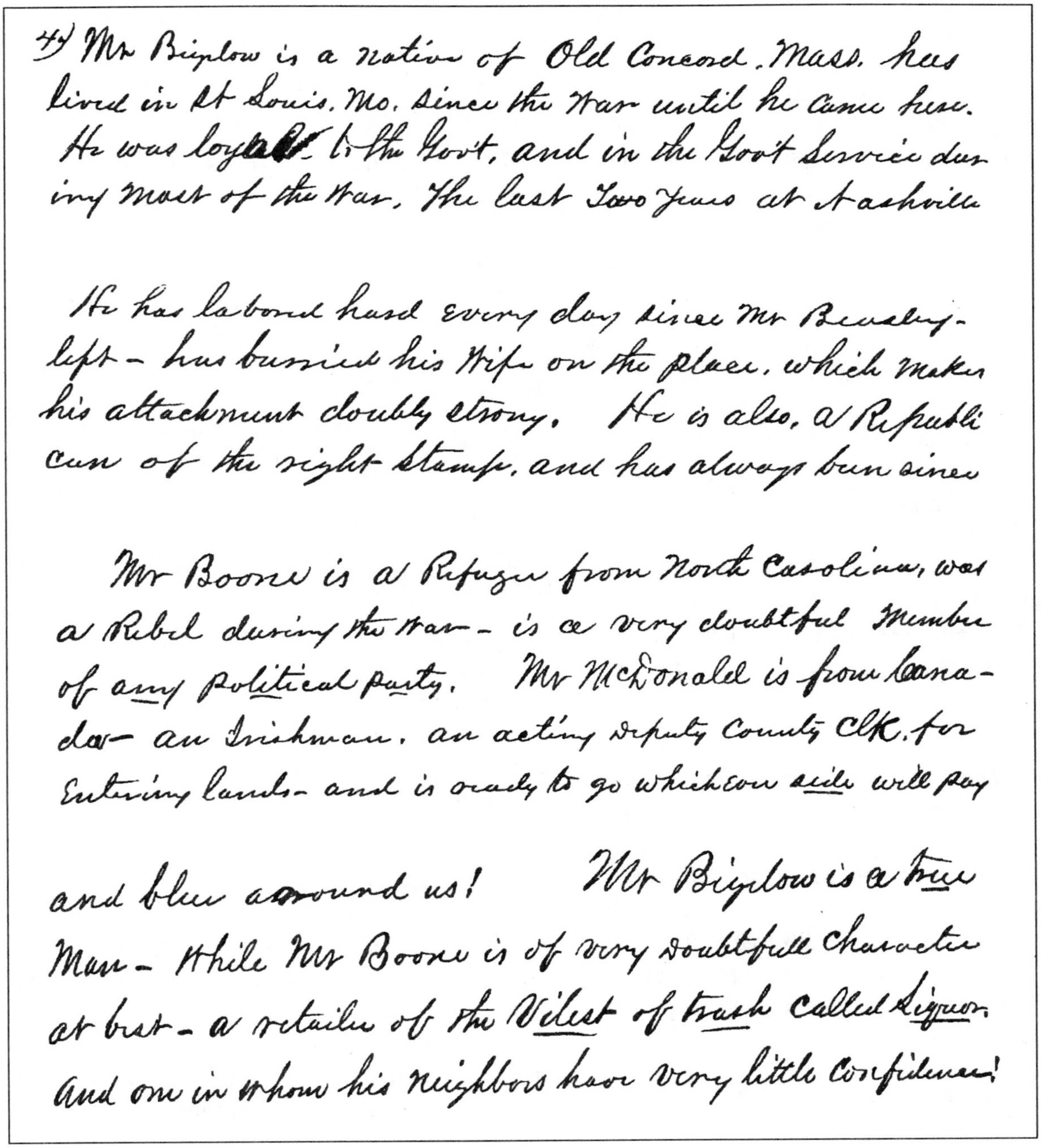
4) Mr Biglow is a native of Old Concord. Mass. has lived in St Louis. Mo. since the War until he came here. He was loyal to the Gov't, and in the Gov't Service during most of the War. The last Two years at Nashville

He has labored hard every day since Mr Beasley left – has buried his Wife on the place. which makes his attachment doubly strong. He is also, a Republican of the right Stamp, and has always been since

Mr Boone is a Refugee from North Carolina, was a Rebel during the War – is a very doubtful Member of any political party. Mr McDonald is from Canada – an Irishman. an acting Deputy County Clk. for Entering lands – and is ready to go whichever side will pay

and blue around us! Mr Biglow is a true Man – While Mr Boone is of very doubtfull Character at best – a retailer of the Vilest of trash called Liquor. And one in whom his neighbors have very little Confidence!

Figure 9-26. Excerpts from testimony given during a homestead claim. The witness was obviously in favor of Mr. Bigelow, whose claim was being contested by Mr. Boone and Mr. McDonald.

then qualify to continue with the claim, having to meet the same requirements. Once the final certificate was received, it entitled the claimant to a patent for his homestead.

A patent could also be obtained by "proving up" for $1.25 an acre before the designated five (or three) years had passed. This took place when the claimant wanted to sell the land and move on, knowing the improvements had made the land worth more on the open market than the required payment to the government. "Proving up" could not take place until at least fourteen months of residence had passed. Unlike bounty lands and registered claims, the sale of a homestead parcel was prohibited and not recognized in court if the patent had not yet been issued. Assignments were not allowed. The property could be mortgaged, but only for purposes of improvement to the property or home.

At the end of the required residency period, the claimant was required to publish an intention to close on the property. This allowed others the opportunity to dispute the validity of the claim before the final certificate was issued. Announcements were made in various ways, including newspapers and miscellaneous postings.

The filing requirements for homesteads make them one of the most detailed records ever created for land. Homestead files contain proof of residence. They also attest to improvements made, describing houses built, wells dug, crops planted, trees cleared, and fences built. At times, they also discuss family members and others who resided on the property. When the claimant passed away, the widow and/or heirs completed the process, recording death dates and relationships. They also contain the testimonies of witnesses and information concerning military service.

The files also provide information on citizenship status. They describe when and where the declaration of intention was filed, as well as any subsequent actions involved in the naturalization process. These records can show the claimant residing in earlier locations—places not previously suspected. This opens up additional sources for research. They can also indicate which port an ancestor arrived at, and occasionally give a precise place of origin.

The final proof documents show name, age, marital status, postal address, descriptions of the house and parcel of land, information on arrival and settlement dates, citizenship status, and crop descriptions. They also include witnesses' testimony.

A completed homestead file will include almost all of the items mentioned here. For those not completed, there may be detailed explanations of why it was rejected or not completed. Death, relocation to another tract, or a disputed claim involving other parties are typical explanations. Disputed claims are often the most informative. When citizenship is questioned, records can be extremely detailed concerning places of origin and times and places of arrival in the United States. A cancelled entry can sometimes be more descriptive than a completed one.

Homestead records are housed at the National Archives in Washington, D.C. They have not been microfilmed, nor are they available through other repositories. Copies can be obtained from the National Archives by following the procedures outlined in "Ordering a Land-Entry Case File" in chapter 10, Strategies for Using Federal Land Records. The original files are organized by land office and final certificate number. Those cancelled are kept separately from those that were accepted. If the tract books indicate a cancelled claim, this needs to be designated when ordering the case file. "Cancelled" applies to claims that were forfeited, rejected, or otherwise not accepted.

For more detailed readings on homesteads, consult F.G. Adams' *Homestead Guide of Kansas and Nebraska,* Benjamin Horace Hibbard's *A History of Public Land Policies,* and Paul W. Gates' *History of Public Land Law.* Additional works are cited at the end of this chapter.

GRADUATION ACT

As it became evident that certain lands were more valuable and more in demand than others, the Graduation Act was adopted. This act did not create new types of records, but rather adjusted the pricing structure of unwanted or less desirable public lands on the cash-entry market.

The Graduation Act originated in 1854. Under this act, lands that had been on the open market for ten years or more were gradually decreased in price. Prices were lowered to $1 per acre for lands on the market for over ten years, 75 cents for lands not claimed after fifteen years, 50 cents for those over twenty years, 25 cents for those lands not purchased after twenty-five years, and a mere 12 ½ cents per acre for lands vacant after thirty years.

There were restrictions, however. Buyers were required to live on or own a farm adjacent to the property purchased, and a limit of 320 acres was set for any one individual. The Graduation Act was repealed by Congress in 1862. Lands under this act are included with the records of cash entries.

TOWNSITE RECORDS

County and town governments were issued preemption rights as early as 1824. Acreages varied, from 160 acres upward. While many towns failed to take advantage of this gratuity, those that did were still subject to normal claim procedures under the Preemption Act, and created no new or different record sources than those already in place. Special tract books do exist for some townsites. They were generally created by state or town officials, and are mostly found in state or local repositories. Some for Nevada and other selected states can be found in the National Archives II, in College Park, Maryland.

MINERAL ENTRIES

Mineral entries, though not as broad in personal content as homestead files, still contain a significant amount of information. Because many of the claims were filed in the nineteenth and twentieth centuries, better assessment was made during the application process. More meticulous procedures meant more records were created. (See figures 9-27 through 9-29.)

The Land Ordinance of 1785 specified that one-third of all mineral lands were to be reserved for the United States. Legislation in 1807, directed mostly at lead deposits in the Indiana Territory and the Great Lakes region, provided for leasing of those mineral lands. The importance of lead was heightened at the time by the impending War of 1812.

Few records were created for mineral lands until after the California gold rush. The gold rush sparked government recognition of various problems. It suddenly became evident that there was no adequate program in place to monitor the booming interest in mining while protecting the rights of legitimate claimants. An Act of 26 July 1866 finally provided the first means for mining claimants to actually receive patent on their mineral lands. Previously, only leases had been given.

Naturalizations or declarations proved for mineral claims are usually the most detailed of any federal land program before 1908. Preprinted forms often define the exact town in addition to the country of origin. Birthplace in the United States was often requested as well.

Two types of mining claims existed—those for lode claims and those for placer claims. Lode claims are those with a lode, ledge, or vein of mineral-bearing rock, such as gold, silver, or tin. These claims were restricted to 1,500 feet along the vein and 300 feet width on each side. This calculated to be a little over ten acres for the maximum claim. Local laws, however, could be more restrictive

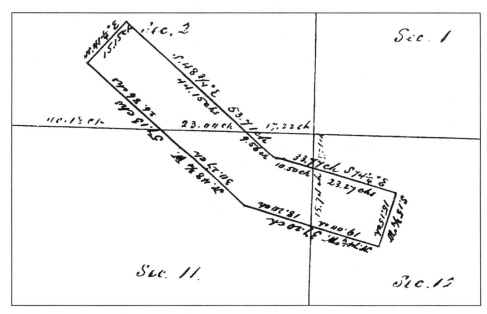

Figure 9-27. A lode claim plat. It shows an indiscriminate survey of lands surveyed by township, range, and section.

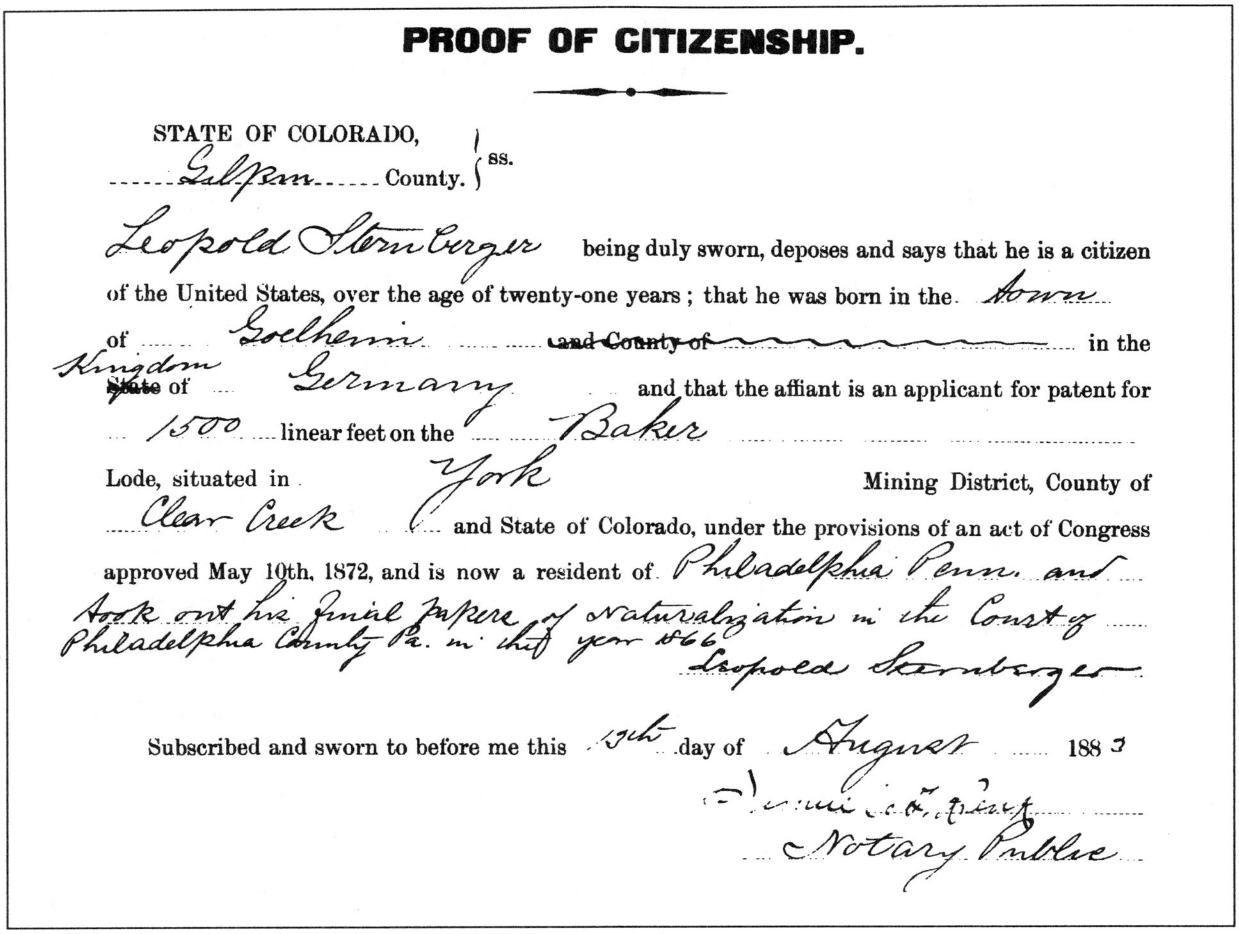

PROOF OF CITIZENSHIP.

STATE OF COLORADO,
............_Gilpin_............ County. } ss.

Leopold Sternberger being duly sworn, deposes and says that he is a citizen of the United States, over the age of twenty-one years ; that he was born in the _Town_ of ...._Goelheim_........... ~~and County of~~ .... in the ~~State~~ _Kingdom_ of ....._Germany_..... and that the affiant is an applicant for patent for ....._1500_.....linear feet on the _Baker_ Lode, situated in _York_ Mining District, County of _Clear Creek_ and State of Colorado, under the provisions of an act of Congress approved May 10th, 1872, and is now a resident of _Philadelphia Penn. and took out his final papers of Naturalization in the Court of Philadelphia County Pa. in this year 1866_

Leopold Sternberger

Subscribed and sworn to before me this _5th_ day of _August_ 188 _3_

....
Notary Public

Figure 9-28. Proof of citizenship from the York Mining District in Colorado, dated 1883. Leopold Sternberger testified in it that he was born in Goelheim, Germany, and had been naturalized in Philadelphia in 1866.

than federal laws, and were usually supported by the federal government.

Placer claims are for minerals not found in veins. They were restricted to twenty acres for individuals, and 160 acres for associations or groups of individuals.

Under the Act of 1866, lode claims were required to have at least $1,000 worth of improvements in order to receive patent. The length of a patented claim could not exceed two hundred feet at that time, and a cost of $5 per acre was assessed for the patent. A second act was passed in 1870, introducing placer claims. Placer claims were charged $2.50 per acre for patent.

Designations of mineral lands were made by the surveyor. If lands were determined to be mineral lands, a mineral claim was necessary. Non-

mineral lands, however, could also be obtained through a mineral entry. The government allowed agricultural development on the surface of mineral lands, as long as mineral resources remained preserved and untapped.

As with most federal land entries, the applicant for mineral lands had to be twenty-one years old and a citizen of the United States, or have declared intention to become such. In the instance of unincorporated associations, each individual involved was required to prove the same. If incorporated, they needed proper registration according to territory, state, or federal governments. Therefore, each individual involved in the corporation may not have proven their declaration or citizenship. For those who did prove citizenship, the forms were often preprinted to include spaces for the exact name of the town as well as the country. This makes mineral claims one of the best land sources for tracing immigrant origins.

Coal lands were separated from other mineral lands beginning in 1864, having their own entries after 1873. Coal claims were a maximum of 160 acres for individuals and 320 acres for associations or groups. When an association of persons, not less than four in total, had expended a minimum of $5,000 in improvements to the coal mining claim, their acreage could be increased to a maximum of 640 acres. Except for this increase, only one coal entry could be entered by any individual or association. The cost was a minimum of $20 per acre for lands closer than fifteen miles to a railroad and a minimum of $15 an acre for those farther away. The increased acreage for coal claims was necessary because larger amounts of coal had to be mined to make a claim financially successful.

The General Mining Law of 1872 further defined mineral lands as containing *any* "valuable minerals." It also extended the length for lode claims to 1,500 feet in length and 600 feet in width. Claims had to be improved by a value of $500 each year, with over $100 worth of assessments performed in order to receive or retain patent.

Although the allowances and restrictions varied through the years, mining claims in the 1800s can be one of the most useful sources for historical and genealogical research. Claims did not always go to patent, but mining records should be explored by anyone suspecting that his or her ancestors were involved in mining occupations.

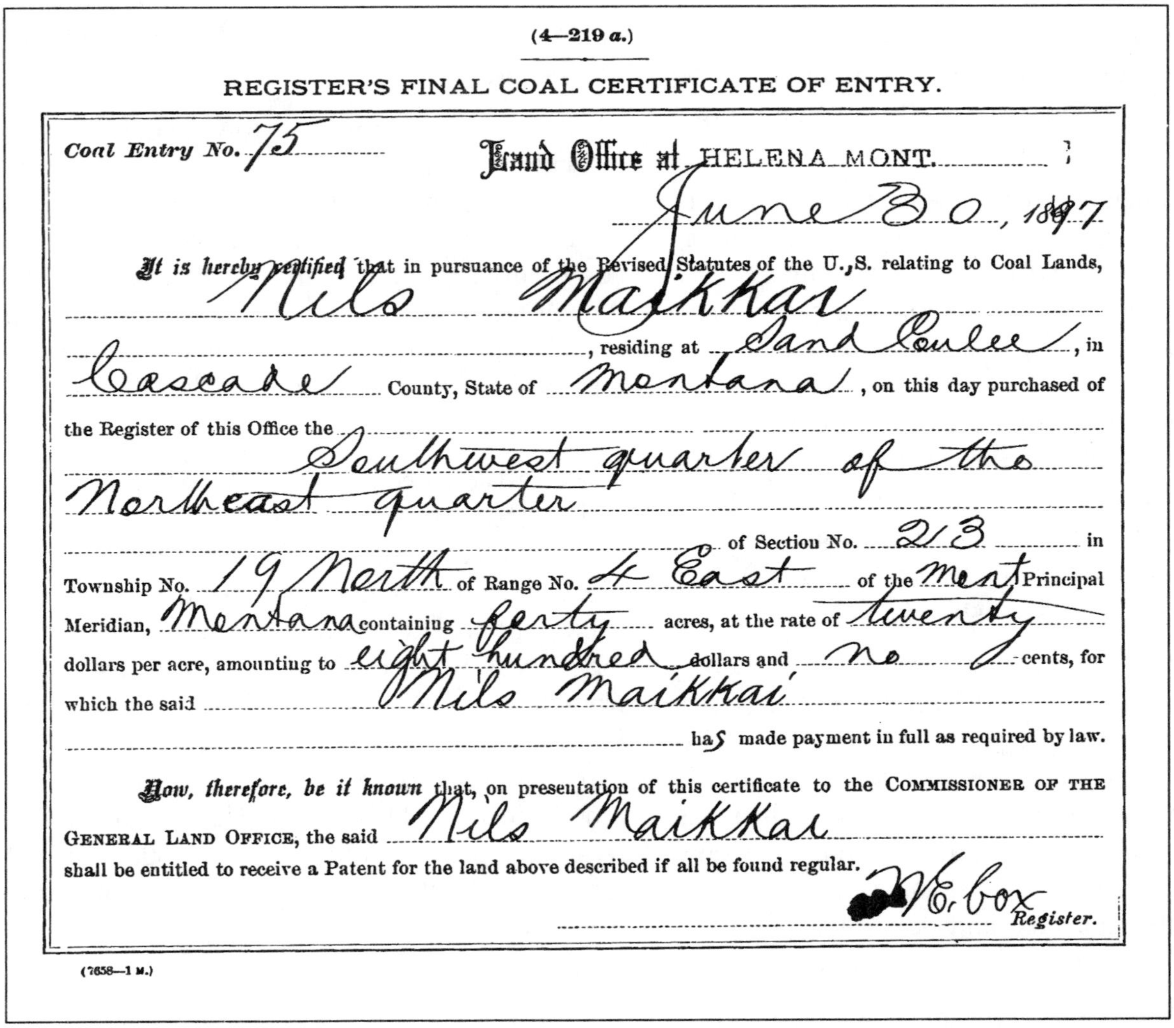
(4—219 *a*.)

REGISTER'S FINAL COAL CERTIFICATE OF ENTRY.

Coal Entry No. 75 — Land Office at HELENA MONT.

June 30, 1897

It is hereby certified that in pursuance of the Revised Statutes of the U. S. relating to Coal Lands, Nils Maikkar, residing at Sand Coulee, in Cascade County, State of Montana, on this day purchased of the Register of this Office the Southwest quarter of the Northeast quarter of Section No. 23 in Township No. 19 North of Range No. 4 East of the Mont Principal Meridian, Montana containing forty acres, at the rate of twenty dollars per acre, amounting to eight hundred dollars and no cents, for which the said Nils Maikkai has made payment in full as required by law.

Now, therefore, be it known that, on presentation of this certificate to the COMMISSIONER OF THE GENERAL LAND OFFICE, the said Nils Maikkal shall be entitled to receive a Patent for the land above described if all be found regular.

W. E. Cox *Register.*

(7658—1 M.)

Figure 9-29. A typical coal mining application.

Mineral claims before 1908 are housed in the National Archives in Washington, D.C. They are not indexed, but can be accessed by using the tract books and ordering the land-entry case file. Currently, mining claims have not been microfilmed. Local land offices sometimes kept copies for reference. The duplicates are then found in the state offices of the Bureau of Land Management, along with most mineral, oil, and gas claims since 1908. Many local offices have mining claim indexes for their states.

TIMBER CULTURE ACT

Enacted in 1873, the Timber Culture Act was similar to the Homestead Law in that only filing fees were required. The purchase of the property was earned rather than bought. Up to 160 acres could be entered if the claimant planted a minimum of forty acres with new trees. The property had to be "naturally" void of any timber at the time of the claim. Unlike homesteading, however, no actual residence was required.

The claimant had to be at least twenty-one years old and prove citizenship or declaration of intention. Trees could be planted no further than twelve feet apart, and had to be kept in a healthy and growing condition for at least ten years in order to receive final patent. An amendment in 1878 required that claimants entering a full 160 acres produce 6,750 "living thrifty" trees by the end of the first eight years. Successful completion of the requirements was more difficult than expected, and of almost 260,000 entries, only twenty-five percent ever received patent.

Many of the records created are similar to homestead records. Property descriptions, testimonies of claimant and witnesses, residences, ages, citizenship information, assessments of the condition of the property and trees, and other miscellaneous papers can all be found in the case files. A widow who continued her late husband's claim provided proof of the marriage and death. On occasion, heirs also followed through on a claim.

Records for claims presented under the Timber Culture Act are housed at the National Archives.

They are filed according to their respective land office, and can be accessed by using the tract books to order the land-entry case file. (To learn more about ordering these case files, refer to chapter 10, Strategies for Federal Land Records.) Timber Culture Act records are not indexed or microfilmed, and are not available at any other repository. Some state offices of the Bureau of Land Management may possess duplicate records.

TIMBER AND STONE LAW

Under the 1878 Timber and Stone Law, all nonmineral surveyed lands on public domain which were considered to have no agricultural value except for timber and stone could be sold at appraised value, but at no less than $2.50 per acre. The law excluded all areas with special restrictions and lands considered to have "valuable mineral" qualities. The stone claims filed were usually for quarry purposes.

Only one entry could be filed under this law, and only for a maximum of 160 acres. The acreage claimed could not combine with existing acreage for a total of more than 320 acres. Associations and corporations were also allotted the same rights, though each person within the organization had to qualify individually. This generated further information about each individual, not just the controlling partner.

Records created by the Timber and Stone Law include testimonies from witnesses and claimants, asking each their age and residence (figure 9-30). The claimant's birthplace is also requested. A note at the bottom of the testimony sheet states, "In case the party is of foreign birth, a certified transcript from the court records of his declaration of intention to become a citizen, or naturalization, or a copy thereof, certified by the officer taking this proof, must be filed with the case." Dates of arrival, lengths of residence, and descriptions of land are all among the papers created by timber and stone lands.

Records for claims presented under the Timber and Stone Law are housed at the National Archives. They are filed according to their respective

TIMBER AND STONE LANDS.

TESTIMONY OF CLAIMANT.

_____ Eliga A. Hixon _____, being called as a witness in support of his application to purchase the __ N.W.¼ of S.W.¼ & S.½ of S.W.¼ __

of Section ____ 4 ____, Township __ 9 South __, Range __ 28 East __,

testifies as follows:

QUESTION 1. What is your age, post-office address, and where do you reside?

ANSWER ___ 48 years. St. Augustine Fla. St. Augustine Fla. ___

QUES. 2. Are you a *native born* citizen of the United States; and if so, in what State or Territory were you born?*

ANS. ___ Yes. Florida ___

QUES. 3. Are you the identical person who applied to purchase this land on the _____ day of _____, 1_____, and made the sworn statement assigned by law before the Register (or Receiver) on that day?

ANS. ___ Yes ___

QUES. 4. Are you acquainted with the land above described by personal inspection of each of its smallest legal subdivisions?

ANS. ___ Yes ___

QUES. 5. When and in what manner was such inspection made?

ANS. ___ June 18" 1906. by going over it. ___

QUES. 6. Is the land occupied; or are there any improvements on it not made for ditch or canal purposes, or which were not made by or do not belong to you?

ANS. ___ No. ___ No. ___

QUES. 7. Is the land fit for cultivation, or would it be fit for cultivation if the timber were removed?

ANS. ___ some parts might be. but very small. No better if timber were removed ___

QUES. 8. What is the situation of this land, and what is the nature of the soil, and what causes render the land unfit for cultivation?

ANS. ___ than deep creek swamp. poor sandy. swampy & sandy soil. ___

Figure 9-30. Typical claimant testimony from the Timber and Stone Law.

land office, and can be accessed by using the tract books to identify an ancestor and order the land-entry case file. They are not indexed or microfilmed, nor are they available through any other repository, except state offices of the Bureau of Land Management that may contain duplicates.

DESERT LAND LAW

The Desert Land Law first appeared in 1875, as special legislation for Lassen County, California, in response to the arid conditions found there on federal lands. This act provided for up to 640 acres at $1.25 per acre, and the land had to be shown irrigable within the first two years. What differentiated this law from many other acts of the same era were the residency requirements and the acreage that was admissible. While a person still had to be twenty-one years old and at least a declared citizen of the United States, he or she did not have to reside on the property being claimed.

The official Desert Land Act itself (not the Desert Land Law) was enacted on 3 March 1877. This official act added another year for reclamation to the earlier Desert Land Law. Instead of two years for irrigation production, three were allowed beyond the year of the original claim. When filing, a minimum of 25 cents per acre was required. Only after reclamation had been proven and one-eighth of the claim had been cultivated could an additional one dollar per acre be remitted to receive patent. Additional legislation in 1891 required an annual accounting for reclamation efforts of at least one dollar per acre.

The Act of 30 August 1890 had further affected the Desert Land Act by placing a ceiling on all federal land purchases at 320 acres. Coal entries and donation lands were the only other acts which allowed more than 320 acres. Any new entries for any act following that date in 1890 were also restricted to the lesser amount of 320 acres.

This program was generally considered a failure. Beginning with the Carey Act in 1894, reclamation responsibilities began to be placed in the hands of the states. By 1902, the federal treasury began to provide funds for the development of arid or semi-arid lands throughout the United States.

The Desert Land Law created a mixture of records, similar to the Homestead Act and the Timber and Stone Law. Included are proof of citizenship, descriptions of property and conditions thereon, proof of cultivation efforts and irrigation progress, fulfillment of financial requirements, and assessment of the property rated as unfit for cultivation. All of these records can help provide missing clues about the individuals involved.

Records for claims presented under the Desert Land Law are housed at the National Archives. They are filed according to their respective land office, and can be accessed by using tract books to

identify an ancestor's involvement, then ordering the land-entry case file. They have not been microfilmed and are not available through any other repository, except state offices of the Bureau of Land Management, which may contain duplicates of the original claims.

AGRICULTURAL COLLEGE SCRIP

Another act through which individuals could purchase federal lands was an act providing lands for "Colleges for Agricultural and Mechanic Arts." The Morrill Act of 1862 provided 30,000 acres per senator or representative to each state in the Union. The land was used to finance the construction of agricultural and mechanical arts colleges. Public-land states chose their own acreage from within the boundaries of their own states. State-land states, and public-land states with insufficient acreage remaining, were issued scrip for equivalent lands in other public-land states. The revenues generated went to the state which issued the scrip, helping to fund the building of the designated colleges.

Issued in increments of 160 acres, agricultural college scrip was similar to scrip for military bounty lands. It could be used in place of any other act involving federal land purchases, except for mineral lands or homesteads; thus, the records take on the characteristics of the acts under which the scrip was redeemed. Some were used for preemption purposes, some for cash entries, etc. Receipts, applications, citizenship information, claimant's testimony, testimonies from witnesses, and much more can also be found.

Records for the claims under the Agricultural College Scrip Act are located in the National Archives. They are separated from the land office records, creating a collection of their own. Scrip was issued to the following states, with the number of claims listed in parentheses:

Alabama (1,500)	North Carolina (1,688)
Arkansas (937)	New Jersey (1,312)
Connecticut (1,125)	New Hampshire (937)

Delaware (563)   New York (6,187)

Florida (562)   Ohio (3,938)

Georgia (1,687)   Pennsylvania (4,875)

Illinois (3,000)   Rhode Island (750)

Indiana (2,438)   South Carolina (1,125)

Kentucky (2,062)   Tennessee (1,875)

Louisiana (1,312)   Texas (1,125)

Maine (1,312)   Vermont (937)

Maryland (1,311)   Virginia (1,875)

Massachusetts (2,250)   West Virginia (937)

Mississippi (1,312)

Knowledge of a person's involvement with agricultural scrip can generally be obtained only through the use of tract books for the area in which that person lived. They are filed numerically, and there is no other index currently available. They have not been microfilmed, and are housed only at the National Archives. (See figure 9-31.)

RAILROAD GRANTS

Railroad grants are one of the most well-known forms of land disbursement in history, yet provide the fewest clues for researchers. Lands were granted to various railroad companies by the U.S. government as a form of monetary contribution to the building and expansion of the American West. Since cash was not readily available at the time, land was donated to the companies, to be sold to assist in the necessary financing of railroad construction.

As early as 1850, lands were donated for railroad development. By 1871, however, it was apparent that railroads were not using the lands for financing. Rather, they were holding onto the lands as a corporate investment, creating a monopoly unmatched for over a century. The railroads had been required to dispose of their lands within the

first three years, at $1.25 per acre. Through mortgaging and other loopholes, they were able to skirt these requirements. Congress immediately suspended all future railroad grants and began assessing possible forfeitures. One railroad, the Oregon and California, eventually forfeited more than 2 million acres to the government after failing to act on lands they had been granted.

Though they played a fascinating role in the economic and political history of America, railroad grants created very few records about individuals. The railroads were formed as corporations in order to receive their grants. Their own disbursement, then, was through the individual, or private sector, of land transactions. By selling the land, deeds were created just as if they were from person to person, not affecting the federal land system or generating any additional records after being granted to the railroad. (See section 4 for further information regarding individual lands.)

DONATION LANDS

Donation lands affected Florida, the Oregon and Washington Territories, and New Mexico. Lands were given to settlers in return for settlement, cultivation, and fortification commitments. Each claimant also generated a land-entry case file, which will often contain the most detailed and specific records ever produced by the federal land system.

Donation lands were granted in Florida under the Armed Occupation Act. Designed to populate and fortify the eastern peninsula against Indian attacks, the claimants were required simply to maintain constant residence, begin cultivation, and be prepared to defend the area against unwanted harassment. Organized according to land office, the Armed Occupation Act records usually include the following information:

- Application for a permit to settle

- Various affidavits

- Final certificates

- Notes from the land agent

- Final proofs of settlement and cultivation

Land Scrip No. *723*   for "One Quarter Section."

Colleges for Agriculture and Mechanic Arts.

ACT OF CONGRESS, JULY 2, 1862

For *State of New Jersey*

Whereas, in pursuance of the Act of Congress approved July 2, 1862, entitled "An act donating Public Lands to the several States and Territories which may provide Colleges for the benefit of Agriculture and the Mechanic Arts." The State of *New Jersey* has accepted the Grant provided by the said act, and, under the same, has consequently a legal claim to *Two Hundred and Ten Thousand* acres, not locatable by the State itself, but liable to transfer, and may be located by the Assignees of said STATE, according to assignment, attested by two witnesses, in the form on the back of this instrument; the locations by Assignees in satisfaction of the claim above mentioned, to be made in virtue of a regular Series of Scrip, a part of which is this:

Land Scrip No. *723* for "One Quarter Section."

Therefore be it known, That this SCRIP, when duly assigned and attested by two witnesses, under such authority of the said State as the act of the Legislature thereof may designate, may be surrendered at any Land Office of the UNITED STATES in satisfaction of a location of "One Quarter" of a Section" or for any quantity in one legal sub-division less than "One Quarter" Section," where such location is taken in full for "One Quarter" Section"—the location to be restricted to vacant public lands subject to entry at private sale at $1.25 per acre, MINERAL LANDS EXCLUDED; and whilst the aggregate location of all the claims under the said act may be taken in any of the TERRITORIES without limitation as to the quantity located in any one of them, yet, in virtue of express limitation in the Statute, "not more than One Million Acres" of the total aggregate Scrip-issue under said act can be located within the limits "of any one of the States."

Given under my hand and seal of the Department of the Interior on the *Twenty second* day of *July* A. D. *1863*, and of the Independence of the United States the *Eighty eighth*.

M Edmunds
Commissioner of the General Land Office.

W. T. Otto
Acty, Secretary of the Interior.

Recorded, Vol. 75 Page 79.

Figure 9-31. Though issued for New Jersey, this agricultural college scrip could be redeemed in almost any federal-land state. The sale would then be credited to New Jersey.

- Citizenship information

- Powers of attorney

(The permit shows the name of the applicant, marital status, date of initial residency, and a description of the property.)

The original records for the Armed Occupation Act are housed at the National Archives. They are organized by their respective land office, have not yet been microfilmed, and are not available through any other repository.

The lands donated in the Oregon and Washington Territories were simply termed the "donation lands." They were designed to encourage stable settlement and fortification against the British, with whom an agreement had been reached for possession of that territory in 1846. Originating with the Act of 27 September 1850, free lands were provided to all white or mixed-blood settlers who arrived in the Oregon Territory before 1 December 1855. The main requirements were four years of residence and cultivation, setting the stage for eventual homestead acts.

There were two separate provisions for donation lands: one for those who had arrived before 1 December 1850, and a second for those who arrived between 1 December 1850 and 1 December 1853. An act in 1853 extended the latter provision's arrival time to 1 December 1855. Depending on the family status (i.e., married, widowed, orphaned, or single) and the date of arrival, applicants were given up to 640 acres of land. Thus, marriage, death, and citizenship information can often be found in the case files for donation lands (figure 9-32). This is the only source through which a man could claim additional acreage if he were married.

The Donation Land Act placed limits on the date of arrival, but not on the date of application. For example, if a person arrived in the territory in 1854, at the age of only three years, he might apply for donation lands in 1872 when turning twenty-one. He might also have waited until age

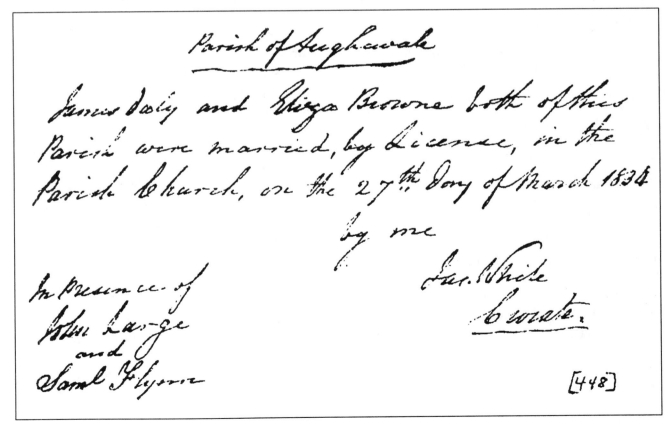

Figure 9-32. From the Oregon Donation Land Claim papers, a marriage record sent from Ireland to prove the marital status of James Daly and Eliza Browne.

thirty-five to apply, as long as he had originally arrived within the specified time period. Uniquely, the first provision only required the applicant to be eighteen years of age, a first in legislative acts for federal lands. The second provision reverted to the customary age of twenty-one.

Donation lands in the Oregon and Washington Territories involved people from all over the world. Records include the following:

- Name of the applicant
- Birth year or age
- Birthplace (usually county and state/country)
- Marriage date and place
- Given name of wife
- Date of arrival in the territory
- Date and court of naturalization
- Record of land improvements

As the state of Washington was separated in 1853, the same legislation continued to govern the records created there.

The original records for the donation lands in Oregon and Washington are housed at the National Archives. They have also been microfilmed, filling 108 rolls. Microfilm versions are available at:

- The National Archives
- The Family History Library
- The Oregon State Archives
- The National Archives branch in Seattle
- Various major university libraries

All Oregon and Washington donation lands have been abstracted and indexed by the Bureau of Land Management. The abstracts contain the dates of claims, descriptions of property, and note pertinent genealogical information such as names, birth years, and birthplaces. These abstracts have been microfilmed and are available through the repositories listed above.

The Oregon donation lands have also been abstracted and indexed by the Oregon State Archives and published by the Genealogical Forum of Oregon. The publication includes five volumes titled *Genealogical Material in Oregon Donation Land Claims.* Indexing these five volumes is a two-volume set titled *Index of Oregon Donation Land Claims.* Also of value is the *Washington Territory Donation Land Claims.* These three publications will identify the certificate number and the land office where the claim was filed. This information will then assist in locating the original papers on microfilm. Most of the valuable information is already contained in the abstracts, however.

Donation lands in New Mexico were similar to the Oregon and Washington Territories. However, only 160 acres could be received in New Mexico. Donation lands were given to two groups of settlers. The first group included those residing in the territory prior to 1 January 1853 who were still residing there in July of 1854, when the legislation was passed. The second group encompassed those moving into the territory between 1 January 1853 and 1 January 1858. Cultivation and residence were required for a minimum of four years, and claims could only take place on surveyed land. The residence and cultivation requirement could have been completed before legislation was introduced, as long as the requirements were met. However, claimants of Spanish or Mexican land grants could not file for donation claims. Also, donation land recipients could not file for preemption or homestead claims. Donation land records for New Mexico are housed at the Bureau of Land Management in Santa Fe. They are also available at the University of New Mexico in Albuquerque.

CONGRESSIONAL COLLECTIONS

Records of federal land disbursement were also created by non-land-oriented government entities. Claims were presented as a form of appeal to the Senate or House of Representatives, generating documents that can reveal additional clues about one's ancestry.

Certainly the most well known of these collections is the *American State Papers.* Divided into ten different classes, the most voluminous and informative is class 8, Public Lands. This class consists of eight volumes and ranges in dates from 1789 to 1837. Within its pages are found the minutes of various congressional sessions during that era, detailing claims presented for every type of land issue imaginable. (Also see page 135.)

Private land claims and preemptions occupy much of the agenda found in the *American State Papers,* with references to many unsuccessful claimants which will not be found elsewhere. References are also made to the refugees from Canada and Nova Scotia, military bounty lands, and a fragment of Indian claims. The *American State Papers* also include the following:

- Petitions of inhabitants

- Discussions of litigation surrounding the validity of claims

- Documentation of arrivals into geographic areas

- Discussions of boundary disputes

- Land cessions and annexations

- Discussions of neighbors and associates

- More detailed testimonies than land-entry case files

This was a step beyond the normal procedures for many land acts, and the information can be rich in both historical and genealogical content. These books also include information on some land issues for state-land states.

The *American State Papers,* published by Gales and Seaton, can be found at most state libraries

---

114   *T E R R I T O R I A L   P A P E R S*

your memorialists further pray, that no innovation be made in the judicial system which might compel the attendance of . the citizens of this country to the discussion of claims existing within the Territory before·any tribunal beyond its limits—For it must be self evident to the honorable Congress, that to drag the planters of this country to a distance of 2000 miles from their homes, there to await the decision of their fate, would be to them nothing less than deplorable ruin—and the certain consequence of such a measure united to the second grade of government would be rapid depopulation and ruin of this weak and defenceless Territory.

And your memorialists, as in duty bound, &c.

Dated in the Missisippi Territory, *December 6th,* A. D. 1800.

Eunice McIntosh	John Ellis
William McIntosh	Elias Fisher
James McIntosh	T. Hutchins
William Williams	Cha^a Miller
Israel Leonard	John Callahan
Ithamar Andrews	Joseph W A Lloyd
John Hollands	James Harwick
Thos Burling	Richd Butler
Benjⁿ Farrar	

[Section 2 of Subscribers to Memorial [61]]

William Conner	Justus Andrews
Jno Collins	Giles Andrews
Isaac Gaillard	Ithamar Andrews
Abram Ellis	William Robertson
Benj^a Kilgore	James Nicholson
Nathan Dix	James Cook

[Section 3 of Subscribers to Memorial]

Wm Thomas	[H. Ferguson [62]]
Hezekiah Brigg	Robt. Currie
Stephen Jett	John Whitten
Wm F. Burch	[Richard Farrar [62]]
Thomas Spain	Mordecai Throckmorton
Wm Newman	Wm Miller
Robt Throckmorton	

Figure 9-33. Petitioners listed in the Territorial Papers.

---

and universities, and is available at the National Archives and the Family History Library. It is also available on microfilm through the latter two repositories. Each volume is separately indexed, though a more complete index is found in *Grassroots of America,* by Phillip W. McMullin.

The *Territorial Papers* are similar to the *American State Papers,* containing minutes of the territorial matters presented before Congress. The records contain numerous petitions for a variety of issues (figure 9-33). The petitions often include the names of the earliest land holders. They document individuals on federal lands before a designated office was established to record such arrangements. At times, the petitions provide detailed descriptions of the migrations of an entire group of individuals.

The *Territorial Papers* encompass numerous volumes, organized by geographic region. Some volumes contain records from more than one region. They are available at most state libraries and universities, as well as the Family History Library and the National Archives.

TOWNSHIP PLATS

Township plats are organized according to meridian rather than the local land office. They will generally show all of the lands within the township, and may have more than one plat for each. The duplicate copies will often exclude railroad purchases, Indian lands, school lands, and other extras. The shapes of the individual boundaries are also visible, usually including swamps, rivers, and mountains. (See figure 9-34.)

Township plats are less informative than tract books, although they are useful in unique ways. By showing an entire township on a single page, as well as a variety of land subdivisions, they are easier to use when searching a broad and general area for an ancestor. Many times the owner's name will be listed. Although some do not include this information, most strategies involving township plats depend on these names being shown for each section.

Multiple copies of the plats were made, and while one copy was sent to the General Land Office, the others were used by the local land office and surveyors. Though the applicant's name is not found on all copies, it should almost always be found on the copy used by the local land office for reference. Some copies only list the final certificate number and the acreage. Most township plat maps will not give the date of purchase, the land office, or other information necessary for ordering the land-entry case files. That information will usually need to be found in the tract books.

Township plats are available for many of the federal-land states, though the custody of these records is mixed. Three copies were originally produced for each plat. One was the headquarters' copy, sent to the General Land Office; one was for the local land office; and one was for reference by the state or territorial government. The headquarters' copy and the local land office copies have been integrated for states whose records are housed at the National Archives. These states are:

Alabama	Missouri
Illinois	Ohio
Indiana	Oklahoma
Iowa	Oregon
Kansas	Washington
Mississippi	Wisconsin

The records for these states have been microfilmed. They are available through the National Archives, the Family History Library, and most state archives for the states included. The Bureau of Land Management office for each state also will usually have a copy of these films. The originals are housed at the National Archives II in College Park, Maryland. This is where the National Archives maintains most cartographic records.

Plats not in possession of the National Archives are housed at the Bureau of Land Management-Eastern States Office in Alexandria, Virginia. They have not been microfilmed, but copies can be requested for a modest fee. The Bureau of Land Management also possesses duplicate township plat books for many of the states housed at the National Archives. The plat maps included at the Bureau of Land Management-Eastern States Office are for the following states:

Alabama	Montana
Alaska	Nebraska
Arizona	Nevada
Arkansas	New Mexico
California	North Dakota
Colorado	Oklahoma
Florida	Oregon

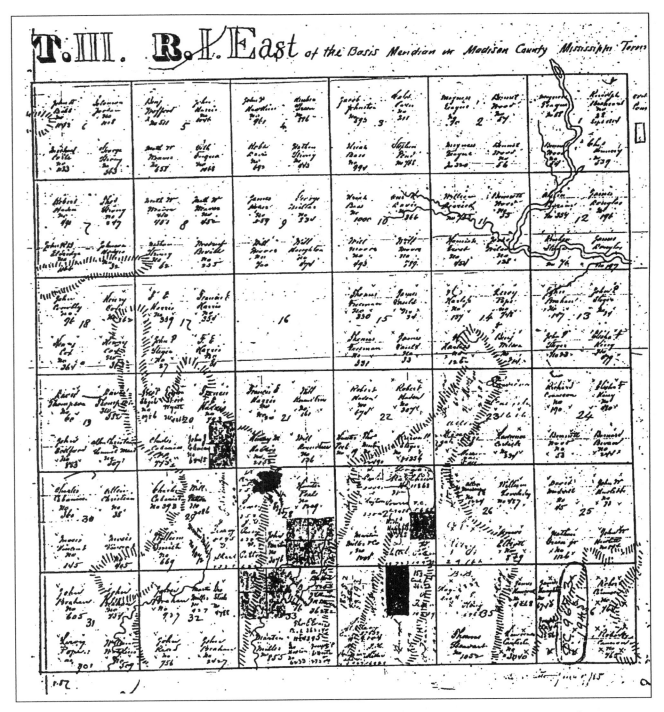

Figure 9-34. A township plat map showing names and final certificate numbers for each quarter-section.

Idaho	South Dakota
Louisiana	Utah
Michigan	Washington
Minnesota	Wisconsin
Mississippi	Wyoming

Many of the western states' plats have been reproduced on microfiche by the Bureau of Land Management. Contact the Bureau of Land Management in Denver for availability. Most individual states also have one of the three original copies. They are usually kept at a designated state land agency or state archive. Reproductions and originals can be found at the National Archives branches in Denver, San Francisco, and Seattle. Because township plats are organized by meridian, the tract book guide in appendix A will greatly facilitate research in these records.

There are a variety of plats in addition to township plats. Separate plats exist for mineral claims, townsites, and private land claim surveys. Townsite plats are available for selected states and towns at the National Archives. Many are for the post-1908 era, though they do include some scattered maps as early as 1817. Many of these towns are found in the *List of Townsite Plats of Towns and Cities Throughout the Public Domain, Mainly West of the Mississippi River, 1825–1935*. This list, prepared by the BLM, is housed at the National Archives II.

Private land claims plats for the following states are housed at the National Archives:

Arizona	Illinois
California	Louisiana
Colorado	Missouri
Florida	New Mexico

Mineral plats are also available there for the following states:

Alabama	Nevada
Alaska	New Mexico
Arizona	Oregon
Arkansas	South Dakota
California	Utah
Colorado	Washington
Idaho	Wyoming
Montana	

AMNESTY PAPERS

Amnesty papers, more properly titled *Case Files of Applications from Former Confederates for Presidential Pardons, 1865–1867,* are a little-used source for land and property research. At the conclusion of the Civil War, amnesty was granted to most of the southern supporters, although certain classes of individuals were excluded. Among these excluded classes were people who performed acts of treason or rebellion, and "voluntary participants in the rebellion who had real property valued at more than $20,000." (See figure 9-35.)

All who were excluded from the initial pardon were required to make special application directly to the President of the United States. Presidents in office during this time were Abraham Lincoln and Andrew Johnson. Almost 14,000 applications were received. Approximately half of them were related to the property clause described above.

If an ancestor had significant property holdings before the Civil War, and his or her origins are unknown or questioned, amnesty papers should be seriously consulted. Many applicants were successful merchants who helped in ways other than through direct military service. Hence, pensions and service records may not have been created for them. Their applications usually included the following information:

• Description of places of origin

• Age

• Date of arrival at current residence

• Detailed reasons for assistance to the Confederacy (many state that they were forced to contribute)

Amnesty papers have been microfilmed by the National Archives, where the original records are also housed. They are also available at the Family History Library, and at branch facilities of both repositories. They are organized into the following groups:

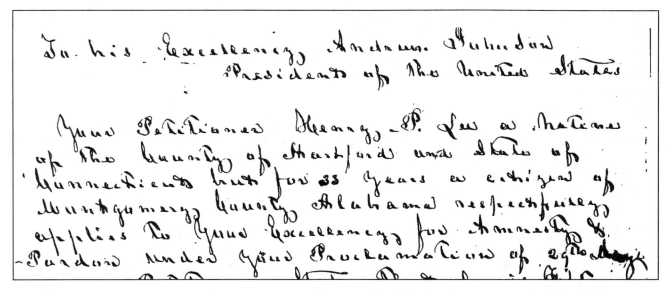

Figure 9-35. From the Amnesty Papers of Alabama, this document concerns Henry P. Lee, a native of Hartford, Connecticut.

Group One

Alabama	Missouri
Arkansas	North Carolina
Florida	South Carolina
Georgia	Tennessee
Kentucky	Texas
Louisiana	Virginia
Maryland	West Virginia
Mississippi	

Group Two

California	Michigan
Delaware	Nebraska
District of Columbia	New Jersey
Illinois	New Mexico Territory
Indiana	New York
Iowa	Ohio
Kansas	Pennsylvania
Massachusetts	Rhode Island

Group Three

Applications by persons who designated no state or territory.

Group one occupies seventy-two rolls of microfilm, while groups two and three are combined on one roll. The areas indicate the residence at the time the application was made.

BUREAU OF LAND MANAGEMENT

The Bureau of Land Management has been the governing agency for federal land issues since the early 1800s. Originally founded in 1812, it was first called the General Land Office. It was a division of the treasury until 1849, when it became part of the Department of the Interior. Though many of the earliest records have been transferred from its jurisdiction, it continues to be one of the most active instigators of preservation and organization among federal land records. Federal lands are no longer available in the continental United States except under certain mining laws and exchange programs. The BLM's role is now primarily to oversee 270 million acres of public land and more than 570 million acres of federally owned mineral lands. It preserves, protects, and environmentally manages wilderness areas and endangered archaeological sites.

The Bureau of Land Management-Eastern States Office supervises federal-land states east of the Mississippi River and the first tier of states west of that same river. The remaining states are under the jurisdiction of their own state bureaus, except for a few that share a common office.

Montana, North Dakota, and South Dakota are grouped together and are administered from the main office in Montana. New Mexico, Kansas, and Oklahoma are governed from New Mexico. Oregon and Washington are directed from Oregon. Wyoming and Nebraska are governed from Wyoming. All other states have their own offices. Records kept by the Bureau of Land Management for pre-1908 claims include field notes, survey plats, tract books, and patents.

Patents to federal lands for the entire United States are still housed with the Bureau of Land Management. While the patent is not as informative as the case file, there are definite advantages to requesting a copy from the appropriate office. Many states have patent indexes for lands within their domain. These indexes allow easy access to the actual patent, which contains all of the information necessary to order the land-entry case file. (For further information about ordering a land-entry case file, see chapter 10, Strategies for Federal Land Records.)

The Bureau of Land Management is in the process of producing one of the most beneficial indexes ever created for federal lands. The General Land Office Automated Retrieval System, also called "GLOARS," represents the culmination of both dedicated service and advancing technology spanning over a decade. It uses optical discs to store information about each and every patent available at the Eastern States Office.

Patents are first optically scanned. When the document is displayed on the computer screen, specific information is extracted and entered into a database for indexing. The indexed information is directly linked to the image of the patent. After being checked for accuracy, the information is stored on optical discs. Using GLOARS, a name can then be entered and all pertinent information

can be retrieved. In addition, an image of the patent can be viewed and printed for further reference. It can also be printed on parchment paper, becoming an heirloom.

GLOARS will eventually cover every state under the jurisdiction of the Bureau of Land Management-Eastern States Office. Its first objective is to include all homesteads and cash entries prior to 1908. Iowa, Indiana, and Illinois are the last states to be completed. The indexing allows a state-by-state search, or a search of the entire region. Searches also can be made by name, document number, land office, property description, county, document type, or any combination thereof. The information displayed contains everything needed to order the land-entry case file.

Computer users can log into this system from their home or work by establishing an account with the Eastern States Office. The system can then be searched much the same as if on location. In addition, if an entry is found, a copy can be sent directly to the user's fax machine. If the user does not have a fax machine, a copy can be ordered while online and sent to the user the following business day. There are fees involved, although there is a practice area that is free of charge. Fees include connect time and printing or output charges. For more information about GLOARS, contact the Bureau of Land Management-Eastern States Office.

GLOARS is also in the process of producing CD-ROMs for each of the completed states. These CDs can be purchased through the Government Printing Office and through various private vendors. Each state is on a separate CD, and includes only the index portion of GLOARS. This allows individuals access to the indexed information without accruing online charges. Once the information has been sorted and the appropriate entry has been found, online time is then reduced to simply ordering the patent.

For a list of BLM offices and addresses, see "Repositories," below. Statewide or local land office patent indexes can eliminate a tremendous amount of research in the tract books. However, it is important to realize that patent indexes also neglect to identify millions of unsuccessful applicants who did not complete the patent process. For each of these applicants, there was still a case file created. All post-1908 transactions are indexed for every federal-land state. The information can be accessed through the applicable bureau overseeing each particular state.

The Bureau of Land Management also assists with present-day mineral and oil leases. The bureau serves the community in a variety of ways, including public recreation and wilderness areas. Like the National Archives and the Family History Library, it is a major source of information concerning land and property records which may have involved our ancestors.

REPOSITORIES

General

Bureau of Land Management
Eastern States Office
7450 Boston Boulevard
Springfield, VA 22153

Government Printing Office
Superintendent of Documents
P.O. Box 371954
Pittsburgh, PA 15250-7954

National Archives and Records Administration
Textual Reference Branch (NNR1)
Washington, D.C. 20408

National Archives and Records Administration
Cartographic Division (NNR2)
8601 Adelphi Road
College Park, MD 20740-6001

National Archives, New England Region
380 Trapelo Road
Waltham, MA 02154
(Serves Connecticut, Maine, Massachusetts, New Hampshire, Rhode Island, and Vermont.)

National Archives, Northeast Region
Bldg. 22, Military Ocean Terminal
Bayonne, NJ 07002-5388
(Serves New Jersey, New York, Puerto Rico, and the Virgin Islands.)

National Archives, Mid-Atlantic Region
9th and Market Streets, Room 1350
Philadelphia, PA 19107
(Serves Pennsylvania, Delaware, Maryland, Virginia, and West Virginia.)

National Archives, Southeast Region
1557 St. Joseph Avenue
East Point, GA 30344
(Serves North Carolina, South Carolina, Florida, Georgia, Alabama, Mississippi, Tennessee, and Kentucky.)

National Archives, Great Lakes Region
7358 South Pulaski Road
Chicago, IL 60629
(Serves Illinois, Indiana, Ohio, Michigan, Minnesota, and Wisconsin.)

National Archives, Central Plains Region
2312 East Bannister Road
Kansas City, MO 64131
(Serves Iowa, Nebraska, Kansas, and Missouri.)

National Archives, Southwest Region
501 West Felix Street
P.O. Box 6216
Fort Worth, TX 76115
(Serves Arkansas, Louisiana, Texas, Oklahoma, and New Mexico.)

National Archives, Rocky Mountain Region
Bldg. 48, Denver Federal Center
P.O. Box 25307
Denver, CO 80225
(Serves North Dakota, South Dakota, Montana, Wyoming, Colorado, and Utah.)

National Archives, Pacific Southwest Region
24000 Avila Road
P.O. Box 6719
Laguna Niguel, CA 92677-6719
(Serves Arizona; southern California counties of Imperial, Inyo, Kern, Los Angeles, Orange, Riverside, San Bernardino, San Diego, San Luis

Obispo, Santa Barbara, and Ventura; and Clark County, Nevada.)

National Archives, Pacific Sierra Region
1000 Commodore Drive
San Bruno, CA 94066
(Serves California counties not listed above, Nevada [except Clark County], Hawaii, and the Pacific Ocean area.)

National Archives, Pacific Northwest Region
6125 Sand Point Way, NE
Seattle, WA 98115
(Serves Idaho, Washington, and Oregon.)

Alabama

Alabama Department of Archives and History
624 Washington Street
Montgomery, AL 36130

University of Alabama Library
Special Collections
P.O. Box 870266
Tuscaloosa, AL 35487-0266

Alaska

Bureau of Land Management
Alaska State Office
222 W. 7th Avenue, No. 13
Anchorage, AK 99513

Alaska State Archives and Record
Management Services
141 Willoughby Avenue
Juneau, AK 99801-1720

Alaska Historical Society
524 West 4th Avenue, Suite 208
Anchorage, AK 99501

Arizona

Bureau of Land Management
Arizona State Office
3707 North 7th Street
Phoenix, AZ 85011

Arizona Historical Society
949 E. Second Street
Tucson, AZ 85719

Arizona Department of Library and Archives
1700 West Washington
Phoenix, AZ 85007

Arkansas

Arkansas State Land Commission
State Capitol
Little Rock, AR 72206

Arkansas History Commission
One Capitol Mall
Little Rock, AR 72201

California

Bureau of Land Management
California State Office
2800 Cottage Way, E-2841
Sacramento, CA 95825

California State Archives
Office of Secretary of State
1020 O Street
Room 130
Sacramento, CA 95814

University of California-Berkeley
Bancroft Library
Berkeley, CA 94720

Colorado

Bureau of Land Management
Colorado State Office
2850 Youngfield Street
Lakewood, CO 80215

Colorado State Archives
1313 Sherman Street
Denver, CO 80203

Denver Public Library
Social Sciences and Genealogy Department
1357 Broadway
Denver, CO 80203

Florida

Florida State Archives and the
State Library of Florida
Division of Library and Information Services
500 South Bronough Street
Tallahassee, FL 32399

University of Florida
P.K. Yonge Library
Special Collections/Florida History
Gainesville, FL 32611

University of West Florida
John C. Pace Library
Pensacola, FL 32514

Idaho

Bureau of Land Management
3380 Americana Terrace
Boise, ID 83706

Idaho State Historical Society
The Library and Archives Genealogical Library
325 West State Street
Boise, ID 83702

Illinois

Illinois State Archives
Archives Building
Spring and Edwards
Springfield, IL 62756

Illinois State Library
Second and Capitol Streets
Springfield, IL 62756

Newberry Library
60 West Walton Street
Chicago, IL 60610

Indiana

Indiana State Archives
Commission on Public Records
140 North Senate Avenue
Indianapolis, IN 46204

Indiana State Library
140 North Senate Avenue
Indianapolis, IN 46204

Allen County Public Library
Genealogy Department
900 Webster Street
Fort Wayne, IN 46802

Iowa

State Historical Society of Iowa
Research Library
402 Iowa Avenue
Iowa City, IA 52240

State Historical Society of Iowa Library
Capitol Complex
Des Moines, IA 50319

Kansas

Kansas State Historical Society
120 West 10th Avenue
Topeka, KS 66612

Kansas Genealogical Society
700 Avenue G and Vine Street
P.O. Box 103
Dodge City, KS 67801

Louisiana

Louisiana State Archives and Records
Office of the Secretary of State
3851 Essen Lane
P.O. Box 94125
Baton Rouge, LA 70804-9125

Loyola University of New Orleans
6363 St. Charles Avenue
P.O. Box 198
New Orleans, LA 70118

Southern University
John B. Cade Library
Southern Br. PO
Baton Rouge, LA 70813

New Orleans Public Library
Louisiana Division
219 Loyola Avenue
New Orleans, LA 70140

Tulane University
Howard-Tilton Memorial Library
New Orleans, LA 70118-5682

Louisiana State Museum
Louisiana Historical Center Library
751 Chartres Street
New Orleans, LA 70176

Michigan

State Archives of Michigan
717 West Allegan Street
Lansing, MI 48918

Library of Michigan
Michigan Library and Historical Center
717 Allegan Street
Lansing, MI 48909

Minnesota

Minnesota Historical Society Research Center
(State Archives)
1500 Mississippi Street
St. Paul, MN 55101

Minnesota Historical Society
690 Cedar Street
St. Paul, MN 55101

Mississippi

Mississippi Archives and Library Division
Mississippi Dept. of Archives and History
P.O. Box 571
Jackson, MS 39205-0571

University of Southern Mississippi
McCain Library and Archives
Hattiesburg, MS 39410

Missouri

Missouri State Archives
P.O. Box 778
Jefferson City, MO 65102

Missouri Historical Society
Jefferson Memorial Building
Forest Park
St. Louis, MO 63103

Montana

Bureau of Land Management
Montana State Office
222 North 32nd Street
Billings, MT 59107

Montana Historical Society
225 North Roberts
Helena, MT 59601

Nebraska

Nebraska State Historical Society
P.O. Box 82554
1500 R Street
Lincoln, NE 68501

Nebraska State Genealogical Society
P.O. Box 5608
Lincoln, NE 68505

Nevada

Bureau of Land Management
Nevada State Office
850 Harvard Way
Reno, NV 89520

Nevada State Library
Capitol Complex
401 North Carson Street
Carson City, NV 89710

Nevada State Archives
Division of Archives and Records
101 South Fall Street
Carson City, NV 89710

New Mexico

Bureau of Land Management
New Mexico State Office
1474 Rodeo Road
Santa Fe, NM 87505

New Mexico Records Center and Archives
404 Montezuma
Santa Fe, NM 87501

Center for Southwest Research
University of New Mexico-General Library
Albuquerque, NM 87131-1466

New Mexico State Library
Southwest Room
325 Don Gaspar Avenue
Santa Fe, NM 87503

North Dakota

State Archives and Historical Research Library
State Historical Society of North Dakota
612 East Boulevard Avenue
Bismark, ND 58505-0179

North Dakota State Library
Liberty Memorial Building
Capitol Grounds
Bismark, ND 58505

Ohio

Ohio Historical Society
Archives-Library
1985 Velma Avenue
Columbus, OH 43211

State Library of Ohio
Genealogy Division
65 South Front Street
Columbus, OH 43215

Western Reserve Historical Society
10825 East Boulevard
Cleveland, OH 44106

Oklahoma

Oklahoma Department of Libraries
Division of State Archives and Records
200 NE 18th Street
Oklahoma City, OK 75105

Oklahoma Historical Society
2100 North Lincoln Boulevard
Oklahoma City, OK 73105

Oregon

Bureau of Land Management
Oregon State Office
1300 NE 44th Avenue
Portland, OR 97213

Oregon State Archives
800 Summer Street NE
Salem, OR 97310

Oregon Historical Society Library
1230 SW Park Avenue
Portland, OR 97205

South Dakota

South Dakota State Historical Society
(State Archives)
Cultural Heritage Center
900 Governors Drive
Pierre, SD 57501-2294

The Center for Western Studies
Box 727, Augustana College
Sioux Falls, SD 57197

Utah

Bureau of Land Management
Utah State Office
324 South State Street
Salt Lake City, UT 84111

Family History Library
35 North West Temple
Salt Lake City, UT 84101

Utah State Archives and Records Service
Archives Building, State Capitol
Salt Lake City, UT 84114

Washington

Washington State Archives
P.O. Box 9000
12th and Washington Streets
Olympia, WA 98111

Washington State Library
Capital Campus
State Library Building
Washington/Northwest Room
Olympia, WA 98504

Wisconsin

State Historical Society of Wisconsin
816 State Street
Madison, WI 53706-1488

Wisconsin State Genealogical Society
2109 Twentieth Avenue
Monroe, WI 53566

Wyoming

Bureau of Land Management
Wyoming State Office
P.O. Box 1828
2515 Warren Avenue
Cheyenne, WY 82003

Wyoming State Archives and Historical Dept.
Barrett Building
Cheyenne, WY 82002

FOR FURTHER REFERENCE

Adams, F.G. *Homestead Guide for Kansas and Nebraska.* Waterville, Kans.: F.G. Adams, 1873.

Ainsworth, Fern. *Private Land Claims: Illinois, Indiana, Michigan and Wisconsin.* Natchitoches, La.: the author, ca. 1980.

Ainsworth, Fern. *Private Land Claims: Mississippi and Missouri.* Natchitoches, La.: the author, n.d.

Ainsworth, Fern. *Private Land Claims: Alabama, Arkansas, Florida.* Natchitoches, La.: the author, 1978.

Barr, Charles B. *Townships and Legal Descriptions of Land.* Independence, Mo.: the author, 1989.

Beahan, Gary W. *Missouri's Public Domain: United States Land Sales, 1818–1922.* Jefferson City, Mo.: Records Management and Archives Service, 1980.

Brown, Jean C. *Oklahoma Research: The Twin Territories.* Sapulpa, Okla.: the author, 1975.

Burke, Thomas A. *Ohio Lands: A Short History.* Columbus, Ohio: Auditor of State, 1991.

Carlson, Theodore L. *Illinois Military Tract: A Study of Land Occupation, Utilization and Tenure.* Urbana: University of Illinois Press, 1951.

Carstensen, Vernon. *The Public Lands: Studies in the History of the Public Domain.* Madison: University of Wisconsin Press, 1968.

Carter, Clarence Edwin, ed. *Territorial Papers of the United States.* Washington, D.C.: Government Printing Office, 1948–.

Christensen, Katheren. *Arkansas Military Bounty Grants (War of 1812).* Hot Springs: Arkansas Ancestors, 1971.

Coggins, George Cameron, and Charles F. Wilkinson. *Federal Public Land and Resources Law.* Mineola, N.Y.: The Foundation Press, 1981.

Coren, Robert W., et al. *Guide to the Records of the United States Senate at the National Archives.* Washington, D.C.: U.S. Government Printing Office, 1989.

Donaldson, Thomas. *The Public Domain: Its History, with Statistics.* Washington, D.C.: Government Printing Office, 1880.

Dunaway, Maxine. *Missouri Military Land Warrants, War of 1812.* Springfield, Mo.: the author, 1985.

Fox, Michael. *Maps and Atlases Showing Land Ownership in Wisconsin.* Madison: State Historical Society of Wisconsin, 1978.

Gates, Paul W. *Fifty Million Acres: Conflicts Over Kansas Land Policy, 1854–1890.* Ithaca, N.Y.: Cornell University Press, 1954.

Gates, Paul W. "Public Land Disposal in California." *Agricultural History* 49 (1975).

Gates, Paul W., et al. *History of Public Land Law Development.* Washington, D.C.: Government Printing Office, 1968.

Genealogical Material in Oregon Donation Land Claims. Portland, Oreg.: Genealogical Forum of Portland, 1957–75.

Green, Charles L. *The Administration of the Public Domain in South Dakota.* Pierre, S.D.: Hipple Printing, 1939.

Guide to Genealogical Research in the National Archives. Washington, D.C.: National Archives Trust Fund Board, 1983.

Gurley, Lottie LeGett. *Genealogical Material in Oregon Provisional Land Claims, 1845–1849.* Portland, Oreg.: Genealogical Forum of Portland, 1982.

Hahn, Marilyn Davis. *Old Cahaba Land Office Records and Military Warrants, 1817–1853.* (Alabama.) Birmingham, Ala.: Banner Press, 1982.

Hahn, Marilyn Davis. *Old Sparta and Elba Land Office Records and Military Warrants, 1822–1860.* (Alabama.) Easley, S.C.: Southern Historical Press, 1983.

Hahn, Marilyn Davis. *Old St. Stephens Land Office Records and American State Papers: Public Lands, Vol.1, 1768–1888.* Easley, S.C.: Southern Historical Press, 1983.

Hibbard, Benjamin Horrace. *A History of Public Land Policies.* New York: MacMillan, 1924.

Hundley, Debra. *A Study of Slave and Non-Slave Property Values in Early South Carolina.* Provo, Utah: Brigham Young University, 197–.

Hutchinson, William Thomas. *The Bounty Lands of the American Revolution in Ohio.* New York: Arno Press, 1979.

Irons, Victoria, and Patricia C. Brennan. *Descriptive Inventory of the Archives of the State of Illinois.* Springfield: Illinois State Archives, 1978.

Jackson, Ronald Vern. *Ohio Military Land Warrants, 1789–1801.* Bountiful, Utah: Accelerated Indexing Systems, n.d.

Kirkham, E. Kay. *The Land Records of America and Their Genealogical Value.* Salt Lake City: Deseret Book, 1964.

Lanza, Michael L. *Agrarianism and Reconstruction Politics: The Southern Homestead Act.* Baton Rouge: Louisiana State University Press, 1990.

Lindgren, H. Elaine. *Land in Her Own Name: Women as Homesteaders in North Dakota.* Fargo: North Dakota Institute for Regional Studies, 1991.

Lux, Leonard. *The Vincennes Donation Lands.* Indianapolis: Indiana Historical Society Publications, Vol. 25, item 4.

Mayer, Carl, and George Riley. *Public Domain-Private Dominion: A History of Public Mineral Policy in America.* N.p., 1985.

McMullin, Phillip W. *Grassroots of America.* Salt Lake City: Gendex, 1972.

Muhn, James, and Hanson R. Stuart. *Opportunity and Challenge: The Story of the BLM.* Washington, D.C.: Government Printing Office, 1988.

Nelson, Robert. *The Making of Federal Coal Policy.* N.p., 1983.

Oberly, James W. *Sixty Million Acres: American Veterans and Public Lands Before the Civil War.* Kent, Ohio: Kent State University Press, 1990.

Peters, William E. *Ohio Lands and Their Subdivisions.* Athens, Ohio: the author, 1930.

Peters, William S., and Maxine C. Johnson. *Public Lands in Montana: Their History and Current Significance.* Missoula, Mont.: Bureau of Business and Economic Research, 1959.

Rand McNally. *Commercial Atlas and Marketing Guide.* U.S. 127th ed. 1996.

Riegel, Mayburt Stephenson. *Early Ohioans' Residences from the Land Grant Records.* Mansfield: Ohio Genealogical Society, 1976.

Robbins, Roy M. *Our Landed Heritage: The Public Domain, 1776–1936.* Princeton, N.J.: Princeton University Press, 1942.

Rohrbough, Malcolm J. *The Land Office Business: The Settlement and Administration of American Public Lands, 1789–1837.* New York: Oxford University Press, 1968.

Sheldon, Addison E. *Land Systems and Land Policies in Nebraska: A History of Nebraska Land, Public Domain and Private Property.* Lincoln: Nebraska State Historical Society, 1936.

Sherman, C.E. *Original Ohio Land Subdivisions.* Columbus: Ohio State Reformatory, 1925.

Smith, Clifford Neal. *Federal Land Series.* Chicago: American Library Association, 1972–.

Socolofsky, Homer. "Land Disposal in Nebraska, 1854–1906: The Homestead Story." *Nebraska History* 48 (1967).

Stephenson, Richard W. *Land Ownership Maps.* Washington, D.C.: Library of Congress, 1967.

Survey of Federal Archives in Louisiana: Land Claims and Other Documents. Baton Rouge, La.: Historical Records Survey, 1940.

Szucs, Loretto Dennis, and Sandra Luebking, eds. "Research in Land and Tax Records." In *The Source: A Guidebook of American Genealogy.* Rev. ed. Salt Lake City: Ancestry, 1997.

Szucs, Loretto Dennis, and Sandra Luebking. *The Archives: A Guide to the National Archives Field Branches.* Salt Lake City: Ancestry, 1988.

United States Congress. *American State Papers.* Washington, D.C.: Gales and Seaton, 1832–61.

United States Congress. *War of 1812 Bounty Lands in Illinois: With an Introduction by James D. Walker.* Thomson, Ill.: Heritage House, 1977.

Volkel, Lowell M., indexer. *War of 1812 Bounty Lands in Illinois.* Thomson, Ill.: Heritage House, 1977. (See entry under United States Congress.)

Wardell, Patrick G. *War of 1812: Virginia Bounty Land and Pension Applicants.* Bowie, Md.: 1987.

Water, Margaret R. *Indiana Land Entries.* Knightstown, Ind.: Bookmark, 1977.

Waterfield, Marjorie Featheringill. *Petition to Partition Land Records: Land Records Often Overlooked by Genealogists.* Bowling Green, Ohio: the author, 1988.

Watkins, T.H., and Charles S. Watson, Jr. *The Land No One Knows: America and the Public Domain.* San Francisco: Sierra Club Books, 1975.

Westphall, Victor. *The Public Domain in New Mexico, 1854–1891.* Albuquerque: University of New Mexico, 1965.

White, C. Albert. *A History of the Rectangular Survey System.* Washington, D.C.: Government Printing Office, 1991.

White, Virgil D. *Genealogical Abstracts of Revolutionary War Pension Files.* 4 vols. Waynesboro, Tenn.: National Historical Publishing Co., 1990–92.

_____. *Index to War of 1812 Pension Files.* Waynsesboro, Tenn.: National Historical Publishing Co., 1989.

_____. *Index to Mexican War Pension Files.* Waynesboro, Tenn.: National Historical Publishing Co., 1989.

Yoshpe, Harry P., and Philip P. Brower, comps. *Preliminary Inventory of the Land-Entry Papers of the General Land Office (Preliminary Inventory No. 22).* Washington, D.C.: National Archives, 1949.

10

Strategies for Federal Land Records

ORDERING LAND-ENTRY CASE FILES

All case files, whether accepted or rejected, are currently held at the National Archives in Washington, D.C. They were moved there in 1996 from a branch repository in Suitland, Maryland. Because of the way in which these files are currently organized, it is essential to provide the following information when requesting copies:

- Name of land office

- Land description (in township, range, and section)

- Final certificate number or patent number

- Authority under which the land was acquired (i.e., homestead, cash, bounty-land warrant, mining claim)

Direct requests for land-entry case files to:

> National Archives (NNR1)
> Textual Reference Branch
> Washington, D.C. 20408

Typical Strategy for Identifying and Ordering a Land-Entry Case File

These steps are based upon the possibility that no indexes exist for a state or county in which an ancestor lived. Should indexes be available, use only the steps needed to obtain the missing information before ordering.

Step One

Identify the present-day county that the ancestor lived in. Commercial guidebooks and atlases can define the counties that towns are now a part of. One of the best is Rand McNally's *Commercial Atlas and Marketing Guide.* Bullinger's *Postal and Shipper's Guide for the United States and Canada* is also useful for small towns that are unincorporated or not likely to be found on current maps. It also includes many areas that no longer have a zip code. *Ancestry's Red Book: American State, County and Town Sources,* edited by Alice Eichholz, and The Everton Publishers' *The Handybook for Genealogists* are both helpful in following the division and creation of new counties. The best source for county boundary evolutions is William Dollarhide and William Thorndale's *Map Guide to the U.S. Federal Censuses.*

The United States Geological Survey (USGS) produces a variety of maps and gazetteers that can help identify some of the most remote geographical names. Omnigraphics, Inc., has produced a set of eleven volumes titled *Omni Gazetteer of the United States.* The first nine volumes are divided according to geographical region, and then by state; they list even the smallest spring and ridge known for each area (figure 10-1). Volume ten is a national index, and volume eleven is an appendix. Most state libraries and universities possess copies of the Omni gazetteer.

If the ancestor's location is not already known, further research in other record sources will be

OMNI GAZETTEER OF THE UNITED STATES • 367 • Montana   Red Top Creek—Rimrocks

Name (ZIP) or Variant Name	Type or Pop.	County	USGS Map (7.5' series)	Lat/Long Coordinates	Source(s) & Other Data
Red Top Creek	stream	Lincoln	Mount Baldy	4845 44N-1155451W	G
Redtap Creek—See American Creek					
Red Top Creek Campground	locale	Lincoln	Mount Baldy	4845 40N-1155505W	G
Red Top Hill	summit	Powder River	Coleman Draw	4532 19N-1060523W	G; el 3621
Red Top Mtn	summit	Lincoln	Mount Baldy	4845 05N-1155853W	G; el 6226
Redwater	pop. pl.	Dawson			F
Redwater Creek—See Redwater River					
Redwater River	stream	McCone	Poplar	4803 41N-1051236W	G; BGN 1967
Red Water Well	well	Carbon	Red Pryor Mt	4503 33N-1082450W	G; el 5147
Redwater Well	well	McCone	Hertz School	4706 01N-1055342W	G; el 2815
Reed Butte	summit	Ravalli	Grayhorse Creek	4630 32N-1135842W	G; el 4739
Reed Canyon—See Maryott Gulch					
Reed Coulee	valley	Fergus	Grand Island	4738 53N-1084858W	G; BGN 1983
Reed Creek	stream	Yellowstone	Bull Mountain	4602 59N-1074514W	G
Reeder Creek	stream	Park	Miner	4510 42N-1105725W	G
Reeder Place	locale	Madison	Home Park Ranch	4502 59N-1120004W	G
Reed Hill	summit	Fergus	P N Ranch	4740 46N-1093800W	G
Reed Hill	summit	Judith Basin	Woodhurst Mt	4656 09N-1101545W	G
Reed Lake	lake	Missoula	Carlton Lake	4640 15N-1141404W	G
Reedpoint: obs. name—See Reed Point					
Reedpoint—See Reed Point (Reedpoint Postoffice)					
Reed Point Cem	cemetery	Sweet Grass	Reed Point	4542 12N-1093344W	G
Reed Point Ditch	canal	Stillwater	Reed Point	4542 29N-1093344W	G
Reed Point (Reedpoint Postoffice)	pop. pl.	Stillwater	Reed Point	4542 34N-1093229W	G F; el 3744
Reed's Fort—See Lewistown					
Reef, The	spring	Lewis and Clark	Wolf Creek	4706 50N-1120636W	G
Reef Creek	stream	Lewis and Clark	Prairie Reef	4733 32N-1130143W	G
Reef Creek	stream	Powell	Morrell Lake	4721 32N-1132420W	G
Reefs, The	spring	Meagher	Rinrock Divide	4622 18N-1103232W	G
Reese Anderson Creek	stream	Powell	Deer Lodge	4623 34N-1123932W	G
Reese Canyon	valley	Silver Bow	Homestake	4559 08N-1122841W	G
Reese Creek	stream	Gallatin	Belgrade	4550 29N-1110839W	G
Reese Creek	stream	Meagher	Charcoal Gulch	4638 07N-1104655W	G
Reese Creek	stream	Yellowstone Nat F.	Electric Peak	4503 55N-1104627W	G
Reese Creek Sch	hist. pl.	Gallatin			H
Reese Creek Sch	school	Gallatin	Flathead Pass	4552 34N-1110448W	G
Reese Ditch	canal	Gallatin	Gallatin Gateway	4534 16N-1111212W	G
Rees Hills	spring	Meagher	Wolf Hill	4613 04N-1103933W	G
Reeve Coulee	valley	Toole	Berkholder Rsvr	4844 46N-1111937W	G
Revenue Mine	mine	Madison	Maltbys Mound	4532 04N-1114612W	G
Reverend Madison Historical Monmt	park	Stillwater	Roscoe NW	4527 20N-1092651W	G
Reverse B Bar X Ranch	locale	Toole	Beaupre Coulee	4857 57N-1113811W	G
Review Mountain	ridge	Flathead	Tuchuck Mt	4855 27N-1144034W	G; BGN 1969; el 7285
Rexford 59930	140	Lincoln	Beartrap Mt	4852 22N-1151322W	G F C
Rexford	pop. pl.	Lincoln	Rexford	4852 48N-1151220W	G F
Rey Creek	stream	Gallatin	Logan	4554 42N-1112805W	G
Reynold Draw	valley	Custer	Horton	4620 21N-1060406W	G
Reynolds, Mount	summit	Hill	Bearpaw Lake	4819 40N-1093735W	G; BGN 1961
Reynolds City	locale	Powell	Elevation Mt	4649 16N-1131710W	G F
Reynolds Creek	stream	Gallatin	Horseshoe Creek	4554 29N-1111058W	G
Reynolds Creek	stream	Glacier	Logan Pass	4840 02N-1133743W	G; BGN 1929
Reynolds Creek	stream	Meagher	Castle Town	4624 21N-1104137W	G
Reynolds Creek	stream	Meagher	Monument Peak	4657 29N-1110157W	G
Reynolds Creek	stream	Ravalli	Lick Creek	4556 49N-1134302W	G
Reynolds Hill	summit	Phillips	Herman Point	4741 01N-1073953W	G; el 2509
Reynolds Mtn	summit	Glacier	Logan Pass	4840 19N-1134321W	G; BGN 1929; el 9125
Reynolds Mtn	summit	Meagher	Monument Peak	4655 22N-1110236W	G; el 7175
Reynolds Mountain—See Reynolds, Mount					
Reynolds Peak	flat	Meagher	Monument Peak	4656 24N-1110114W	G
Reynolds Pass—See Raynolds Pass					
Rhine, The—See Halfway Creek					
Rhoda Lake	lake	Judith Basin	Yogo Peak	4658 08N-1103545W	G; el 8255
Rhodes	locale	Flathead	Rhodes	4816 45N-1142824W	G F; el 3261
Rhodes Draw	valley	Flathead	Rhodes	4816 41N-1142841W	G
Rhubarb Patch Trail	trail	Beaverhead	Elkhorn Hot Springs	4526 24N-1130504W	G
Rhue Creek	stream	Chouteau	Warrick	4803 23N-1093616W	G
Ribbon Gulch	valley	Liberty	Haystack Butte	4851 55N-1111200W	G
Rice Coulee	valley	Rosebud	Ashland NE	4541 11N-1061558W	G
Rice Creek	stream	Custer	Kinsey	4632 35N-1054415W	G
Rice Creek	stream	Lincoln	Libby	4829 08N-1153031W	G
Rice Creek	stream	Missoula	Seeley Lake W	4712 48N-1133117W	G
Rice Creek	stream	Park	Cottonwood Rsvr	4604 00N-1104246W	G
Rice Draw	valley	Sanders	Heron	4802 22N-1155453W	G
Rice Draw Trail	trail	Sanders	Heron	4800 37N-1155556W	G
Rice Lake	lake	Powell	Ovando	4705 34N-1131042W	G
Rice Ranch	locale	Gallatin	Manhattan SW	4548 36N-1112940W	G
Rice Rsvr	reservoir	Chouteau	Rice Reservoir	4740 11N-1104832W	G; el 3354

Figure 10-1. A page from the *Omni Gazetteer of the United States.*

necessary to avoid page-by-page searches of tract books for an entire state or group of states. Occasionally, statewide or land office indexes have been compiled for easier reference. They usually at least provide the legal land description which allows precise access to the tract books discussed in step three. Also refer to the "GLOARS" index under Bureau of Land Management in chapter 9, Records Generated by Federal Lands.

Step Two

The tract books need to be researched next. Unless a specific legal description of the land is known, tract books can be very cumbersome and tedious to research. Appendix A includes a Tract Book Guide to help determine land descriptions for each present-day county among the federal-land states. For each county it provides the northern-, southern-, eastern-, and western-most township and range involved in the tract books. It also identifies the applicable meridian(s) for the county. Read the introduction to appendix A to understand the extent of its accuracy and important overlap policies.

Step Three

The existing tract books for the entire public domain have been microfilmed. They are organized according to meridian within each state, and thereafter by township, range, and section. Townships and ranges are given for each microfilm number. The information obtained from indexes or the Tract Book Guide can then be matched against the listed townships and ranges, and the correct film(s) retrieved or ordered. (Because many states have only one meridian, the meridian might be assumed and not be specifically identified in a repository catalog. Since the tract books are not organized by county, but by township and range, small segments of several microfilms might have to be researched to cover one county.)

Search the pages that contain the pertinent legal descriptions in the tract books for the county involved, looking for the ancestor's name. If a land description was obtained from an index or deed, search for the pages with that precise description, looking for the ancestor's name. Once found, the entry should provide the patent and/or final certificate number, the authority under which the claim was made (homestead, cash entry, etc.), and verify the legal land description more precisely. Sometimes the entry will also provide the name of the land office.

It is possible that an ancestor will appear in multiple entries for any given area. Research the surrounding legal descriptions to find all possible entries for each individual. A person may have been involved in other transactions for nearby parcels of land that left more descriptive types of entries. It is important to locate the first in a series of attempted entries because it will likely contain the most information; subsequent files may have relied on information already presented during earlier attempts. Remember, cancelled or rejected entries can sometimes contain more information than those that were readily accepted.

Step Four

For many states, such as North Dakota, the land office is not recorded on the pages of the tract book entries. The land office boundary is the primary organization structure for the original case files at the National Archives. To help identify the appropriate land office, a series of Land Office Boundary Maps for each state appear in appendix B. They show land office jurisdictions in relation to present-day counties. The land office is the final piece of information needed to order the case file.

Step Five

Indicate the land office, land description, final certificate or patent number, and authority or type of claim in a request to:

> National Archives (NNR1)
> Textual Reference Branch
> Washington, D.C. 20408

Remember that archives staff are not professional researchers. It is unfair to suggest to them that they assess a pedigree for potential solutions. Be considerate of their time and effort by including only the necessary information to retrieve the re-quested file. Sharing background information about an ancestor's life will only delay the response and confuse the staff's interpretation of the request. Provide only the information listed above. Photocopies of patents or index information will help in case the retrieved file does not match the request.

Step Six

The National Archives' staff will attempt to locate the requested file. If it is found, a price for copies will be determined by the size of the file. The inquirer is notified of the cost involved. Depending on the volume of requests in the upcoming years, your inquiry may be handled by a private company subcontracted by the National Archives for the purpose of photocopying. The procedures, however, will likely remain the same.

Step Seven

Upon being notified of the cost for the file, send the appropriate funds. Be sure to request that the entire case file be copied. What may seem trivial and unimportant to an agent or staff member who is copying the file may actually coincide with information previously gathered.

Then simply wait for the copies to arrive.

GRAPHING TOWNSHIP, RANGE, AND SECTION

Just as platting of metes and bounds can help solve difficult research problems, graphing township, range, and section can also be extremely valuable. Graphing helps to segregate common surnames and to associate ancestors with others of the same or different surname. If three William Johnsons live in the same township, it is helpful to know where the one with a wife named Susanna lived in relation to the William whose wife was Sarah, and which other Johnsons might be related or associated with each. Such questions are just a few of those that can be answered by graphing township, range, and section.

6	5	4	3	2	1
7	8	9	10	11	12
18	17	16	15	14	13
19	20	21	22	23	24
30	29	28	27	26	25
31	32	33	34	35	36

Figure 10-2. Standard township numbering

As mentioned in chapter 8, the numbering system for a township plays an important role in graphing (figure 10-2). Township numbering differs throughout meridians in Ohio and Louisiana, though it is consistent in the remaining states. The following example uses the standard township numbering to illustrate how graphing can help further identify an individual.

Example

John Miller and Rebecca Kirby were identified in a biographical sketch in Iowa as having originated from Macon County, Illinois. John was further identified as sharing the same name as his father. Research in the early censuses of Macon County, Illinois determined that there were four John Millers residing in the same township at the same time. Two were of the correct age to have been the ancestor, and two were of the correct age to have been the father.

Only one of the elder John Millers left a will. In it he referred to lands still owned in Somerset County, Pennsylvania. His wife was listed as Ann, though no children were identified by name. If he was the ancestor, links in Pennsylvania records

could add several generations to the family. An early county history also identified one early John Miller as having arrived with others from North Carolina around 1826. Was the ancestral John Miller the son of John Miller and Ann from Somerset County, Pennsylvania, or was he the son of John Miller from North Carolina?

It was estimated that the ancestral John Miller and Rebecca were married around 1821, bcause children were listed in the biography as having been born starting in 1822. The 1830 census did not specifically help because each of the younger John Millers had more than an appropriate number of people in his household. Either could have been the ancestor, and likely had farmhands included in his household. Which one was the ancestor? Who was the other younger John Miller? A cousin, perhaps? Or was he not related at all? Such situations are frequently encountered during common-surname research.

By assessing all of the Miller grants and deeds for Macon County, several clues were noticed. One was that John and Rebecca were noted in numerous transactions. John and Ann were also identified, as was John Miller in several instances without a spouse mentioned. A John and Susanna Miller were also found in a couple of transactions. Thus, three of the spouses had been identified: Ann, Rebecca, and Susanna.

One deed, from 1830, indicated that John and Rebecca had arrived recently from Gallatin County in Illinois. Marriage records in that county showed John Miller marrying Rebecca White in 1828, just two years before the 1830 deed in Macon County. Apparently, both younger John Millers were married to a Rebecca: one to Rebecca Kirby and one to Rebecca White. Because one John and Rebecca appeared in the deeds of Macon County as early as 1824, it was supposed that they were not one and the same.

The various deeds and grants were gathered and graphed according to township, section, and range. First, John and Ann were placed. Two cash entries and several deeds suggested that he was always located in sections eleven and fourteen

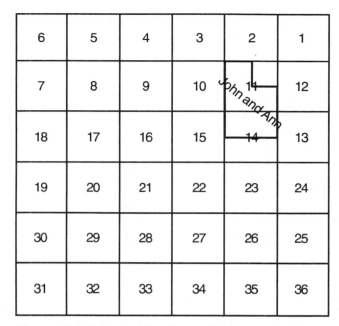

Figure 10-3. John and Ann located in the township.

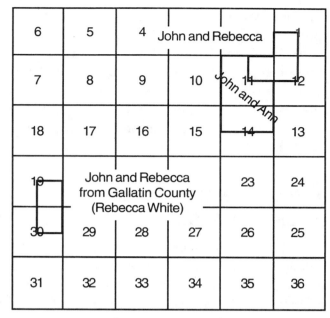

Figure 10-3. The Johns and Rebeccas located in the township.

(figure 10-3). This began to give him additional identity, instead of just having been in Macon County.

The deeds and grants for all Johns and Rebeccas were next graphed. As suspected, they involved two very different locations within the township. One group of records was located in sections nineteen and thirty. This group included the one deed that defined John and Rebecca from Gallatin County, indicating that this pair were John Miller and Rebecca White. The other group of records for a John and Rebecca was located in sections eleven and twelve (figure 10-4).

This placement more clearly shows the distinction of the two Johns and Rebeccas, and associates one pair directly next to John and Ann. The remaining deeds and grants (those without a spouse listed) were next placed on the graph. This was done to insure that there were no other possible associations. Another John, likely the one from North Carolina, was located in sections seven and eight. The other deeds were obviously the same Johns who had already been associated with a spouse; these were additional deeds describing property already graphed through other deeds (figure 10-5).

Graphing helped segregate and associate the families encountered. Other possible scenarios include the comparison of other Millers living near John and Ann to determine if any went to Iowa where the ancestral John and Rebecca eventually settled. Even comparing neighbors with different surnames might be helpful in establishing migra-

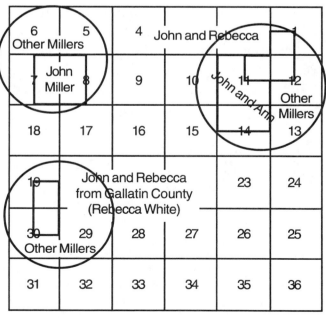

Figure 10-5. The remaining deeds and grants located in the township.

tion patterns for groups of individuals. Graphing a group of neighbors around the ancestor and then matching them with ancestral candidates in other areas can prove the correct connection. In summary, constant comparison by reading complete deed or grant descriptions and then graphing the results will also often help prove or disprove a suspected relationship.

OTHER STRATEGIES FOR FEDERAL LANDS

A variety of strategies can be implemented based upon the circumstances encountered. Strategies for federal lands are similar in concept to those for state lands or individual lands. They all rely upon the creativity of the user to bring about answers that were never intended when the record was originally created. Below is a list of some basic strategies and points to remember.

- Chronological aspects of records need to be analyzed. A dated patent does not indicate the date on which a person arrived in the area. Cash entries, register books, and even a simple receipt can help place an ancestor in a place at an earlier or later time.

- Land-entry case files can be used to help identify citizenship status, where a declaration of intention took place, and sometimes can specify where an ancestor was born.

- Identify prerequisites for any given type of claim with which an ancestor was involved. For example, if an ancestor received certain acreage under the Donation Land Act in Oregon, the amount of that acreage could help determine the date of his arrival in the Oregon Territory, even without the land-entry case file. His marital status could also be determined by the acreage he received.

- Most early inhabitants held land. Land grants can serve as a substitute for censuses that were lost or destroyed. Land records were not restricted to a decennial year, but were generated each and every day, so they can also fill in the years between censuses.

- Watch for second applications for bounty land from the federal government. If an ancestor failed under earlier qualifications, he may have tried again later as the qualifications were reduced; or he may have received some land under an earlier act, then qualified to apply for additional land under later acts.

- Always look for multiple grants. The earliest grants may have generated more information.

- Remember that the date of patent is not the date of application. An ancestor may have been in a location several years earlier than originally thought. Search both documents.

- When indexes are available, search all entries for a specific surname, not just the ancestor. Compare others and their lands with the ancestor's land description. People of the same names receiving grants in the same areas might indicate a relationship.

- Signatures, when not marked with an "X," can help identify different people with the same name. The fact that one could spell well and another could not may also help segregate individuals with common names.

There is an endless number of additional strategies to be considered. Creativity is the key to maximizing the potential of land records. Land records were not designed to give specific answers to genealogical researchers. The answers need to be extracted.

FOR FURTHER REFERENCE

Andriot, Jay, comp. *Township Atlas of the United States*. McLean, Va.: Documents Index, 1991.

Carter, Fran. *Searching American Land and Deed Records*. Orting, Wash.: Heritage Quest, 1991.

Eakle, Arlene. *Solving American Pedigrees: American Property Records, Land and Tax Records*. Salt Lake City: Genealogical Institute, 1973.

Eichholz, Alice, ed. *The Red Book: American State, County and Town Sources*. Rev. ed. Salt Lake City: Ancestry, 1992.

Elliott, Wendy L. *Using Land Records to Solve Research Problems*. Bountiful, Utah: American Genealogical Lending Library, 1987.

Everton Publishers. *The Handybook for Genealogists*. 8th ed. Logan, Utah: The Everton Publishers, 1995.

Gates, Paul W. *History of Public Land Law Development*. Washington, D.C.: U.S. Government Printing Office, 1968.

Greenwood, Val. *The Researcher's Guide to American Genealogy*. Baltimore: Genealogical Publishing Co., 1990.

Hibbard, Benjamin Horrace, Ph.D. *A History of the Public Land Policies*. New York: The MacMillan Company, 1924.

Kirkham, E. Kay. *Land Records of America*. Salt Lake City: Deseret Book Co., 1964.

"Land and Tax Records." In *The Source: A Guidebook of American Genealogy*. Edited by Loretto Dennis Szucs and Sandra Hargreaves Luebking. Rev. ed. Salt Lake City: Ancestry, 1997.

Omni Gazetteer of the United States. Detroit: Omnigraphics, Inc., 1991.

Postal and Shipper's Guide for the United States and Canada. Westwood, N.J.: Bullinger's Guides, Inc.

Rand McNally. *Commercial Atlas and Marketing Guide*. U.S. 127th ed., 1996.

Read, Helen Hunt. *Property Deeds for Genealogy*. Toledo, Ohio: the author, 1985.

Thorndale, William, and William Dollarhide. *Map Guide to the U.S. Federal Censuses*. Baltimore: Genealogical Publishing Co., 1987.

Wattles, Wm. C. *Land Survey Descriptions*. Los Angeles: Title Insurance and Trust Co., 1970.

Section 4:
Individual Lands

An Introduction to Individual Lands

The term "individual lands" (also "private lands") refers to the lands in all land transactions following the initial sale by federal or state governments. Individual lands are sold between individuals or companies through various types of deeds, usually with no inclusion of government. These deeds are the most familiar and commonly used land sources in research. They are generally uniform in content throughout both federal and state-land states, yet they come in a variety of types.

Individual lands usually retain the same organization as the original patent. If located in a federal-land state, the land will be described according to the rectangular measurements of township, range, and section. If located in a state-land state, the land will usually retain the variation of metes and bounds or town lots employed by that geographical area. (See chapter 5, Organization of State Lands, and chapter 8, Organization of Federal Lands, for more detailed information about these descriptions.)

At first glance, it would seem that deed records are monotonous, uninformative documents that merely exist as one type among the many routine transactions entered into by our ancestors. A more careful study of these records, however, illustrates a gold mine of information, including associations, relatives, and patterns pertaining to the lives of our ancestors and the places they lived.

Deeds were drawn up by individuals, then transcribed into deed books at the recorder's office. Often, the originals were written in ranchers' tally books on treated goat hide (which lasts longer than any paper) or on the back of other paper documents, and sometimes they were simply made verbally before witnesses, to be recorded later. For this reason, the information in many deeds, including names and signatures, comprises transcriptions, not originals.

The types of records generated by deeds include power of attorney, escheatment, dower release, mortgage, executing of probate, and a variety of other records. There are even versions of modern prenuptial agreements. Creative strategies for individual lands involve many of those presented for state and federal lands. There are additional strategies that can be applied to individual land research. Some of these strategies are shared in chapter 12, Strategies for Individual Lands.

Land deeds, in their many forms, all contribute to the great amount of information that can be derived about our ancestors. The following chapters in this section discuss, in more detail, the various forms of deeds, the records they generate, and the strategies involved in researching them.

11

Records Generated by Individual Lands

Individual lands rarely involved the detailed acquisition process encountered with most federal or state lands. However, because of the variety of record types, these documents can provide as many or more clues than their counterparts. Since most Americans owned at least some land prior to the twentieth century, individual lands are a way of tracking ancestors when no other record was left behind. Even if a person received a federal or state land grant, that grant was eventually sold or devised to someone else through the individual land system.

The process for obtaining title to individual lands was much less structured than for federal or state lands. A deed could be transacted between almost any two parties, for a variety of reasons. Mortgage, inheritance, and sale are the most common. However, many other types of records can also be found among deeds.

Individual lands were usually registered at a county recorder's office or through the county court clerk. Exceptions from the county jurisdiction were mostly in New England, where some states recorded their land deeds through the town clerk. A summary of the agency in charge of deeds for each state is on the following page. Because the agency in charge of land records was separate from other agencies in the courthouse, land records can sometimes be found to have survived when other records were destroyed.

Prior to the twentieth century, almost any official agency could be turned to for the recording of deeds. If, for example, the county recorder was elsewhere on the one day the grantee was in town, the deed might then have been recorded among the records of another official agency, sometimes in another building.

Researching land deeds can be one of the easiest tasks to undertake, though it can be one of the most intimidating searches for those who are considering land records for the first time. Therefore, a basic overview of records and indexing systems is presented in this chapter.

DEEDS AND RELATED RECORDS

The method of transferring title for individual lands is by deed. Deeds, though full of technical and legal jargon, can include some of the most valuable information available to researchers. Learning what to pay attention to and what to disregard is half of the battle. The following is a list of items to consider:

- Names of the grantee and grantor
- Watercourses
- Bordering neighbors
- Witnesses
- Description and acreage
- Consideration (payment)
- Dates (written and recorded)
- Dower release

Offices Responsible for Recording Land Deeds

Alabama
Probate Court. Watch for multiple courthouses in each county.

Alaska
District Recorder

Arizona
County Recorder

Arkansas
Circuit Court Clerk

California
County Recorder

Colorado
County Recorder

Connecticut
Town Clerk

Delaware
County Recorder

Florida
Circuit Court Clerk

Georgia
Court of Ordinary Clerk

Hawaii
Register of Conveyances in Honolulu

Idaho
County Recorder

Illinois
County Recorder

Indiana
County Recorder

Iowa
County Recorder

Kansas
County Clerk

Kentucky
County Recorder

Louisiana
Clerk of Courts

Maine
Clerk of Courts

Maryland
Clerk of Court

For Baltimore: Clerk of Superior Court

Massachusetts
Registry of Deeds

Watch for multiple courthouses in counties.

Michigan
Register of Deeds

Minnesota
Register of Deeds

Mississippi
Clerk of Chancery Court

Missouri
County Recorder

Montana
County Clerk

Nebraska
Register of Deeds

Nevada
County Recorder

New Hampshire
Town clerk until 1769; the county recorder thereafter.

New Jersey
County Register in Camden, Essex, Hudson, Passaic, and Union Counties. All others with County Clerk.

New Mexico
County Recorder

New York
County Recorder

North Carolina
Register of Deeds

North Dakota
Register of Deeds

Ohio
County Recorder

Oklahoma
County Clerk

Oregon
Mixture. Contact County Clerk for details.

Pennsylvania
County Recorder

Rhode Island
County Recorder

South Carolina
Clerk of Courts

South Dakota
Register of Deeds

Tennessee
Register of Deeds

Texas
County Clerk

Utah
County Recorder

Vermont
Town Clerk and County Clerk

Virginia
Richmond is divided between Chancery Court and Hustins Court. Elsewhere it is the County Circuit Court.

Washington
County Auditor

West Virginia
County Clerk

Wisconsin
Register of Deeds

Wyoming
County Clerk

- Previous owners' names
- Authority of deed (what type)
- County and state of residence
- Signatures

The purpose of the deed can determine how the information should be interpreted. During the course of researching land deeds, various forms of land-related documents will appear. For better reference and understanding, several of the most common documents are briefly described below.

The most common type of deed is the **quit claim** deed. This deed relinquishes any and all rights held by the seller to the buyer. Obligations on both sides are usually inclusive of heirs or assignees. This does not guarantee that the seller is the sole owner, and only relinquishes the seller's interest in the said lands; thus, the key word is rights, not title.

Fee simple is a frequently encountered term; it is similar to a quit claim. Fee simple is used most often in terms of inheritance, and is more absolute, without restrictions.

The above two terms derive from an era in which the British crown was considered actual owner of the land. Purchasers merely had an estate in that land, which could usually be bought or sold, inherited, or otherwise conveyed to or from another party.

Mortgages are very common among all of the states. In states such as Pennsylvania, mortgage companies have been in existence since the early 1700s. A mortgage should not be confused with the outright purchase of a piece of property. A mortgage was security for a loan, using the property as collateral. If the terms of the mortgage were fulfilled, the deed was null and void and the title was retained by the grantor. If the terms were not met, the grantee/lender then held legal possession of the property, to dispose of as he wished. If you find that an individual sold the same piece of property three times, read the deeds closely. Two of the transactions were likely mortgages. A term often associated with mortgages in indexes

is *exon*, which is an abbreviation for "exonerated." It indicates a complete release from contract, either by fulfillment or by forfeiture.

Power of attorney was sometimes given by the grantee or grantor to another individual. This status allowed that individual to act in behalf of the issuer. Many times power of attorney was given because a person did not live in the vicinity where the deed took place. Therefore, the power of attorney may list the absentee as being "of Baltimore," for example, although the deed took place in Nashville. The appointed friend or relative in Nashville acted according to that power of attorney. This power does not imply the occupational status of an attorney, but simply requests that someone act for and in behalf of an absent party.

Dower right, according to Barbara Jean Evans' *A to Zax: A Comprehensive Dictionary for Genealogists and Historians*, is "that portion of an estate which is given to a widow by law from her deceased husband's estate to be used for her lifetime." This dower right is present for a portion of all real and personal property shared by a couple. When a deed was sold, most areas required the wife to release her dower right before the sale could become final, thus disclosing her given name. Dower rights can also further identify males sharing the same name. For example, Joseph Green and Rebecca can be distinguished from Joseph Green and Ann. (See figure 11-1.)

Escheat is another term seen in deeds, especially among the original thirteen colonies. It indicates a deed transaction from an individual to the state by reason of default. This could be due to property abandonment or because of death with no legal heirs.

Primogeniture indicated the right of the first-born male to inherit all real property upon the death of his father. This practice can be useful in determining relationships when exact deeds between father and son did not survive or were not recorded. If the son sold more property than he bought, he may have inherited through primogeniture. By comparing the deeds of possible

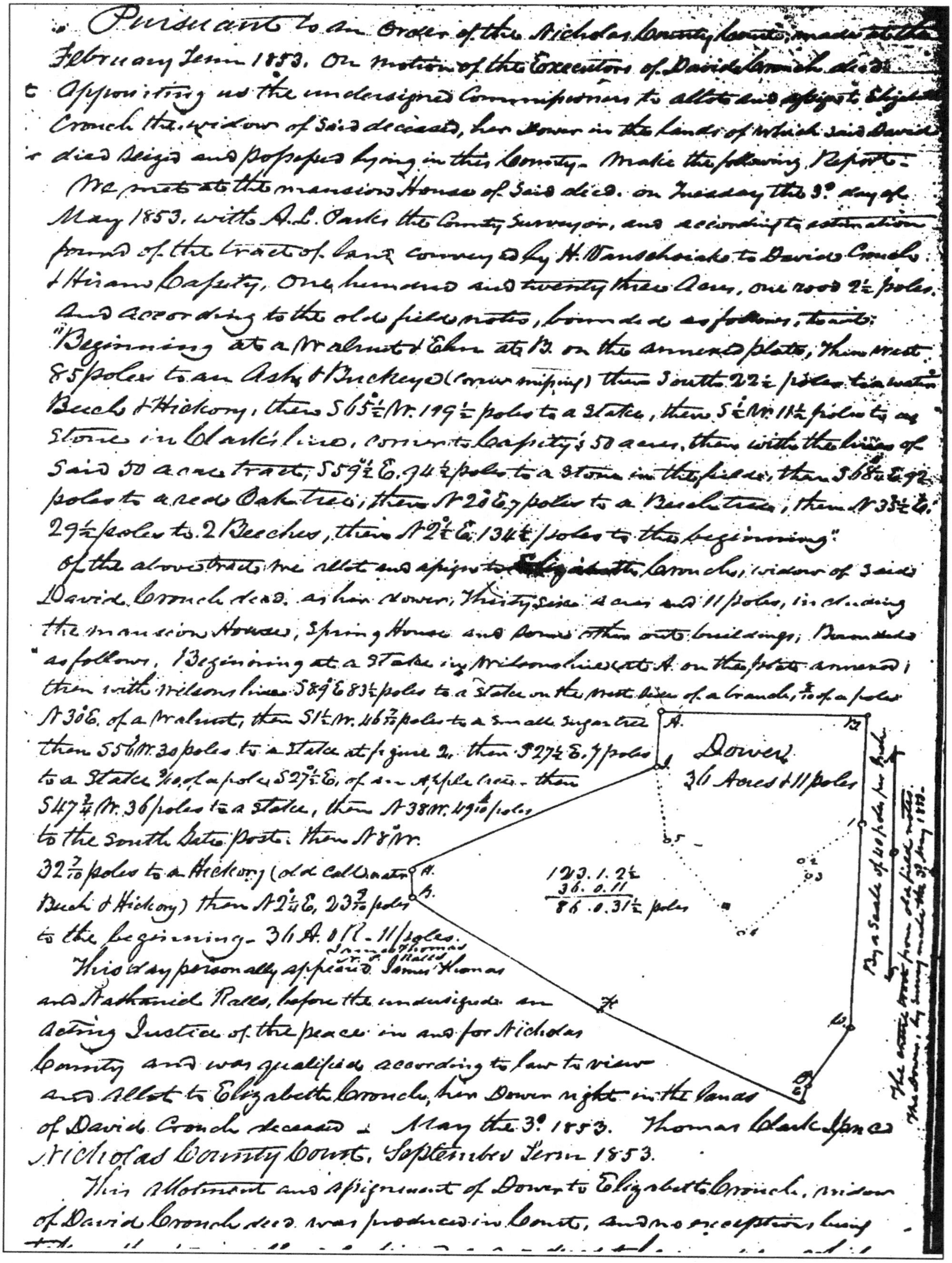

Pursuant to an Order of the Nicholas County Court, made at the February Term 1853. On motion of the Executors of David Crouch decd. Appointing us the undersigned Commissioners to allot and assign to Elizabeth Crouch the widow of said deceased, her Dower in the lands of which said David died seized and possessed lying in this County. Make the following Report:

We met at the mansion House of said decd. on Tuesday the 3d day of May 1853. with A. L. Parks the County Surveyor, and according to estimation found of the tract of land conveyed by H. Vanschoick to David Crouch & Hiram Cafferty, One hundred and twenty three Acres, one rood 2½ poles. And according to the old field notes, bounded as follows, to wit: "Beginning at a Walnut & Elm at B. on the annexed plat, thence west 85 poles to an Ash & Buckeye (corner missing) then South 22½ poles to a water Beech & Hickory, thence S 65½ W. 19½ poles to a Stake, thence S ½ W. 11½ poles to a Stone in Clark's line, corner to Cafferty's 50 acres, then with the lines of said 50 acre tract, S 59½ E. 94½ poles to a stone in the field, then S 68½ E 92 poles to a red Oak tree; thence N 20 E 7 poles to a Beech tree; then N 33½ E. 29½ poles to 2 Beeches, then N 2½ E. 134½ poles to the beginning."

Of the above tract we allot and assign to Elizabeth Crouch, widow of said David Crouch decd. as her dower, Thirty six acres and 11 poles, including the mansion House, Spring House and some other out buildings; Bounded as follows, Beginning at a Stake in Wilsons line at A. on the plat annexed; then with Wilsons line S 89 E 83½ poles to a Stake on the west line of a branch, ⅔ of a pole N 30 E. of a Walnut, then S 1½ W. 46 7/10 poles to a small sugar tree then S 56 W. 30 poles to a Stake at figure 2. then S 27½ E. 7 poles to a Stake 3/10 of a pole S 27½ E. of an Apple tree then S 47¾ W. 36 poles to a stake, then N 38 W. 49 6/10 poles to the South Gate post. then N 8 W. 32 7/10 poles to a Hickory (old call water Beech & Hickory) then N 2¼ E, 23 9/10 poles to the beginning. 36 A. 0 R. 11 poles.

This day personally appeared James Thomas and Nathaniel Rallo, before the undersigned an acting Justice of the peace in and for Nicholas County and was qualified according to law to view and allot to Elizabeth Crouch, her Dower right in the lands of David Crouch deceased. May the 3d 1853. Thomas Clark J.P.

Nicholas County Court, September Term 1853.

This Allotment and assignment of Dower to Elizabeth Crouch, widow of David Crouch decd. was produced in Court, and no exceptions being

Figure 11-1. A deed demonstrating dower distribution.

fathers, the property descriptions might be matched and the identity of the father determined.

Warranty deeds express the guarantee that the grantor holds official title and can legally sell the piece of property. Should a dispute arise, the responsibility to protect the rights of the grantee belongs solely to the grantor.

Prenuptial agreements were not commonplace, though they cannot be considered uncommon either. They can often be found in Virginia counties where large estates were inherited. Most referred specifically to the wife, who may have accumulated large property holdings, either through heirship or widowhood. The agreement secured her interests in the property and insured distribution of her late husband's estate only to his and the wife's children.

For love and affection is a term often encountered in land deeds as the consideration or payment for which the property was sold. It does not necessarily indicate a specific relationship. It may, in fact, refer only to a special friendship. It usually warrants further investigation of the association between the two parties. These deeds often occur between a parent and child, or between siblings.

Various other types of deeds can also be found. Some deeds arrange for the care and upkeep of parents until their death in exchange for property. Sheriff's deeds distribute lands that were repossessed for delinquent taxes. For further explanations of miscellaneous types of deeds, see Fran Carter's *Searching American Land and Deed Records*, and Barbara Jean Evans' *A to Zax: A Comprehensive Dictionary for Genealogists and Historians*. Valuable definitions and descriptions can also be found in E. Kay Kirkham's *Land Records of America,* "Land and Tax Records" in *The Source: A Guidebook of American Genealogy,* and Val Greenwood's *The Researcher's Guide to American Genealogy*.

Deeds in America have been recorded since the first charter was granted. Most colonial deeds have been transferred to state archives or similar repositories, while many post-colonial deeds remain in the custody of their respective counties or towns. Title companies and insurance companies have accumulated extensive collections through the years and can be helpful when courthouses have been destroyed.

Deeds were seldom recorded at the time of sale. Deeds recorded more than eighty years after the actual transaction took place have been found. Before the twentieth century, most areas did not require deeds to be filed at any specific time. It was only when an action caused concern, or when there was a question about the legitimacy of the transaction, that some earlier deeds were finally recorded. For example, Mr. B may have bought land from Mr. A in 1812. Later, in 1836, Mr. B wanted to sell the property to Mr. C. However, the recorder knew only that the land had belonged to Mr. A. Proof was presented, and the earlier deed would then be recorded for A to B at the same time as the deed between B and C. At times, deeds were not recorded until a question of probate arose. Numerous other scenarios also existed. When fire or flood destroyed records, people were often asked to bring in evidence of their transactions and rerecord them. Careful attention should always be given to searching the deed books well after an ancestor left the area or passed away.

In addition to town- or county-generated land records, three other sources warrant mention here: manors, plantations, and land companies.

Manors were large tracts of land given to individuals. They were similar to charters, but on a much smaller basis. They were administered with characteristics similar to the feudal system in England. The owner of the manor would often lease lands within his manor in exchange for percentages of crops and labor. Manors were found mostly in the earliest settlements along the east coast, from Maryland northward. Some can also be found in northern Virginia.

Many manors, such as the Carrollton Manor in Carroll County, Maryland, kept their own records of land leases. They recorded crop productivity and a variety of other matters for each and every family. Their records are not part of the town or county records. Rather, they are often now found in local historical societies and state archive facilities, having been donated by descendants of manor owners. Many have also been transcribed or abstracted. They can be found at local and state libraries and at the Family History Library. An excellent reference for understanding more about the concept of manors is Sung Bok Kim's *Landlord and Tenant in Colonial New York: Manorial Society, 1664–1775.*

Most **plantations** were located in the southern states, from Virginia southward. Like manors, they were large tracts of land granted to one individual. Unlike manors, the plantations came to be staffed predominantly by slaves and involved less individual leasing. Plantations often kept their own records of administration, which included mostly personal information and crop production data. Land was seldom transferred or assigned except through the process of sharecropping and share tenancy.

Records for plantations are not centrally located. They are scattered about in museums, historical societies, and some state archives. They are not usually found among other deed records in county or town jurisdictions, and no specific inventory has ever been produced. When found, however, these records can reveal births, deaths, marriages, show family units, and document the transfer or sale of slaves.

Land companies were created when a group of investors pooled their financial resources, bought large tracts of land at reduced prices, then subdivided the land for resale. Sometimes these companies were awarded significant portions of newly opened territory. They operated in a manner similar to a marketing management firm—promoting, surveying, and distributing the lands. In these circumstances, land companies were usually financially responsible for the sale of a minimum acreage, then only for the exact acreage sold above that minimum.

Records generated by land companies are similar to those for plantations. They were not as well preserved, since they were not considered as official as those created by government entities. Land company records are often found in local libraries, museums, university manuscript collections, and state archives. The best reference for understanding more about land companies, their structure and influence on America, is Shaw Livermore's *Early American Land Companies: Their Influence on Corporate Development.*

LAND OWNERSHIP MAPS

While township plat maps focus on congressional townships, land ownership maps focus on civil townships. Land ownership maps are usually very neat and legible. Some are indexed, though many are not. Some illustrate only the names and approximate locations of residence, while others define exact portions of each township and section. (See figure 11-2.)

The Library of Congress houses more than 1,400 land ownership maps for at least portions of all states except Wyoming. The maps represent approximately one-third of the counties in the United States, and are dated mostly from 1840 to 1900. All maps have been microfiched and are available at the National Archives, the Library of Congress, and the Family History Library. For further information, see Richard W. Stephenson's *Land Ownership Maps: A Checklist of Nineteenth Century United States County Maps in the Library of Congress.*

INDEXES

Since land deeds are recorded chronologically by the date of registration, not the date of transaction, they can be among the most difficult records to search without the aid of an index. Though some indexes can prove very useful, some can be very disappointing or frustrating to search. Seeing an index invokes optimism about finding an ancestor's name. However, an ancestor may not always be listed where the researcher thinks he or she should be in an index. Each has its own peculiarities.

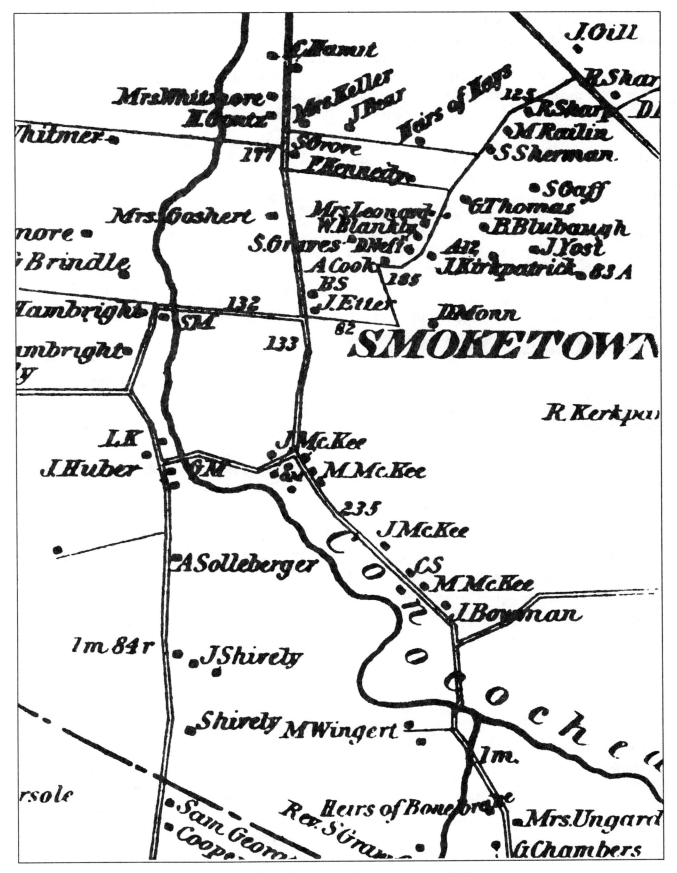

Figure 11-2. A land ownership map from Franklin County, Pennsylvania, 1858.

Grantee and grantor indexes are usually available for most deed books, though they vary in style from one county to another. (The grantee is the buyer, the grantor is the seller.) Grantee indexes are sometimes referred to as "indirect" indexes, while grantor indexes are sometimes referred to as "direct."

Indexes have been devised by various individuals and companies, though the perfect index has yet to be created. Some indexes, as logical as they seem after they are understood, can appear illogical and confusing at first glance. Some popular methods of indexing land deeds are discussed below.

The **running index** is the most common index encountered. Entries are arranged in alphabetical order by the first letter of the surname only. Within each letter the information is recorded chronologically. The first letter of each surname is assigned a page number to begin on. As the records are accumulated, they are placed on the appropriate page. When the information exceeds the allot-

ted page numbers, a notation at the bottom of the page refers the reader to the continuing page number. This usually refers to another letter of the alphabet, stating "continued after 'b'," or "see 'j'." Remember that these added pages will be out of order.

Cumulative indexes encompass a series of years, such as 1782 to 1787, 1787 to 1792, and so on. Within each group of years the names are listed alphabetically or chronologically. Some indexes are simple variations of the running indexes. Within each beginning letter of the surnames they are sometimes listed according to the first letter of the given name. Thus, within the surnames of the letter "A," they are organized by all given names starting with "A," then the given names of "B," etc.

Running Index Sample

A

Charles Anderson from James Whitfield	1797
Benjamin Arliss from George Furth	1799
Charles Anderson from Samuel Taylor	1799
Charles Anderson from Samuel Taylor	1800
John Alston from Peter Sims	1804
Seyborn Armstrong from Carl Berg	1806
Charles Anderson from John Anderson	1806

B

Carl Berg from William Toliver	1793
Charles Berg from Joseph Toliver	1797
Charles Berg from Zadock Davis	1799

C

Cumulative Index Sample

<u>1782–1787</u>

A

Stephen Ames to Jeptha Strate	A:23
Charles Adderbury to John White	A:68
Stephen Ames to Horatio Miles	A:101

B

Samuel Bradford to William Suter	A:53
Peter Bradford to George Howland	A:59
Lemuel Bogg to Henry Stanford	A:79

<u>1787–1795</u>

A

Stephen Ames to Joseph Berry	A:433
John Ames to Henry Griggs	B:3
Charles Adderbury to Miles White	B:47

B

Peter Bradford to James Caldwell	A:456
Peter Bradford to Francis Caldwell	A:457
Samuel Bradford to James Caldwell	A:461

<u>1795–1799</u>

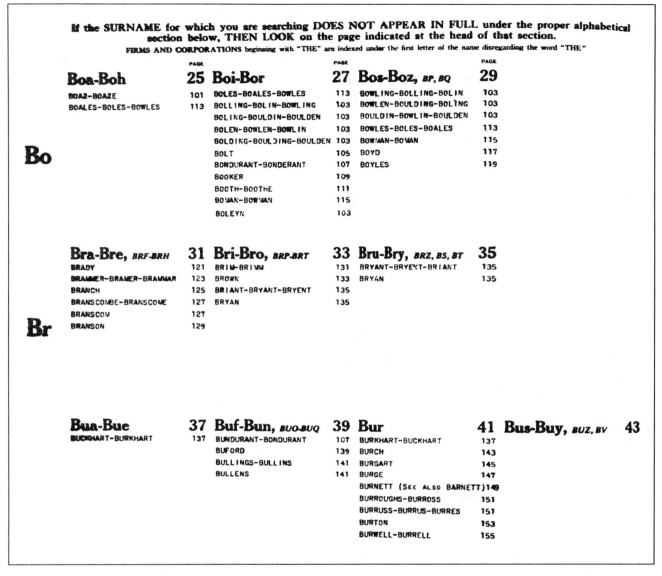

If the SURNAME for which you are searching DOES NOT APPEAR IN FULL under the proper alphabetical section below, THEN LOOK on the page indicated at the head of that section.

FIRMS AND CORPORATIONS beginning with "THE" are indexed under the first letter of the name disregarding the word "THE"

Bo

Boa-Boh	**25**		Boi-Bor	**27**		Bos-Boz, *BP, BQ*	**29**
BOAZ-BOAZE	101		BOLES-BOALES-BOWLES	113		BOWLING-BOLLING-BOLIN	103
BOALES-BOLES-BOWLES	113		BOLLING-BOLIN-BOWLING	103		BOWLEN-BOULDING-BOLING	103
			BOLING-BOULDIN-BOULDEN	103		BOULDIN-BOWLIN-BOULDEN	103
			BOLEN-BOWLEN-BOWLIN	103		BOWLES-BOLES-BOALES	113
			BOLDING-BOULDING-BOULDEN	103		BOWMAN-BOWAN	115
			BOLT	105		BOYD	117
			BONDURANT-BONDERANT	107		BOYLES	119
			BOOKER	109			
			BOOTH-BOOTHE	111			
			BOWAN-BOWMAN	115			
			BOLEYN	103			

Br

Bra-Bre, *BRF-BRH*	**31**		Bri-Bro, *BRP-BRT*	**33**		Bru-Bry, *BRZ, BS, BT*	**35**
BRADY	121		BRIM-BRIVM	131		BRYANT-BRYENT-BRIANT	135
BRAMMER-BRAMER-BRAMMAR	123		BROWN	133		BRYAN	135
BRANCH	125		BRIANT-BRYANT-BRYENT	135			
BRANSCOMBE-BRANSCOME	127		BRYAN	135			
BRANSCOM	127						
BRANSON	129						

Bua-Bue	**37**		Buf-Bun, *BUO-BUQ*	**39**		Bur	**41**		Bus-Buy, *BUZ, BV*	**43**
BUCKHART-BURKHART	137		BUNDURANT-BONDURANT	107		BURKHART-BUCKHART	137			
			BUFORD	139		BURCH	143			
			BULLINGS-BULLINS	141		BURGART	145			
			BULLENS	141		BURGE	147			
						BURNETT (SEE ALSO BARNETT)	149			
						BURROUGHS-BURROSS	151			
						BURRUSS-BURRUS-BURRES	151			
						BURTON	153			
						BURWELL-BURRELL	155			

Figure 11-3. An example of the Cott indexing method. Common surnames are given their own categories, while others are grouped together.

Cott System indexes are the most common commercial indexing systems among deed records. They were devised by companies for indexing land deeds and other similar transactions undertaken by a variety of businesses or government agencies. This system organizes entries by the first three letters of the surname. Common surnames are given their own category, while others within those first three letters are grouped together. All are placed chronologically within groups. (See figure 11-3.)

Though there are a variety of indexing methods that may seem confusing, most questions can be answered by looking through the various pages of the index for the missing data. If "J" does not follow "I," it does not mean that there were no surnames that started with "J"; it likely means they are located somewhere else in the alphabet lineup of that particular index.

CONCLUSION

Though some individuals from the past left behind very few traces of their lives, it is probable that they at least held title to land. More than eighty-five percent of our ancestors who lived before 1900 owned land at one time. Whether that land was obtained at a high price or was obtained at no charge, it was always later sold through a type of deed. Searching deed indexes can sometimes be confusing, but more often will be rewarding. With a little extra effort, names can usually be located.

There is a variety of deeds, and understanding their purpose can help improve the interpretation of the events that took place and the clues that may actually be there.

Some additional terms that may prove helpful are *liber*, which means "volume"; *et alii* (usually shortened to *et al.*), which means "and others"; and *et ux*, which means "and wife."

For information on a variety of strategies to employ when working with land deeds, see chapter 12, Strategies for Individual Lands. Also refer to Research in Land and Tax Records in *The Source: A Guidebook of American Genealogy*, William Dollarhide's many articles on land and property found in the *Genealogy Bulletin*, and Helen Hunt Read's *Property Deeds for Genealogy*. For complete references to these works and others, see "For Further Reference," below.

REPOSITORIES

For a list of designated repositories for each state, see page 184.

FOR FURTHER REFERENCE

Carter, Fran. *Searching American Land and Deed Records*. Orting, Wash.: Heritage Quest, 1991.

Evans, Barbara Jean. *A to Zax: A Comprehensive Dictionary for Genealogists and Historians*. 3rd ed. Alexandria, Va.: Hearthside Press, 1995.

Eichholz, Alice, ed. *The Red Book*. Salt Lake City: Ancestry, 1994.

The Handybook for Genealogists. 8th ed. Logan, Utah: The Everton Publishers, 1995.

Greenwood, Val D. *The Researcher's Guide to American Genealogy*. Baltimore: Genealogical Publishing Co., 1990.

Kirkham, E. Kay. *Land Records of America*. Salt Lake City: Deseret Book Co., 1964.

Leary, Helen, and Maurice R. Stirewalt, eds. *North Carolina Research: Genealogy and Local History*. Raleigh: North Carolina Genealogical Society, 1980.

Read, Helen Hunt. *Property Deeds for Genealogy*. Toledo, Ohio: the author, 1985.

"Research in Land and Tax Records." In *The Source: A Guidebook of American Genealogy*. Edited by Loretto Dennis Szucs and Sandra Hargreaves Luebking. 2nd ed. Salt Lake City: Ancestry, 1997.

Stephenson, Richard W. *Land Ownership Maps*. Washington, D.C.: Library of Congress, 1967.

Also see "For Further Reference" in chapters 5 through 10 for a variety of resources that apply to individual lands.

12

Strategies for Individual Land Records

GRANTEE/GRANTOR PATTERNS

Strategies for federal- and state-land states, as listed in chapters 7 and 10, can also be applied to individual lands. There are a few strategies, however, that apply more specifically to individual lands. One is the observation of patterns among individuals listed in the indexes.

Associations are among the most vital clues in genealogical or historical research. Too often, attention is only given to relationships; associations are ignored. While many individuals left their homes, they did not usually travel alone. Friends, neighbors, religious groups, and relatives with other surnames are among the many associates with whom people migrated. By identifying these associations, the ancestor's place of origin can be more precisely confirmed.

For example, if the previous origin of James Smith of Tipton County, Indiana, is being researched, records can be found for James Smiths in almost every city or county east of the Mississippi River. Distinguishing his origins could seem hopeless. However, what if the same James Smith of Tipton County, Indiana, could be found frequently associated in deeds with a Stanley Seymour and Ichabod Kennedy, and all three were found residing earlier in the same town in Connecticut? Through further research in Connecticut, this evidence could help prove James Smith's origin. Such evidence becomes a basis for choosing to research in Connecticut rather than another area.

Associations can be derived through almost any record source, though most easily through land records. Searches in the grantee and grantor indexes should never be restricted to the ancestor only. Even with names such as Smith or Williams, each and every individual with that surname should be carefully studied for a pattern of associations. The following is a classic example of relationships being determined by association with a third party.

Example

Abraham Milton was identified living in Smalltown, Nebraska. A review of the grantee and grantor indexes showed him to never have bought or sold land with another Milton. Careful studies of all his deeds showed no witnesses or bordering properties containing the surname Milton. He appeared to have no close connections with any other Milton in the area.

By studying all of the Milton deeds for this particular county, the following names were noted from the grantee list:

Abraham Milton	from	**John Wilkins**
Jeremiah Milton	from	Peter Towland
Peter Milton	from	Greenbury Adams
Jacob Milton	from	Samuel Secord
Jeremiah Milton	from	Francis Grosberg

Abraham Milton	from	William Smith
John Milton	from	Peter Towland
Jacob Milton	from	**John Wilkins**
Jeremiah Milton	from	Greenbury Adams
Peter Milton	from	**John Wilkins**
Peter Milton	from	Samuel Secord
Abraham Milton	from	James Brubaker
Isaac Milton	from	**John Wilkins**
Jacob Milton	from	Henry Chauncey

While this list confirms that Abraham did not transact land with another Milton, it shows a very interesting pattern of association. Abraham Milton received land from John Wilkins. Jacob Milton, Peter Milton, and Isaac Milton all received land from John Wilkins as well. Thus, Abraham Milton was indirectly associated with Jacob, Peter, and Isaac Milton through a common individual.

In this particular case, a review of the probate records for the county showed that John Wilkins had a deceased daughter named Lucretia Milton, who had been the wife of Jacob Milton. John Wilkins left personal and real property to his grandchildren Abraham, Peter, and Isaac Milton, children of his deceased daughter Lucretia.

Patterns are the key to most clues that exist in land records. The will of John Wilkins would never have been researched to find the father of Abraham Milton were it not for the name patterns and associations in the deed index. No logic existed until patterns were identified.

GENERAL STRATEGIES

In addition to identifying patterns from grantee and grantor indexes, other strategies can also be used for individual lands. Some are duplicates of state and federal land record strategies, though many are unique to individual lands. They can be summarized as follows:

- Compare property descriptions. If there are similar names for people that are spelled differently, comparing descriptions will often identify them as the same person.

- Land deeds can serve as a census substitute. Censuses were taken in decennial years, but land deeds were recorded at the time of registration. They can also identify when a person arrived in or departed from an area.

- Consideration is important. Was the property sold for love and affection, or was it for $1,000? Such a clue indicates a possible relationship, though it should be further supported with other evidence.

- A wife's name can often be discerned in the grantor records where she released her dower rights to the property being sold. (The lack of a wife's name does not necessarily indicate that she was deceased, or that the male was single at that time.)

- Always assess the date the deed was written versus the date it was recorded. The difference may further define the years of an ancestor's activity.

- Unlike federal lands and many state lands, an individual did not have to be a resident of the United States to buy a piece of property from another individual; nor was the person required to have declared his intention to become a citizen.

- Compare the acreage bought with the acreage sold. Such a comparison may yield clues to inheritance or similar circumstances. If more was sold than bought, perhaps some of the property previously belonged to parents or to a wife through previous marriage or inheritance.

- Filing was not required at the time of the actual transaction, so the deed may not have been recorded for many years. Search at least twenty years beyond the last known date of an ancestor's existence in an area. Also, if more was bought than was sold, who might be in possession of the remainder? Is it possible that it was recorded much later?

- If a courthouse is found to have burned, perhaps an ancestor's deed was taken in afterwards and rerecorded. This could have been years after the original filing date.

- Most state grants can also be found listed in county and town grantee/grantor indexes. In addition to the surname, look under corporations, businesses, state of, town of, and under the name of the state.

- "Et al." and "et ux," when found in the index, can indicate that further clues may exist in the document. Et al. means "and others." Who are these others? Siblings selling a joint inheritance, perhaps? Et ux means "and wife." This could then disclose the given name of the wife, helping further differentiate people with the same name, or simply provide a name that had been previously unknown.

- Power of attorney was often given to a friend or known acquaintance. The person may have been a friend of a friend. Regardless, if the recipient of that power was not an attorney or did not advertise such services, a potential association or relationship should be explored.

- Determine the legal age for the state being researched. Most require a person to be at least eighteen or twenty-one to appear on a deed, either as a witness or as a transacting party. Minors who sold inheritance did so through a guardian. In those circumstances, the minor may not have been listed in the grantor index; the transaction may be under the guardian's name.

- Some deeds, especially in the New England area, can identify the occupation of both the grantor and grantee. This helps discern them from others with the same name.

- County boundaries were constantly changing as new counties were created. Carefully consider which county you should be researching for each time period.

For additional strategies and case studies, see chapter 7, Strategies for State Land Records, and chapter 10, Strategies for Federal Land Records.

Also see Helen Hunt Read's *Property Deeds for Genealogy* and Val Greenwood's *The Researcher's Guide to American Genealogy*. "Research in Land and Tax Records" in *The Source* is always an excellent reference as well.

FOR FURTHER REFERENCE

Carter, Fran. *Searching American Land and Deed Records*. Orting, Wash.: Heritage Quest, 1991.

Dollarhide, William, and William Thorndale. *Map Guide to U.S. Federal Censuses*. Baltimore: Genealogical Publishing Co., 1987.

Eakle, Arlene. *Solving American Pedigrees: American Property Records, Land and Tax Records*. Salt Lake City: Genealogical Institute, 1973.

Eichholz, Alice, ed. *The Red Book: American State, County and Town Sources*. Rev. ed. Salt Lake City: Ancestry, 1992.

Elliott, Wendy L. *Using Land Records to Solve Research Problems*. Bountiful, Utah: American Genealogical Lending Library, 1987.

Gates, Paul W. *History of Public Land Law Development*. Washington, D.C.: U.S. Government Printing Office, 1968.

Greenwood, Val D. *The Researcher's Guide to American Genealogy*. Baltimore: Genealogical Publishing Co., 1990.

The Handybook for Genealogists. 8th ed. Logan, Utah: The Everton Publishers, 1995.

"How to Plat a Deed." *Eswau Huppeday, Bulletin of the Broad River Genealogical Society* 1 (1) (February 1981).

Kirkham, E. Kay. *Land Records of America*. Salt Lake City: Deseret Book Co., 1964.

Lawson, Charles E. *Surveying Your Land: A Common Sense Guide to Surveys, Deeds, and Title Searches*. Woodstock, Vt.: The Countryman Press, 1990.

Leary, Helen F.M., and Maurice R. Stirewalt, eds. *North Carolina Research, Genealogy and Local History*. Raleigh: The North Carolina Genealogical Society, 1980. Has excellent material that can be applied to almost any land research—federal, state, or individual.

Miller, James W., Jr. "Platting Land Grants and Deeds." *The North Carolina Genealogical Society Journal* 16 (2) (May 1990).

Read, Helen Hunt. *Property Deeds for Genealogy.* Toledo, Ohio: the author, 1985.

Szucs, Loretto Dennis, and Sandra Hargreaves Luebking, eds. *The Source: A Guidebook of American Genealogy.* Rev. ed. Salt Lake City: Ancestry, 1997.

Section 5:
Special Interest

An Introduction to Special Interest Lands

The concept of individual land ownership was foreign to most Native Americans until it was introduced by the Europeans. This naiveté can be perceived as positive in terms of communal organization and in the concept of "shared land equals shared responsibility." Security and success were found in the accomplishments of the entire tribe. This cultural adherence was difficult to maintain among the rapidly expanding "white" society, where success was measured in terms of property and monetary wealth. Voluntarily or not, Native Americans were soon involved in a variety of land transactions under a variety of circumstances.

The government of the United States recognized the titles of previous Spanish, French, and Mexican occupants. Treaties with Native Americans were handled differently, however. The Pueblo Indians were the only Native Americans to be considered a foreign sovereign by the United States, and thus were recognized in the private claims courts of New Mexico Territory. Indian mission lands and reservations were also dealt with by private land claims courts. Most other tribes relinquished their rights to tribal lands in exchange for relocation further west, and/or for repatriation into a "civilized" society. Usually, minimal monetary compensation for the tribe, and occasionally for individuals, accompanied the agreement.

Allotment records, federal scrip acts, leases, and other records were among the many land records generated. Though not as informative and consistently recorded as other land records, records created by Native American land issues often help reconstruct neighborhoods and fill in possible relationships and associations that will help bridge generations and establish correct migration groups. Cultural circumstances have generated unique sets of records, whether the allottee actually received the land or not.

Because many of the land-related records for Native Americans were recorded separately from ordinary federal transactions, they justify segregation from all other sections of this book, including pre-U.S. possession. This chapter, however, does not cover even a modest amount of the land collections available for this unique group of individuals. Rather, it is hoped that it will be an introduction—a beginning to build from and add to, spurring recognition of the value of Native American documents in genealogical research.

13

Native American Land Records

Treaties with Native Americans were initially negotiated between individual settlers (those who were considerate enough to do so) and the Native Americans occupying the lands at the time of settlement. These treaties were for small parcels of land rather than entire territories. Confusion and chaos quickly resulted from the uncoordinated efforts of these individuals, their well-meaning intentions notwithstanding. Foreign governments that claimed regional jurisdiction at the time refused to acknowledge most individual treaties. In fact, the British eventually outlawed entering into a treaty not performed by their own appointed emissaries.

As the United States gained independence and began to expand westward, lands continued to be acquired from the Indians by treaties with government-appointed officials. The land was then distributed through federal programs to non-Indian settlers. Conversely, the acquisition of land by Native Americans did not begin in earnest until the 1830s, in treaties with the Creeks and Chickasaws. Native Americans acquired land in a variety of ways, though most commonly as follows:

ACQUISITION

- Allotments of specific land to tribes and individual tribal members
- Scrip, which could be used by an individual to locate on any available tract in designated areas

Allotment had taken hold as a practice by the 1830s. It provided individual tracts of land for Native Americans being displaced because of land cessions to the United States. It was also theorized that allotments would help them integrate more quickly into the "civilized" culture of whites by having actual ownership and the ability to perform land transactions. Though the government had allotted them land, Native Americans were, in reality, expected to sell quickly and move on. Often the tracts would be immediately sold to raise funds for this removal. Land speculators and non-Indian settlers were the only beneficiaries of the earliest allotments.

Later, under the Dawes Act (1893), lands allotted to individuals were held in trust, to be disbursed only after a twenty-five-year moratorium had passed. This was done in the belief that the land would later be handled more wisely by the recipients. The government acted as "guardian" until the Native Americans could better understand white society and its economic system. It was also done to protect recipients from the hordes of land speculators who took advantage of the circumstances faced by earlier allotees.

After 1901, it was possible to sell inherited lands out of trust before the trust period was completed. By 1907, all allotted lands could be dispersed if a fee patent was issued by the government, or if the agent deemed such actions in the allottee's best interest. There were two types of patents that allowed resale by individual Native

Americans: fee patents and trust patents. Trust patents indicated the right to patent, while a fee patent was actual title to the property.

Scrip was also given to Native Americans, such as the Choctaws and Chippewas. It was also distributed to "half-breeds," some of whom were not necessarily living on tribal lands when the treaty was signed. Scrip allowed the recipient to select public lands rather than be assigned specifically defined allotments. The selections were restricted to designated areas, depending on the treaty. For example, scrip given under the Choctaw Treaty of 1830 had to be redeemed for lands in Mississippi, Louisiana, Alabama, or Arkansas. Scrip lands had to be located and defined by the recipient before the rights to that property could be resold. It was then sold by deed, the same as any individual transaction.

Records were generated for Native Americans as they received land, mostly through allotments and scrip. Records were also generated as they dispersed those lands. This dispersal was mostly undertaken in the ways described below.

DISPERSAL

- Allotted lands still within the twenty-five-year moratorium could be leased

- After twenty-five years had expired or a trust patent was obtained, direct sale of the property could be made

- Sale of surplus tribal lands could be made after allotments to individuals were completed, with the approval of Congress

Leases of Indian allotments were frequently made by the 1890s. They first came into effect with the establishment of the Trade and International Act of 1834. Reservation land could not be sold without the consent of Congress, though leasing to outsiders was permitted. The lease price was established by the quality of the land and could be bartered rather than sold for a fixed market value. Leases were usually made for a term of ninety-nine years and are often found recorded among land deeds for each particular county or town. These

records will document that the property was being leased, from whom, the length of lease, and that the property was still under the twenty-five-year term stipulated in the Dawes Act.

Direct sale of Native American lands could take place once the right to patent was obtained or the actual patent was issued. Seldom did Native Americans actually patent the property allotted them. Once the right to patent was vested, the lands were usually sold to white settlers or speculators. These procedures were similar to the assignments made by bounty-land warrant recipients to a third party. If a fee patent had not yet been issued, the resale of Native American allotments was usually documented in federal records of the Bureau of Land Management or the Bureau of Indian Affairs as the initial transaction for that piece of property.

Surplus tribal allotments usually existed after individual allotments had been made. These excess lands were often sold to non-Indian settlers or companies on behalf of the tribe. Monies collected were used for a variety of purposes, including the cost of administering allotments. Trust lands were not subject to preemption, nor could bounty-land warrants or scrip be used as payment.

RECORD COLLECTIONS

Native American tribes are too numerous to represent all of their records here with due justice. However, certain record collections concerning Native American land transactions warrant inclusion in this book. These records derive from two sources:

- The Bureau of Land Management (Record Group 49)

- The Bureau of Indian Affairs (Record Group 75)

Other records were generated at individual state levels of government and through various Native American agencies, but their scattered storage and accountability prevent uniform coverage in any single volume.

Records Generated by the Bureau of Land Management

Most pre-1908 records generated by the Bureau of Land Management are held at the National Archives in Washington, D.C., in Record Group 49. Additional duplicate records can be found in many individual state offices of that same bureau. The Native American records held at the National Archives can be viewed as two different groups: records grouped on a nationwide, multi-state, or tribal basis; and records organized according to individual land offices within each state. The former group is the focus for purposes of this book, and examples of the most informative records follow.

Indian Reserve Files

One of the largest nationwide collections is called the Indian Reserve Files. Indian Reserve Files are groups of miscellaneous papers generated by a variety of different legislative actions. They include allotment records, reports of Indian commissions, patents, and special agent reports on fraudulent claims. Correspondence, copies of wills to support the relationship of heirs, interviews with local residents, and a combination of other records are also included. All were generated through land-related procedures.

There are twenty-two boxes of Indian Reserve Files. They are not indexed, nor are they organized in any particular way. While this makes it difficult to search for a particular ancestor, the following guide has been derived from covers on the boxes and from further assessment of grouped contents inside each box.

Box 1

Reports of Seattle allotments; allotment applications in Oregon, Washington, and California; Roseburg allotments in Oregon; The Dalles allotments in Oregon; miscellaneous allottments for Arizona, Michigan, Idaho, Montana, Nevada, and New Mexico. (See figure 13-1.)

Box 2

Miscellaneous information on the Brothertons, Chippewas and Munsee, Delaware, Great and Little Osage, and the Crow; several Cherokee land claims; cancelled Chickasaw patents; land claims of the Delaware in Kansas.

Box 3

Chickasaw cession letters, 1837–39; Records of the Surveyor-General at Pontotoc, Mississippi; miscellaneous records of the Commissioner of Indian Affairs concerning the Chickasaw; adjusted accounts of Chickasaw cession certificates, 1837–48.

Box 4

Chickasaw cession letters in Mississippi; Chickasaw cession accounts in Alabama. These records are organized according to the year in which the receiver's office obtained them (mostly the 1840s). This was usually the same year they were produced.

Box 5

Chickasaw cession contracts of survey; Chickasaw letters; Choctaw line surveys; Chickasaw registers, patents, and letters, 1833–38 (dates on these can be misleading, as the actions were taken later in the 1840s).

Box 6

Chickasaw correspondence (written mostly by "whites"), 1839–43; approved list of Chickasaw orphan lands; orphan land certificates 1–204; letters concerning Creeks and Creek orphans. (See figure 13-2.)

Box 7

Creek contracts, 1842–1907; correspondence regarding Chippewas, Ottawas, and Pottawatomies, 1847–55.

Box 8

Choctaw Indian Lands, 1842–83; miscellaneous Choctaw letters, 1809–45; Choctaw orphan lands in Mississippi, 1820–40.

Box 9

Choctaw Orphan lands, 1850–1900; Crow Creek Agency records (which include Sioux Land Certificates, sample copied); Kansas trust lands.

```
Tommy Joby All.    Affidavit.      2.

     That Jennie All died many years ago (exact date unknown), unmarried and
without issue, leaving as her heirs at law her father, Joby All, and her
mother, Sallie All, who were each entitled to an undivided one half interest
in and to her estate.
     That Johnny All died while Special Allotting Agent George Keepers was in the
Suiattle Valley, in 1902 or 1903, unmarried and without issue;  that he left as
his heirs at law his father, Joby All, and his mother, Sallie All, who were
each entitled to an undivided one half interest in and to his estate.
     That George All Died one week after Special Allotting Agent George Keepers
left the Suiattle Valley, in 1903, unmarried and without issue, leaving as his
heirs at law his father, Joby All and his mother, Sallie All, who were each
entitled to an undivided one half interest in and to his estate.
     That Mike All died eight years ago, in 1908, unmarried and without issue,
leaving as his heirs at law his father, Joby All, and his mother, Sallie All,
who were each entitled to an undivided one half interest in and to his estate.
     That Joby All died on January 25, 1912, leaving as his heirs at law his wife,
Sallie All, and three children, Tommy Joby All, Son; Julia Moses, wife of
William Moses, daughter;  and Susie Moses, wife of Charles Moses, Daughter;
That xxxxxxxxx there were no other children nor any representatives of any
deceased children of the said Joby All living at the date of his death;  that
the said Sallie All is entitled to an undivided one third interest in and to
the estate of the said Joby All, and that the said Tommy Joby All and the said
Julia Moses and the said Susie Moses are each entitled to an undivided two-
ninths interest in and to the estate of the said Joby All, deceased.
```

Figure 13-1. From the "Reports of Seattle Allotments" in Box 1 of the Indian Reserve Files. Most records in these files are not typescripts such as this, though many contain similar information.

Indian "B" Files

The records of the next five boxes are simply labeled "B files." They belong to the Bureau of Land Management, Division B. The recorder of lands was assigned this division. The "B files" include mostly issues of scrip, mixed blood and otherwise. They involve the Creek, Pottawatomie, Sioux, Chippewa, and several other tribes. They are in no apparent order and have no known index or cross-reference.

Box 10	**Box 13**
1–122	632–995
Box 11	**Box 14**
123–241	997–1036
Box 12	
242–631	

Box 15

Includes 1038–1054 of the "B files"; a variety of Indian claims; miscellaneous information concerning the Kaskaskias, Peorias, Piankeshaws and Weas, Kansas trust, Cheyenne, and Arapahoe.

Box 16

Packets on the Kickapoo Indians; Ottawa reservations in Illinois; Sac and Fox grants in Illinois; Indian reservations in Idaho, Illinois, and Florida, including some maps (several with tags stating "moved to cartographic branch"); papers concerning the Miami Treaty.

Box 17

Sac and Fox records in Mississippi, Missouri and Iowa, including approvals for land records; Sac and Fox allotments as found in the Nemaha Half-Breed Book; secretaries' letters cancelling selections of "Chips" (Chippewas) in Saginaw.

Box 18

More secretaries' letters cancelling selections of Chippewas in Saginaw; papers concerning the Shawnee Treaty and lands therefrom; papers concerning Black Bob's Band (the fraud scheme of the century).

Box 19

Papers concerning the Stockbridge and Munsee in Wisconsin (Winnebagos).

Box 20

Turtle Mountain; Winnebago Trust; Lac Court Orielles; mixed blood Chippewas; lists of accounts for various land offices for land sales during 1839 and 1840 (these papers have no apparent relation to Indian lands); accounting adjustments for land sales in the state of Alabama, 1842 (also with no apparent connection to or exclusiveness to Indian lands).

Box 21

Correspondence from various agencies, some concerning Indian bounty lands; copy of patents issued to fictitious persons of the Winnebago tribe.

Box 22

Papers concerning the Wyandott Treaty of 1855 and lands thereon; absentee Wyandott selections; a few papers on the Nisqually or Lischi; miscellaneous documents on the Upper Sandusky; absentee Cheyenne and Arapahoe.

Almost all of the Indian Reserve File boxes have numerous entries with miniature plats enclosed. These plats/maps can be extremely helpful when reconstructing neighborhoods of Native American families as they existed before removal. Indian Reserve Files have not been microfilmed, and they are only available at the National Archives in downtown Washington, D.C.

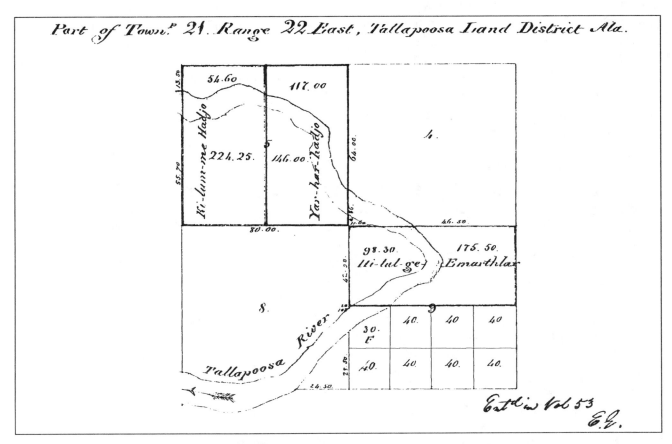

Figure 13-2. From "Letters Concerning Creeks" in Box 6 of the Indian Reserve Files. This letter concerned the allotments of Ki-lum-me-Hadjo. The plat, however, showed his allotment next to Yar-har-Hadjo, perhaps indicating a relationship.

Scrip

Scrip was issued only through acts of Congress and therefore comprises a federal record. Scrip was not issued by agencies except in their role as mediators between individual Native Americans and the government. Records of the Bureau of Land Management that pertain to scrip are housed at the National Archives. While some are recorded among individual land office records, the following collections are filed in a general category:

Sioux Half-Breed Scrip. Congressional acts of 17 July 1854 and 19 May 1858 provided scrip for "half-breeds" or mixed bloods of the "Dacotah or Sioux Nation of Indians" in exchange for their rights to reservation land. Records include powers of attorney, applications for specific locations of land, and patents. Powers of attorney and the applications are the most important records (figure 13-3). Most of these applications were made after removal to new areas. Thus, the records show current residence as well as previous residences, and often they show power of attorney used to successfully acquire the land. Several cases identify family members who remained in the area as recipients of that power of attorney. Testimonies are sometimes present in the files. These records have not been microfilmed, and they are available only at the National Archives.

Choctaw Scrip. Choctaw scrip was implemented by acts of Congress in 1842 and 1845. The scrip certificates are mixed with several other types of documents, including correspondence between agents and bureau officials. Almost one thousand different certificates and accompanying documents exist (figure 13-4). Some show only the name of the individual and to whom he was assigning the scrip. Others show minor and orphan children and identify the father under whom they were qualifying.

Power of attorney, scrip certificates, testimonies, and assignments to "whites" are generally included among Choctaw scrip files. They are not specifically indexed, but there is a List of Choctaw Scrip Certificates that was created in 1854. It is included in the files, which occupy six linear feet of space, and provides names and certificate numbers to allow easier access.

Chippewa Half-Breed Scrip. Half-breed scrip exists for the Chippewas of the Lake Superior, Pembina, and Red Lake bands. These records combined affected fewer than five hundred individuals. Heads of households and individual mixed bloods over the age of twenty-one could qualify.

Know all Men by these Presents, That We Henry H. Titus and Belle P. Titus his wife two of the County of Lyon in the State of Minnesota have made, constituted and appointed, and by these presents do make, constitute and appoint Byron M. Smith of Hennepin county, in the State of Minnesota our true and lawful attorney, for us and in our name, place and stead, to enter into and upon, and take possession of any and all pieces and parcels of land, or the timber and other materials thereon, in the .... of ...., which we now own, or which we may hereafter acquire or become seized of, or in which we may now or hereafter be in any way interested; under and by virtue of location of Sioux (or Dakota), Half Breed Scrip, No. 250 Letter "A" for 40 acres issued to the said Henry H. Titus formerly of Shakopee Minn. under ACT of July 17, 1854, United States Statutes at large. Page 304, chapter 83, authorizing the issuance of said scrip in exchange for lands of the Sioux Half Breed Resverve at Lake Pipin, Minnesota; and to prosecute and defend any and all suits at law, in the courts of said .... of .... or of the United States, relating to the title to said lands; and we further authorize and empower our said

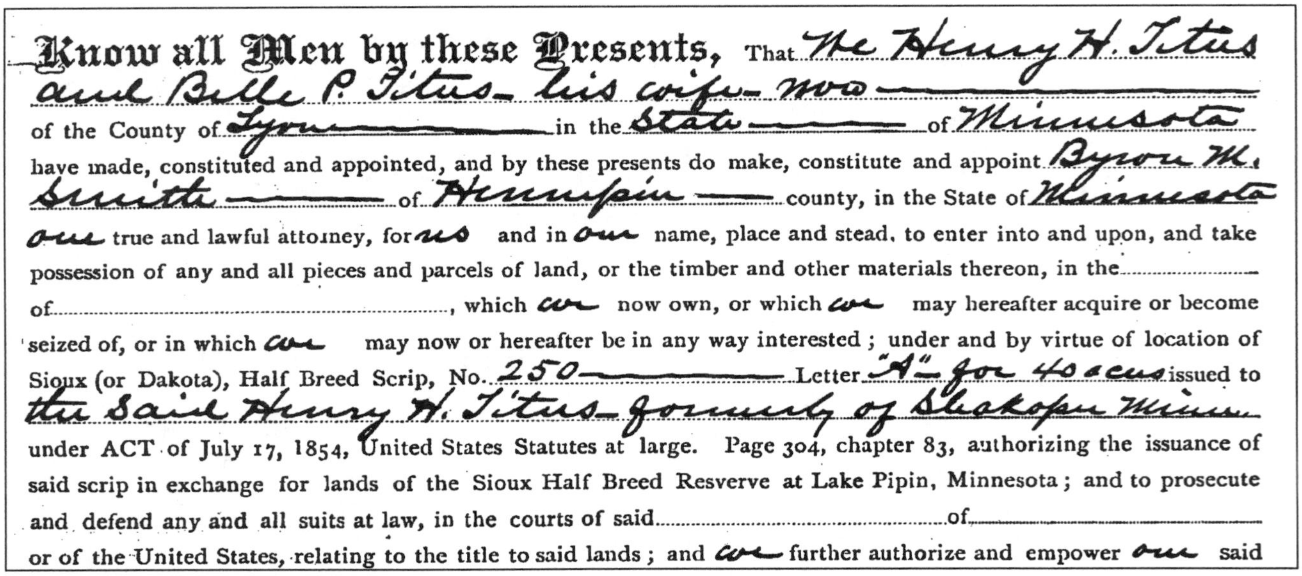

Figure 13-3. From the "Sioux Half-Breed Scrip" files at the National Archives. This example shows information contained in powers of attorney.

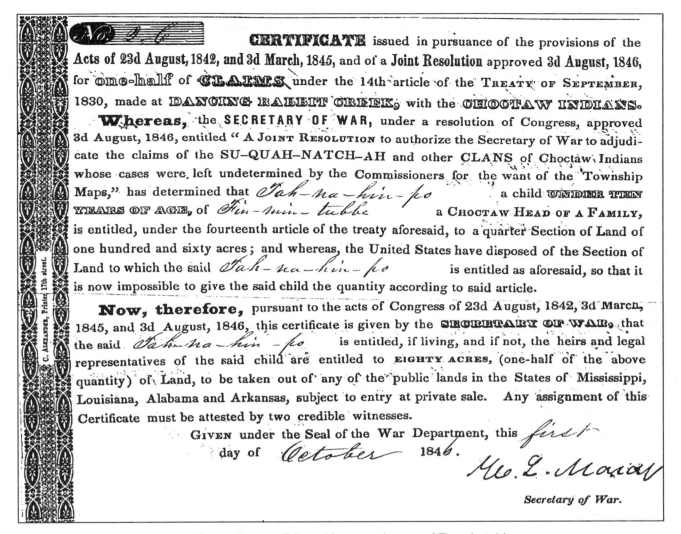

Figure 13-4. Choctaw scrip certificate showing Tah-na-hin-po as the son of Fin-min-tubbe.

Special Acts Series

The Special Acts Series occupies seventeen linear feet of shelf space and mostly involves scrip issues and allotment conflicts. The first several boxes are labeled by case number; records are then grouped categorically (for example, Ft. Jackson-Imperial Valley surveys in California are found grouped together, as are Lewis and Clark issues).

Records of this series include abandoned military reserves, Indian treaties, reservation issues, and more. They all concern the application for scrip under special acts of Congress for the complaints being issued by Native Americans. Of particular interest in these records are the evidence of mixed-blood relationships. Qualification processes for allotments sometimes overlooked the mixed bloods living outside reservations and white settlers who had become part of the tribes. Many mixed bloods and whites were not fully aware of their possible inclusion until after allotments had already been issued.

There is no index to the complete Special Acts Series, other than the non-alphabetized grouping of subjects. Some individual indexes are provided with particular groups of records. The records have not been microfilmed and are only available at the National Archives. For those patient enough to search the topics of each box and then search the papers among the appropriate topic, significant clues about Native American ancestry can be revealed. (See figures 13-5 and 13-6.)

Tract Books

Tract books exist separately for allotments on many Indian reservations. They can provide the following information:

- Name of the allottee
- Patent number
- Rate of land
- Property description
- The assignee of the property

Depending on the state being researched, the records are held at either the National Archives or the Bureau of Land Management. To understand more about the role of tract books and for a listing of tract book holdings for these two repositories, see chapter 9, Records Generated by Federal Lands.

Township Plat Maps

Township plat maps are extremely valuable when researching Native American ancestry. They can show allotments obtained by family members located next to each other and help reconstruct entire neighborhoods. Identification of an ancestor may help associate him or her with a specific band within a tribe; this helps to more accurately identify origins in other areas and opens up additional sources for research. Some land offices diligently recorded Native American allotments on plat maps, while others recorded only the name of the final patentee. Since many Native Americans assigned their allotments to a third party, the final patentee was often a white settler or land speculation company. (See figure 13-7.) For further information on township plat maps, see chapter 9, Records Generated by Federal Lands.

In General

Reservation lands eventually acquired by the federal government were usually dispersed for cash entry or homestead claims only. One-hundred-and-sixty-acre increments were provided for actual settlers; they were off-limits to speculators. These records originated with the federal government. They are recorded among the tract books with all other federal transactions, and they generated a land-entry case file. They are not segregated and are identified only by the legal description of location.

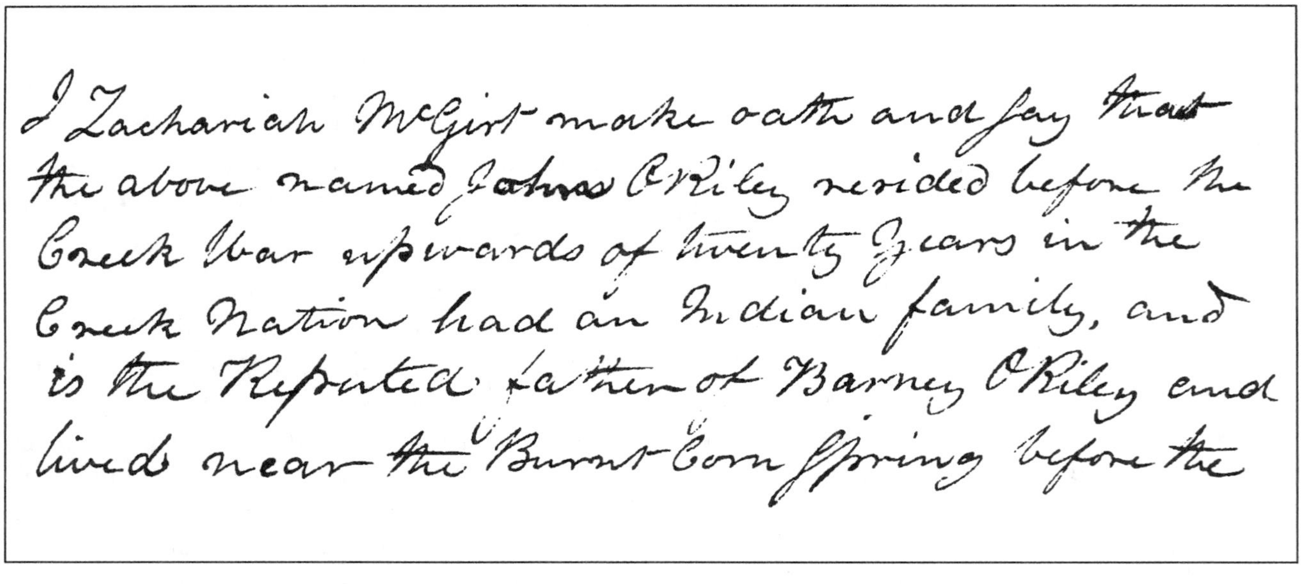
I Zachariah McGirt make oath and say that
the above named Johns O'Riley resided before the
Creek War upwards of twenty years in the
Creek Nation had an Indian family, and
is the Reputed father of Barney O'Riley and
lived near the Burnt Corn Spring before the

Figure 13-5. From the Special Acts Series, testimony concerning the intermarriage of John O'Riley and the mixed-blood status of Barney O'Riley, his "reputed" son.

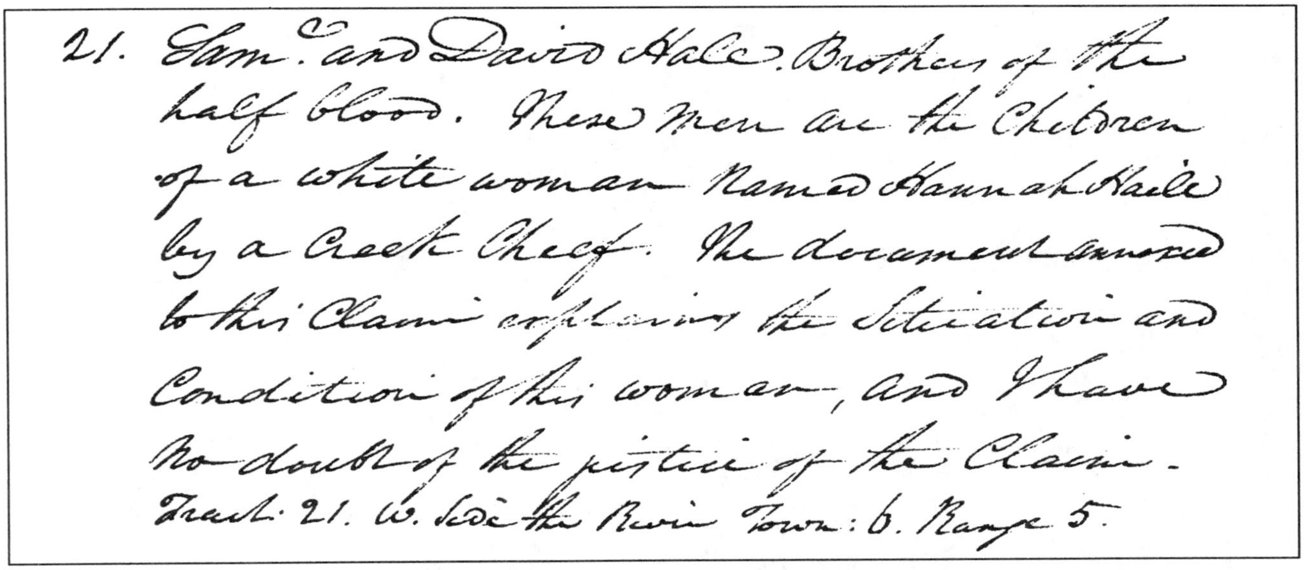

21. Sam[?] and David Hale[?] Brothers of the half blood. These men are the Children of a white woman named Hannah Haile by a Creek Chief. The document annexed to this Claim explaining the Situation and Condition of this woman, and I have No doubt of the justice of the Claim. Tract. 21. W. Side the River Town: 6. Range 5.

Figure 13-6. From an abstract listing of "Claims of Creek Indians" in the Special Acts Series.

Some individual Native Americans purchased lands through the standard procedures of federal land programs such as homesteads or cash purchases. In these circumstances Native American records are grouped with all other claimants for the same program. They were considered American citizens, and therefore they generated no new litigation for naturalization or for proof of declaration of intention to become a citizen. Often, there is no indication in these types of records that the claimant is of Native American heritage.

Records Generated by the Bureau of Indian Affairs

The Bureau of Indian Affairs was established in 1824 as a branch of the War Department. In 1849, it was transferred, along with the Bureau of Land Management, to the Department of the Interior. It was officially known as the Office of Indian Affairs until 1947. Though it was established in 1824, it was not until 1846 that a subdivision specifically dedicated to land was created.

Numerous collections generated by the Bureau of Indian Affairs address the issues of Native American land and property. Some merely comprise correspondence that confirms assignments and other miscellaneous issues. For example, there are 528 volumes of press copies for outgoing letters alone

between 1870 and 1908. No indexes are available for most of these types of records, and to search through them for family information is usually overwhelming. Some records only provide the name of the individual and reference to the land description. While ordinarily helpful, this information usually needs to be known to access these records in the beginning.

The land-related records produced by the Bureau of Indian Affairs are too numerous for a single chapter in any book. Other books being written by various authors will help reveal more about the multitude of records generated by the hundreds of Native American tribes that were within the bounds of the present-day United States. Only a few records are mentioned here.

Allotments

The most important and largest group of land records held by the Bureau of Indian Affairs is the allotments. They are the most numerous land records generated by the Native American population. Distribution of allotments officially ended in 1934, as did most land sales by Native Americans. Edward E. Hill, in his *Guide to Records in the National Archives of the United States Relating to American Indians*, states that "efforts were made to acquire land for Indians rather than to dispose of it" from

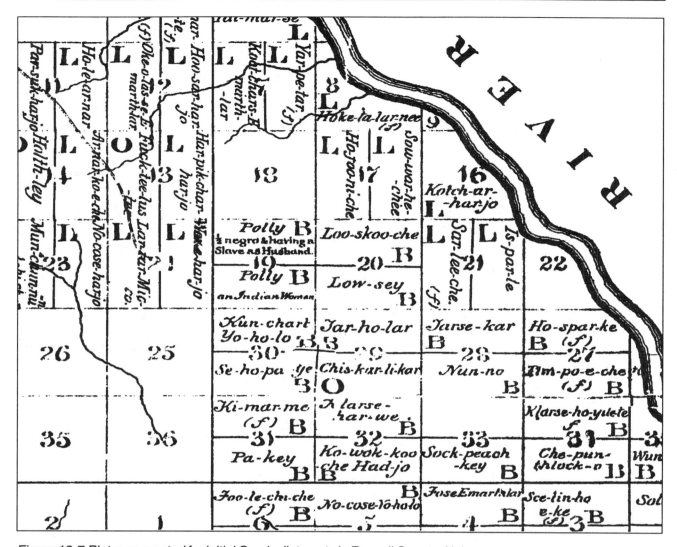

Figure 13-7. Plat map created for initial Creek allotments in Russell County, Alabama.

that time on. Most records described here are summarized in Hill's book, which can be found in most major libraries.

Records of allotments usually include:

- Plats
- Allotment schedules
- Tract books

Plats are mostly housed at the cartographics section of the National Archives in College Park, Maryland. They contain much the same information as do township plat maps (described in chapter 9). Many are individual plat descriptions that

show the allottee and immediate surrounding neighbors. Some are village plats that show an entire region, with names filled in for each individual plat. Most were performed by the Bureau of Land Management, then turned over to the Bureau of Indian Affairs. Some records were duplicated and are found under both departments: Record Group 49 and Record Group 75.

Those plats housed at the Bureau of Indian Affairs include "23 plat books and unbound papers" dating from 1858 to 1923. They concern reservations and individual allotments. Fourteen volumes of plats for the Five Civilized Tribes are also located there. They were produced by the United States Geological Survey from 1897 to

1900, but they do not show individual tracts of land. The last major group involves a set of four binders that contain plats of allotments to nonreservation Indians. All others are included with the allotment schedules.

Allotment schedules record individual allotments to Native Americans. They also record Native American school lands, missions, cemeteries, and other miscellaneous land dealings. They usually include:

- Plats of the land being allotted
- Affidavits of eligibility as a Native American that identify the tribe
- Testimonies of claimant or witnesses
- Name of the allottee
- Household status (such as whether married, age, etc.)
- Description of the land
- Assignee of the allotment
- Information on the twenty-five-year moratorium and any releases from that moratorium

Eligibility as an allottee may have been derived from heirship status, in which case descendance from the original eligible claimant is listed. Allotment schedules also involve homestead entries by certain tribes, records of surveys, scrip stubs that have been redeemed for land, and trust information. They are arranged by allotment number. Edward Hill concedes that "the numbers sometimes were assigned in alphabetical order by name of allottee, or [sometimes] in chronological order, but [more] often there is no discernible pattern to their sequence." A few volumes contain their own indexes, though most are without such a luxury. There are a total of seventy-three volumes in addition to some unbound papers dated 1856 to 1935. They contain both approved and unapproved allotments.

Tract books are further described in this chapter among the records of the Bureau of Land Management and in chapter 9, Records Generated by Federal Lands.

Military Bounty Lands

Military bounty lands were made available to Native Americans for the first time in 1855. Documented service in any war, beginning with the Revolutionary War, entitled the claimant to bounty-land scrip that could be exchanged at any federal land office. The main group of records at the Bureau of Indian Affairs is the Indian Applicants, 1855 to 1882. These records are also indexed from 1855 to 1875.

Regular applications are mixed with all other bounty-land applications in Record Group 15, which belongs to the Department of Veterans Affairs (formerly the Veterans Administration). For further information on Military Bounty Lands, see chapter 9, Records Generated by Federal Lands. Warrants that were eventually surrendered for land are in Record Group 49, which belongs to the Bureau of Land Management.

Conclusion

There are several sources to consider that are not mentioned here, such as tribal agency records. Once an allotment was assigned or patented, it was considered private property and was handled the same as any other individual land transaction. Research in the county deed books can follow the chain of title through time. These records do not usually indicate Native American involvement, though a few deeds have been known to state "of Indian blood," or words of similar terminology.

Several publications can assist in tracing the land and property of Native Americans. Perhaps the most helpful resource is Edward E. Hill's *Guide to Records in the National Archives Relating to American Indians*. Another highly recommended source is *Atlas of American Indian Affairs*, by Francis Paul Prucha. This latter book illustrates cessions of Native American land from colonial times to the present. Also see Barry T. Klein's *Reference Encyclopedia of the American Indian*. Another helpful reference for Native American research is "Tracking Native American Ancestry" in *The Source: A Guidebook of American Genealogy*.

FOR FURTHER REFERENCE

Bledsoe, Samuel T. *Indian Land Laws, Being a Treatise on Indian Land Titles in Oklahoma.* Kansas City, Mo.: Venn Law Books, 1913.

Brophy, William A., and Sophie D. Aberle. *The Indian: America's Unfinished Business.* Norman: University of Oklahoma Press, 1966.

Carlson, Leonard A. *Indians, Bureaucrats, and Land: The Dawes Act and the Decline of Indian Farming.* Westport, Conn.: Greenwood Press, 1981.

DeRosier, Arthur H., Jr. *The Removal of the Choctaw Indians.* Knoxville: The University of Tennessee Press, 1970.

De Vorsey, Louis, Jr. *The Indian Boundary in the Southern Colonies, 1763–1775.* Chapel Hill: The University of North Carolina Press, 1961.

Forbes, Jack D. *The Indian in America's Past.* Norman: University of Oklahoma Press, n.d.

Gibson, Arrell M. *The Chickasaws.* Norman: University of Oklahoma Press, 1971.

Green, Michael D. *Indians of North America: The Creeks.* New York: Chelsea House Publishers, n.d.

Hill, Edward E., comp. *Guide to Records in the National Archives Relating to Native Americans.* Washington, D.C.: National Archives Trust Fund Board, 1981.

_____, comp. *Preliminary Inventory of the Records of the Bureau of Indian Affairs.* 2 vols. Washington, D.C.: National Archives Trust Fund Board, 1965.

Hodge, Frederick W., ed. *Handbook of American Indians North of Mexico.* 2 vols. Reprint. New York: Pageant Books, 1959.

Johnson, Steven L. *Guide to American Indian Documents in the Congressional Serial Set: 1817–1899.* New York: Clearwater Publishing Co., 1977.

Kirkham, E. Kay. *Our Native Americans and Their Records of Genealogical Value.* 2 vols. Logan, Utah: The Everton Publishers, 1980–83.

Morris, John W., et al. *Historical Atlas of Oklahoma.* 2nd ed. Norman: University of Oklahoma Press, 1976.

Oklahoma Historical Society. *Catalogue of Microfilm Holdings: Indian Archives Collection.* Oklahoma City: Oklahoma Historical Society, 1989.

Parker, Linda S. *Native American Estate: The Struggle Over Indian and Hawaiian Lands.* Honolulu: University of Hawaii Press, 1989.

Radford, Dwight, and Pat Smith. "Scots-Irish as Muscogee (Creek)." *The Irish at Home and Abroad* 3 (1): 14–19. This periodical contains articles on Scots-Irish as Chickasaw, Choctaw, and other Native American affiliations.

Smith, Dwight L. *Indians of the United States and Canada: A Bibliography.* 2 vols. Santa Barbara, Calif.: ABC-CLIO, 1974, 1983.

Speck, Gordon. *Breeds and Half-Breeds.* New York: C. N. Potter, 1969.

"Tracking Native American Ancestry." In *The Source: A Guidebook of American Genealogy.* Edited by Loretto Dennis Szucs and Sandra Hargreaves Luebking. 2nd ed. Salt Lake City: Ancestry, 1997.

United States Department of Commerce. *Federal and State Indian Reservations and Indian Trust Areas.* Washington, D.C.: U.S. Government Printing Office, n.d.

Watson, Ian. *Catawba Indian Genealogy.* Geneseo, N.Y.: Department of Anthropology, State University of New York, 1995.

Watson, Larry S., ed. *Creek-Choctaw-Chickasaw Land Fraud in Public Land Sales: Public Land Series No. 1.* Reprint. Yuma, Ariz.: Histree, 1990.

Young, Mary Elizabeth. *Redskins, Ruffleshirts and Rednecks: Indian Allotments in Alabama and Mississippi, 1830–1860.* Norman: University of Oklahoma Press, 1961.

Appendix A:
Tract Book and Township Plat Map Guide to Federal Land States

Tract books comprise the only nationwide index for all attempted federal land sales, successful or unsuccessful. They are the basis for ordering land-entry case files, which often provide the most beneficial information of any land records, and are discussed more fully in chapter nine. Because they are organized by property description, not by name of claimant, they are difficult to access when detailed commercial atlases are not readily available. This guide has been designed to provide easier access to the portions of tract books that pertain only to ancestors' areas of residence, and similarly to help with access to the township plat maps which are arranged according to meridian and property description.

This guide includes all federal-land states and their respective counties. It helps determine more precisely the coordinates needed for research, based upon the present-day county boundaries of the location in which an ancestor may have lived. Columns in it define the north-, south-, east-, and western-most township and range for each county. Certain criteria were used to determine the coordinates listed: the county boundaries, when involving half of a township or range, have been extended to the full width of that coordinate. Thus, the coordinates listed in this guide will extend over, rather than undercut, the current boundaries of the county; this insures the entire county will be researched effectively, but also creates circumstances that the reader should be aware of. These circumstances are best described in the illustration at right.

The tract books for the entire United States, except Alaska and Missouri, are contained on 1,265 rolls of microfilm which are available from the National Archives and from the Family History Library of The Church of Jesus Christ of Latter-day Saints in Salt Lake City, Utah. Although the tract books for Alaska and Missouri are missing, those states have been included in this guide to facilitate usage if copies of these records are uncovered in the future, and to help with access to township plat maps. (For Missouri, refer to a statewide index of federal land purchases, 1818 to 1893, available at the State Archives in Jefferson City, Missouri. This collection is also on microfilm at the Family History Library.)

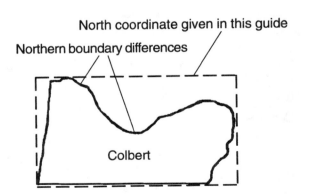

The coordinates given in this guide are defined by the farthest north, south, east, and west boundaries of the county. Thus, the area searched will overlap rather than undercut the current boundaries of the county

Tract books for some states, such as Alabama and Ohio, are organized by land office. Others are grouped for the entire state. Use of the land office boundary maps in appendix B will help those needing land office descriptions. Also, township and range descriptions in Ohio often differ from those found elsewhere in the country. Maps and additional explanations for these areas are included in this guide immediately following the listings for the state of Ohio.

Some general considerations for researching tract books:

- A county can involve more than one meridian or land office.

- County boundaries changed through the years. Be certain that present-day boundaries are accurately identified. (See chapter 10.)

- If a search is unsuccessful, check surrounding counties as well. An ancestor may have lived on the border and been recorded in another area.

- A single township and range coordinate may involve several pages in the tract book. Don't look at just one.

- The name of the land office is often omitted from tract book pages. Cross reference the land office by using appendix B.

For further information concerning tract books and their contents, refer to chapter 9, Records Generated by Federal Lands.

Alabama

County	North	South	East	West	Meridian
Autauga	20N	16N	16E	11E	St. Stephens
Baldwin	4N	9S	7E	1W	St. Stephens
Barbour	13N	8N	30E	23E	St. Stephens
Bibb	24N	22N	12E	7E	St. Stephens
Bibb	21S	22S	4W	7W	Huntsville
Blount	9S	14S	3E	4W	Huntsville
Bullock	15N	11N	26E	21E	St. Stephens
Butler	11N	7N	16E	12E	St. Stephens
Calhoun	12S	17S	10E	5E	Huntsville
Chambers	24N	20N	29E	25E	St. Stephens
Cherokee	6S	12S	12E	8E	Huntsville
Chilton	24N	20N	16E	11E	St. Stephens
Choctaw	15N	9N	1E	5W	St. Stephens
Clarke	12N	3N	5E	2W	St. Stephens
Clay	18S	22S	9E	5E	Huntsville
Cleburne	12S	18S	13E	7E	Huntsville
Coffee	7N	3N	22E	19E	St. Stephens
Colbert	2S	5S	9W	15W	Huntsville
Conecuh	9N	3N	14E	6E	St. Stephens
Coosa	24N	21N	20E	16E	St. Stephens

Alabama (cont.)

County	North	South	East	West	Meridian
Covington	6N	1N	18E	14E	St. Stephens
Crenshaw	12N	6N	19E	16E	St. Stephens
Cullman	8S	13S	2E	5W	Huntsville
Dale	7N	3N	26E	23E	St. Stephens
Dallas	19N	13N	13E	6E	St. Stephens
Dekalb	2S	9S	11E	5E	Huntsville
Elmore	20N	17N	22E	17E	St. Stephens
Escambia	3N	1N	13E	5E	St. Stephens
Etowah	10S	14S	8E	3E	Huntsville
Fayette	13S	17S	9W	13W	Huntsville
Franklin	6S	8S	10W	16W	Huntsville
Geneva	3N	1N	25E	19E	St. Stephens
Greene	22S	22S	13W	14W	Huntsville
Greene	24N	18N	4E	2W	St. Stephens
Hale	23N	18N	6E	2E	St. Stephens
Henry	9N	4N	30E	26E	St. Stephens
Houston	4N	1N	30E	23E	St. Stephens
Jackson	1S	6S	10E	3E	Huntsville
Jefferson	14S	20S	1E	8W	Huntsville
Lamar	12S	17S	14W	17W	Huntsville
Lauderdale	1S	4S	7W	16W	Huntsville
Lawrence	3S	8S	6W	9W	Huntsville
Lee	20N	17N	30E	24E	St. Stephens
Limestone	1S	5S	3W	7W	Huntsville
Lowndes	16N	12N	16E	12E	St. Stephens
Macon	18N	15N	26E	20E	St. Stephens
Madison	1S	6S	3E	2W	Huntsville
Marengo	18N	12N	6E	1W	St. Stephens
Marion	9S	13S	11W	16W	Huntsville
Marshall	5S	11S	5E	1E	Huntsville
Mobile	2N	9S	1E	4W	St. Stephens
Monroe	10N	3N	11E	3E	St. Stephens
Montgomery	18N	12N	21E	16E	St. Stephens
Morgan	4S	8S	1W	5W	Huntsville
Perry	22N	16N	10E	6E	St. Stephens
Pickens	18S	22S	13W	17W	Huntsville
Pickens	24N	23N	1E	3W	St. Stephens
Pike	13N	8N	24E	19E	St. Stephens
Randolph	18S	22S	14E	10E	Huntsville
Russell	18N	13N	31E	26E	St. Stephens
St.Clair	12S	19S	6E	1E	Huntsville
Shelby	17S	22S	3E	5W	Huntsville

Alabama (cont.)

County	North	South	East	West	Meridian
Shelby	24N	24N	16E	11E	St. Stephens
Sumter	23N	16N	2E	4W	St. Stephens
Talladega	15S	22S	8E	2E	Huntsville
Tallapoosa	24N	18N	24E	20E	St. Stephens
Tuscaloosa	17S	22S	5W	12W	Huntsville
Tuscaloosa	24N	23N	7E	3E	St. Stephens
Walker	12S	17S	4W	10W	Huntsville
Washington	8N	2N	2E	5W	St. Stephens
Wilcox	15N	10N	12E	4E	St. Stephens
Winston	9S	12S	6W	10W	Huntsville

Alaska

	North	South	East	West	Meridian
Southeastern					
South Central					
Southwestern					
Central Plateau					
Arctic Slope					

Arizona

County	North	South	East	West	Meridian
Apache	42N	4N	31E	22E	Gila & Salt River
Cochise	12S	24S	32E	19E	Gila & Salt River
Coconino	42N	10N	15E	10W	Gila & Salt River
Gila	12N	5S	23E	6E	Gila & Salt River
Graham	3N	11S	31E	19E	Gila & Salt River
Greenlee	5N	11S	32E	28E	Gila & Salt River
Lapaz	11N	4S	11W	24W	Gila & Salt River
Maricopa	8N	10S	13E	10W	Gila & Salt River
Mohave	42N	10N	2W	23W	Gila & Salt River
Navajo	42N	2N	23E	15E	Gila & Salt River
Pima	11S	23S	18E	10W	Gila & Salt River
Pinal	1N	10S	18E	2E	Gila & Salt River
Santa Cruz	20S	24S	18E	10E	Gila & Salt River
Yavapai	25N	6N	8E	10W	Gila & Salt River
Yuma	1N	16S	11W	25W	Gila & Salt River
Navajo Indian Reservation	14N	1N	10W	6W	Navajo

Arkansas

County	North	South	East	West	Meridian
Arkansas	2S	9S	1W	6W	Fifth Principal
Ashley	15S	19S	4W	10W	Fifth Principal
Baxter	21N	16N	11W	15W	Fifth Principal
Benton	21N	17N	27W	34W	Fifth Principal
Boone	21N	17N	18W	22W	Fifth Principal
Bradley	12S	18S	9W	12W	Fifth Principal
Calhoun	11S	17S	12W	16W	Fifth Principal
Carroll	21N	17N	22W	27W	Fifth Principal
Chicot	13S	19S	1E	3W	Fifth Principal
Clark	5S	11S	17W	23W	Fifth Principal
Clay	21N	18N	9E	3E	Fifth Principal
Cleburne	12N	9N	8W	12W	Fifth Principal
Cleveland	7S	11S	9W	13W	Fifth Principal
Columbia	15S	20S	18W	23W	Fifth Principal
Conway	9N	5N	14W	19W	Fifth Principal
Craighead	16N	13N	7E	1E	Fifth Principal
Crawford	13N	8N	27W	33W	Fifth Principal
Crittenden	9N	3N	10E	6E	Fifth Principal
Cross	9N	6N	5E	1E	Fifth Principal
Dallas	7S	10S	12W	18W	Fifth Principal
Desha	7S	13S	2E	5W	Fifth Principal
Drew	11S	15S	4W	9W	Fifth Principal
Faulkner	8N	3N	11W	15W	Fifth Principal
Franklin	13N	6N	26W	29W	Fifth Principal
Fulton	21N	19N	5W	11W	Fifth Principal
Garland	1N	4S	17W	22W	Fifth Principal
Grant	3N	7S	11W	15W	Fifth Principal
Greene	19N	16N	8E	2E	Fifth Principal
Hempstead	9S	14S	23W	28W	Fifth Principal
Hot Spring	3S	6S	16W	22W	Fifth Principal
Howard	5S	11S	27W	30W	Fifth Principal
Independence	15N	11N	2W	8W	Fifth Principal
Izard	18N	14N	7W	11W	Fifth Principal
Jackson	14N	9N	1W	5W	Fifth Principal
Jefferson	3S	7S	4W	11W	Fifth Principal
Johnson	13N	8N	21W	25W	Fifth Principal
Lafayette	15S	20S	22W	27W	Fifth Principal
Lawrence	18N	15N	3E	3W	Fifth Principal
Lee	3N	1N	6E	1W	Fifth Principal
Lincoln	6N	10N	2W	9W	Fifth Principal
Little River	10S	14S	27W	33W	Fifth Principal
Logan	9N	4N	22W	29W	Fifth Principal

Arkansas(cont.)

County	North	South	East	West	Meridian
Lonoke	5N	2S	6W	10W	Fifth Principal
Madison	19N	13N	23W	28W	Fifth Principal
Marion	21N	17N	14W	18W	Fifth Principal
Miller	13S	20S	25W	28W	Fifth Principal
Mississippi	16N	10N	13E	8E	Fifth Principal
Monroe	4N	4S	1E	4W	Fifth Principal
Montgomery	1N	4S	23W	27W	Fifth Principal
Nevada	9S	15S	20W	23W	Fifth Principal
Newton	17N	13N	19W	24W	Fifth Principal
Ouachita	11S	15S	14W	19W	Fifth Principal
Perry	5N	2N	15W	22W	Fifth Principal
Phillips	1S	6S	5E	1W	Fifth Principal
Pike	5S	9S	22W	28W	Fifth Principal
Poinsett	12N	10N	7E	1E	Fifth Principal
Polk	1N	6S	28W	32W	Fifth Principal
Pope	12N	6N	17W	22W	Fifth Principal
Prairie	5N	2S	3W	7W	Fifth Principal
Pulaski	4N	2S	10W	16W	Fifth Principal
Randolph	21N	18N	3E	4W	Fifth Principal
Saint Francis	6N	3N	6E	1W	Fifth Principal
Saline	2N	3S	12W	19W	Fifth Principal
Scott	5N	1S	26W	32W	Fifth Principal
Searcy	17N	13N	14W	18W	Fifth Principal
Sebastian	9N	4N	29W	32W	Fifth Principal
Sevier	7S	11S	28W	33W	Fifth Principal
Sharp	21N	15N	3W	7W	Fifth Principal
Stone	18N	13N	8W	13W	Fifth Principal
Union	15S	20S	9W	18W	Fifth Principal
Van Buren	13N	9N	12W	17W	Fifth Principal
Washington	18N	13N	28W	33W	Fifth Principal
White	10N	5N	3W	10W	Fifth Principal
Woodruff	9N	4N	1W	4W	Fifth Principal
Yell	7N	1N	18W	25W	Fifth Principal

California

County	North	South	East	West	Meridian
Alameda	1N	5S	5E	5W	Mount Diablo
Alpine	12N	6N	22E	17E	Mount Diablo
Amador	10N	5N	17E	9E	Mount Diablo
Butte	27N	17N	8E	2W	Mount Diablo
Calaveras	7N	1S	18E	9E	Mount Diablo

California(cont.)

County	North	South	East	West	Meridian
Colusa	18N	13N	1E	8W	Mount Diablo
Contra Costa	3N	2S	4E	5W	Mount Diablo
Del Norte	19N	12N	6E	2W	Humboldt
El Dorado	14N	8N	19E	8E	Mount Diablo
Fresno	4S	23S	33E	10E	Mount Diablo
Glenn	22N	18N	1W	10W	Mount Diablo
Humboldt	12N	5S	7E	3W	Humboldt
Imperial	9S	18S	24E	9E	San Bernardino
Inyo	6S	24S	46E	29E	Mount Diablo
Inyo	30N	20N	13E	1E	San Bernardino
Kern	25S	32S	40E	17E	Mount Diablo
Kern	11N	9N	7W	24W	San Bernardino
Kings	17S	24S	23E	15E	Mount Diablo
Lake	20N	9N	5W	11W	Mount Diablo
Lassen	39N	22N	17E	6E	Mount Diablo
Los Angeles	8N	5S	7W	20W	San Bernardino
Madera	2S	13S	27E	13E	Mount Diablo
Marin	6N	1S	5W	11W	Mount Diablo
Mariposa	1N	8S	24E	14E	Mount Diablo
Mendocino	25N	11N	9W	19W	Mount Diablo
Mendocino	5S	5S	5W	1W	Humbolt
Merced	3S	13S	18E	7E	Mount Diablo
Modoc	48N	39N	17E	5E	Mount Diablo
Mono	9N	5S	38E	21E	Mount Diablo
Monterey	12S	24S	16E	1W	Mount Diablo
Napa	12N	4N	2W	7W	Mount Diablo
Nevada	19N	14N	18E	6E	Mount Diablo
Orange	2S	9S	5W	11W	San Bernardino
Placer	17N	10N	18E	5E	Mount Diablo
Plumas	30N	20N	17E	5E	Mount Diablo
Riverside	1S	8S	24E	7W	San Bernardino
Sacramento	10N	2N	9E	1E	Mount Diablo
San Benito	11S	20S	12E	3E	Mount Diablo
San Bernardino	19N	1S	26E	8W	San Bernardino
San Bernardino	25S	32S	47E	40E	Mount Diablo
San Diego	7S	18S	8E	4W	Mount Diablo
San Francisco	1S	2S	5W	6W	Mount Diablo
San Joaquin	5N	5S	9E	4E	Mount Diablo
San Luis Obispo	25S	32S	22E	6E	Mount Diablo
San Luis Obispo	11N	9N	25W	36W	San Bernardino
San Mateo	3S	9S	3W	6W	Mount Diablo
Santa Barbara	32S	32S	18E	17E	Mount Diablo

California(cont.)

County	North	South	East	West	Meridian
Santa Barbara	11N	3N	24W	36W	San Bernardino
Santa Clara	5S	12S	7E	3W	Mount Diablo
Santa Cruz	8S	12S	3E	4W	Mount Diablo
Shasta	39N	28N	6E	11W	Mount Diablo
Sierra	22N	18N	17E	8E	Mount Diablo
Siskiyou	48N	37N	4E	12W	Mount Diablo
Siskiyou	19N	9N	8E	4E	Humboldt
Solano	8N	2N	4E	5W	Mount Diablo
Sonoma	12N	3N	5W	16W	Mount Diablo
Stanislaus	3N	9S	14E	4E	Mount Diablo
Sutter	17N	11N	4E	1W	Mount Diablo
Tehama	30N	23N	6E	11W	Mount Diablo
Trinity	40N	25N	5W	12W	Mount Diablo
Trinity	9N	5S	8E	5E	Humboldt
Tulare	14S	24S	37E	22E	Mount Diablo
Tuolumne	7N	3S	25E	12E	Mount Diablo
Ventura	9N	1S	17W	24W	San Bernardino
Yolo	12N	6N	4E	5W	Mount Diablo
Yuba	20N	13N	8E	3E	Mount Diablo

Colorado

County	North	South	East	West	Meridian
Adams	1S	3S	57W	68W	Sixth Principal
Alamosa	26S	29S	72W	73W	Sixth Principal
Alamosa	40N	36N	12E	9E	New Mexico Principal
Arapahoe	4S	5S	57W	68W	Sixth Principal
Archuleta	36S	32S	4E	5W	New Mexico Principal
Baca	28S	35S	41W	50W	Sixth Principal
Bent	21S	27S	48W	53W	Sixth Principal
Boulder	3N	1S	69W	74W	Sixth Principal
Chaffee	11S	15S	76W	82W	Sixth Principal
Chaffee	51N	48N	10E	5E	New Mexico Principal
Cheyenne	12S	16S	41W	51W	Sixth Principal
Clear Creek	2S	5S	72W	76W	Sixth Principal
Conejos	36N	32N	11E	3E	New Mexico Principal
Costilla	27S	35S	70W	75W	Sixth Principal
Crowley	18S	22S	55W	59W	Sixth Principal
Custer	21S	25S	69W	73W	Sixth Principal
Custer	46N	44N	12E	11E	New Mexico Principal
Delta	10S	15S	91W	98W	Sixth Principal
Delta	51N	51N	6W	13W	New Mexico Principal

Colorado(cont.)

County	North	South	East	West	Meridian
Denver	3S	4S	67W	68W	Sixth Principal
Dolores	42N	37N	9W	20W	New Mexico Principal
Douglas	6S	10S	65W	71W	Sixth Principal
Eagle	2S	8S	79W	87W	Sixth Principal
Elbert	6S	13S	57W	65W	Sixth Principal
El Paso	10S	17S	60W	69W	Sixth Principal
Fremont	16S	20S	68W	73W	Sixth Principal
Fremont	51N	47N	12E	9E	New Mexico Principal
Garfield	1N	8S	86W	104W	Sixth Principal
Gilpin	1S	3S	72W	74W	Sixth Principal
Grand	6N	4S	74W	83W	Sixth Principal
Gunnison	9S	15S	81W	90W	Sixth Principal
Gunnison	51N	45N	6E	7W	New Mexico Principal
Hinsdale	45N	36N	1W	7W	New Mexico Principal
Huerfano	23S	31S	62W	73W	Sixth Principal
Jackson	12N	4N	75W	85W	Sixth Principal
Jefferson	2S	10S	69W	71W	Sixth Principal
Kiowa	17S	20S	41W	54W	Sixth Principal
Kit Carson	6S	11S	42W	51W	Sixth Principal
Lake	8S	11S	78W	82W	Sixth Principal
La Plata	39N	32N	5W	14W	New Mexico Principal
Larimer	12N	4N	68W	78W	Sixth Principal
Las Animas	26S	35S	51W	69W	Sixth Principal
Lincoln	6S	17S	52W	59W	Sixth Principal
Logan	12N	6N	48W	55W	Sixth Principal
Mesa	8S	15S	90W	104W	Sixth Principal
Mesa	2N	4S	3E	3W	Ute Principal
Mesa	51N	49N	14W	20W	New Mexico Principal
Mineral	43N	36N	2E	2W	New Mexico Principal
Moffat	12N	3N	89W	104W	Sixth Principal
Montezuma	39N	32N	10W	20W	New Mexico Principal
Montrose	51N	45N	6W	20W	New Mexico Principal
Morgan	6N	1N	55W	60W	Sixth Principal
Otero	21S	27S	54W	59W	Sixth Principal
Ouray	47N	42N	6W	11W	New Mexico Principal
Park	6S	15S	71W	79W	Sixth Principal
Phillips	9N	6N	42W	47W	Sixth Principal
Pitkin	8S	12S	81W	90W	Sixth Principal
Prowers	21S	27S	41W	47W	Sixth Principal
Pueblo	18S	26S	60W	69W	Sixth Principal
Rio Blancho	3N	4S	86W	104W	Sixth Principal
Rio Grande	41N	37N	8E	3E	New Mexico Principal

Colorado(cont.)

County	North	South	East	West	Meridian
Routt	12N	1S	83W	89W	Sixth Principal
Saguache	24S	26S	72W	73W	Sixth Principal
Saguache	48N	41N	12E	1W	New Mexico Principal
San Juan	43N	39N	5W	10W	New Mexico Principal
San Miguel	45N	41N	8W	20W	New Mexico Principal
Sedgwick	12N	9N	42W	47W	Sixth Principal
Summit	2S	8S	75W	81W	Sixth Principal
Teller	11S	16S	68W	71W	Sixth Principal
Washington	5N	5S	49W	56W	Sixth Principal
Weld	12N	1N	56W	68W	Sixth Principal
Yuma	5N	5S	42W	48W	Sixth Principal

Florida

County	North	South	East	West	Meridian
Alachua	6S	12S	22E	17E	Tallahassee
Baker	2N	4S	22E	19E	Tallahassee
Bay	2N	6S	12W	17W	Tallahassee
Brevard	20S	30S	38E	34E	Tallahassee
Bradford	4S	8S	22E	19E	Tallahassee
Broward	48S	52S	43E	35E	Tallahassee
Calhoun	2N	3S	7W	11W	Tallahassee
Charlotte	40S	42S	27E	20E	Tallahassee
Citrus	16S	21S	21E	15E	Tallahassee
Clay	4S	9S	27E	22E	Tallahassee
Collier	46S	53S	34E	25E	Tallahassee
Columbia	2N	8S	19E	15E	Tallahassee
Dade	52S	65S	42E	35E	Tallahassee
Dixie	8S	13S	14E	9E	Tallahassee
De Soto	36S	39S	27E	23E	Tallahassee
Duval	2N	4S	29E	22E	Tallahassee
Escambia	6N	3S	29W	34W	Tallahassee
Flagler	9S	14S	32E	28E	Tallahassee
Franklin	5S	10S	1W	10W	Tallahassee
Gadsden	3N	1S	1W	7W	Tallahassee
Gilchrist	6S	10S	16E	13E	Tallahassee
Glades	38S	42S	34E	28E	Tallahassee
Gulf	3S	9S	8W	12W	Tallahassee
Hamilton	2N	2S	17E	11E	Tallahassee
Hardee	33S	36S	27E	23E	Tallahassee
Hendry	43S	48S	34E	28E	Tallahassee
Hernando	21S	23S	22E	16E	Tallahassee

Florida (cont.)

County	North	South	East	West	Meridian
Highlands	33S	39S	34S	28E	Tallahassee
Hillsborough	27S	32S	22E	17E	Tallahassee
Holmes	7N	4N	13W	17W	Tallahassee
Holmes	6N	3N	18W	18W	Tallahassee
Indian River	30S	33S	40E	34E	Tallahassee
Jackson	7N	2N	6W	14W	Tallahassee
Jefferson	3N	4S	7E	3E	Tallahassee
Lafayette	3S	7S	14E	10E	Tallahassee
Lake	14S	25S	30E	24E	Tallahassee
Lee	43S	48S	27E	20E	Tallahassee
Leon	3N	2S	3E	5W	Tallahassee
Levy	10S	17S	19E	12E	Tallahassee
Liberty	2N	6S	3W	9W	Tallahassee
Madison	3N	2S	11E	5E	Tallahassee
Manatee	33S	37S	22E	16E	Tallahassee
Marion	11S	17S	26E	18E	Tallahassee
Martin	37S	40S	43E	37E	Tallahassee
Monroe	54S	68S	34E	21E	Tallahassee
Nassau	5N	2S	28E	22E	Tallahassee
Okaloosa	6N	2S	22W	25W	Tallahassee
Okeechobee	33S	38S	37E	31E	Tallahassee
Orange	20S	24S	34E	27E	Tallahassee
Osceola	25S	32S	34E	27E	Tallahassee
Palm Beach	41S	47S	43E	35E	Tallahassee
Pasco	23S	26S	22E	15E	Tallahassee
Pinellas	27S	33S	17E	15E	Tallahassee
Polk	25S	32S	32E	22E	Tallahassee
Putnam	8S	13S	28E	22E	Tallahassee
St. Johns	3S	10S	31E	26E	Tallahassee
St. Lucie	34S	37S	41E	37E	Tallahassee
Santa Rosa	6N	3S	26W	31W	Tallahassee
Sarasota	36S	41S	22E	16E	Tallahassee
Seminole	19S	21S	33E	29E	Tallahassee
Sumter	18S	25S	23E	20E	Tallahassee
Suwannee	1S	7S	15E	11E	Tallahassee
Taylor	2S	9S	10E	3E	Tallahassee
Union	4S	6S	22E	17E	Tallahassee
Volusia	12S	21S	35E	27E	Tallahassee
Wakulla	2S	6S	2E	5W	Tallahassee
Walton	2N	2S	16W	17W	Tallahassee
Walton	6N	3S	18W	21W	Tallahassee
Washington	5N	1S	12W	17W	Tallahassee

Idaho

County	North	South	East	West	Meridian
Ada	5N	3S	4E	1W	Boise
Adams	22N	13N	3E	5W	Boise
Bannock	5S	13S	39E	34E	Boise
Bear Lake	9S	16S	46E	42E	Boise
Benewah	47N	43N	1E	6W	Boise
Bingham	3N	6S	41E	29E	Boise
Blaine	7N	9S	29E	13E	Boise
Boise	12N	3N	13E	2E	Boise
Bonner	63N	53N	3E	6W	Boise
Bonneville	3N	4S	46E	34E	Boise
Boundary	65N	60N	3E	6W	Boise
Butte	10N	1S	32E	23E	Boise
Camas	6N	2S	17E	12E	Boise
Canyon	6N	1S	1W	6W	Boise
Caribou	5S	11S	46E	37E	Boise
Cassia	9S	16S	29E	19E	Boise
Clark	14N	8N	41E	29E	Boise
Clearwater	41N	34N	15E	1W	Boise
Custer	18N	3N	26E	10E	Boise
Elmore	9N	7S	13E	2E	Boise
Franklin	12S	16S	42E	37E	Boise
Fremont	16N	7N	46E	37E	Boise
Gem	14N	6N	2E	3W	Boise
Gooding	3S	9S	16E	12E	Boise
Idaho	38N	21N	18E	4W	Boise
Jefferson	8N	4N	38E	32E	Boise
Jerome	7S	11S	21E	16E	Boise
Kootenai	54N	47N	1E	6W	Boise
Latah	44N	37N	1E	6W	Boise
Lemhi	27N	11N	30E	14E	Boise
Lewis	36N	31N	3E	3W	Boise
Lincoln	3S	7S	23E	16E	Boise
Madison	7N	4N	43E	37E	Boise
Minidoka	3S	10S	26E	22E	Boise
Nez Perce	38N	29N	1E	6W	Boise
Oneida	11S	16S	37E	30E	Boise
Owyhee	4N	16S	12E	6W	Boise
Payette	9N	5N	1W	5W	Boise
Power	4S	12S	35E	28E	Boise
Shoshone	54N	42N	11E	1E	Boise
Teton	8N	2N	46E	43E	Boise
Twin Falls	6S	16S	21E	12E	Boise

Idaho(cont.)

County	North	South	East	West	Meridian
Valley	22N	9N	15E	2E	Boise
Washington	17N	10N	1E	7W	Boise

Illinois

County	North	South	East	West	Meridian
Adams	2N	3S	5W	9W	Fourth Principal
Alexander	14S	17S	1W	4W	Third Principal
Bond	7N	4N	2W	5W	Third Principal
Boone	46N	43N	4E	3E	Third Principal
Brown	1N	2S	1W	4W	Fourth Principal
Bureau	18N	14N	11E	6E	Fourth Principal
Calhoun	8S	13S	1W	3W	Fourth Principal
Carroll	25N	23N	7E	2E	Fourth Principal
Cass	19N	17N	8W	13W	Third Principal
Champaign	22N	17N	11E	7E	Third Principal
Champaign	22N	18N	14W	14W	Second Principal
Christian	16N	11N	1E	4W	Third Principal
Clark	12N	9N	10W	14W	Second Principal
Clay	5N	2N	8E	5E	Third Principal
Clinton	3N	1S	1W	5W	Third Principal
Coles	14N	11N	11E	7E	Third Principal
Coles	13N	11N	14W	14W	Second Principal
Cook	42N	35N	15E	9E	Third Principal
Crawford	9N	5N	10W	14W	Second Principal
Cumberland	11N	9N	11E	7E	Third Principal
De Kalb	42N	37N	5E	3E	Third Principal
De Witt	21N	19N	5E	1E	Third Principal
Douglas	16N	14N	11E	7E	Third Principal
Douglas	16N	14N	14W	14W	Second Principal
Du Page	40N	37N	11E	9E	Third Principal
Edgar	16N	12N	10W	14W	Second Principal
Edwards	2N	3S	11E	10E	Third Principal
Edwards	2N	3S	14W	14W	Second Principal
Effingham	9N	6N	7E	4E	Third Principal
Fayette	9N	4N	4E	1W	Third Principal
Ford	29N	23N	11E	7E	Third Principal
Ford	23N	23N	14W	14W	Second Principal
Franklin	5S	7S	4E	1E	Third Principal
Fulton	8N	3N	5E	1E	Fourth Principal
Gallatin	7S	11S	10E	8E	Third Principal
Greene	12N	8N	10W	13W	Third Principal

Illinois(cont.)

County	North	South	East	West	Meridian
Grundy	34N	31N	8E	6E	Third Principal
Hamilton	3S	7S	7E	5E	Third Principal
Hancock	7N	3N	5W	9W	Fourth Principal
Hardin	11S	12S	10E	7E	Third Principal
Henderson	12N	8N	4W	6W	Fourth Principal
Henry	18N	14N	5E	1E	Fourth Principal
Iroquois	29N	24N	11E	10E	Third Principal
Iroquois	29N	24N	10W	14W	Second Principal
Jackson	7S	11S	1W	5W	Third Principal
Jasper	8N	5N	11E	8E	Third Principal
Jasper	9N	5N	14W	14W	Second Principal
Jefferson	1S	4S	4E	1E	Third Principal
Jersey	9N	6N	10W	13W	Third Principal
Jo Daviess	29N	26N	5E	2W	Fourth Principal
Johnson	11S	14S	4E	2E	Third Principal
Kane	42N	38N	8E	6E	Third Principal
Kankakee	32N	29N	14E	9E	Third Principal
Kendall	37N	35N	8E	6E	Third Principal
Knox	13N	9N	4E	1E	Fourth Principal
Lake	46N	43N	12E	9E	Third Principal
LaSalle	36N	29N	5E	1E	Third Principal
Lawrence	5N	2N	10W	13W	Second Principal
Lee	39N	37N	2E	1E	Third Principal
Lee	22N	19N	11E	8E	Fourth Principal
Livingston	30N	25N	8E	3E	Third Principal
Logan	22N	17N	1W	4W	Third Principal
Macon	18N	14N	4E	1W	Third Principal
Macoupin	12N	7N	6W	9W	Third Principal
Madison	6N	3N	5W	10W	Third Principal
Marion	4N	1N	4E	1E	Third Principal
Marshall	30N	29N	1E	3W	Third Principal
Marshall	13N	12N	10E	8E	Fourth Principal
Mason	23N	19N	5W	11W	Third Principal
Massac	14S	17S	6E	3E	Third Principal
McDonough	7N	4N	1W	4W	Fourth Principal
McHenry	46N	43N	9E	5E	Third Principal
McLean	26N	21N	6E	1W	Third Principal
Menard	20N	17N	5W	8W	Third Principal
Mercer	15N	13N	1W	6W	Fourth Principal
Monroe	1N	5S	7W	11W	Third Principal
Montgomery	12N	7N	1W	5W	Third Principal
Morgan	16N	13N	8W	13W	Third Principal

Illinois(cont.)

County	North	South	East	West	Meridian
Moultrie	15N	12N	6E	4E	Third Principal
Ogle	42N	40N	2E	1E	Third Principal
Ogle	25N	22N	11E	7E	Fourth Principal
Peoria	11N	7N	9E	5E	Fourth Principal
Perry	4S	6S	1E	4W	Third Principal
Piatt	21N	16N	6E	4E	Third Principal
Pike	3S	7S	2W	8W	Fourth Principal
Pope	11S	17S	7E	5E	Third Principal
Pulaski	14S	17S	2E	1W	Third Principal
Putnam	33N	31N	1W	2W	Third Principal
Putnam	14N	14N	10E	9E	Fourth Principal
Randolph	4S	8S	5W	10W	Third Principal
Richland	5N	2N	11E	8E	Third Principal
Richland	5N	2N	14W	14W	Second Principal
Rock Island	21N	16N	3E	6W	Fourth Principal
St. Clair	2N	3S	6W	10W	Third Principal
Saline	7S	10S	7E	5E	Third Principal
Sangamon	18N	13N	1W	8W	Third Principal
Schuyler	3N	1S	3E	4W	Fourth Principal
Scott	15N	13N	11W	13W	Third Principal
Shelby	14N	9N	6E	1E	Third Principal
Stark	14N	12N	7E	5E	Fourth Principal
Stephenson	29N	26N	9E	5E	Fourth Principal
Tazewell	26N	22N	2W	7W	Third Principal
Union	11S	13S	1E	3W	Third Principal
Vermilion	24N	18N	10W	14W	Second Principal
Wabash	2N	3S	11W	14W	Second Principal
Warren	12N	8N	1W	3W	Fourth Principal
Washington	1N	3S	1W	5W	Third Principal
Wayne	2N	3S	9E	5E	Third Principal
White	3S	7S	10E	8E	Third Principal
White	3S	5S	14W	14W	Second Principal
Whiteside	22N	19N	7E	2E	Fourth Principal
Will	37N	32N	15E	9E	Third Principal
Williamson	8S	10S	4E	1E	Third Principal
Winnebago	46N	43N	2E	1E	Third Principal
Winnebago	29N	26N	11E	10E	Fourth Principal
Woodford	28N	25N	2E	4W	Third Principal

Indiana

County	North	South	East	West	Meridian
Adams	28N	25N	15E	13E	Second Principal
Allen	32N	29N	15E	11E	Second Principal
Bartholomew	10N	7N	7E	4E	Second Principal
Benton	26N	24N	6W	10W	Second Principal
Blackford	24N	22N	11E	10E	Second Principal
Boone	20N	17N	2E	2W	Second Principal
Brown	10N	7N	4E	1E	Second Principal
Carroll	26N	23N	1E	3W	Second Principal
Cass	28N	25N	3E	1W	Second Principal
Clark	2N	3S	10E	5E	Second Principal
Clay	13N	9N	5W	7W	Second Principal
Clinton	23N	20N	2E	2W	Second Principal
Crawford	1S	4S	2E	2W	Second Principal
Daviess	5N	1N	5W	8W	Second Principal
Dearborn	7N	3N	1W	3W	First Principal
Decatur	12N	8N	11E	8E	Second Principal
De Kalb	35N	33N	15E	12E	Second Principal
Delaware	22N	19N	11E	8E	Second Principal
Dubois	1N	3S	3W	6W	Second Principal
Elkhart	38N	35N	7E	4E	Second Principal
Fayette	15N	13N	13E	11E	Second Principal
Floyd	1S	4S	7E	4E	Second Principal
Fountain	22N	18N	6W	9W	Second Principal
Franklin	12N	10N	13E	11E	Second Principal
Franklin	10N	8N	1W	3W	First Principal
Fulton	31N	29N	5E	1E	Second Principal
Gibson	1N	4S	8W	14W	Second Principal
Grant	25N	22N	9E	6E	Second Principal
Greene	8N	6N	3W	7W	Second Principal
Hamilton	20N	17N	6E	3E	Second Principal
Hancock	17N	15N	8E	5E	Second Principal
Harrison	1S	6S	5E	2E	Second Principal
Hendricks	17N	14N	2E	2W	Second Principal
Henry	19N	16N	12E	8E	Second Principal
Howard	24N	22N	6E	1E	Second Principal
Huntington	29N	26N	10E	8E	Second Principal
Jackson	7N	3N	6E	2E	Second Principal
Jasper	33N	27N	5W	7W	Second Principal
Jay	24N	22N	15E	12E	Second Principal
Jefferson	5N	2N	12E	8E	Second Principal
Jennings	9N	4N	10E	7E	Second Principal
Johnson	14N	11N	5E	3E	Second Principal

Indiana(cont.)

County	North	South	East	West	Meridian
Knox	5N	1N	6W	12W	Second Principal
Kosciusko	34N	30N	8E	4E	Second Principal
La Grange	38N	36N	11E	8E	Second Principal
Lake	38N	31N	7W	10W	Second Principal
La Porte	38N	32N	1W	4W	Second Principal
Lawrence	6N	3N	2E	2W	Second Principal
Madison	22N	17N	8E	6E	Second Principal
Marion	17N	14N	5E	2E	Second Principal
Marshall	35N	32N	4E	1E	Second Principal
Martin	5N	1N	3W	5W	Second Principal
Miami	29N	25N	6E	3E	Second Principal
Monroe	10N	6N	2E	2W	Second Principal
Montgomery	20N	17N	3W	6W	Second Principal
Morgan	14N	11N	2E	2W	Second Principal
Newton	32N	27N	8W	10W	Second Principal
Noble	35N	33N	11E	8E	Second Principal
Ohio	4N	3N	1W	3W	First Principal
Orange	3N	1S	2E	2W	Second Principal
Owen	12N	9N	2W	6W	Second Principal
Parke	17N	14N	6W	9W	Second Principal
Perry	3S	8S	1W	4W	Second Principal
Pike	1N	3S	6W	9W	Second Principal
Porter	38N	32N	5W	7W	Second Principal
Posey	3S	8S	12W	14W	Second Principal
Pulaski	31N	29N	1W	4W	Second Principal
Putnam	16N	12N	2W	5W	Second Principal
Randolph	21N	18N	15E	12E	Second Principal
Randolph	19N	16N	1W	1W	First Principal
Ripley	10N	6N	13E	10E	Second Principal
Rush	15N	12N	11E	8E	Second Principal
St. Joseph	38N	34N	4E	1W	Second Principal
Scott	5N	2N	8E	6E	Second Principal
Shelby	14N	11N	8E	5E	Second Principal
Spencer	4S	8S	3W	8W	Second Principal
Starke	34N	32N	1W	4W	Second Principal
Steuben	38N	36N	15E	12E	Second Principal
Sullivan	9N	6N	8W	11W	Second Principal
Switzerland	6N	3N	12E	12E	Second Principal
Switzerland	4N	1N	1E	4W	First Principal
Tippecanoe	24N	21N	3W	6W	Second Principal
Tipton	23N	21N	6E	3E	Second Principal
Union	15N	13N	14E	13E	Second Principal

Indiana(cont.)

County	North	South	East	West	Meridian
Union	12N	10N	1W	2W	First Principal
Vanderburgh	4S	8S	9W	11W	Second Principal
Vermillion	20N	14N	9W	10W	Second Principal
Vigo	13N	10N	7W	11W	Second Principal
Wabash	30N	26N	8E	5E	Second Principal
Warren	23N	20N	6W	10W	Second Principal
Warrick	3S	7S	6W	9W	Second Principal
Washington	4N	1S	6E	2E	Second Principal
Wayne	18N	15N	15E	12E	Second Principal
Wayne	15N	12N	1W	2W	First Principal
Wells	28N	25N	13E	10E	Second Principal
White	28N	25N	2W	6W	Second Principal
Whitley	33N	30N	11E	8E	Second Principal

Iowa

County	North	South	East	West	Meridian
Adair	77N	74N	30W	33W	Fifth Principal
Adams	73N	71N	32W	35W	Fifth Principal
Allamakee	100N	96N	2W	6W	Fifth Principal
Appanoose	70N	67N	16W	19W	Fifth Principal
Audubon	81N	78N	34W	37W	Fifth Principal
Benton	86N	82N	9W	12W	Fifth Principal
Black Hawk	90N	87N	11W	14W	Fifth Principal
Boone	85N	82N	25W	28W	Fifth Principal
Bremer	93N	91N	11W	14W	Fifth Principal
Buchanan	90N	87N	7W	10W	Fifth Principal
Buena Vista	93N	90N	35W	38W	Fifth Principal
Butler	93N	90N	15W	18W	Fifth Principal
Calhoun	89N	86N	31W	34W	Fifth Principal
Carroll	85N	82N	33W	36W	Fifth Principal
Cass	77N	74N	34W	37W	Fifth Principal
Cedar	82N	79N	1W	4W	Fifth Principal
Cerro Gordo	97N	94N	19W	22W	Fifth Principal
Cherokee	93N	90N	39W	42W	Fifth Principal
Chickasaw	97N	94N	11W	14W	Fifth Principal
Clarke	73N	71N	24W	27W	Fifth Principal
Clay	97N	94N	35W	38W	Fifth Principal
Clayton	95N	91N	1E	6W	Fifth Principal
Clinton	83N	80N	7E	1E	Fifth Principal
Crawford	85N	82N	37W	41W	Fifth Principal
Dallas	81N	78N	26W	30W	Fifth Principal

Iowa(cont.)

County	North	South	East	West	Meridian
Davis	70N	67N	12W	15W	Fifth Principal
Decatur	70N	67N	24W	27W	Fifth Principal
Delaware	90N	87N	3W	6W	Fifth Principal
Des Moines	72N	68N	1W	4W	Fifth Principal
Dickinson	100N	98N	35W	38W	Fifth Principal
Dubuque	90N	87N	4E	2W	Fifth Principal
Emmett	100N	98N	31W	34W	Fifth Principal
Fayette	95N	91N	7W	10W	Fifth Principal
Floyd	97N	94N	15W	18W	Fifth Principal
Franklin	93N	90N	19W	22W	Fifth Principal
Fremont	70N	67N	40W	44W	Fifth Principal
Green	85N	82N	29W	32W	Fifth Principal
Grundy	89N	86N	15W	19W	Fifth Principal
Guthrie	81N	78N	30W	34W	Fifth Principal
Hamilton	89N	86N	22W	26W	Fifth Principal
Hancock	97N	94N	23W	26W	Fifth Principal
Hardin	89N	86N	19W	22W	Fifth Principal
Harrison	81N	78N	41W	45W	Fifth Principal
Henry	73N	70N	5W	7W	Fifth Principal
Howard	100N	97N	11W	14W	Fifth Principal
Humboldt	93N	91N	27W	30W	Fifth Principal
Ida	89N	86N	39W	41W	Fifth Principal
Iowa	81N	78N	9W	12W	Fifth Principal
Jackson	87N	84N	7E	1E	Fifth Principal
Jasper	81N	78N	17W	21W	Fifth Principal
Jefferson	73N	71N	8W	11W	Fifth Principal
Johnson	81N	77N	5W	8W	Fifth Principal
Jones	86N	83N	1W	4W	Fifth Principal
Keokuk	77N	74N	10W	13W	Fifth Principal
Kossuth	100N	94N	27W	30W	Fifth Principal
Lee	69N	65N	2W	7W	Fifth Principal
Linn	86N	82N	5W	8W	Fifth Principal
Louisa	76N	73N	1W	5W	Fifth Principal
Lucas	73N	71N	20W	23W	Fifth Principal
Lyon	100N	98N	43W	49W	Fifth Principal
Madison	77N	74N	26W	29W	Fifth Principal
Mahaska	77N	74N	14W	17W	Fifth Principal
Marion	77N	74N	18W	21W	Fifth Principal
Marshall	85N	82N	17W	20W	Fifth Principal
Mills	73N	71N	40W	44W	Fifth Principal
Mitchell	100N	97N	15W	19W	Fifth Principal
Monona	85N	82N	42W	47W	Fifth Principal

Iowa(cont.)

County	North	South	East	West	Meridian
Monroe	73N	71N	16W	19W	Fifth Principal
Montgomery	73N	71N	36W	39W	Fifth Principal
Muscatine	78N	76N	1E	4W	Fifth Principal
O'Brien	97N	94N	39W	42W	Fifth Principal
Osceola	100N	98N	39W	42W	Fifth Principal
Page	70N	67N	36W	39W	Fifth Principal
Palo Alto	97N	94N	31W	34W	Fifth Principal
Plymouth	93N	90N	43W	49W	Fifth Principal
Pocahontas	93N	90N	31W	34W	Fifth Principal
Polk	81N	78N	22W	25W	Fifth Principal
Pottawatamie	77N	74N	38W	44W	Fifth Principal
Poweshiek	81N	78N	13W	16W	Fifth Principal
Ringgold	70N	67N	28W	31W	Fifth Principal
Sac	89N	86N	35W	38W	Fifth Principal
Scott	80N	77N	5E	1E	Fifth Principal
Shelby	81N	78N	37W	41W	Fifth Principal
Sioux	97N	94N	43W	49W	Fifth Principal
Story	85N	82N	21W	24W	Fifth Principal
Tama	86N	82N	13W	16W	Fifth Principal
Taylor	70N	67N	32W	35W	Fifth Principal
Union	73N	71N	28W	31W	Fifth Principal
Van Buren	70N	67N	8W	11W	Fifth Principal
Wapello	73N	71N	12W	15W	Fifth Principal
Warren	77N	74N	22W	25W	Fifth Principal
Washington	77N	74N	6W	9W	Fifth Principal
Wayne	70N	67N	20W	23W	Fifth Principal
Webster	90N	86N	27W	30W	Fifth Principal
Winnebago	100N	98N	23W	26W	Fifth Principal
Winneshiek	100N	96N	7W	10W	Fifth Principal
Woodbury	89N	86N	42W	48W	Fifth Principal
Worth	100N	98N	19W	22W	Fifth Principal
Wright	93N	90N	23W	26W	Fifth Principal

Kansas

County	North	South	East	West	Meridian
Allen	23S	26S	21E	17E	Sixth Principal
Anderson	19S	23S	21E	17E	Sixth Principal
Atchison	5S	7S	22E	17E	Sixth Principal
Barber	30S	35S	10W	15W	Sixth Principal
Barton	16S	20S	11W	15W	Sixth Principal
Bourbon	23S	27S	25E	21E	Sixth Principal

Kansas(cont.)

County	North	South	East	West	Meridian
Brown	1S	4S	18E	15E	Sixth Principal
Butler	23S	29S	8E	3E	Sixth Principal
Chase	18S	22S	9E	6E	Sixth Principal
Chautauqua	32S	35S	13E	8E	Sixth Principal
Cherokee	32S	35S	25E	21E	Sixth Principal
Cheyenne	1S	5S	37W	42W	Sixth Principal
Clark	30S	35S	21W	25W	Sixth Principal
Clay	5S	10S	9E	4E	Sixth Principal
Cloud	5S	8S	1W	5W	Sixth Principal
Coffey	19S	23S	17E	13E	Sixth Principal
Comanche	31S	35S	16W	20W	Sixth Principal
Cowley	30S	35S	8E	3E	Sixth Principal
Crawford	27S	31S	25E	21E	Sixth Principal
Decatur	1S	5S	26W	30W	Sixth Principal
Dickinson	11S	16S	5E	1E	Sixth Principal
Doniphan	1S	4S	23E	19E	Sixth Principal
Douglas	11S	15S	21E	17E	Sixth Principal
Edwards	23S	26S	16W	20W	Sixth Principal
Elk	28S	31S	13E	8E	Sixth Principal
Ellis	11S	15S	16W	20W	Sixth Principal
Ellsworth	14S	17S	6W	10W	Sixth Principal
Finney	21S	26S	27W	34W	Sixth Principal
Ford	25S	29S	21W	26W	Sixth Principal
Franklin	15S	19S	21E	17E	Sixth Principal
Geary	10S	13S	8E	4E	Sixth Principal
Gove	11S	15S	26W	31W	Sixth Principal
Graham	6S	10S	21W	25W	Sixth Principal
Grant	27S	30S	35W	39W	Sixth Principal
Gray	24S	29S	27W	30W	Sixth Principal
Greeley	16S	20S	39W	43W	Sixth Principal
Greenwood	22S	28S	13E	8E	Sixth Principal
Hamilton	21S	26S	39W	43W	Sixth Principal
Harper	31S	35S	5W	9W	Sixth Principal
Harvey	22S	24S	2E	3W	Sixth Principal
Haskell	27S	30S	31W	34W	Sixth Principal
Hodgeman	21S	24S	21W	26W	Sixth Principal
Jackson	5S	9S	16E	12E	Sixth Principal
Jefferson	7S	12S	20E	16E	Sixth Principal
Jewell	1S	5S	6W	10W	Sixth Principal
Johnson	12S	15S	25E	21E	Sixth Principal
Kearny	21S	26S	35W	38W	Sixth Principal
Kingman	27S	30S	5W	10W	Sixth Principal

Kansas(cont.)

County	North	South	East	West	Meridian
Kiowa	27S	30S	16W	20W	Sixth Principal
Labette	31S	35S	21E	17E	Sixth Principal
Lane	16S	20S	27W	30W	Sixth Principal
Leavenworth	7S	12S	23E	20E	Sixth Principal
Lincoln	10S	13S	6W	10W	Sixth Principal
Linn	19S	23S	25E	21E	Sixth Principal
Logan	11S	15S	32W	38W	Sixth Principal
Lyon	15S	21S	13E	10E	Sixth Principal
Marion	17S	22S	5E	1E	Sixth Principal
Marshall	1S	5S	10E	6E	Sixth Principal
McPherson	17S	21S	1W	5W	Sixth Principal
Meade	30S	35S	26W	30W	Sixth Principal
Miami	15S	19S	25E	21E	Sixth Principal
Mitchell	6S	9S	6W	10W	Sixth Principal
Montgomery	31S	35S	17E	13E	Sixth Principal
Morris	14S	17S	9E	5E	Sixth Principal
Morton	31S	35S	39W	43W	Sixth Principal
Nemaha	1S	5S	14E	11E	Sixth Principal
Neosho	27S	30S	21E	17E	Sixth Principal
Ness	16S	20S	21W	26W	Sixth Principal
Norton	1S	5S	21W	25W	Sixth Principal
Osage	13S	18S	17E	13E	Sixth Principal
Osborne	6S	10S	11W	15W	Sixth Principal
Ottawa	9S	12S	1W	5W	Sixth Principal
Pawnee	20S	23S	15W	20W	Sixth Principal
Phillips	1S	5S	16W	20W	Sixth Principal
Pottawatomie	6S	10S	12E	6E	Sixth Principal
Pratt	26S	29S	11W	15W	Sixth Principal
Rawlins	1S	5S	31W	36W	Sixth Principal
Reno	22S	26S	4W	10W	Sixth Principal
Republic	1S	4S	1W	5W	Sixth Principal
Rice	18S	21S	6W	10W	Sixth Principal
Riley	6S	11S	9E	4E	Sixth Principal
Rooks	6S	10S	16W	20W	Sixth Principal
Rush	16S	19S	16W	20W	Sixth Principal
Russell	11S	15S	11W	15W	Sixth Principal
Saline	12S	16S	1W	5W	Sixth Principal
Scott	16S	20S	31W	34W	Sixth Principal
Sedgwick	25S	29S	2E	4W	Sixth Principal
Seward	31S	35S	31W	34W	Sixth Principal
Shawnee	10S	13S	17E	12E	Sixth Principal
Sheridan	6S	10S	25W	30W	Sixth Principal

Kansas (cont.)

County	North	South	East	West	Meridian
Sherman	6S	10S	36W	42W	Sixth Principal
Smith	1S	5S	11W	15W	Sixth Principal
Stafford	21S	25S	11W	15W	Sixth Principal
Stanton	27S	30S	39W	43W	Sixth Principal
Stevens	31S	35S	35W	39W	Sixth Principal
Sumner	30S	35S	2E	4W	Sixth Principal
Thomas	6S	10S	30W	36W	Sixth Principal
Trego	11S	15S	21W	25W	Sixth Principal
Wabaunsee	10S	15S	13E	8E	Sixth Principal
Wallace	11S	15S	37W	43W	Sixth Principal
Washington	1S	5S	5E	1E	Sixth Principal
Wichita	16S	20S	35W	38W	Sixth Principal
Wilson	27S	30S	17E	13E	Sixth Principal
Woodson	23S	26S	17E	13E	Sixth Principal
Wyandotte	10S	12S	25E	23E	Sixth Principal

Louisiana

Parish	North	South	East	West	Meridian
Acadia	7S	11S	3E	3W	Louisiana
Allen	2S	7S	2W	7W	Louisiana
Ascension	10S	11S	15E	13E	Louisiana
Ascension	8S	11S	6E	1E	St. Helena
Assumption	12S	17S	15E	12E	Louisiana
Avoyelles	4N	2S	8E	2E	Louisiana
Beauregard	2S	7S	6W	13W	Louisiana
Bienville	18N	14N	4W	10W	Louisiana
Bossier	24N	15N	10W	14W	Louisiana
Caddo	24N	14N	11W	16W	Louisiana
Calcasieu	7S	11S	5W	14W	Louisiana
Caldwell	15N	11N	6E	2E	Louisiana
Cameron	11S	17S	3W	15W	Louisiana
Catahoula	11N	3N	9E	5E	Louisiana
Claiborne	24N	19N	3W	8W	Louisiana
Concordia	9N	1S	10E	6E	Louisiana
DeSoto	16N	10N	10W	16W	Louisiana
East Baton Rouge	4S	8S	3E	2W	St. Helena
East Carroll	24N	18N	14E	10E	Louisiana
East Feliciana	1S	4S	4E	2W	St. Helena
Evangeline	1S	6S	3E	2W	Louisiana
Franklin	16N	10N	10E	5E	Louisiana
Grant	9N	5N	3E	6W	Louisiana

Louisiana(cont.)

Parish	North	South	East	West	Meridian
Iberia	11S	18S	12E	5E	Louisiana
Iberville	7S	12S	14E	8E	Louisiana
Iberville	8S	10S	2E	1W	St. Helena
Jackson	17N	14N	1E	4W	Louisiana
Jefferson	13S	21S	25E	22E	Louisiana
Jefferson	12S	13S	10E	9E	St. Helena
Jefferson Davis	7S	11S	2W	7W	Louisiana
Lafayette	8S	12S	6E	2E	Louisiana
Lafourche	13S	23S	24E	15E	Louisiana
LaSalle	11N	4N	4E	1E	Louisiana
Lincoln	20N	17N	1W	5W	Louisiana
Livingston	5S	10S	7E	2E	St. Helena
Madison	18N	14N	15E	9E	Louisiana
Morehouse	24N	18N	10E	4E	Louisiana
Natchitoches	13N	4N	3W	10W	Louisiana
Orleans	10S	14S	15E	11E	St. Helena
Ouachita	20N	15N	5E	1E	Louisiana
Plaquemines	14S	23S	29E	24E	Louisiana
Plaquemines	14S	23S	20E	12E	St. Helena
Pointe Coupee	1N	6S	11E	7E	Louisiana
Rapides	6N	2S	4E	6W	Louisiana
Red River	14N	11N	8W	12W	Louisiana
Richland	19N	14N	10E	4E	Louisiana
Sabine	10N	3N	9W	14W	Louisiana
St. Bernard	13S	16S	20E	12E	St. Helena
St. Charles	12S	16S	23E	19E	Louisiana
St. Charles	12S	13S	9E	7E	St. Helena
St. Helena	1S	4S	6E	3E	St. Helena
St. James	12S	13S	18E	15E	Louisiana
St. James	10S	12S	6E	3E	St. Helena
St. John the Baptist	12S	13S	19E	18E	Louisiana
St. John the Baptist	9S	12S	9E	6E	St. Helena
St. Landry	2S	9S	7E	1W	Louisiana
St. Martin (1)	7S	11S	11E	5E	Louisiana
St. Martin (2)	12S	15S	14E	10E	Louisiana
St. Mary	13S	18S	14E	6E	Louisiana
St. Tammany	4S	10S	15E	9E	St. Helena
Tangipahoa	1S	9S	9E	7E	St. Helena
Tensas	15N	9N	15E	9E	Louisiana
Terrebonne	15S	22S	20E	11E	Louisiana
Union	24N	19N	4E	3W	Louisiana
Vermilion	10S	17S	5E	3W	Louisiana

Louisiana(cont.)

Parish	North	South	East	West	Meridian
Vernon	4N	2S	5W	12W	Louisiana
Washington	1S	4S	14E	9E	St. Helena
Webster	24N	17N	8W	11W	Louisiana
West Baton Rouge	5S	8S	13E	10E	Louisiana
West Carroll	24N	19N	12E	8E	Louisiana
West Feliciana	1S	4S	1W	5W	St. Helena
Winn	13N	9N	1E	6W	Louisiana

Michigan

County	North	South	East	West	Meridian
Alcona	28N	25N	9E	5E	Michigan
Alger	50N	44N	13W	22W	Michigan
Allegan	4N	1N	11W	17W	Michigan
Alpena	32N	29N	9E	5E	Michigan
Antrim	32N	29N	5W	9W	Michigan
Arenac	20N	18N	7E	3E	Michigan
Baraga	52N	47N	30W	35W	Michigan
Barry	4N	1N	7W	10W	Michigan
Bay	18N	13N	6E	3E	Michigan
Benzie	27N	25N	13W	16W	Michigan
Berrien	3S	8S	17W	21W	Michigan
Branch	5S	8S	5W	8W	Michigan
Calhoun	1S	4S	4W	8W	Michigan
Cass	5S	8S	13W	16W	Michigan
Charlevoix	40N	32N	4W	13W	Michigan
Cheboygan	39N	33N	1E	3W	Michigan
Chippewa	50N	41N	8E	7W	Michigan
Clare	20N	17N	3W	6W	Michigan
Clinton	8N	5N	1W	4W	Michigan
Crawford	28N	25N	1W	4W	Michigan
Delta	43N	37N	17W	24W	Michigan
Dickinson	44N	39N	27W	30W	Michigan
Eaton	4N	1N	3W	6W	Michigan
Emmet	39N	34N	4W	6W	Michigan
Genesee	9N	5N	8E	5E	Michigan
Gladwin	20N	17N	2E	2W	Michigan
Gogebic	50N	43N	38W	49W	Michigan
Grand Traverse	30N	25N	9W	12W	Michigan
Gratiot	12N	9N	1W	4W	Michigan
Hillsdale	5S	9S	1W	4W	Michigan
Houghton	56N	47N	32W	37W	Michigan

Michigan(cont.)

County	North	South	East	West	Meridian
Huron	19N	15N	16E	9E	Michigan
Ingham	4N	1N	2E	2W	Michigan
Ionia	8N	5N	5W	8W	Michigan
Iosco	24N	21N	9E	5E	Michigan
Iron	46N	41N	31W	37W	Michigan
Isabella	16N	13N	3W	6W	Michigan
Jackson	1S	4S	2E	3W	Michigan
Kalamazoo	1S	4S	9W	12W	Michigan
Kalkaska	28N	25N	5W	8W	Michigan
Kent	10N	5N	9W	12W	Michigan
Keweenaw	66N	56N	27W	38W	Michigan
Lake	20N	17N	11W	14W	Michigan
Lapeer	10N	6N	12E	9E	Michigan
Leelanau	35N	28N	11W	15W	Michigan
Lenawee	5S	9S	5E	1E	Michigan
Livingston	4N	1N	6E	3E	Michigan
Luce	50N	45N	8W	12W	Michigan
Mackinac	44N	39N	3E	12W	Michigan
Macomb	5N	1N	14E	12E	Michigan
Manistee	24N	21N	13W	17W	Michigan
Marquette	52N	42N	23W	30W	Michigan
Mason	20N	17N	15W	18W	Michigan
Mecosta	16N	13N	7W	10W	Michigan
Menominee	41N	32N	24W	29W	Michigan
Midland	16N	13N	2E	2W	Michigan
Missaukee	24N	21N	5W	8W	Michigan
Monroe	5S	9S	10E	6E	Michigan
Montcalm	12N	9N	5W	10W	Michigan
Montmorency	32N	29N	4E	1E	Michigan
Muskegon	12N	9N	13W	18W	Michigan
Newaygo	16N	11N	11W	14W	Michigan
Oakland	5N	1N	11E	7E	Michigan
Oceana	16N	13N	15W	19W	Michigan
Ogemaw	24N	21N	4E	1E	Michigan
Ontonagon	54N	46N	37W	44W	Michigan
Osceola	20N	17N	7W	10W	Michigan
Oscoda	28N	25N	4E	1E	Michigan
Otsego	32N	29N	1W	4W	Michigan
Ottawa	9N	5N	13W	17W	Michigan
Presque Isle	38N	33N	8E	2E	Michigan
Roscommon	24N	21N	1W	4W	Michigan
Saginaw	13N	9N	6E	1E	Michigan

Michigan (cont.)

County	North	South	East	West	Meridian
Saint Clair	8N	2N	17E	13E	Michigan
Saint Joseph	5S	8S	9W	13W	Michigan
Sanilac	14N	9N	17E	12E	Michigan
Schoolcraft	47N	39N	13W	18W	Michigan
Shiawassee	8N	5N	4E	1E	Michigan
Tuscola	15N	10N	11E	7E	Michigan
Van Buren	1S	4S	13W	18W	Michigan
Washtenaw	1S	4S	7E	3E	Michigan
Wayne (Detroit)	1S	5S	13E	8E	Michigan
Wexford	24N	21N	9W	12W	Michigan

Minnesota

County	North	South	East	West	Meridian
Aitkin	52N	43N	22W	27W	Fourth Principal
Anoka	34N	30N	22W	25W	Fourth Principal
Becker	142N	138N	36W	43W	Fifth Principal
Beltrami	158N	146N	30W	38W	Fifth Principal
Benton	38N	36N	28W	32W	Fourth Principal
Big Stone	124N	120N	44W	49W	Fifth Principal
Blue Earth	109N	105N	25W	29W	Fifth Principal
Brown	112N	108N	30W	35W	Fifth Principal
Carlton	49N	46N	16W	21W	Fourth Principal
Carver	117N	114N	23W	26W	Fifth Principal
Cass	146N	133N	25W	31W	Fifth Principal
Chippewa	119N	115N	37W	43W	Fifth Principal
Chisago	37N	33N	19W	22W	Fourth Principal
Clay	142N	137N	44W	48W	Fifth Principal
Clearwater	152N	143N	36W	38W	Fifth Principal
Cook	66N	58N	6E	5W	Fourth Principal
Cottonwood	108N	105N	34W	38W	Fifth Principal
Crow Wing	138N	131N	25W	29W	Fifth Principal
Dakota	117N	112N	16W	21W	Fifth Principal
Dodge	108N	105N	16W	18W	Fifth Principal
Douglas	130N	127N	36W	40W	Fifth Principal
Faribault	104N	101N	24W	28W	Fifth Principal
Fillmore	104N	101N	8W	13W	Fifth Principal
Freeborn	104N	101N	19W	23W	Fifth Principal
Goodhue	114N	109N	13W	18W	Fifth Principal
Grant	130N	127N	41W	44W	Fifth Principal
Hennepin	120N	116N	20W	24W	Fifth Principal
Houston	104N	101N	3W	7W	Fifth Principal

Minnesota(cont.)

County	North	South	East	West	Meridian
Hubbard	145N	139N	32W	35W	Fifth Principal
Isanti	37N	34N	22W	25W	Fourth Principal
Itasca	150N	144N	25W	29W	Fifth Principal
Itasca	62N	53N	22W	27W	Fourth Principal
Jackson	104N	101N	34W	38W	Fifth Principal
Kanabec	42N	38N	22W	25W	Fourth Principal
Kandiyohi	122N	117N	33W	36W	Fifth Principal
Kittson	164N	159N	45W	51W	Fifth Principal
Koochiching	160N	151N	25W	29W	Fifth Principal
Koochiching	71N	63N	22W	27W	Fourth Principal
Lac Qui Parle	121N	116N	41W	46W	Fifth Principal
Lake	66N	52N	6W	11W	Fourth Principal
Lake of the Woods	163N	157N	30W	36W	Fifth Principal
Le Sueur	112N	109N	23W	26W	Fifth Principal
Lincoln	113N	109N	44W	47W	Fifth Principal
Lyon	113N	109N	40W	43W	Fifth Principal
Mohnomen	146N	143N	39W	42W	Fifth Principal
Marshall	158N	154N	39W	50W	Fifth Principal
Martin	104N	101N	29W	33W	Fifth Principal
McLeod	117N	114N	27W	30W	Fifth Principal
Meeker	121N	117N	29W	32W	Fifth Principal
Mille Lacs	43N	36N	25W	27W	Fourth Principal
Morrison	133N	127N	29W	31W	Fifth Principal
Morrison	42N	39N	28W	32W	Fourth Principal
Mower	104N	101N	14W	18W	Fifth Principal
Murray	108N	105N	39W	43W	Fifth Principal
Nicollet	111N	108N	26W	32W	Fifth Principal
Nobles	104N	101N	39W	43W	Fifth Principal
Norman	146N	143N	43W	49W	Fifth Principal
Olmstead	108N	104N	11W	15W	Fifth Principal
Otter Tail	137N	131N	36W	44W	Fifth Principal
Pennington	154N	152N	39W	45W	Fifth Principal
Pine	45N	38N	16W	22W	Fourth Principal
Pipestone	108N	105N	44W	47W	Fifth Principal
Polk	154N	147N	39W	50W	Fifth Principal
Pope	126N	123N	36W	40W	Fifth Principal
Ramsey	30N	28N	22W	23W	Fourth Principal
Red Lake	152N	150N	40W	45W	Fifth Principal
Redwood	114N	109N	34W	39W	Fifth Principal
Renville	116N	112N	31W	38W	Fifth Principal
Rice	112N	109N	19W	22W	Fifth Principal
Rock	104N	101N	44W	47W	Fifth Principal

Minnesota(cont.)

County	North	South	East	West	Meridian
Roseau	164N	159N	35W	44W	Fifth Principal
Saint Louis	71N	48N	12W	21W	Fourth Principal
Scott	115N	113N	21W	25W	Fifth Principal
Sherburne	35N	32N	26W	31W	Fourth Principal
Sibley	114N	112N	25W	31W	Fifth Principal
Stearns	126N	121N	27W	35W	Fifth Principal
Steele	108N	105N	19W	21W	Fifth Principal
Stevens	126N	123N	41W	44W	Fifth Principal
Swift	122N	120N	37W	43W	Fifth Principal
Todd	133N	127N	32W	35W	Fifth Principal
Traverse	129N	125N	45W	49W	Fifth Principal
Wabasha	111N	108N	9W	14W	Fifth Principal
Wadena	138N	134N	33W	35W	Fifth Principal
Waseca	108N	105N	22W	24W	Fifth Principal
Washington	32N	27N	20W	21W	Fourth Principal
Watonwan	107N	105N	30W	33W	Fifth Principal
Wilkin	136N	130N	45W	48W	Fifth Principal
Winona	108N	105N	4W	10W	Fifth Principal
Wright	122N	118N	23W	28W	Fifth Principal
Yellow Medicine	117N	113N	38W	47W	Fifth Principal

Mississippi

County	North	South	East	West	Meridian
Adams	9N	3N	1W	5W	Washington
Alcorn	1S	4S	9E	5E	Chickasaw
Amite	4N	1N	6E	1E	Washington
Attala	16N	12N	9E	3E	Choctaw
Benton	1S	6S	3E	1W	Chickasaw
Bolivar	26N	20N	5W	10W	Choctaw
Calhoun	11S	14S	1E	3W	Chickasaw
Calhoun	25N	22N	10E	8E	Choctaw
Carroll	21N	16N	6E	1E	Choctaw
Chickasaw	22N	22N	13E	11E	Choctaw
Chickasaw	12S	14S	5E	2E	Chickasaw
Choctaw	19N	15N	11E	8E	Choctaw
Claiborne	14N	10N	5E	1W	Washington
Clarke	10N	10N	6W	9W	St. Stephens
Clarke	4N	1N	18E	14E	Choctaw
Clay	15S	17S	7E	3E	Chickasaw
Clay	22N	19N	16E	12E	Choctaw
Coahoma	30N	25N	2W	7W	Choctaw

Mississippi(cont.)

County	North	South	East	West	Meridian
Copiah	12N	8N	11E	5E	Washington
Copiah	2N	1N	1E	4W	Choctaw
Covington	10N	6N	14W	17W	St. Stephens
De Soto	1S	4S	5W	10W	Chickasaw
Forrest	5N	1S	12W	15W	St. Stephens
Franklin	7N	4N	6E	1E	Washington
George	1S	3S	4W	9W	St. Stephens
Greene	5N	1N	4W	8W	St. Stephens
Grenada	23N	21N	7E	2E	Choctaw
Hancock	5S	10S	14W	17W	St. Stephens
Harrison	4S	8S	9W	13W	St. Stephens
Hinds	8N	3N	2E	4W	Choctaw
Hinds	16N	13N	5E	5E	Washington
Holmes	17N	12N	5E	2W	Choctaw
Humphreys	17N	13N	1W	5W	Choctaw
Issaquena	18N	17N	3E	3E	Washington
Issaquena	13N	9N	5W	10W	Choctaw
Itawamba	7S	11S	11E	7E	Chickasaw
Jackson	4S	8S	4W	9W	St. Stephens
Jasper	10N	10N	9W	13W	St. Stephens
Jasper	14N	1N	13E	10E	Choctaw
Jefferson	10N	8N	5E	2W	Washington
Jefferson Davis	9N	5N	16W	20W	St. Stephens
Jones	10N	6N	10W	14W	St. Stephens
Kemper	12N	9N	19E	14E	Choctaw
Lafayette	6S	10S	1W	5W	Chickasaw
LaMar	5N	1S	14W	16W	St. Stephens
Lauderdale	8N	5N	19E	14E	Choctaw
Lawrence	9N	4N	12E	10E	Washington
Lawrence	9N	5N	20W	21W	St. Stephens
Leake	12N	9N	9E	6E	Choctaw
Lee	7S	11S	7E	5E	Chickasaw
Leflore	22N	16N	2E	2W	Choctaw
Lincoln	8N	5N	9E	5E	Washington
Lowndes	19N	17N	19E	16E	Choctaw
Lowndes	15S	20S	16W	19W	Huntsville
Madison	12N	7N	5E	2W	Choctaw
Marion	5N	1N	14E	12E	Washington
Marion	5N	1N	17W	20W	St. Stephens
Marshall	1S	6S	1W	5W	Chickasaw
Monroe	12S	16S	10E	6E	Chickasaw
Monroe	12S	16S	16W	19W	Huntsville

Mississippi(cont.)

County	North	South	East	West	Meridian
Montgomery	21N	17N	8E	5E	Choctaw
Neshoba	12N	9N	13E	10E	Choctaw
Newton	8N	5N	13E	10E	Choctaw
Noxubee	16N	13N	19E	15E	Choctaw
Oktibeeha	20N	17N	15E	12E	Choctaw
Panola	28N	27N	3E	2E	Choctaw
Panola	6S	10S	5W	9W	Chickasaw
Pearl River	1S	7S	14W	18W	St. Stephens
Perry	5N	1S	9W	11W	St. Stephens
Pike	4N	1N	9E	7E	Washington
Pontotoc	8S	11S	4E	1E	Chickasaw
Prentiss	4S	7S	9E	5E	Chickasaw
Quitman	29N	26N	1E	2W	Choctaw
Quitman	7S	9S	10W	11W	Chickasaw
Rankin	9N	3N	5E	1E	Choctaw
Scott	9N	5N	9E	5E	Choctaw
Sharkey	14N	10N	5W	7W	Choctaw
Simpson	10N	9N	17W	21W	St. Stephens
Simpson	2N	1N	6E	1E	Choctaw
Smith	10N	10N	13W	16W	St. Stephens
Smith	4N	1N	9E	6E	Choctaw
Stone	2S	4S	9W	13W	St. Stephens
Sunflower	24N	17N	3W	5W	Choctaw
Tallahatchie	26N	23N	3E	2W	Choctaw
Tate	4S	6S	5W	10W	Chickasaw
Tippah	1S	5S	5E	2E	Chickasaw
Tishomingo	1S	7S	11E	9E	Chickasaw
Tunica	2S	7S	10W	13W	Chickasaw
Union	6S	8S	5E	1E	Chickasaw
Walthall	4N	1N	13E	10E	Washington
Warren	18N	13N	5E	1E	Washington
Warren	9N	9N	5W	5W	Choctaw
Washington	19N	14N	5W	10W	Choctaw
Wayne	10N	6N	5W	9W	St. Stephens
Wayne	1N	1N	18E	17E	Choctaw
Webster	22N	19N	12E	8E	Choctaw
Wilkinson	5N	1N	1E	5W	Washington
Winston	16N	12N	14E	10E	Choctaw
Yalobusha	26N	23N	7E	4E	Choctaw
Yalobusha	10S	11S	3W	7W	Chickasaw
Yazoo	13N	8N	3E	5W	Choctaw

Missouri

County	North	South	East	West	Meridian
Adair	64N	61N	13W	17W	Fifth Principal
Andrew	61N	58N	33W	37W	Fifth Principal
Atchison	67N	63N	38W	43W	Fifth Principal
Audrian	53N	50N	5W	12W	Fifth Principal
Barry	25N	21N	24W	29W	Fifth Principal
Barton	33N	30N	29W	34W	Fifth Principal
Bates	42N	38N	29W	33W	Fifth Principal
Benton	43N	39N	20W	23W	Fifth Principal
Bollinger	33N	28N	11E	8E	Fifth Principal
Boone	51N	45N	11W	15W	Fifth Principal
Buchanan	58N	55N	33W	38W	Fifth Principal
Butler	26N	22N	8E	4E	Fifth Principal
Caldwell	57N	55N	26W	29W	Fifth Principal
Callaway	49N	44N	7W	11W	Fifth Principal
Camden	40N	36N	14W	19W	Fifth Principal
Cape Girardeau	33N	29N	15E	11E	Fifth Principal
Carroll	55N	50N	20W	25W	Fifth Principal
Carter	28N	25N	4E	2W	Fifth Principal
Cass	46N	42N	29W	33W	Fifth Principal
Cedar	36N	33N	25W	29W	Fifth Principal
Chariton	56N	51N	16W	21W	Fifth Principal
Christian	28N	25N	18W	24W	Fifth Principal
Clark	67N	63N	5W	9W	Fifth Principal
Clay	54N	50N	30W	33W	Fifth Principal
Clinton	57N	54N	30W	33W	Fifth Principal
Cole	46N	41N	10W	14W	Fifth Principal
Cooper	49N	45N	15W	19W	Fifth Principal
Crawford	40N	35N	2W	5W	Fifth Principal
Dade	33N	30N	25W	29W	Fifth Principal
Dallas	36N	31N	18W	20W	Fifth Principal
Daviess	62N	58N	26W	29W	Fifth Principal
De Kalb	60N	57N	30W	33W	Fifth Principal
Dent	35N	32N	2W	8W	Fifth Principal
Douglas	27N	25N	11W	18W	Fifth Principal
Dunklin	23N	16N	10E	7E	Fifth Principal
Franklin	46N	40N	2E	4W	Fifth Principal
Gasconade	46N	40N	4W	6W	Fifth Principal
Gentry	64N	61N	30W	33W	Fifth Principal
Greene	31N	28N	20W	24W	Fifth Principal
Grundy	63N	60N	22W	25W	Fifth Principal
Harrison	67N	62N	26W	29W	Fifth Principal
Henry	44N	40N	24W	28W	Fifth Principal

Missouri (cont.)

County	North	South	East	West	Meridian
Hickory	38N	35N	20W	24W	Fifth Principal
Holt	63N	58N	37W	41W	Fifth Principal
Howard	52N	48N	14W	18W	Fifth Principal
Howell	27N	21N	7W	10W	Fifth Principal
Iron	35N	30N	4E	2W	Fifth Principal
Jackson	51N	47N	29W	33W	Fifth Principal
Jasper	30N	27N	29W	34W	Fifth Principal
Jefferson	43N	38N	7E	2E	Fifth Principal
Johnson	48N	44N	24W	29W	Fifth Principal
Knox	63N	60N	10W	13W	Fifth Principal
Laclede	36N	32N	12W	17W	Fifth Principal
Lafayette	52N	48N	24W	29W	Fifth Principal
Lawrence	29N	26N	25W	29W	Fifth Principal
Lewis	63N	60N	5W	9W	Fifth Principal
Lincoln	52N	48N	3E	3W	Fifth Principal
Linn	60N	57N	18W	22W	Fifth Principal
Livingston	59N	56N	21W	25W	Fifth Principal
Macon	60N	56N	13W	17W	Fifth Principal
Madison	34N	31N	8E	5E	Fifth Principal
Maries	41N	38N	7W	11W	Fifth Principal
Marion	59N	56N	4W	8W	Fifth Principal
McDonald	23N	21N	29W	34W	Fifth Principal
Mercer	67N	63N	22W	25W	Fifth Principal
Miller	42N	38N	12W	16W	Fifth Principal
Mississippi	28N	22N	18E	14E	Fifth Principal
Moniteau	48N	43N	14W	17W	Fifth Principal
Monroe	56N	53N	7W	12W	Fifth Principal
Montgomery	51N	45N	3W	6W	Fifth Principal
Morgan	45N	40N	16W	19W	Fifth Principal
New Madrid	26N	20N	16E	10E	Fifth Principal
Newton	27N	24N	29W	34W	Fifth Principal
Nodaway	67N	62N	33W	38W	Fifth Principal
Oregon	26N	21N	2W	6W	Fifth Principal
Osage	45N	41N	7W	11W	Fifth Principal
Ozark	24N	21N	11W	16W	Fifth Principal
Pemiscot	21N	16N	14E	10E	Fifth Principal
Perry	37N	33N	14E	8E	Fifth Principal
Pettis	48N	43N	20W	23W	Fifth Principal
Phelps	39N	34N	6W	10W	Fifth Principal
Pike	55N	51N	2E	5W	Fifth Principal
Platte	54N	50N	33W	38W	Fifth Principal
Polk	35N	31N	21W	24W	Fifth Principal

Missouri (cont.)

County	North	South	East	West	Meridian
Pulaski	38N	34N	10W	13W	Fifth Principal
Putnam	67N	64N	16W	22W	Fifth Principal
Ralls	57N	53N	3W	7W	Fifth Principal
Randolph	55N	52N	13W	16W	Fifth Principal
Ray	54N	50N	26W	29W	Fifth Principal
Reynolds	33N	28N	3E	3W	Fifth Principal
Ripley	25N	21N	4E	1W	Fifth Principal
Saint Charles	48N	44N	8E	1E	Fifth Principal
Saint Clair	39N	36N	24W	28W	Fifth Principal
Saint Francois	38N	34N	8E	4E	Fifth Principal
Saint Genevieve	39N	34N	10E	5E	Fifth Principal
Saint Louis	48N	42N	7E	3E	Fifth Principal
Saline	53N	48N	18W	23W	Fifth Principal
Schulyer	67N	64N	13W	16W	Fifth Principal
Scotland	67N	64N	10W	13W	Fifth Principal
Scott	30N	26N	16E	12E	Fifth Principal
Shannon	31N	26N	1W	6W	Fifth Principal
Shelby	59N	56N	9W	12W	Fifth Principal
Stoddard	28N	23N	12E	7E	Fifth Principal
Stone	26N	21N	22W	24W	Fifth Principal
Sullivan	64N	61N	18W	22W	Fifth Principal
Taney	24N	21N	17W	21W	Fifth Principal
Texas	33N	28N	7W	12W	Fifth Principal
Vernon	38N	34N	29W	34W	Fifth Principal
Warren	49N	44N	1W	4W	Fifth Principal
Washington	40N	35N	3E	1W	Fifth Principal
Wayne	30N	26N	9E	3E	Fifth Principal
Webster	32N	28N	16W	19W	Fifth Principal
Worth	67N	65N	30W	33W	Fifth Principal
Wright	32N	28N	12W	16W	Fifth Principal

Montana

County	North	South	East	West	Meridian
Beaverhead	2N	16S	2E	19W	Principal
Big Horn	3N	9S	44E	24E	Principal
Blaine	37N	23N	26E	17E	Principal
Broadwater	12N	1N	5E	1W	Principal
Carbon	2S	9S	29E	16E	Principal
Carter	4N	9S	62E	53E	Principal
Cascade	22N	12N	8E	4W	Principal
Chouteau	29N	19N	17E	2E	Principal
Custer	13N	1N	56E	45E	Principal

Montana (cont.)

County	North	South	East	West	Meridian
Daniels	37N	33N	51E	43E	Principal
Dawson	23N	13N	58E	50E	Principal
Deer Lodge	6N	1S	8W	16W	Principal
Fallon	11N	2N	62E	55E	Principal
Fergus	23N	11N	26E	12E	Principal
Flathead	37N	21N	10W	27W	Principal
Gallatin	5N	15S	7E	2W	Principal
Garfield	26N	13N	44E	30E	Principal
Glacier	37N	30N	5W	19W	Principal
Golden Valley	11N	4N	23E	17E	Principal
Granite	12N	2N	12W	18W	Principal
Hill	37N	28N	17E	8E	Principal
Jefferson	9N	1S	1W	8W	Principal
Judith Basin	19N	11N	16E	8E	Principal
Lake	26N	16N	16W	23W	Principal
Lewis & Clark	26N	8N	2E	12W	Principal
Liberty	37N	28N	7E	2E	Principal
Lincoln	37N	25N	24W	34W	Principal
Madison	1N	13S	3E	9W	Principal
McCone	27N	16N	50E	42E	Principal
Meagher	15N	5N	11E	1E	Principal
Mineral	20N	11N	22W	32W	Principal
Missoula	21N	11N	14W	25W	Principal
Musselshell	11N	5N	31E	22E	Principal
Park	5N	9S	15E	6E	Principal
Petroleum	21N	12N	31E	24E	Principal
Phillips	37N	20N	35E	22E	Principal
Pondera	31N	26N	2E	13W	Principal
Powder River	1S	9S	54E	45E	Principal
Powell	21N	6N	6W	16W	Principal
Prairie	16N	10N	56E	45E	Principal
Ravalli	10N	4S	16W	23W	Principal
Richland	28N	19N	59E	50E	Principal
Roosevelt	32N	26N	59E	46E	Principal
Rosebud	13N	7S	45E	31E	Principal
Sanders	29N	16N	21W	34W	Principal
Sheridan	37N	31N	58E	51E	Principal
Silver Bow	5N	2S	5W	12W	Principal
Stillwater	4N	7S	23E	13E	Principal
Sweet Grass	5N	7S	18E	12E	Principal
Teton	27N	20N	2E	11W	Principal
Toole	37N	29N	3E	4W	Principal

Montana (cont.)

County	North	South	East	West	Meridian
Treasure	8N	2N	38E	32E	Principal
Valley	37N	22N	45E	34E	Principal
Wibaux	19N	10N	61E	57E	Principal
Wheatland	12N	6N	18E	12E	Principal
Yellowstone	8N	4S	34E	22E	Principal

Nebraska

County	North	South	East	West	Meridian
Adams	8N	5N	9W	12W	Sixth Principal
Antelope	28N	23N	5W	8W	Sixth Principal
Arthur	20N	17N	35W	40W	Sixth Principal
Banner	20N	17N	53W	57W	Sixth Principal
Blaine	24N	21N	21W	25W	Sixth Principal
Boone	22N	17N	5W	8W	Sixth Principal
Box Butte	28N	24N	46W	52W	Sixth Principal
Boyd	35N	32N	9W	16W	Sixth Principal
Brown	33N	25N	20W	24W	Sixth Principal
Buffalo	12N	8N	13W	19W	Sixth Principal
Burt	24N	20N	12E	8E	Sixth Principal
Butler	17N	13N	4E	1E	Sixth Principal
Cass	13N	10N	14E	9E	Sixth Principal
Cedar	33N	28N	3E	1W	Sixth Principal
Chase	8N	5N	36W	42W	Sixth Principal
Cherry	35N	25N	25W	40W	Sixth Principal
Cheyenne	17N	12N	46W	52W	Sixth Principal
Clay	8N	5N	5W	8W	Sixth Principal
Colfax	20N	16N	4E	2E	Sixth Principal
Cuming	24N	21N	7E	4E	Sixth Principal
Custer	20N	13N	17W	25W	Sixth Principal
Dakota	29N	27W	10E	6E	Sixth Principal
Dawes	35N	29N	47W	52W	Sixth Principal
Dawson	12N	9N	19W	26W	Sixth Principal
Deuel	14N	12N	41W	46W	Sixth Principal
Dixon	32N	27N	7E	3E	Sixth Principal
Dodge	20N	17N	10E	5E	Sixth Principal
Douglas	16N	14N	14E	8E	Sixth Principal
Dundy	4N	1N	36W	42W	Sixth Principal
Fillmore	8N	5N	1W	4W	Sixth Principal
Franklin	4N	1N	13W	16W	Sixth Principal
Frontier	8N	5N	24W	30W	Sixth Principal
Furnas	4N	1N	21W	25W	Sixth Principal
Gage	6N	1N	9E	5E	Sixth Principal

Nebraska(cont.)

County	North	South	East	West	Meridian
Garden	24N	15N	40W	46W	Sixth Principal
Garfield	24N	21N	13W	16W	Sixth Principal
Gosper	8N	5N	21W	24W	Sixth Principal
Grant	24N	21N	35W	40W	Sixth Principal
Greeley	20N	17N	9W	12W	Sixth Principal
Hall	12N	9N	9W	12W	Sixth Principal
Hamilton	14N	9N	5W	8W	Sixth Principal
Harlan	4N	1N	17W	20W	Sixth Principal
Hayes	8N	5N	31W	35W	Sixth Principal
Hitchcock	4N	1N	31W	35W	Sixth Principal
Holt	34N	25N	9W	16W	Sixth Principal
Hooker	24N	21N	31W	35W	Sixth Principal
Howard	16N	13N	9W	12W	Sixth Principal
Jefferson	4N	1N	4E	1E	Sixth Principal
Johnson	6N	4N	12E	9E	Sixth Principal
Kearney	8N	5N	13W	16W	Sixth Principal
Keith	16N	12N	35W	42W	Sixth Principal
Keya Paha	35N	32N	17W	24W	Sixth Principal
Kimball	16N	12N	53W	57W	Sixth Principal
Knox	33N	29N	2W	8W	Sixth Principal
Lancaster	12N	7N	9E	5E	Sixth Principal
Lincoln	16N	9N	26W	35W	Sixth Principal
Logan	20N	17N	26W	29W	Sixth Principal
Loup	24N	21N	17W	20W	Sixth Principal
Madison	24N	21N	1W	4W	Sixth Principal
McPherson	20N	17N	30W	35W	Sixth Principal
Merrick	16N	11N	3W	8W	Sixth Principal
Morrill	24N	17N	47W	52W	Sixth Principal
Nance	18N	15N	4W	8W	Sixth Principal
Nemaha	6N	4N	16E	12E	Sixth Principal
Nuckolls	4N	1N	5W	8W	Sixth Principal
Otoe	9N	7N	15E	9E	Sixth Principal
Pawnee	3N	1N	12E	9E	Sixth Principal
Perkins	12N	9N	35W	42W	Sixth Principal
Phelps	8N	5N	17W	20W	Sixth Principal
Pierce	28N	25N	1W	4W	Sixth Principal
Platte	20N	16N	1E	4W	Sixth Principal
Polk	16N	13N	1W	4W	Sixth Principal
Red Willow	4N	1N	26W	30W	Sixth Principal
Richardson	3N	1N	19E	13E	Sixth Principal
Rock	33N	25N	17W	20W	Sixth Principal
Saline	8N	5N	4E	1E	Sixth Principal

Nebraska(cont.)

County	North	South	East	West	Meridian
Sarpy	14N	12N	14E	10E	Sixth Principal
Saunders	17N	12N	10E	5E	Sixth Principal
Scotts Bluff	24N	20N	52W	57W	Sixth Principal
Seward	12N	9N	4E	1E	Sixth Principal
Sheridan	35N	24N	40W	46W	Sixth Principal
Sherman	16N	13N	13W	16W	Sixth Principal
Sioux	35N	24N	53W	57W	Sixth Principal
Stanton	24N	21N	3E	1E	Sixth Principal
Thayer	4N	1N	1W	4W	Sixth Principal
Thomas	24N	21N	26W	30W	Sixth Principal
Thurston	27N	24N	10E	5E	Sixth Principal
Valley	20N	17N	13W	16W	Sixth Principal
Washington	20N	17N	13E	9E	Sixth Principal
Wayne	27N	25N	5E	1E	Sixth Principal
Webster	4N	1N	9W	12W	Sixth Principal
Wheeler	24N	21N	9W	12W	Sixth Principal
York	12N	9N	1W	4W	Sixth Principal

Nevada

County	North	South	East	West	Meridian
Carson City	16N	14N	22E	18E	Mount Diablo
Churchill	24N	14N	40E	25E	Mount Diablo
Clark	13S	34S	71E	54E	Mount Diablo
Douglas	15N	8N	24E	18E	Mount Diablo
Elko	47N	26N	70E	44E	Mount Diablo
Esmeralda	7N	11S	43E	32E	Mount Diablo
Eureka	36N	15N	55E	48E	Mount Diablo
Humboldt	47N	31N	44E	24E	Mount Diablo
Lander	36N	14N	48E	37E	Mount Diablo
Lincoln	9N	12S	71E	54E	Mount Diablo
Lyon	22N	7N	29E	20E	Mount Diablo
Mineral	14N	1N	38E	25E	Mount Diablo
Nye	15N	22S	62E	34E	Mount Diablo
Pershing	36N	25N	41E	24E	Mount Diablo
Storey	20N	16N	24E	20E	Mount Diablo
Washoe	47N	15N	25E	18E	Mount Diablo
White Pine	26N	10N	70E	54E	Mount Diablo

New Mexico

County	North	South	East	West	Meridian
Bernalillo	11N	7N	7E	3W	New Mexico Principal
Catron	4N	12S	9W	21W	New Mexico Principal
Chaves	3S	20S	33E	16E	New Mexico Principal
Cibola	13N	4N	2W	21W	New Mexico Principal
Colfax	32N	23N	27E	15E	New Mexico Principal
Curry	9N	1N	37E	31E	New Mexico Principal
De Baca	6N	3S	28E	20E	New Mexico Principal
Dona Ana	15S	29S	5E	4W	New Mexico Principal
Eddy	16S	26S	31E	21E	New Mexico Principal
Grant	13S	28S	8W	21W	New Mexico Principal
Guadalupe	11N	2N	27E	16E	New Mexico Principal
Harding	23N	14N	33E	24E	New Mexico Principal
Hidalgo	18S	34S	13W	21W	New Mexico Principal
Lea	9S	26S	39E	31E	New Mexico Principal
Lincoln	1N	13S	19E	7E	New Mexico Principal
Los Alamos	20N	18N	7E	5E	New Mexico Principal
Luna	20S	29S	5W	13W	New Mexico Principal
McKinley	20N	9N	5W	21W	New Mexico Principal
Mora	23N	18N	24E	12E	New Mexico Principal
Otero	11S	26S	20E	6E	New Mexico Principal
Quay	18N	5N	37E	27E	New Mexico Principal
Rio Arriba	32N	21N	13E	7W	New Mexico Principal
Roosevelt	4N	8S	38E	29E	New Mexico Principal
Sandoval	23N	12N	6E	7W	New Mexico Principal
San Juan	32N	21N	8W	21W	New Mexico Principal
San Miguel	19N	10N	31E	12E	New Mexico Principal
Santa Fe	20N	9N	11E	7E	New Mexico Principal
Sierra	9S	19S	6E	11W	New Mexico Principal
Socorro	4N	9S	9E	8W	New Mexico Principal
Taos	32N	21N	16E	8E	New Mexico Principal
Torrance	9N	1N	15E	5E	New Mexico Principal
Union	32N	18N	37E	28E	New Mexico Principal
Valencia	8N	3N	5E	3W	New Mexico Principal

North Dakota

County	North	South	East	West	Meridian
Adams	132N	129N	91W	98W	Fifth Principal
Barnes	143N	137N	56W	61W	Fifth Principal
Benson	156N	151N	62W	71W	Fifth Principal
Billings	144N	137N	98W	102W	Fifth Principal
Bottineau	164N	159N	74W	83W	Fifth Principal

North Dakota(cont.)

County	North	South	East	West	Meridian
Bowman	132N	129N	99W	107W	Fifth Principal
Burke	164N	159N	88W	94W	Fifth Principal
Burleigh	144N	137N	75W	81W	Fifth Principal
Cass	143N	137N	48W	55W	Fifth Principal
Cavalier	164N	159N	57W	64W	Fifth Principal
Dickey	132N	129N	59W	66W	Fifth Principal
Divide	164N	160N	95W	103W	Fifth Principal
Dunn	150N	141N	91W	97W	Fifth Principal
Eddy	150N	148N	62W	67W	Fifth Principal
Emmans	136N	129N	74W	79W	Fifth Principal
Foster	147N	145N	62W	67W	Fifth Principal
Golden Valley	144N	136N	103W	106W	Fifth Principal
Grand Forks	154N	149N	49W	56W	Fifth Principal
Grant	137N	129N	83W	90W	Fifth Principal
Griggs	148N	144N	58W	61W	Fifth Principal
Hettinger	136N	132N	91W	97W	Fifth Principal
Kidder	144N	137N	70W	74W	Fifth Principal
La Moure	136N	133N	59W	66W	Fifth Principal
Logan	136N	133N	67W	73W	Fifth Principal
McHenry	159N	151N	75W	80W	Fifth Principal
McIntosh	132N	129N	67W	73W	Fifth Principal
McKenzie	154N	145N	93W	104W	Fifth Principal
McLean	150N	143N	78W	91W	Fifth Principal
Mercer	147N	141N	84W	90W	Fifth Principal
Morton	140N	133N	79W	90W	Fifth Principal
Mountrail	158N	150N	88W	94W	Fifth Principal
Nelson	154N	149N	57W	61W	Fifth Principal
Oliver	144N	141N	81W	87W	Fifth Principal
Pembina	164N	159N	50W	56W	Fifth Principal
Pierce	158N	151N	69W	74W	Fifth Principal
Ramsey	158N	151N	60W	66W	Fifth Principal
Ransom	136N	133N	53W	58W	Fifth Principal
Renville	164N	158N	81W	87W	Fifth Principal
Richland	136N	129N	47W	52W	Fifth Principal
Rolette	164N	159N	69W	73W	Fifth Principal
Sargent	132N	129N	52W	58W	Fifth Principal
Sheridan	150N	145N	74W	78W	Fifth Principal
Sioux	134N	129N	79W	90W	Fifth Principal
Slope	136N	133N	98W	107W	Fifth Principal
Stark	141N	137N	91W	99W	Fifth Principal
Steele	148N	144N	54W	57W	Fifth Principal
Stutsman	144N	137N	62W	69W	Fifth Principal

North Dakota (cont.)

County	North	South	East	West	Meridian
Towner	164N	157N	65W	68W	Fifth Principal
Traill	148N	144N	49W	53W	Fifth Principal
Walsh	158N	155N	50W	59W	Fifth Principal
Ward	161N	151N	81W	89W	Fifth Principal
Wells	150N	145N	68W	73W	Fifth Principal
Williams	159N	154N	95W	104W	Fifth Principal

Ohio

County	North	South	East	West	Meridian
Adams			Virginia Military Tract		
Allen	1	4	VIII	IV	E & S of First Principal
Ashland	1	1	XVIII	XX	Western Reserve
Ashland	See Map, p. 257		XV	XVII	Ohio River Survey
Ashtabula	14	8	I	V	Western Reserve
Athens	See Map, p. 257		XI	XV	Ohio River Survey
Auglaize	4	8	VIII	IV	E & S of First Principal
Belmont	See Map, p. 257		II	VI	First Seven Ranges
Brown			Virginia Military Tract		
Butler	IV	IV	See Map, p. 258		Between the Miamis
Butler	See Map, p. 258		5E	1E	Miami River Survey
Butler	III	II	See Map, p. 258		Symmes Purchase
Carroll	See Map, p. 257	IV	VII	First Seven Ranges	
Carroll	See Map, p. 257		IV	VII	Ohio River Survey
Champaign	XIII	X	See Map, p. 258		Between the Miamis
Champaign			Virginia Military Tract		
Clark	X	VIII	See Map, p. 258		Between the Miamis
Clark			Virginia Military Tract		
Clermont			Virginia Military Tract		
Clinton			Virginia Military Tract		
Columbiana	See Map, p. 257		I	III	First Seven Ranges
Columbiana	See Map, p. 257		IV	VII	Ohio River Survey
Coshocton	7	4	IV	IX	U.S. Military District
Crawford	1	4	XVII	XV	E & S of First Principal
Crawford	See Map, p. 257		XX	XXI	Ohio River Survey
Cuyahoga	8	5	X	XV	Western Reserve
Darke	See Map, p. 258		4E	1E	Miami River Survey
Defiance	5	3	V	I	E & N of First Principal
Delaware	6	3	XVI	XX	U.S. Military District
Delaware			Virginia Military Tract		
Erie	6	5	XX	XXIV	Western Reserve
Fairfield	See Map, p. 257		XVII	XXI	Ohio River Survey

Ohio (cont.)

County	North	South	East	West	Meridian
Fayette		Virginia Military Tract			
Franklin	2	1	XVI	XIX	U.S. Military District
Franklin	See Map, p. 257		XXI	XXIII	Ohio River Survey
Franklin		Virginia Military Tract			
Fulton	9	10	4E	1W	Michigan Survey
Fulton	8	6	VIII	IV	E & N of First Principal
Gallia	See Map, p. 257		XIV	XVII	Ohio River Survey
Geauga	10	6	VI	IX	Western Reserve
Greene	VIII	V	See Map, p. 258		Between the Miamis
Greene		Virginia Military Tract			
Guernsey	4	1	I	IV	U.S. Military District
Guernsey	See Map, p. 257		IX	X	Ohio River Survey
Guernsey			VII	VII	First Seven Ranges
Hamilton	See Map, p. 258		2E	1E	Miami River Survey
Hamilton	II	I fr	See Map, p. 258		Symmes Purchase
Hamilton		Virginia Military Tract			
Hancock	2	1	XII	IX	E & N of First Principal
Hancock	1	2	XII	IX	E & S of First Principal
Hardin	3	5	XII	IX	E & S of First Principal
Hardin		Virginia Military Tract			
Harrison	See Map, p. 257		IV	VII	First Seven Ranges
Henry	6	3	VIII	V	E & N of First Principal
Highland		Virginia Military Tract			
Hocking	See Map, p. 257		XV	XIX	Ohio River Survey
Holmes	10	8	IV	IX	U.S. Military District
Holmes	See Map, p. 257		XI	XV	Ohio River Survey
Huron	4	1	XX	XXIV	Western Reserve
Jackson	See Map, p. 257		XVII	XX	Ohio River Survey
Jefferson	See Map, p. 257		I	IV	First Seven Ranges
Knox	9	5	X	XV	U.S. Military District
Knox	18	18	XVII	XIX	Ohio River Survey
Lake	12	9	VI	X	Western Reserve
Lawrence	See Map, p. 257		XV	XIX	Ohio River Survey
Licking	4	1	X	XV	U.S. Military District
Licking	See Map, p. 257		XV	XX	Ohio River Survey
Logan	XV	XIII	See Map, p. 258		Between the Miamis
Logan		Virginia Military Tract			
Logan	See Map, p. 258		VIII	VIII	Miami River Survey
Logan	6	7	IX	VII	E & S of First Principal
Lorain	7	2	XV	XIX	Western Reserve
Lucas	8	6	XI	IX	E & N of First Principal
Lucas	9	10	10E	5E	Michigan Survey

Ohio (cont.)

County	North	South	East	West	Meridian
Lucas			Twelve Mile Reserve		
Madison			Virginia Military Tract		
Mahoning	2	1	I	V	Western Reserve
Mahoning	See Map, p. 257		I	V	First Seven Ranges
Marion	7	7	XIX	XX	U.S. Military District
Marion	4	6	XVII	XIII	E & S of First Principal
Marion			Virginia Military Tract		
Medina	4	1	XIII	XVII	Western Reserve
Meigs	See Map, p. 257		XI	XV	Ohio River Survey
Mercer	4	8	III	I	E & S of First Principal
Mercer	See Map, p. 258		4E	1E	Miami River Survey
Miami	See Map, p. 258		6E	4E	Miami River Survey
Miami	XII	IX	See Map, p. 258		Between the Miamis
Monroe	See Map, p. 257		III	VII	First Seven Ranges
Montgomery	See Map, p. 258		6E	4E	Miami River Survey
Montgomery	VIII	V	See Map, p. 258		Between the Miamis
Morgan	See Map, p. 257		X	XIII	Ohio River Survey
Morrow	8	6	XV	XVIII	U.S. Military District
Morrow	5	6	XVII	XVII	E & S of First Principal
Morrow	See Map, p. 257		XIX	XXI	Ohio River Survey
Muskingum	3	1	V	IX	U.S. Military District
Muskingum	See Map, p. 257		XI	XV	Ohio River Survey
Noble	See Map, p. 257		VII	VII	First Seven Ranges
Noble	See Map, p. 257		VIII	X	Ohio River Survey
Ottawa	8	6	XVII	XIII	E & N of First Principal
Paulding	3	1	IV	I	E & N of First Principal
Perry	See Map, p. 257		XIV	XVII	Ohio River Survey
Pickaway	See Map, p. 257		XX	XXII	Ohio River Survey
Pickaway			Virginia Military Tract		
Pike	See Map, p. 257		XX	XXII	Ohio River Survey
Pike			Virginia Military Tract		
Portage	5	1	VI	IX	Western Reserve
Preble	See Map, p. 258		3E	1E	Miami River Survey
Putnam	2	1	VIII	V	E & N of First Principal
Putnam	1	2	VIII	IV	E & S of First Principal
Richland	See Map, p. 257		XVII	XX	Ohio River Survey
Ross	See Map, p. 257		XX	XXII	Ohio River Survey
Ross			Virginia Military District		
Sandusky	6	4	XVII	XIII	E & N of First Principal
Scioto	See Map, p. 257		XVIII	XXII	Ohio River Survey
Scioto			Virginia Military Tract		
Seneca	3	1	XVIII	XIII	E & N of First Principal

Ohio (cont.)

County	North	South	East	West	Meridian
Shelby	6	8	VII	IV	E & S of First Principal
Shelby	See Map, p. 258		8E	4E	Miami River Survey
Shelby	XIV	XII	See Map, p. 258		Between the Miamis
Stark	See Map, p. 257		VI	X	Ohio River Survey
Summit	5	1	X	XII	Western Reserve
Summit	See Map, p. 257		IX	X	Ohio River Survey
Trumbull	7	3	I	V	Western Reserve
Tuscarawas	10	5	I	IV	U.S. Military District
Tuscarawas	See Map, p. 257		VII	VII	First Seven Ranges
Union	Virginia Military Tract				
Van Wert	1	4	IV	I	E & S of First Principal
Vinton	See Map, p. 257		XV	XIX	Ohio River Survey
Warren	V	IV	See Map, p. 258		Between the Miamis
Warren	III	II	See Map, p. 258		Symmes Purchase
Warren	Virginia Military Tract				
Washington	See Map, p. 257		V	VII	First Seven Ranges
Washington	See Map, p. 257		VIII	XII	Ohio River Survey
Wayne	See Map, p. 257		XI	XV	Ohio River Survey
Williams	8	6	IV	I	E & N of First Principal
Williams	9	10	1W	4W	Michigan Survey
Wood	Twelve Mile Reserve				
Wood	8	3	XII	IX	E & N of First Principal
Wyandot	1	4	XV	XII	E & S of First Principal

Note: The state of Ohio was the first area to be declared "federal land." It was therefore experimental in its organization. Some areas used a township and range structure similar to standard meridians; others used different methods for identifying the individual townships, usually numbered from south to north in columns that each started with number one in a different place, depending on where the southern boundary of the state intersected the column. The circumstances are best described in the maps on pages 257 and 258. For further information about the unique circumstances involved in Ohio's surveys, including duplicate numbering, see C.A. White's *A History of the Rectangular Survey System.*

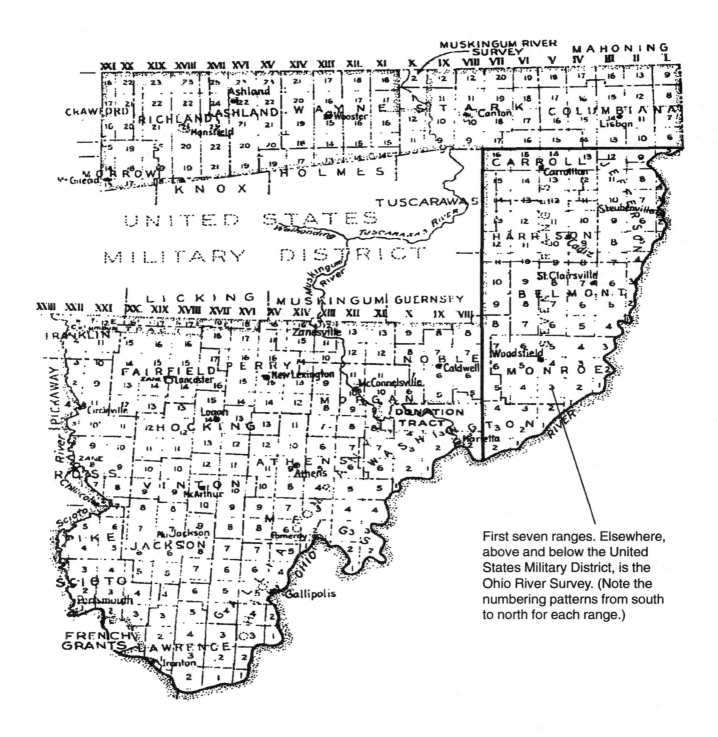

First seven ranges. Elsewhere, above and below the United States Military District, is the Ohio River Survey. (Note the numbering patterns from south to north for each range.)

Map reproduced courtesy of Thomas Aquinas Burke. Originally published in Christopher E. Sherman's *Original Land Subdivisions,* Vol. 3, *Final Report—Ohio Topographic Survey* (Columbus: Ohio Departrment of Natural Resources, 1925. Reprint. 1982.)

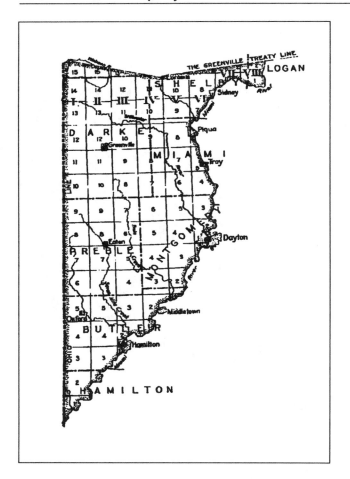 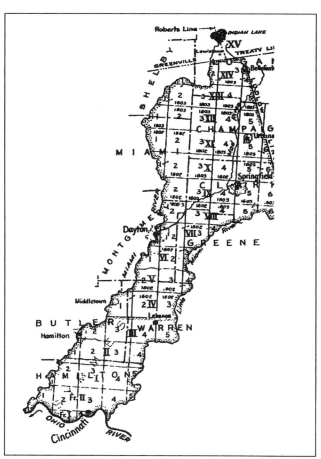

Note the numbering patterns from south to north in the Miami River Survey (left), and the numbering patterns from west to east in the survey Between the Miamis & Sim's Purchase (right). (Maps reproduced courtesy of Thomas Aquinas Burke. Originally published in Christopher E. Sherman's *Original Land Subdivisions,* Vol. 3, *Final Report—Ohio Topographic Survey* [Columbus: Ohio Departrment of Natural Resources, 1925. Reprint. 1982].)

Oklahoma

County	North	South	East	West	Meridian
Adair	19N	14N	27E	24E	Indian
Alfalfa	29N	23N	9W	12W	Indian
Atoka	2N	4S	16E	9E	Indian
Beaver	6N	1N	28E	20E	Cimarron
Beckham	12N	7N	21W	27W	Indian
Blaine	19N	13N	10W	13W	Indian
Bryan	5S	9S	15E	7E	Indian
Caddo	12N	5N	9W	13W	Indian
Canadian	14N	10N	5W	10W	Indian
Carter	1S	5S	3E	3W	Indian
Cherokee	19N	14N	23E	19E	Indian
Choctaw	5S	8S	20E	13E	Indian
Cimarron	6N	1N	9E	1E	Cimarron

Oklahoma(cont.)

County	North	South	East	West	Meridian
Cleveland	10N	5N	1E	4W	Indian
Coal	3N	1S	11E	8E	Indian
Comanche	4N	2S	9W	16W	Indian
Cotton	1S	5S	9W	14W	Indian
Craig	29N	24N	21E	18E	Indian
Creek	19N	14N	12E	6E	Indian
Custer	15N	12N	14W	20W	Indian
Delaware	25N	20N	26E	22E	Indian
Dewey	19N	16N	14W	20W	Indian
Ellis	24N	16N	21W	26W	Indian
Garfield	24N	20N	3W	8W	Indian
Garvin	4N	1N	3E	4W	Indian
Grady	10N	3N	5W	8W	Indian
Grant	29N	25N	3W	8W	Indian
Greer	7N	3N	20W	25W	Indian
Harmon	6N	1N	24W	27W	Indian
Harper	29N	25N	20W	26W	Indian
Haskell	11N	7N	23E	18E	Indian
Hughes	9N	4N	12E	8E	Indian
Jackson	4N	2S	18W	25W	Indian
Jefferson	3S	8S	4W	9W	Indian
Johnston	1S	5S	8E	4E	Indian
Kay	29N	25N	5E	2W	Indian
Kingfisher	19N	15N	5W	9W	Indian
Kiowa	7N	2N	14W	21W	Indian
Latimer	7N	3N	22E	17E	Indian
Le Flore	10N	1N	27E	21E	Indian
Lincoln	17N	12N	6E	2E	Indian
Logan	19N	15N	1E	4W	Indian
Love	6S	10S	4E	3W	Indian
Major	23N	20N	9W	16W	Indian
Marshall	4S	8S	7E	3E	Indian
Mayes	24N	19N	21E	18E	Indian
McClain	10N	5N	3E	4W	Indian
McCurtain	1S	10S	27E	21E	Indian
McIntosh	12N	8N	18E	13E	Indian
Murray	2N	2S	4E	1W	Indian
Muskogee	16N	9N	21E	15E	Indian
Noble	25N	20N	4E	2W	Indian
Nowata	29N	25N	17E	14E	Indian
Okfuskee	13N	10N	12E	6E	Indian
Oklahoma	14N	11N	1E	4W	Indian

Oklahoma(cont.)

County	North	South	East	West	Meridian
Okmulgee	16N	11N	15E	11E	Indian
Osage	29N	20N	12E	2E	Indian
Ottawa	29N	25N	25E	22E	Indian
Pawnee	25N	20N	10E	3E	Indian
Payne	20N	17N	6E	1W	Indian
Pittsburg	10N	2N	18E	12E	Indian
Pontotoc	6N	1N	8E	4E	Indian
Pottawatomie	11N	5N	6E	2E	Indian
Pushmataha	2N	4S	22E	15E	Indian
Roger Mills	18N	11N	21W	26W	Indian
Rogers	24N	19N	18E	14E	Indian
Seminole	12N	5N	8E	5E	Indian
Sequoyah	13N	9N	27E	21E	Indian
Stephens	2N	3S	4W	9W	Indian
Texas	6N	1N	19E	10E	Cimarron
Tillman	2N	5S	14W	20W	Indian
Tulsa	22N	16N	14E	10E	Indian
Wagoner	19N	15N	20E	14E	Indian
Washington	29N	23N	14E	12E	Indian
Washita	11N	7N	14W	20W	Indian
Woods	29N	22N	13W	21W	Indian
Woodward	27N	20N	16W	22W	Indian

Oregon

County	North	South	East	West	Meridian
Baker	6S	15S	48E	35E	Willamette
Benton	10S	15S	3W	8W	Willamette
Clackamas	1S	8S	9E	1W	Willamette
Clatsop	9N	4N	6W	11W	Willamette
Columbia	8N	3N	1W	5W	Willamette
Coos	23S	33S	9W	15W	Willamette
Crook	12S	21S	25E	14E	Willamette
Curry	30S	41S	9W	16W	Willamette
Deschutes	14S	22S	23E	6E	Willamette
Douglas	19S	33S	7E	13W	Willamette
Gilliam	4N	6S	24E	18E	Willamette
Grant	7S	18S	36E	26E	Willamette
Harney	18S	41S	38E	24E	Willamette
Hood River	3N	3S	11E	7E	Willamette
Jackson	30S	41S	4E	4W	Willamette
Jefferson	9S	13S	19E	7E	Willamette

Oregon(cont.)

County	North	South	East	West	Meridian
Josephine	32S	41S	5W	12W	Willamette
Klamath	23S	41S	15E	5E	Willamette
Lake	23S	41S	28E	12E	Willamette
Lane	15S	24S	8E	12W	Willamette
Lincoln	6S	15S	8W	12W	Willamette
Linn	9S	16S	8E	5W	Willamette
Malheur	13S	41S	48E	37E	Willamette
Marion	3S	10S	8E	4W	Willamette
Morrow	5N	7S	29E	23E	Willamette
Multnomah	3N	1S	8E	2W	Willamette
Polk	6S	10S	3W	8W	Willamette
Sherman	3N	5S	20E	14E	Willamette
Tillamook	3N	6S	5W	11W	Willamette
Umatilla	6N	7S	39E	27E	Willamette
Union	4N	7S	44E	33E	Willamette
Wallowa	6N	5S	51E	39E	Willamette
Wasco	2N	8S	20E	8E	Willamette
Washington	3N	3S	1W	6W	Willamette
Wheeler	6S	14S	25E	19E	Willamette
Yamhill	2S	5S	1W	9W	Willamette

South Dakota

County	North	South	East	West	Meridian
Aurora	105N	101N	63W	66W	5th Principal
Beadle	113N	109N	59W	65W	5th Principal
Bennett	39N	35N	33W	40W	6th Principal
Bon Homme	96N	92N	58W	62W	5th Principal
Brookings	112N	109N	47W	52W	5th Principal
Brown	128N	121N	60W	65W	5th Principal
Brule	105N	101N	67W	73W	5th Principal
Buffalo	108N	106N	68W	73W	5th Principal
Butte	14N	7N	9E	1E	Black Hills
Campbell	128N	125N	74W	79W	5th Principal
Charles Mix	100N	93N	61W	72W	5th Principal
Clark	119N	113N	56W	59W	5th Principal
Clay	95N	91N	51W	53W	5th Principal
Codington	119N	116N	51W	55W	5th Principal
Corson	23N	18N	30E	17E	Black Hills
Custer	2S	6S	12E	1E	Black Hills
Davison	104N	101N	60W	62W	5th Principal
Day	124N	120N	53W	59W	5th Principal

South Dakota(cont.)

County	North	South	East	West	Meridian
Deuel	117N	113N	47W	50W	5th Principal
Dewey	17N	9N	31E	22E	Black Hills
Douglas	100N	97N	62W	66W	5th Principal
Edmunds	124N	121N	66W	73W	5th Principal
Fall River	7S	12S	9E	1E	Black Hills
Faulk	120N	117N	66W	72W	5th Principal
Grant	121N	118N	46W	52W	5th Principal
Gregory	100N	95N	65W	73W	5th Principal
Haakon	9N	1N	25E	18E	Black Hills
Hamlin	115N	113N	51W	55W	5th Principal
Hand	116N	109N	66W	70W	5th Principal
Hanson	104N	101N	57W	59W	5th Principal
Harding	23N	15N	9E	1E	Black Hills
Hughes	112N	108N	73W	80W	5th Principal
Hutchinson	100N	97N	56W	61W	5th Principal
Hyde	116N	109N	71W	73W	5th Principal
Jackson	44N	40N	33W	40W	6th Principal
Jackson	1S	4S	25E	18E	Black Hills
Jerauld	108N	106N	63W	67W	5th Principal
Jones	2N	4S	31E	26E	Black Hills
Kingsbury	112N	109N	53W	58W	5th Principal
Lake	108N	105N	51W	54W	5th Principal
Lawrence	7N	2N	5E	1E	Black Hills
Lincoln	100N	96N	48W	51W	5th Principal
Lyman	109N	103N	71W	79W	5th Principal
Marshall	129N	125N	53W	59W	5th Principal
McCook	104N	101N	53W	56W	5th Principal
McPherson	128N	125N	66W	73W	5th Principal
Meade	12N	2N	17E	5E	Black Hills
Mellette	45N	40N	25W	33W	6th Principal
Miner	108N	105N	55W	58W	5th Principal
Minnehaha	104N	101N	47W	52W	5th Principal
Moody	108N	105N	47W	50W	5th Principal
Pennington	6N	4S	17E	1E	5th Principal
Perkins	23N	13N	17E	10E	Black Hills
Potter	120N	117N	73W	80W	5th Principal
Roberts	129N	122N	47W	52W	5th Principal
Sanborn	108N	105N	59W	62W	5th Principal
Shannon	43N	35N	41W	48W	6th Principal
Spink	120N	114N	60W	65W	5th Principal
Stanley	9N	3N	34E	25E	Black Hills
Sully	116N	113N	73W	81W	5th Principal

South Dakota(cont.)

County	North	South	East	West	Meridian
Todd	39N	35N	25W	33W	6th Principal
Tripp	103N	95N	74W	79W	5th Principal
Turner	100N	96N	52W	55W	5th Principal
Union	95N	89N	48W	50W	5th Principal
Walworth	124N	121N	74W	80W	5th Principal
Yankton	96N	92N	54W	57W	5th Principal
Ziebach	17N	7N	24E	17E	Black Hills

Utah

County	North	South	East	West	Meridian
Beaver	25S	30S	4W	20W	Salt Lake
Box Elder	15N	4N	1W	19W	Salt Lake
Cache	14N	7N	5E	3W	Salt Lake
Carbon	12S	15S	18E	6E	Salt Lake
Daggett	3N	2S	25E	17E	Salt Lake
Davis	5N	1N	2E	4W	Salt Lake
Duchesne	9S	11S	17E	9E	Salt Lake
Duchesne	5N	5S	1W	9W	Uintah
Emery	13S	26S	18E	6E	Salt Lake
Garfield	31S	37S	18E	7W	Salt Lake
Grand	16S	26S	26E	16E	Salt Lake
Iron	31S	38S	6W	20W	Salt Lake
Juab	9S	17S	3E	19W	Salt Lake
Kane	38S	43S	11E	9W	Salt Lake
Millard	15S	25S	2W	20W	Salt Lake
Morgan	7N	1N	6E	1E	Salt Lake
Piute	27S	30S	1E	6W	Salt Lake
Rich	14N	5N	8E	4E	Salt Lake
Salt Lake	1N	4S	3E	3W	Salt Lake
San Juan	27S	43S	26E	7E	Salt Lake
Sanpete	12S	20S	5E	1W	Salt Lake
Sevier	20S	26S	5E	6W	Salt Lake
Summit	6N	3S	17E	3E	Salt Lake
Tooele	3N	10S	3W	19W	Salt Lake
Uintah	1N	15S	25E	17E	Salt Lake
Uintah	5N	4S	2E	1W	Uintah
Utah	3S	12S	9E	3W	Salt Lake
Wasatch	2S	10S	9E	3E	Salt Lake
Wasatch	3N	4S	9E	11E	Uintah
Washington	37S	43S	10W	20W	Salt Lake
Wayne	27S	30S	18E	1E	Salt Lake

Utah (cont.)

County	North	South	East	West	Meridian
Weber	8N	5N	5E	4W	Salt Lake

Washington

County	North	South	East	West	Meridian
Adams	20N	15N	38E	28E	Willamette
Asotin	11N	6N	47E	42E	Willamette
Benton	14N	4N	31E	24E	Willamette
Chelan	35N	21N	24E	13E	Willamette
Clallam	34N	28N	2W	16W	Willamette
Clark	7N	1N	4E	1W	Willamette
Columbia	13N	6N	41E	37E	Willamette
Cowlitz	10N	4N	4E	4W	Willamette
Douglas	31N	21N	31E	20E	Willamette
Ferry	40N	27N	37E	32E	Willamette
Franklin	14N	8N	37E	27E	Willamette
Garfield	14N	6N	45E	40E	Willamette
Grant	28N	13N	30E	22E	Willamette
Grays Harbor	24N	15N	4W	13W	Willamette
Island	34N	28N	3E	1W	Willamette
Jefferson	31N	24N	1E	15W	Willamette
King	26N	19N	14E	2E	Willamette
Kitsap	28N	22N	3E	3W	Willamette
Kittitas	24N	15N	23E	10E	Willamette
Klickitat	6N	2N	23E	10E	Willamette
Lewis	15N	11N	11E	5W	Willamette
Lincoln	28N	21N	39E	31E	Willamette
Mason	24N	19N	1W	6W	Willamette
Okanogan	40N	29N	31E	16E	Willamette
Pacific	15N	9N	6W	11W	Willamette
Pend Oreille	40N	30N	45E	41E	Willamette
Pierce	22N	15N	11E	1W	Willamette
San Juan	38N	34N	1W	4W	Willamette
Skagit	37N	33N	17E	1W	Willamette
Skamania	10N	1N	10E	5E	Willamette
Snohomish	32N	27N	15E	3E	Willamette
Spokane	29N	21N	46E	40E	Willamette
Stevens	40N	27N	42E	35E	Willamette
Thurston	20N	15N	5E	4W	Willamette
Wahkiakum	10N	8N	4W	8W	Willamette
Walla Walla	13N	6N	38E	30E	Willamette
Whatcom	40N	37N	17E	3W	Willamette

Washington(cont.)

County	North	South	East	West	Meridian
Whitman	20N	11N	46E	36E	Willamette
Yakima	18N	7N	23E	10E	Willamette

Wisconsin

County	North	South	East	West	Meridian
Adams	20N	14N	7E	4E	Fourth Principal
Ashland	53N	41N	1E	4W	Fourth Principal
Barron	36N	32N	10W	14W	Fourth Principal
Bayfield	52N	43N	3W	9W	Fourth Principal
Brown	25N	21N	22E	19E	Fourth Principal
Buffalo	24N	18N	10W	14W	Fourth Principal
Burnett	42N	37N	14W	20W	Fourth Principal
Calumet	20N	17N	20E	17E	Fourth Principal
Chippewa	32N	28N	5W	10W	Fourth Principal
Clark	29N	23N	1E	4W	Fourth Principal
Columbia	13N	10N	12E	6E	Fourth Principal
Crawford	11N	6N	3W	7W	Fourth Principal
Dane	9N	5N	12E	6E	Fourth Principal
Dodge	13N	9N	17E	13E	Fourth Principal
Door	35N	26N	30E	23E	Fourth Principal
Douglas	50N	43N	10W	15W	Fourth Principal
Dunn	31N	26N	11W	14W	Fourth Principal
Eau Claire	27N	25N	5W	10W	Fourth Principal
Florence	41N	38N	19E	15E	Fourth Principal
Fond du Lac	17N	13N	19E	14E	Fourth Principal
Forest	41N	34N	16E	12E	Fourth Principal
Grant	8N	1N	1W	7W	Fourth Principal
Green	4N	1N	9E	6E	Fourth Principal
Green Lake	17N	14N	13E	11E	Fourth Principal
Iowa	8N	4N	5E	1E	Fourth Principal
Iron	47N	41N	4E	1W	Fourth Principal
Jackson	24N	19N	1E	6W	Fourth Principal
Jefferson	8N	5N	16E	13E	Fourth Principal
Juneau	20N	14N	6E	2E	Fourth Principal
Kenosha	2N	1N	23E	19E	Fourth Principal
Kewanee	25N	21N	26E	23E	Fourth Principal
La Crosse	19N	15N	5W	8W	Fourth Principal
Lafayette	4N	1N	5E	1E	Fourth Principal
Langlade	34N	30N	15E	9E	Fourth Principal
Lincoln	35N	31N	8E	4E	Fourth Principal
Manitowoc	21N	17N	25E	21E	Fourth Principal

Wisconsin(cont.)

County	North	South	East	West	Meridian
Marathon	30N	26N	10E	2E	Fourth Principal
Marinette	38N	29N	24E	17E	Fourth Principal
Marquette	17N	14N	11E	8E	Fourth Principal
Menominee	30N	28N	17E	12E	Fourth Principal
Milwaukee	8N	5N	22E	21E	Fourth Principal
Monroe	19N	15N	1E	5W	Fourth Principal
Oconto	33N	26N	22E	15E	Fourth Principal
Oneida	39N	35N	11E	4E	Fourth Principal
Outagamie	24N	21N	19E	15E	Fourth Principal
Ozaukee	12N	9N	22E	21E	Fourth Principal
Pepin	25N	23N	11W	16W	Fourth Principal
Pierce	27N	24N	15W	20W	Fourth Principal
Polk	37N	32N	15W	20W	Fourth Principal
Portage	25N	21N	10E	6E	Fourth Principal
Price	40N	34N	3E	2W	Fourth Principal
Racine	4N	2N	23E	19E	Fourth Principal
Richland	12N	8N	2E	2W	Fourth Principal
Rock	4N	1N	14E	10E	Fourth Principal
Rusk	36N	33N	3W	9W	Fourth Principal
Saint Croix	31N	28N	15W	20W	Fourth Principal
Sauk	13N	8N	7E	2E	Fourth Principal
Sawyer	42N	37N	3W	9W	Fourth Principal
Shawano	29N	25N	18E	11E	Fourth Principal
Sheboygan	16N	13N	23E	20E	Fourth Principal
Taylor	33N	30N	3E	4W	Fourth Principal
Trempealeau	24N	17N	7W	10W	Fourth Principal
Vernon	14N	11N	1E	7W	Fourth Principal
Vilas	44N	39N	12E	4E	Fourth Principal
Walworth	4N	1N	18E	15E	Fourth Principal
Washburn	42N	37N	10W	13W	Fourth Principal
Washington	12N	9N	20E	18E	Fourth Principal
Waukesha	8N	5N	20E	17E	Fourth Principal
Waupaca	25N	21N	15E	11E	Fourth Principal
Waushara	20N	18N	13E	8E	Fourth Principal
Winnebago	20N	17N	17E	14E	Fourth Principal
Wood	25N	21N	6E	2E	Fourth Principal

Wyoming

County	North	South	East	West	Meridian
Albany	28N	12N	70W	79W	Sixth Principal
Big Horn	58N	49N	86W	97W	Sixth Principal

Wyoming(cont.)

County	North	South	East	West	Meridian
Campbell	58N	41N	69W	76W	Sixth Principal
Carbon	28N	12N	77W	93W	Sixth Principal
Converse	41N	27N	67W	77W	Sixth Principal
Crook	58N	49N	60W	68W	Sixth Principal
Fremont	47N	27N	89W	110W	Sixth Principal
Fremont	8N	2S	6E	6W	Wind River
Goshen	30N	19N	60W	65W	Sixth Principal
Hot Springs	47N	41N	90W	104W	Sixth Principal
Hot Springs	9N	6N	6E	3W	Wind River
Johnson	53N	41N	76W	87W	Sixth Principal
Laramie	19N	12N	60W	70W	Sixth Principal
Lincoln	38N	19N	111W	120W	Sixth Principal
Natrona	41N	29N	77W	89W	Sixth Principal
Niobrara	41N	31N	60W	67W	Sixth Principal
Park	58N	44N	98W	118W	Sixth Principal
Platte	30N	20N	65W	70W	Sixth Principal
Sheridan	58N	53N	76W	92W	Sixth Principal
Sublette	40N	27N	103W	116W	Sixth Principal
Sweetwater	26N	12N	90W	111W	Sixth Principal
Teton	55N	38N	110W	118W	Sixth Principal
Uinta	18N	12N	111W	120W	Sixth Principal
Washakie	48N	41N	86W	97W	Sixth Principal
Weston	48N	41N	60W	68W	Sixth Principal

Appendix B:
Land Office Boundary Maps for All Federal Land States

Most land-entry case files are organized in the National Archives according to land office jurisdictions. Often, however, the land office is omitted from the microfilm tract book reproductions found in most repositories; and when researching the various published land office abstracts that may be available, it is helpful to know which land office an ancestor may have dealt with at a particular time in his or her life. The following maps help identify those land offices.

For each federal land state, this appendix contains a series of maps that begin with the first land office for that region and proceed through approximately 1908. The maps rarely include changes that have taken place since 1908. For a few states, the lack of available information required that only the locations of the land offices be illustrated, without the precise boundaries found in most of the maps. In these circumstances, the researcher needs to be aware that some of the offices shown may have replaced others that are also shown. The dates and locations were derived from the year the land office opened, and do not include dates of mergers or closings. The reader will, however, be able to determine, within a location or two, which office an ancestor would have dealt with.

When the date of a land office's opening is uncertain, the act through which it opened is described. Keep in mind that the actual opening date may have been as much as ten to twelve months after the act of congress. In some instances the date of opening may reflect the date of first entry in the registers of the office.

These maps were produced as closely as possible based upon the township, range, and section numbers encompassed within each land office. The boundary lines have been reproduced as precisely as possible, but allow for the customary margin of error in any such illustration.

The Ohio map series begins with a "pre-land office" era, when lands were segregated for bounty-land distribution and purchases were made from Philadelphia and New York. This was done in order to successfully illustrate the complexities of the state of Ohio and its mixture of federal and state lands.

These maps were originally intended to facilitate research among the land-entry case files, though they can be helpful in numerous ways depending on the ingenuity of the researcher. For further information, see chapter 10, Strategies for Federal Land Records.

Alabama 1
1803–1810

The St. Stephens land office opened 26 December 1806.

Alabama 2
1810–1818

The Huntsville land office opened 27 January 1810.

Alabama 3
1818–1819

The Cahaba land office opened 1 June 1819. It originally opened in Milledgeville, Georgia on 4 August 1817, then moved to the Conecuh Courthouse 20 October 1818 before being established at Cahaba.

Alabama 4
1819–1820

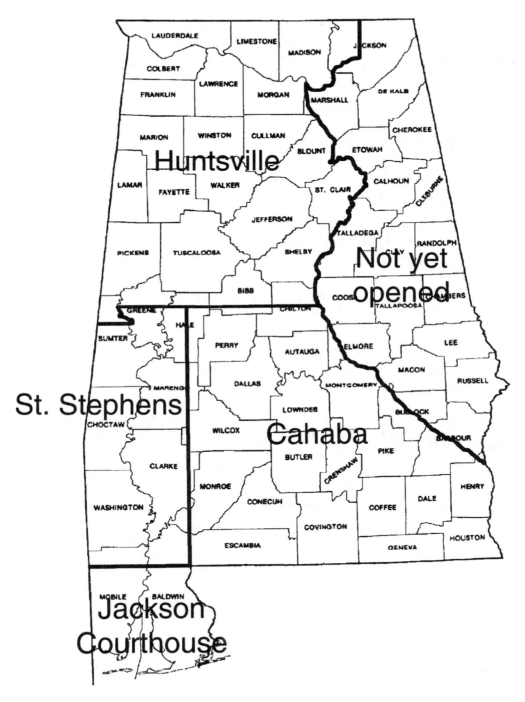

The Jackson Courthouse land office opened 18 May 1819.

Alabama 5
1820–1833

The Tuscaloosa land office opened 2 July 1821.
The Sparta land office opened 1 August 1822.

Alabama 6
1833–1842

The Montevallo land office opened 20 December 1833, and moved to Mardisville
  January 1834.

The Montgomery land office opened 1 January 1834.

The Demopolis land office opened 15 July 1833.

Alabama 7
1842–1866

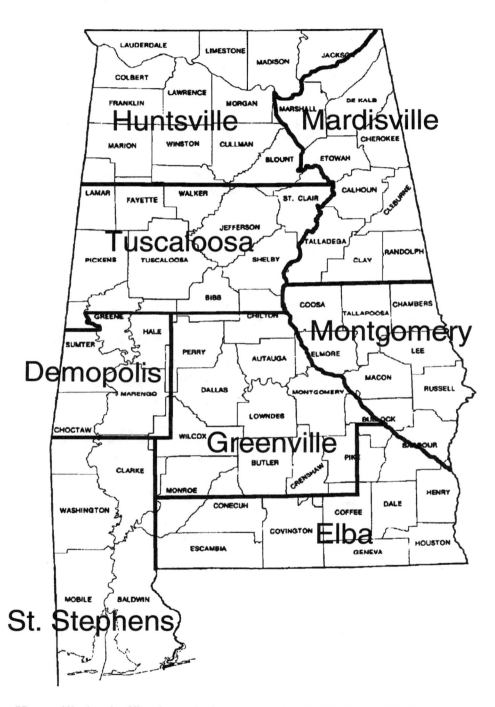

The Huntsville land office boundaries were extended 2 March 1842.

The Sparta land office moved to Elba 1 April 1854.

The Cahaba land office moved to Greenville 15 June 1856.

The Mardisville land office moved to Lebanon 12 April 1842, then to Centre 1 August 1858.

Alabama 8
1866–1867

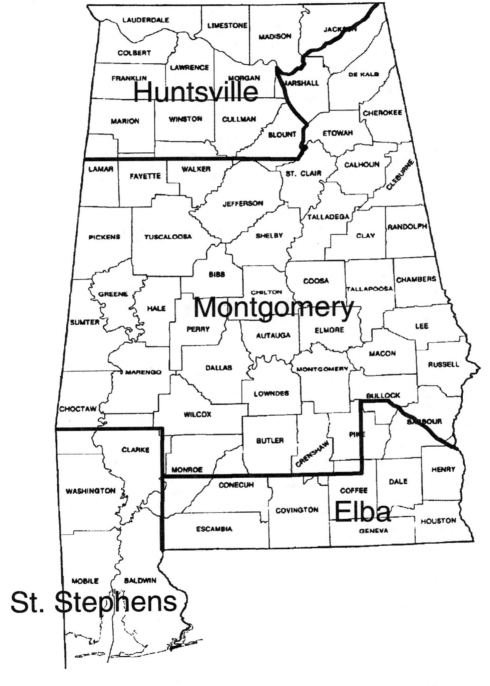

The Tuscaloosa land office merged with Montgomery 30 March 1866.

The Centre land office merged with Huntsville 30 March 1866, then moved to Montgomery 26 May 1866.

The Demopolis land office merged with Montgomery 30 March 1866.

The Greenville land office merged with Montgomery 30 March 1866.

Alabama 9
1867–1872

The Elba land office merged with Montgomery 11 April 1867.
The St. Stephens land office moved to Mobile in 1867.

Alabama 10
1872–1879

The Huntsville land office's boundaries expanded 23 January 1872.

Alabama 11
1879–1905

The Mobile land office merged with Montgomery 28 March 1879.

Alaska
1884–1923

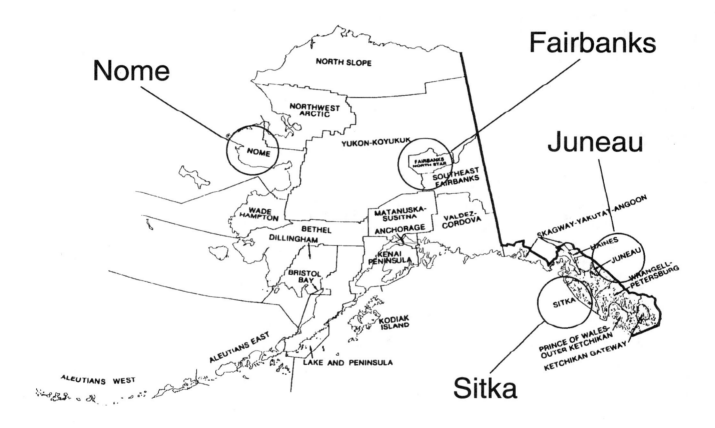

The Sitka land office opened in 1884.
The Juneau land office opened in 1902.
The Nome and Fairbanks land offices opened in 1907.

Arizona 1
1868–1873

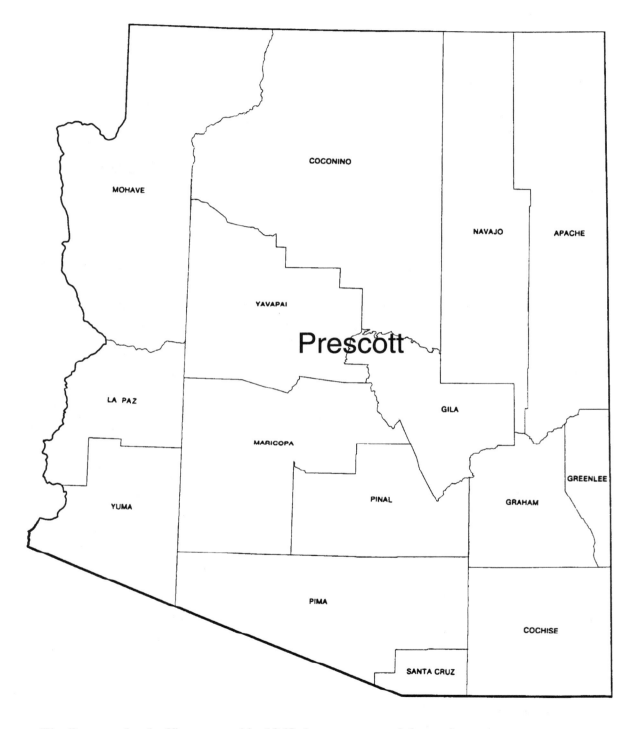

The Prescott land office opened in 1868; it encompassed the entire state.

Arizona 2
1873–1905

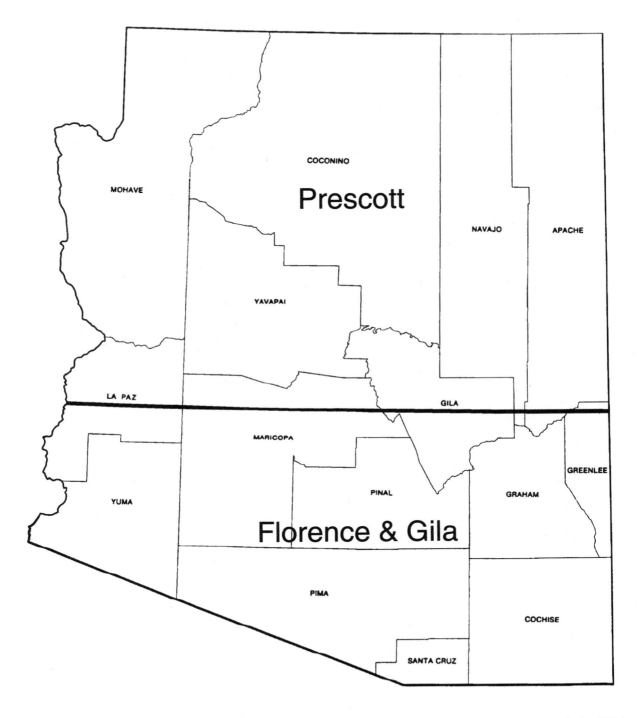

The Florence and Gila land office opened 18 April 1873 and moved to Tucson 21 July 1881.

Arizona 3
1905–

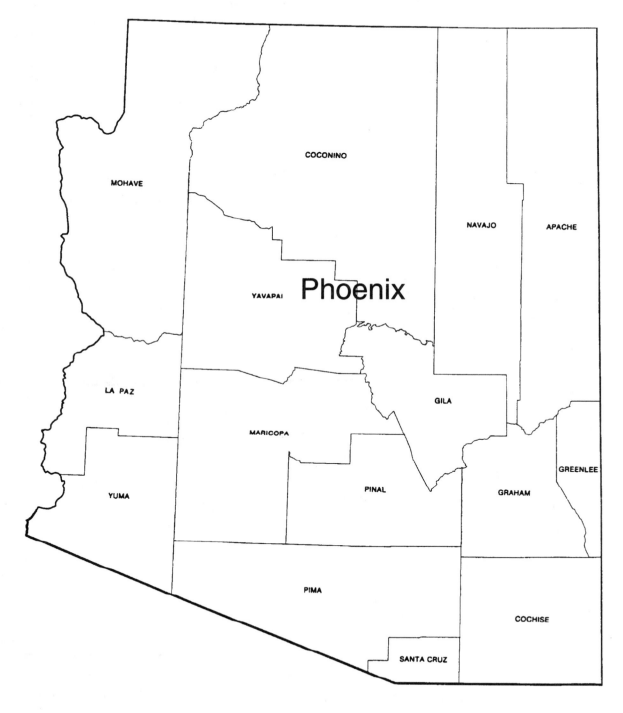

It appears that the Phoenix land office replaced both Prescott and Tucson, opening
in 1905.

Arkansas 1
1820–1825

The Davidsonville land office opened 23 July 1820, then moved to Batesville 13 July 1823.
The Jackson, Missouri, land office opened 29 May 1821.
The Little Rock land office opened 1 September 1821.

Arkansas 2
1825–1826

The Jackson, Missouri, land office merged with Batesville 12 July 1825.

Arkansas 3
1826–1832

The Batesville land office boundaries expanded 5 April 1826.
The Little Rock land office boundaries expanded 5 April 1826.

Arkansas 4
1832–1834

The Fayetteville land office opened 20 Jun 1833.
A Portion of the Batesville land office merged with Little Rock 25 June 1832.
The Washington land office opened 1 November 1832.

Arkansas 5
1834–1838

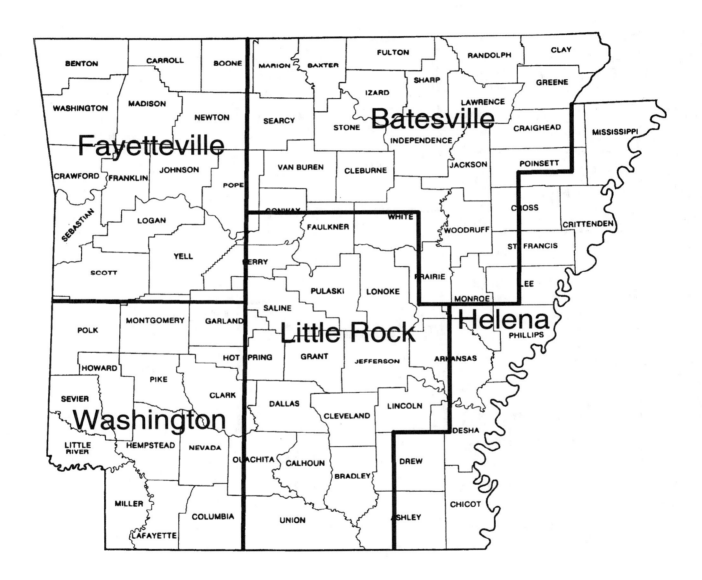

The Helena land office opened 5 November 1834.

Arkansas 6
1838–1845

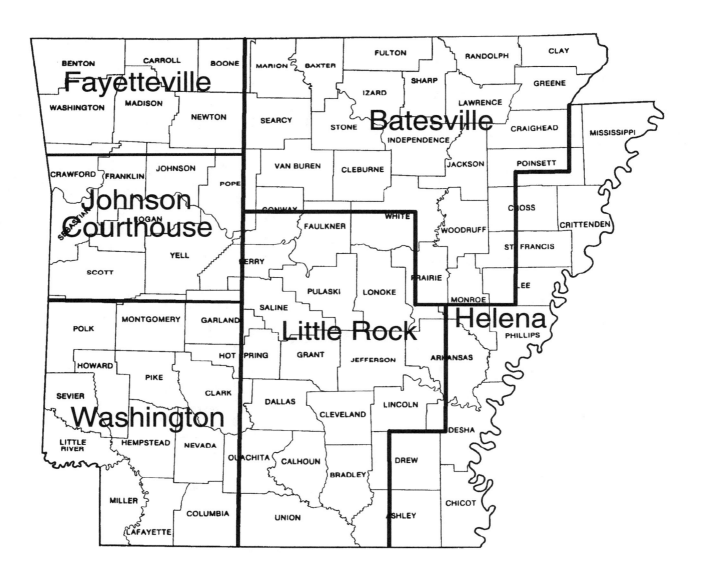

The Johnson Courthouse land office opened 8 April 1839.

Arkansas 7
1845–1860

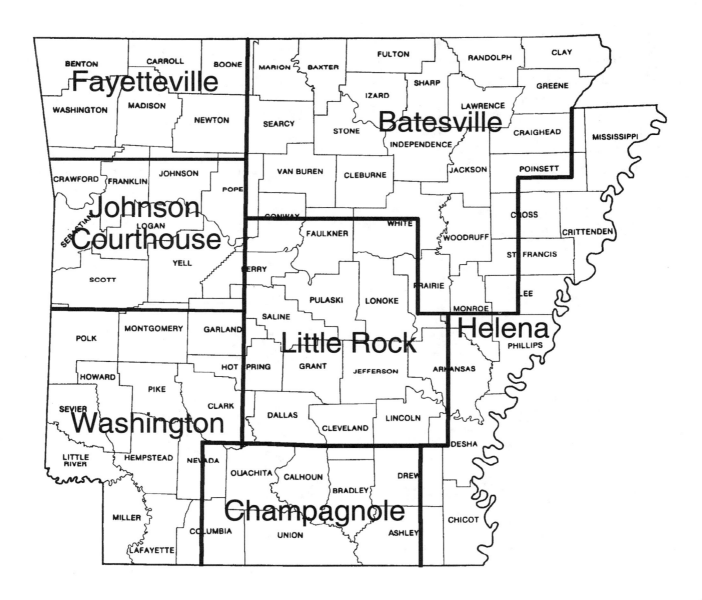

The Champagnole land office opened June 1845.
The Johnson Courthouse land office moved to Clarksville in 1848.

Arkansas 8
1860–1865

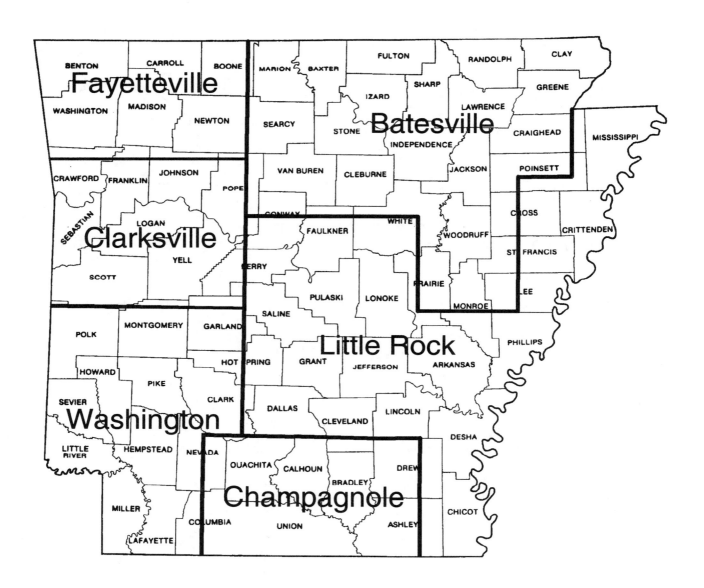

The Fayetteville land office moved to Huntsville 24 September 1860.

Arkansas 9
1865–1871

The Champagnole land office merged with Washington 10 September 1865.
The Batesville land office merged with Little Rock 10 November 1865.
The Huntsville land office merged with Clarksville 10 September 1865.

Arkansas 10
1871–1872

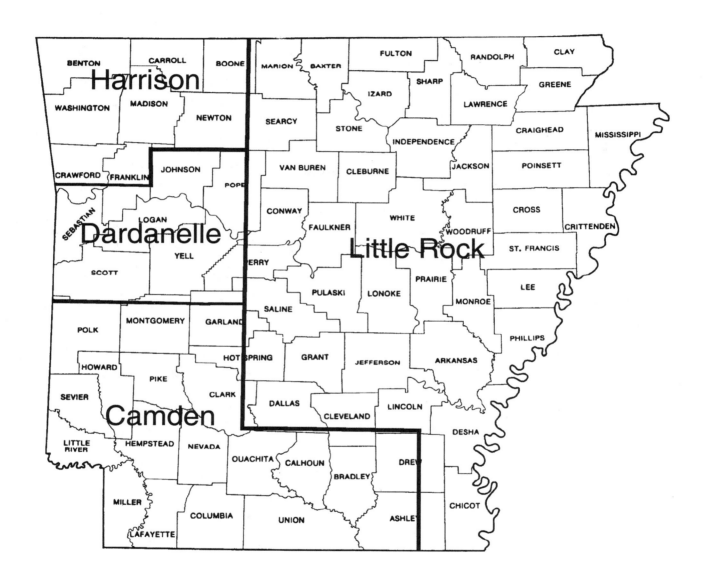

The Clarksville land office closed 8 February 1871.

The Harrison land office opened 27 February 1871.

The Dardanelle land office opened 31 May 1871.

The Washington land office moved to Camden 27 January 1871.

Arkansas 11
1872–1909

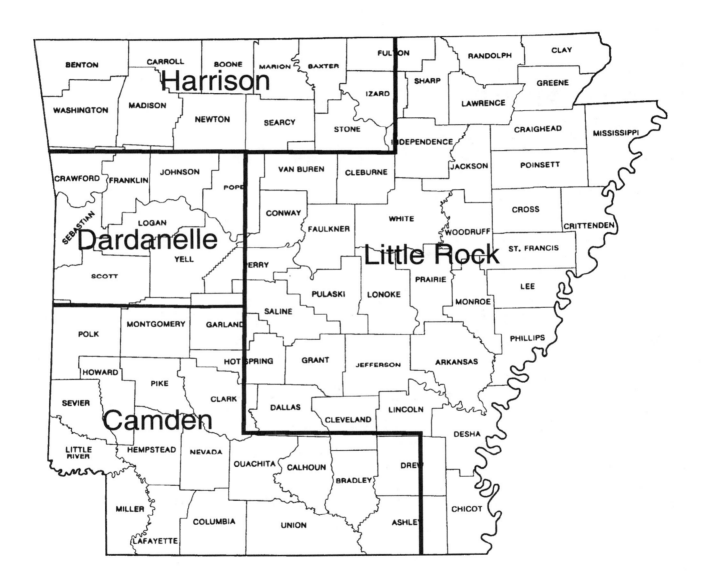

The Harrison land office boundaries expanded 14 March 1872.

California 1
1853–1855

The Benicia land office opened 30 March 1853.
The Los Angeles land office opened by executive order of 21 March 1853.

California 2
1855–1858

The Marysville land office opened 27 April 1855.
The Benicia land office moved to San Francisco 3 November 1857.

California 3
1858–1865

The Humboldt land office opened 24 July 1858.
The Stockton land office opened 1 July 1858.
The Visalia land office opened 10 July 1858.

California 4
1865–1867

The Los Angeles land office merged with San Francisco 26 April 1865.

California 5
1867–1869

The Sacramento land office opened 4 November 1867.

California 6
1869–1870

The Aurora land office opened by executive order of 7 June 1869.
The Los Angeles land office reopened 22 September 1869.

California 7
1870–1874

The Shasta land office opened 17 April 1870, then moved to Redding 13 May 1870.
    Sometime before 1873, the Redding land office moved back to Shasta.
The Susanville land office opened 2 March 1871.
The Aurora land office moved to Independence 31 May 1873.

California 8
1874–1905

The Shasta land office moved to Redding 13 May 1890.

The Independence land office moved to Bodie in 1878, then back to Independence 22 April 1886.

The Humboldt land office moved to Eureka 5 April 1899.

California 9
1905–1916

The Marysville land office merged with Sacramento 1 July 1905.
The Stockton land office merged with Sacramento 2 April 1906.
The Redding land office merged with Sacramento 2 January 1913.

Colorado 1
1863–1867

The Golden City land office opened through an executive order of 11 March 1863, then moved to Denver 15 August 1864.

Colorado 2
1867–1871

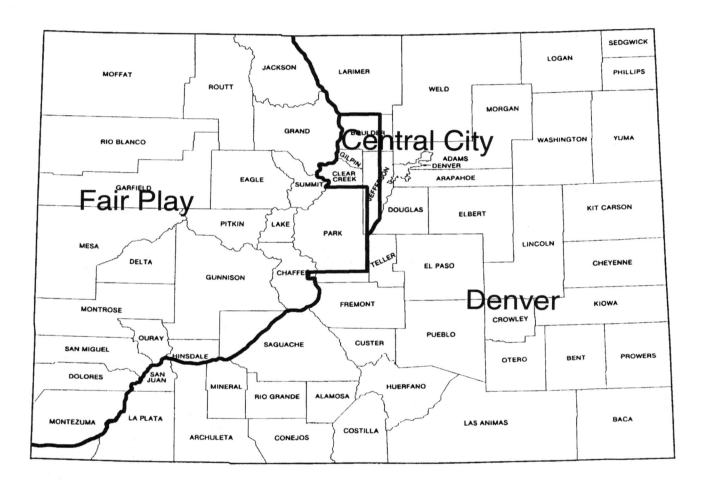

The Fair Play land office opened 23 October 1867.
The Central City land office opened through executive order 31 December 1867.

Colorado 3
1871–1874

The Pueblo land office opened 16 January 1871.

Colorado 4
1875–1877

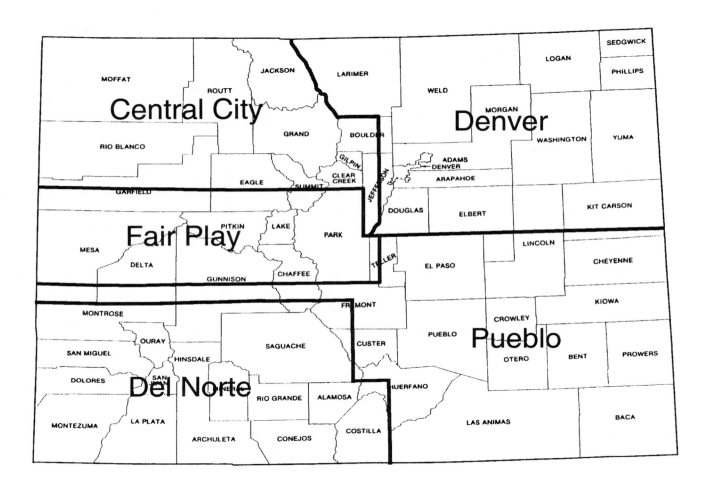

The Del Norte land office opened 22 March 1875.

Colorado 5
1877–1882

The Fair Play land office moved to Leadville 14 April 1879.
The Lake City land office opened 5 May 1877.

Colorado 6
1882–1884

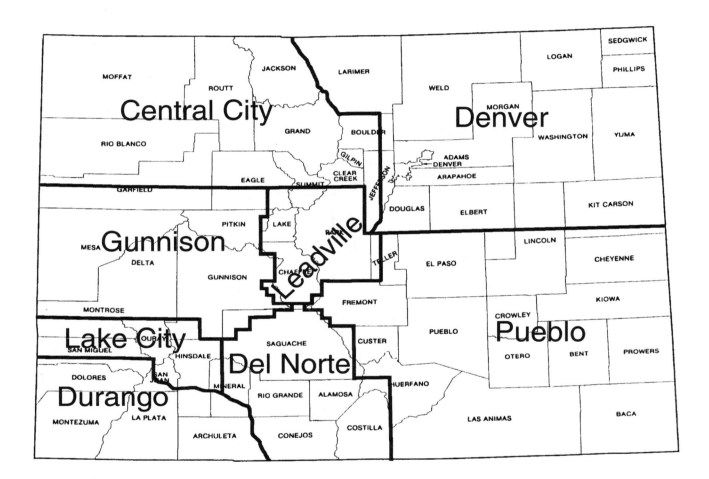

The Gunnison land office opened 2 April 1883.
The Durango land office opened 21 October 1882.

Colorado 7
1884–1887

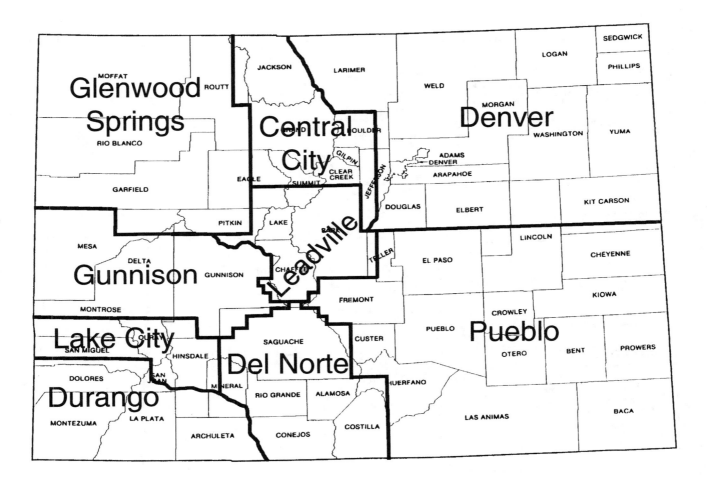

The Glenwood Springs land office opened 10 November 1884.

Colorado 8
1887–1888

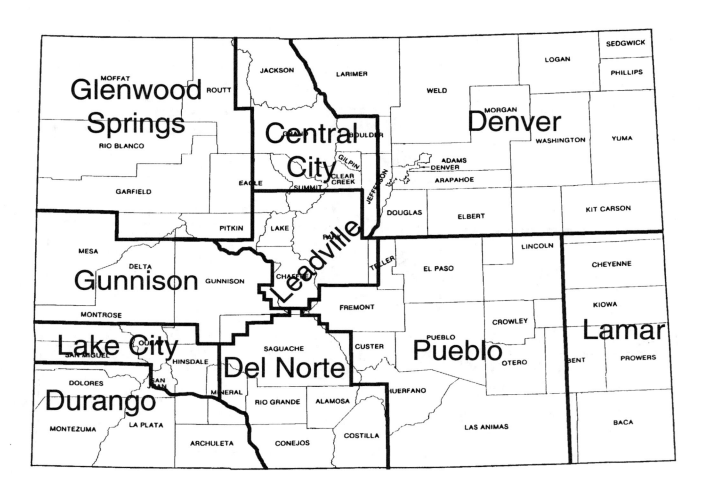

The Lamar land office opened 3 January 1887.

Colorado 9
1888–1890

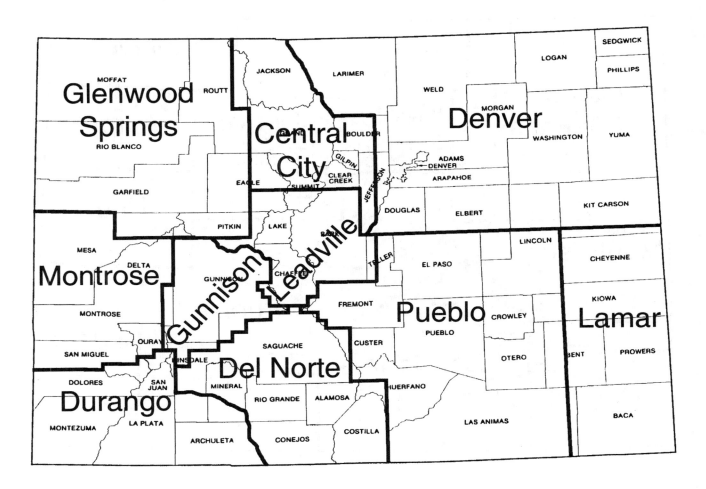

The Montrose land office opened 1 September 1888.

Colorado 10
1890–1894

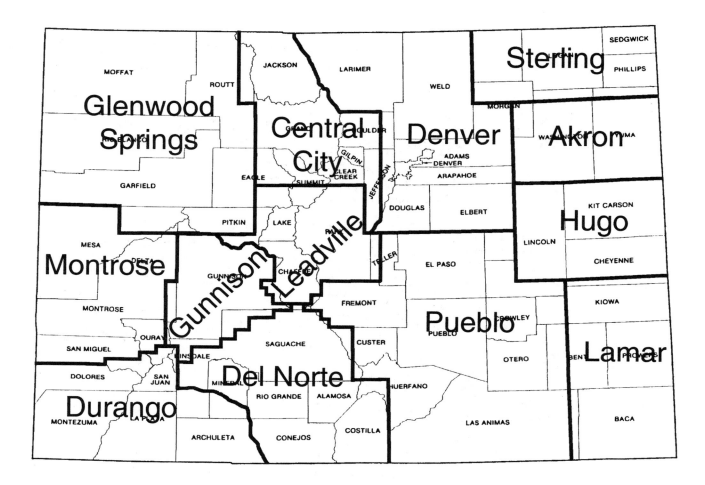

The Sterling land office opened 1 August 1890.
The Akron land office opened 1 August 1890.
The Hugo land office opened 7 September 1890.

Colorado 11
1894–1905

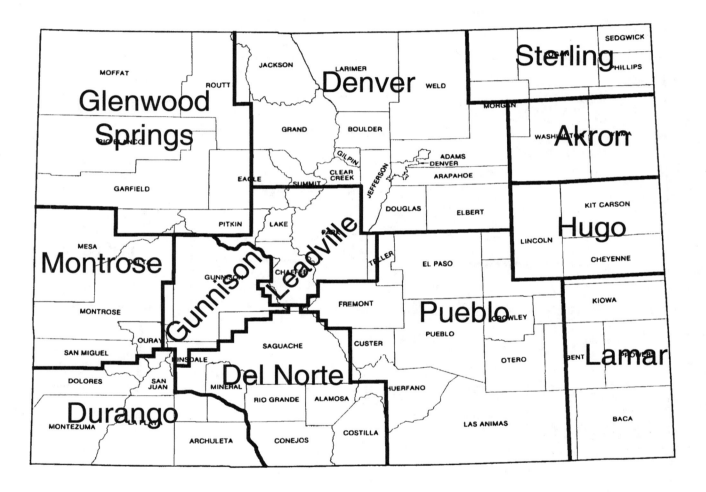

The Central City land office merged with Denver through executive order of 6 January 1894.

Colorado 12
1905–1907

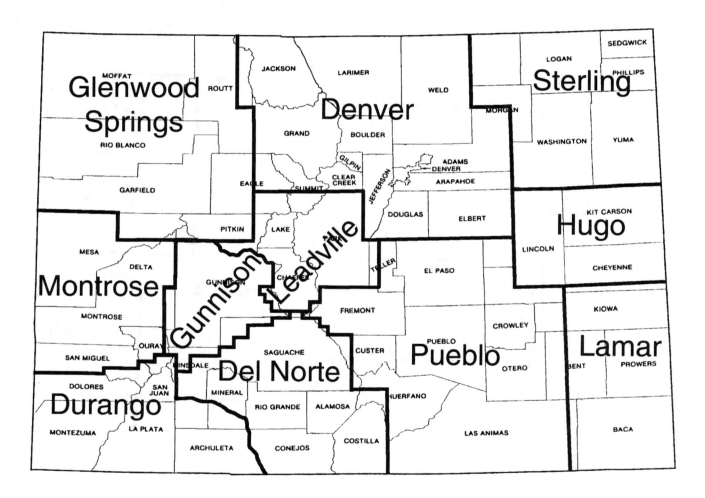

The Akron land office merged with Sterling 1 July 1905.

Colorado 13
1907–1922

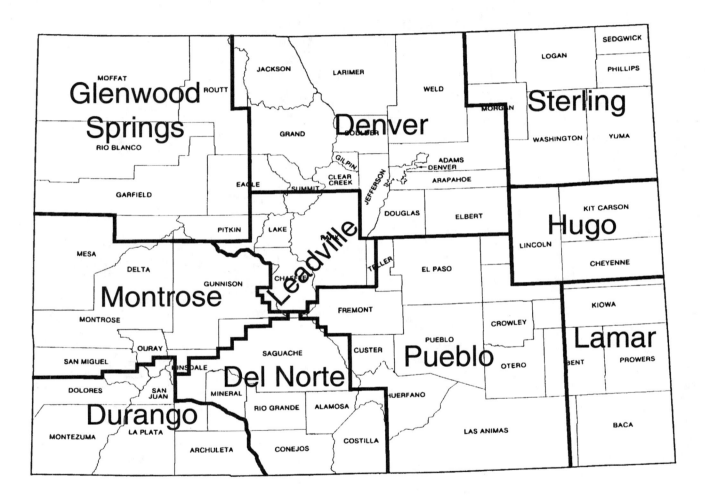

The Gunnison land office merged with Montrose 1 July 1907.

Florida 1
1823–1842

The St. Augustine land office opened 25 September 1825.
The Tallahassee land office opened 16 May 1825.

Florida 2
1842–1854

The Newmansville land office opened in October 1842.

Florida 3
1855–1867

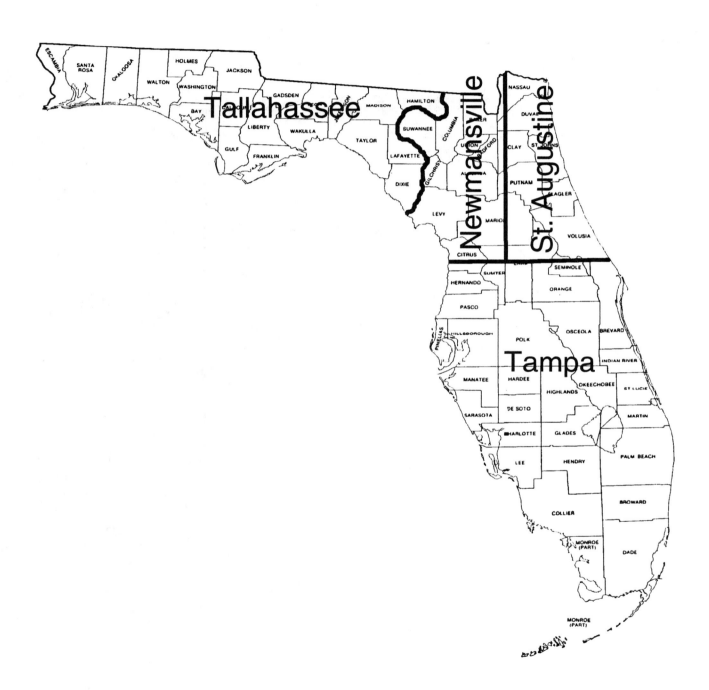

The Tampa land office opened 4 April 1855.

Florida 4
1867–1873

The Newmansville land office merged with Tallahassee 8 May 1867.
The St. Augustine land office merged with Tallahassee 8 May 1867.
The Tampa land office merged with Tallahassee 8 May 1867.

Florida 5
1873–

The Gainesville land office opened 30 April 1873.
The Tallahassee land office merged with Gainesville in 1873/74.

Idaho 1
1866–1879

The Boise land office opened in 1866.
The Lewiston land office opened in 1866.

Idaho 2
1879–1883

The Oxford land office opened in 1879.

Idaho 3
1883–

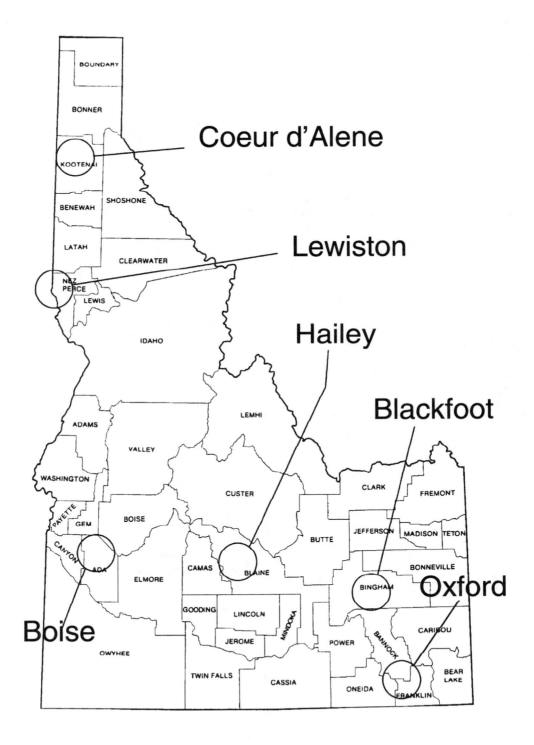

The Hailey land office opened in 1883.
The Coeur d'Alene land office opened in 1884.
The Blackfoot land office opened in 1886.

Illinois 1
1804–1814

The Vincennes, Indiana, land office opened 27 April 1807.
The Kaskaskia land office opened through an Act of 26 March 1804.

Illinois 2
1814–1816

The Shawneetown land office opened 8 July 1814.

Illinois 3
1816–1821

The Edwardsville land office opened 28 October 1816.

Illinois 4
1821–1823

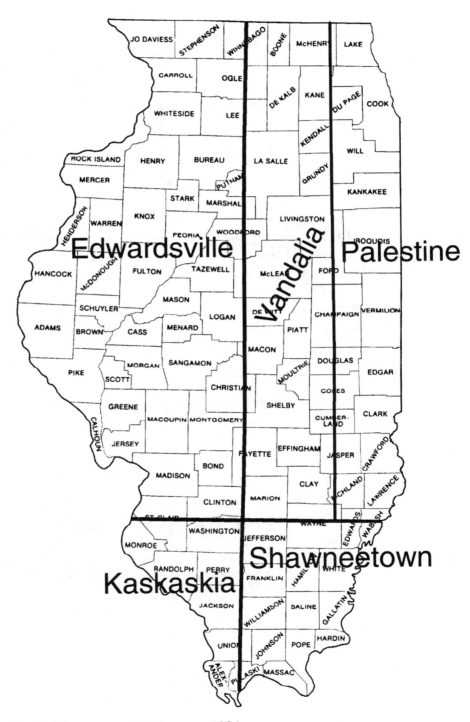

The Vandalia land office opened 15 January 1821.
The Palestine land office opened 23 July 1821.

Illinois 5
1823–1831

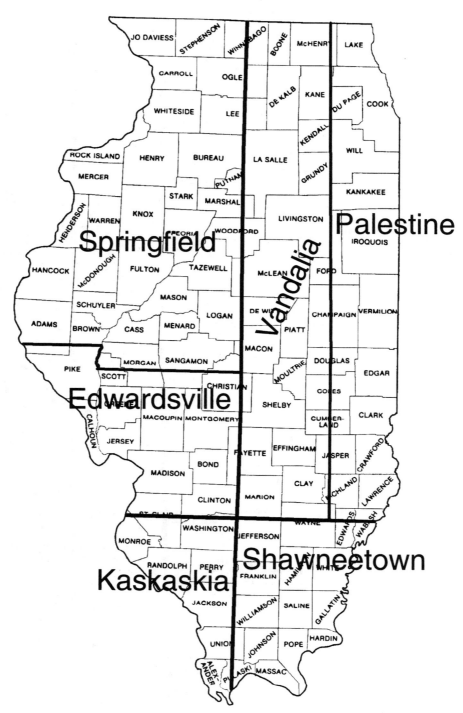

The Springfield land office opened 6 November 1823.

Illinois 6
1831–1833

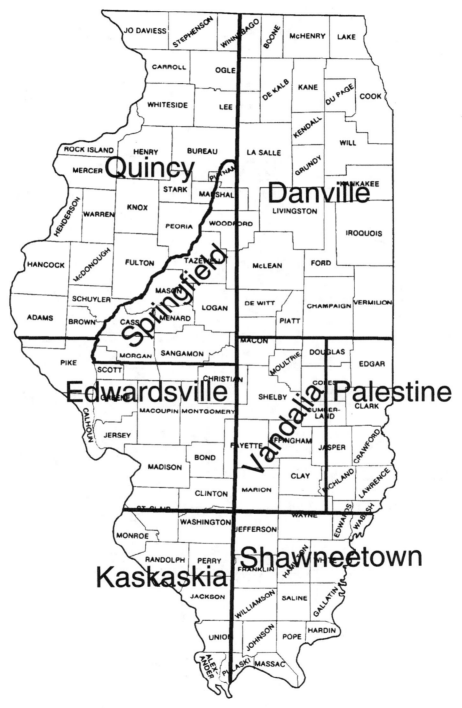

The Quincy land office opened 14 December 1831.
The Danville land office opened 24 August 1831.

Illinois 7
1833–1835

The Vandalia land office expanded through an Act of 2 March 1833.

Illinois 8
1835–1855

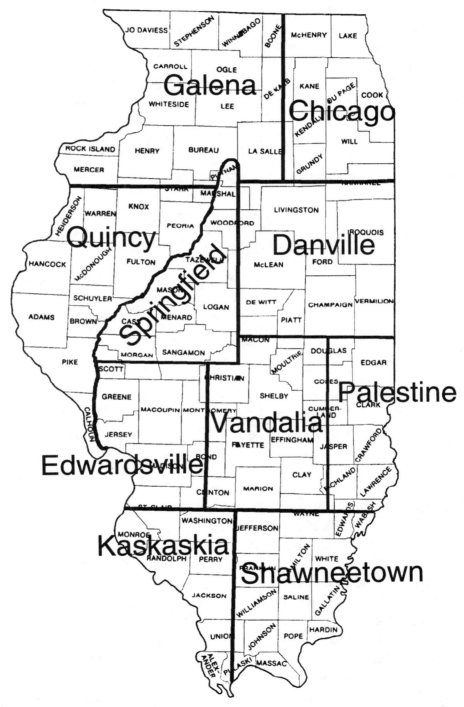

The Galena land office opened 8 June 1835.
The Chicago land office opened 23 May 1835.

Illinois 9
1855–1876

The Dixon, Chicago, and Quincy land
offices merged with Springfield 9 June 1855.

The Danville land office merged with Springfield
5 May 1856.

The Edwardsville and Palestine land offices
merged with Springfield 9 June 1855.

The Vandalia land office merged with
Springfield 8 December 1855.

The Kaskaskia and Shawneetown land offices
merged with Springfield 12 November 1855.

The Springfield land office was merged with the GLO in 1876.

Indiana 1
1805–1808

The Detroit, Michigan, land office opened for northern Indiana under an Act of 3 March 1805. The Vincennes land office opened 27 April 1807.

Indiana 2
1808–1820

The Jeffersonville land office opened 14 April 1808.

Indiana 3
1820–1823

The Terre Haute land office opened 4 September 1820.
The Indianapolis land office opened 3 October 1820.

Indiana 4
1823–1828

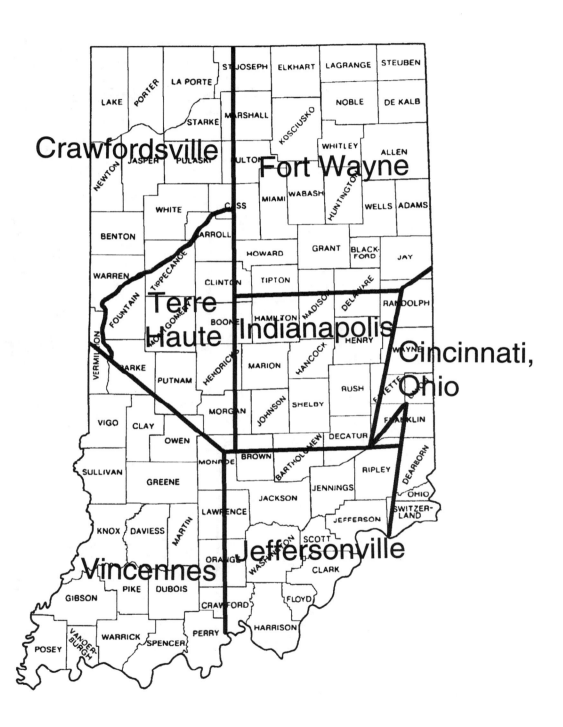

The Crawfordsville land office opened 13 May 1823.
The Fort Wayne land office opened 22 October 1823.

Indiana 5
1828–1833

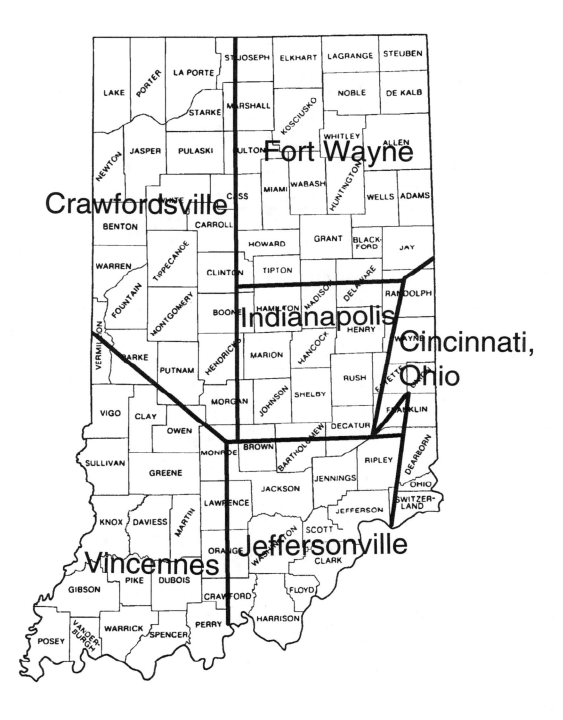

The Terre Haute land office merged with Crawfordsville 28 April 1828.

Indiana 6
1833–1846

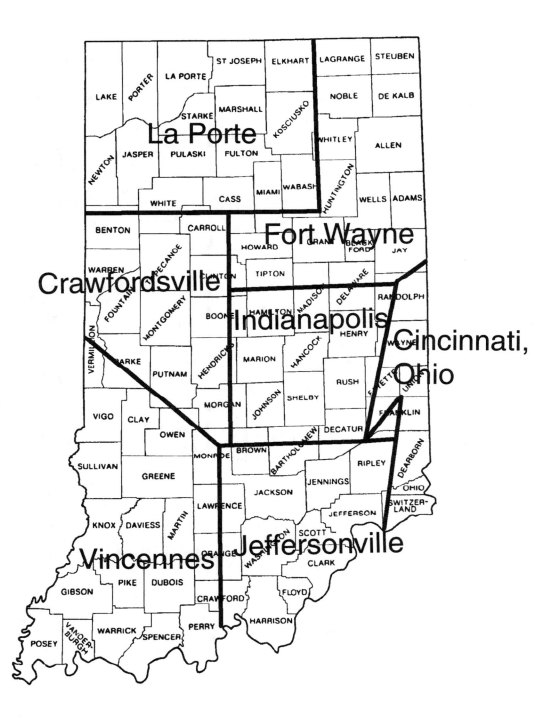

The La Porte land office opened 1 July 1833, then moved to Winamac 16 December 1839.
The Vincennes land office closed from 1840 to 20 April 1853.

Indiana 7
1846–1852

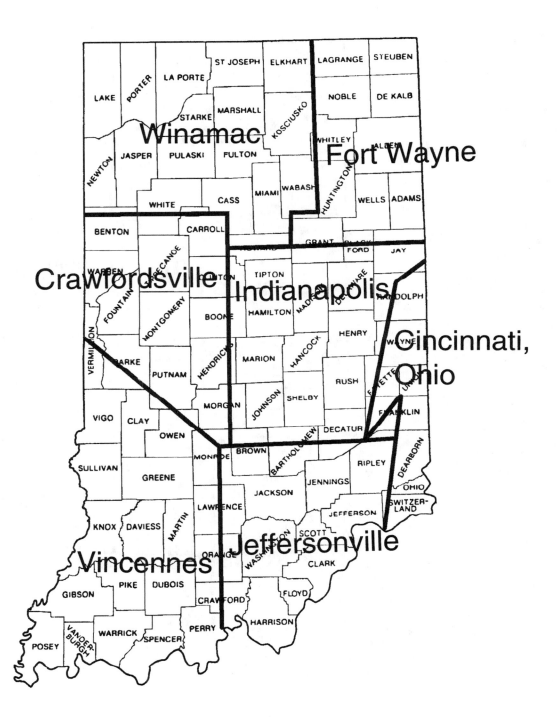

The Fort Wayne land office expanded through the Act of 8 August 1846.
The Vincennes land office closed from 1840 to 20 April 1853.

Indiana 8
1852–1853

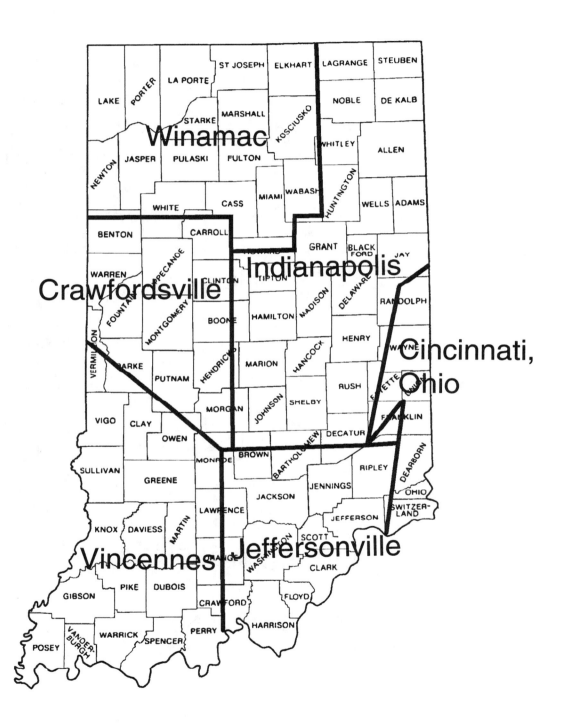

The Fort Wayne land office merged with Indianapolis 12 February 1852.
The Vincennes land office closed from 1840 to 20 April 1853.

Indiana 9
1853–1855

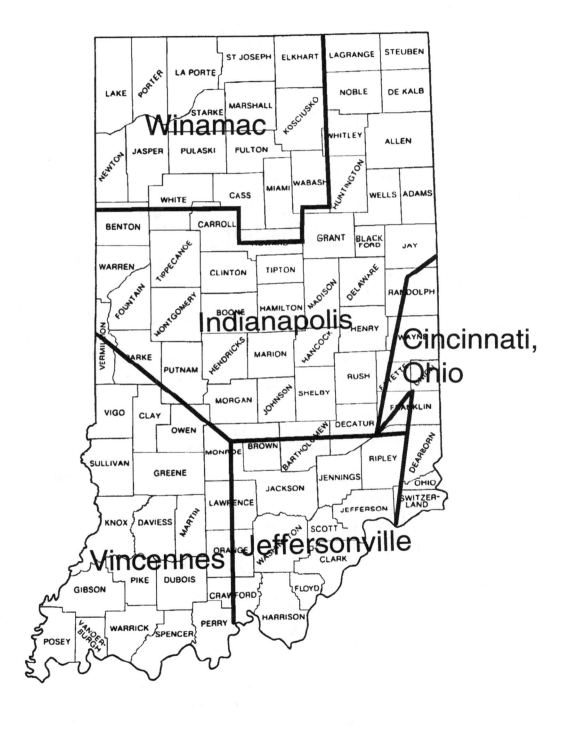

Crawfordsville merged with Indianapolis 7 April 1853.

Indiana 10
1855–1856, 1858–1859, 1861–1876

The Winamac land office merged with Indianapolis in 1855.

The Jeffersonville land office merged with Indianapolis in 1855.

The Vincennes land office merged with Indianapolis 1 September 1855 and was re-established by executive order 22 November 1856. It was closed by executive order 21 June 1858, then re-established by executive order 10 February 1859, remaining open until merging with Indianapolis 20 December 1861.

Indiana 11
1856–1858, 1859–1861

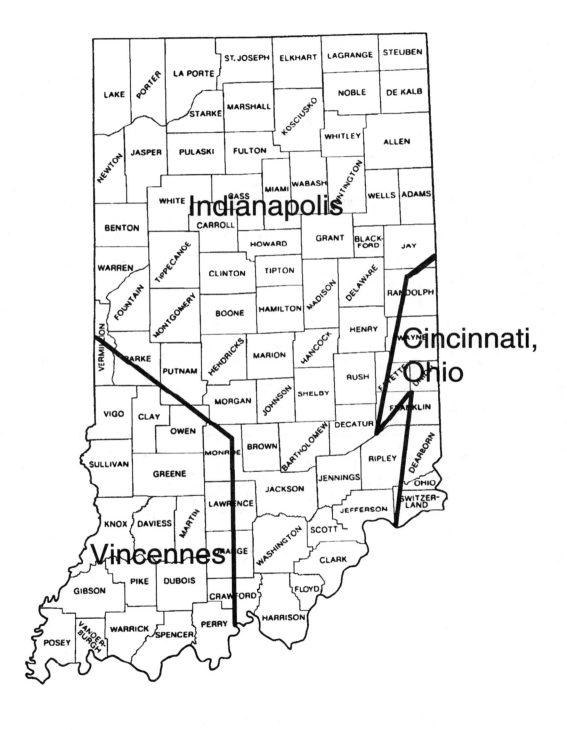

Also see "Indiana 10."

Iowa 1
1838–1846

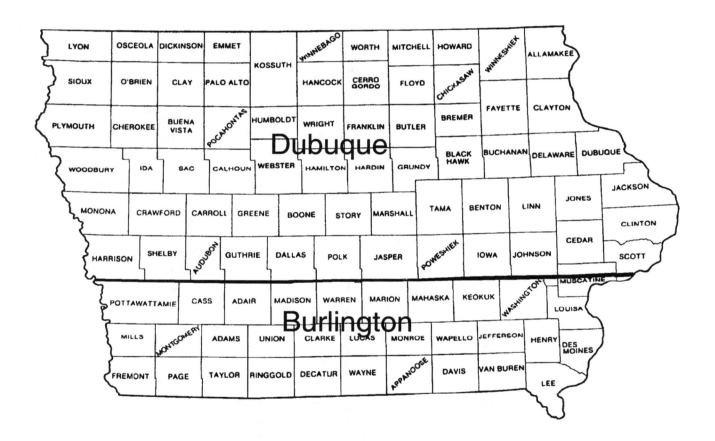

The Dubuque land office opened July 1838, then moved to Marion between 20 February 1843 and 10 July 1843.

The Burlington land office opened July 1838, then moved to Fairfield 1 August 1842.

Iowa 2
1846–1852

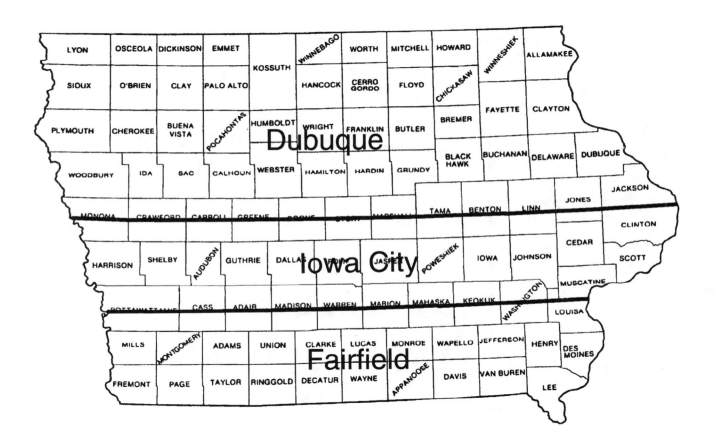

The Iowa City land office opened 5 September 1846.

Iowa 3
1852–1855

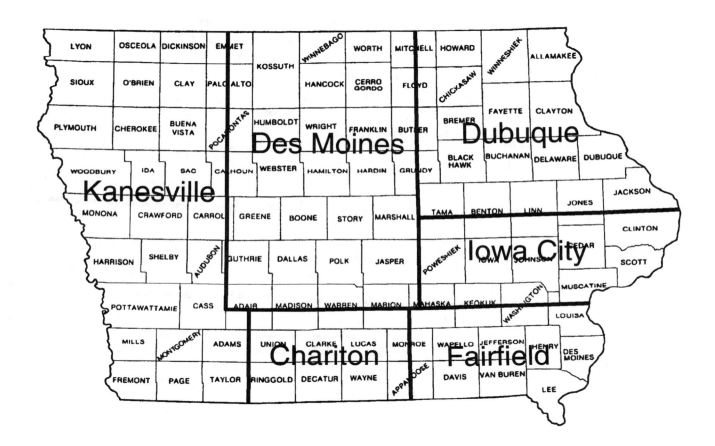

The Kanesville land office opened 28 January 1853.
The Des Moines land office opened 28 January 1853.
The Chariton land office opened 16 October 1852.

Iowa 4
1855–1856

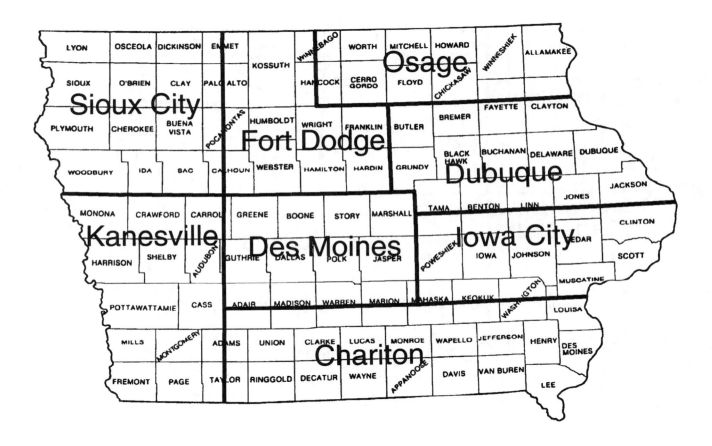

The Sioux City land office opened 31 March 1855.
The Fort Dodge land office opened 26 March 1855.
The Osage land office opened 24 December 1855.
The Fairfield land office merged with Chariton in 1855.

Iowa 5
1856–1859

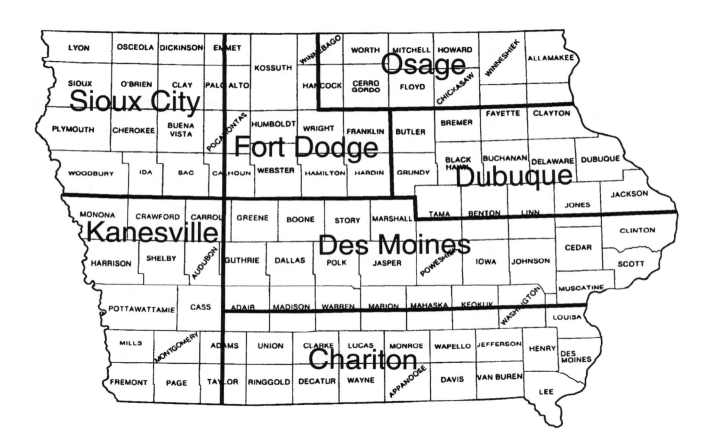

The Iowa City land office merged with Des Moines 15 April 1856.

Iowa 6
1859–1873

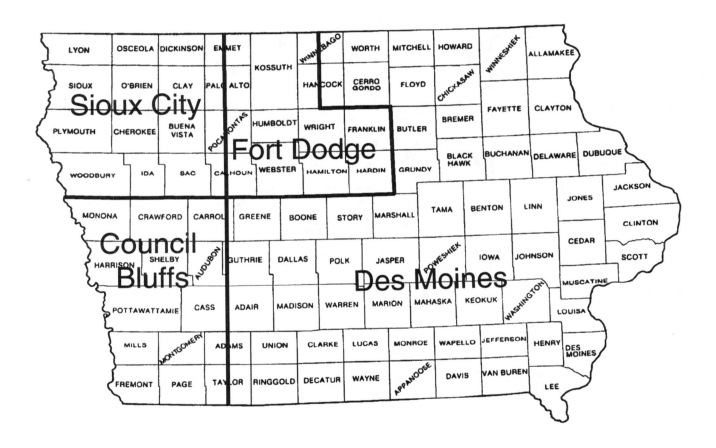

The Osage land office merged with Des Moines 6 July 1859.
The Dubuque land office merged with Des Moines 20 July 1859.
The Chariton land office merged with Des Moines 14 June 1859.
The Kanesville land office moved to Council Bluffs in 1859.

Iowa 7
1873–1877

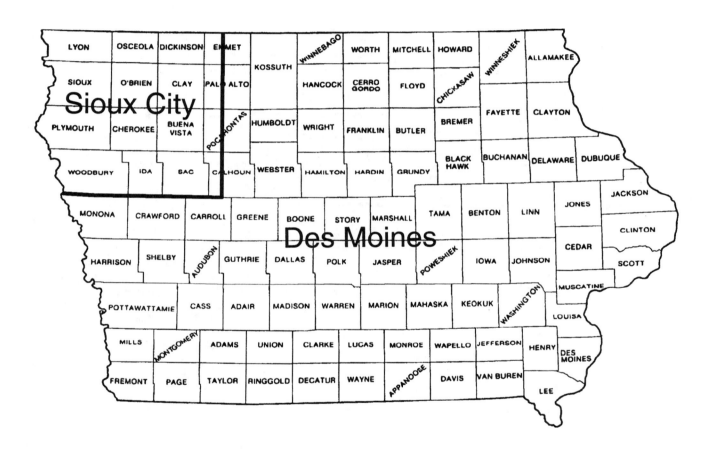

The Fort Dodge land office merged with Des Moines in 1873.
The Council Bluffs land office merged with Des Moines in 1873.

Iowa 8
1877–1910

The Sioux City land office merged with Des Moines in 1877.
Des Moines merged with the GLO 28 February 1910.

Kansas 1
1854–1857

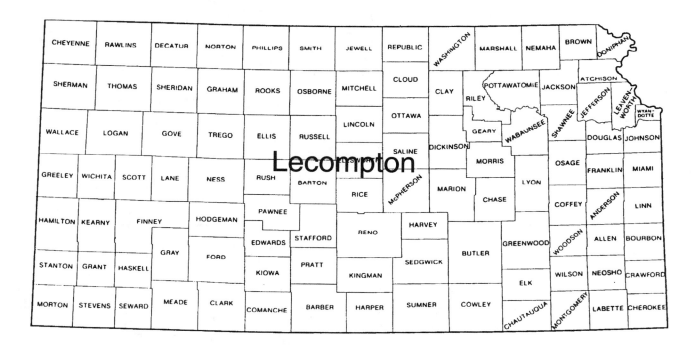

The Lecompton land office opened through the Act of 22 July 1854, encompassing "all of territory to which Indian title has been extinguished."

Kansas 2
1857–1863

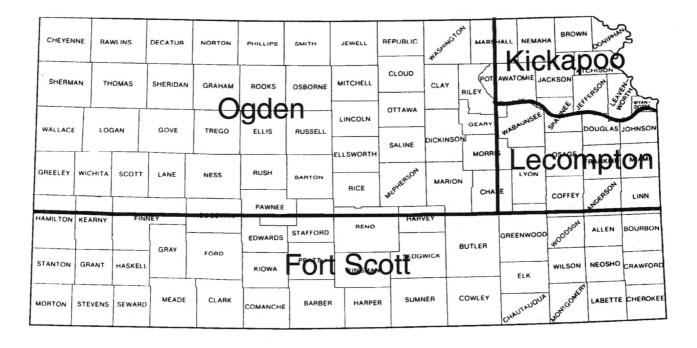

The Ogden land office opened 8 May 1857, then moved to Junction City 6 October 1859.

The Kickapoo land office opened 4 December 1857, then moved to Atchison
  6 September 1861.

The Lecompton land office moved to Topeka through an executive order of 24 July 1861.

The Fort Scott land office opened 20 April 1857; moved to Humboldt 11 September 1861;
  moved to Mapleton 1 November 1861; then moved back to Humboldt 15 May 1862.

Kansas 3
1863–1871

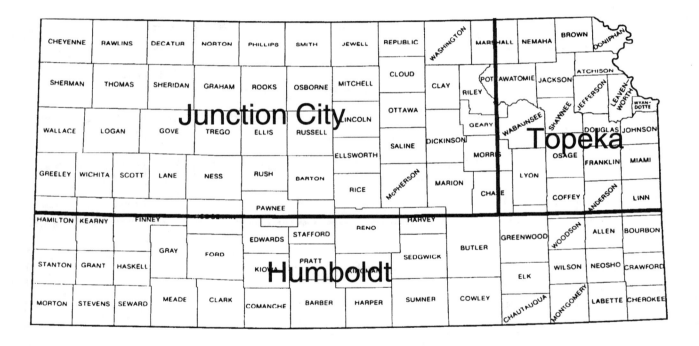

The Atchison land office merged with Topeka through an executive order of 23 October 1863. The Humboldt land office moved to Augusta 1 October 1870.

Kansas 4
1871–1872

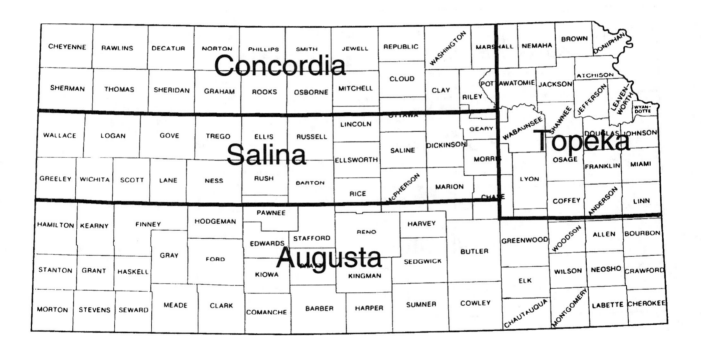

The Junction City land office moved to Salina 1 May 1871.
The Concordia land office opened 16 January 1871.

Kansas 5
1872–1875

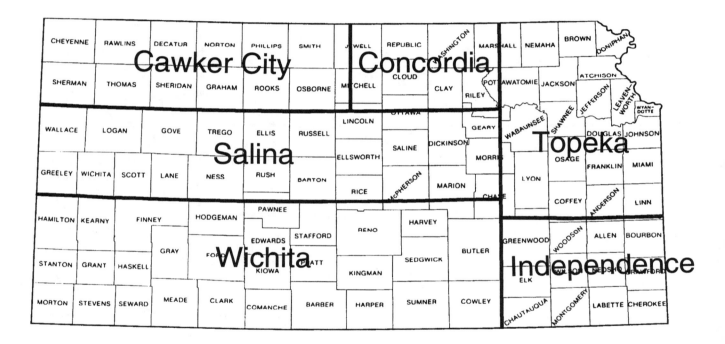

The Cawker City land office opened in June 1872.
The Augusta land office moved to Wichita 20 February 1872.
The Independence land office opened 26 March 1872.

Kansas 6
1875–1881

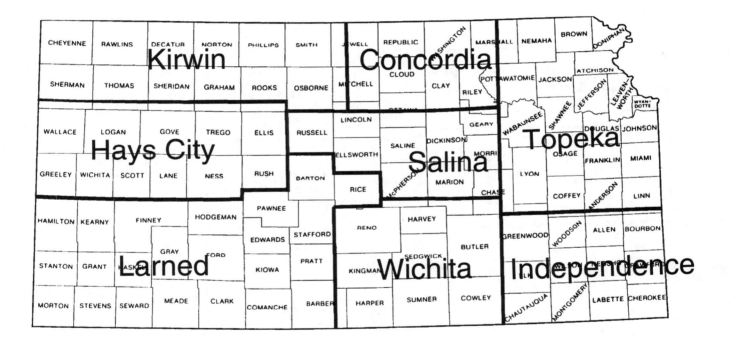

The Cawker City land office moved to Kirwin 4 January 1875.
The Hays City land office opened 8 March 1875, then moved to Wakeeney 20 October 1879.
The Larned land office opened 20 February 1875.

Kansas 7
1881–1883

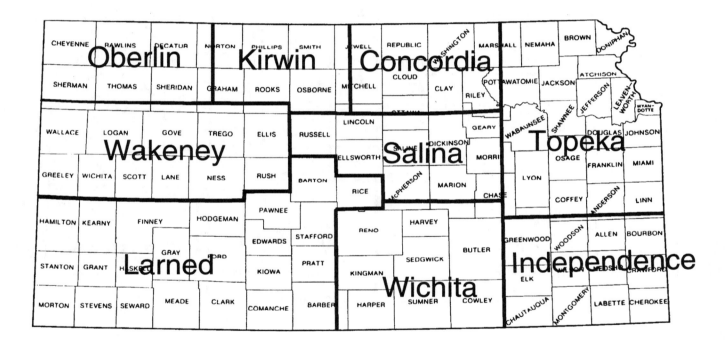

The   Oberlin land office opened 1 August 1881.

Kansas 8
1883–1889

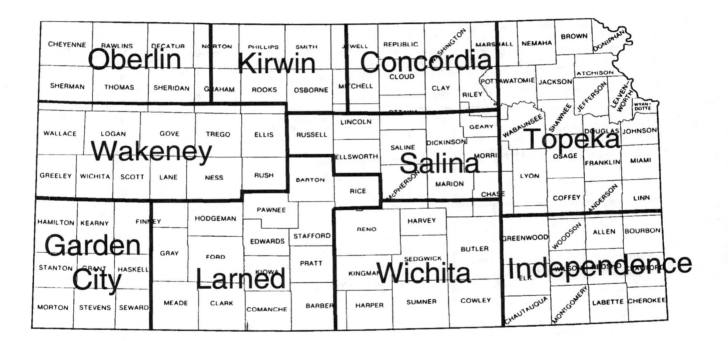

The Garden City land office opened 1 October 1883.

Kansas 9
1889–1893

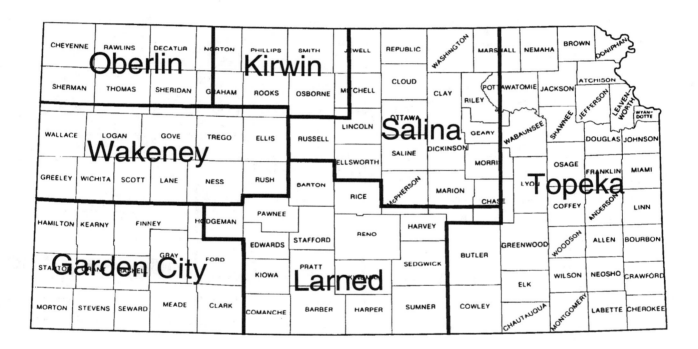

The Concordia land office merged with Salina through an executive order of 20 May 1889.
The Wichita land office merged with Larned through an executive order of 2 August 1889.
The Independence land office merged with Topeka through an executive order of 19
  February 1889.

Kansas 10
1893–1902

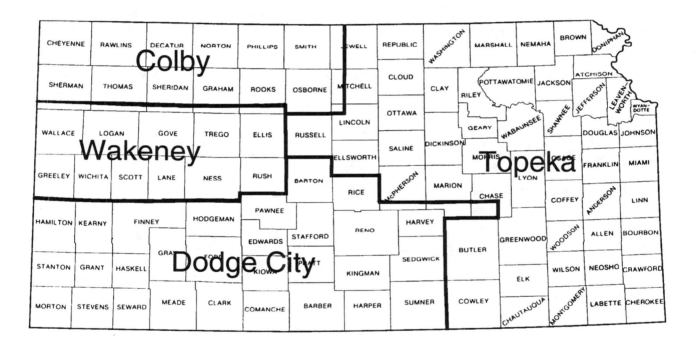

The Oberlin land office moved to Colby 5 February 1894.

The Kirwin land office merged with Colby 5 February 1894.

The Salina land office merged with Topeka through an executive order of 11 September 1893.

The Garden City land office moved to Dodge City 3 February 1894.

The Larned land office merged with Dodge City 3 February 1894.

Kansas 11
1902–1905

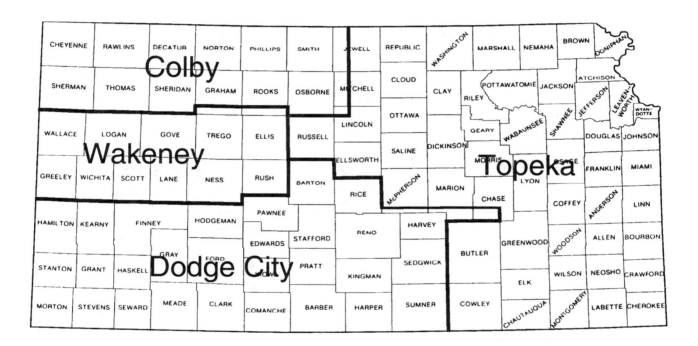

The Colby land office expanded 13 June 1902.

Kansas 12
1905–1908

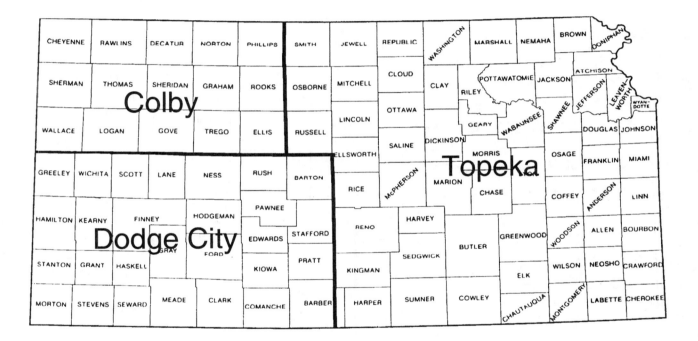

The Wakeeney land office merged with Colby and Dodge City 15 February 1905.
The Topeka land office expanded 15 February 1905.

Kansas 13
1908–1919

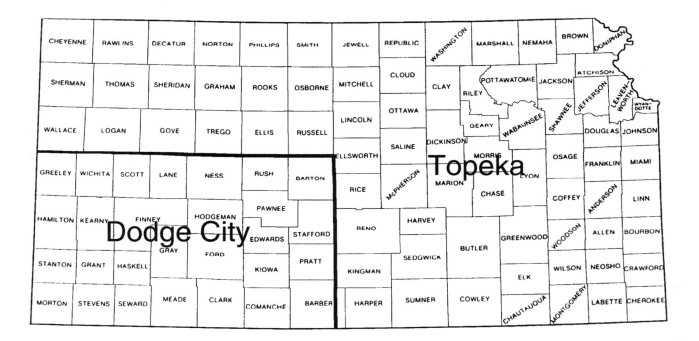

The Colby land office merged with Topeka through an executive order of 7 December 1908. The Dodge City land office merged with Topeka 31 August 1919.

Louisiana 1
1812–1838

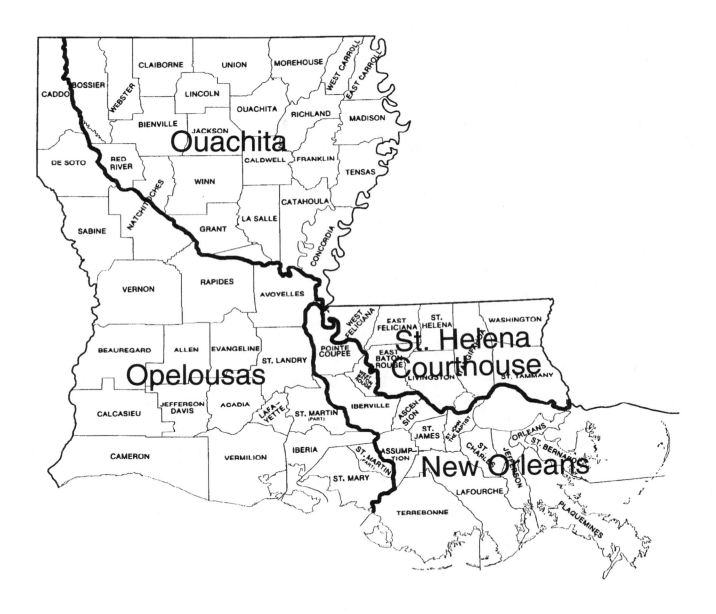

The Ouachita land office opened 1 January 1812.

The Opelousas land office opened 1 January 1812.

The New Orleans land office opened 1 January 1812.

The St. Helena land office opened through an Act of 25 April 1812, then moved to Greensburg through an Act of 3 March 1819.

Louisiana 2
1838–1848

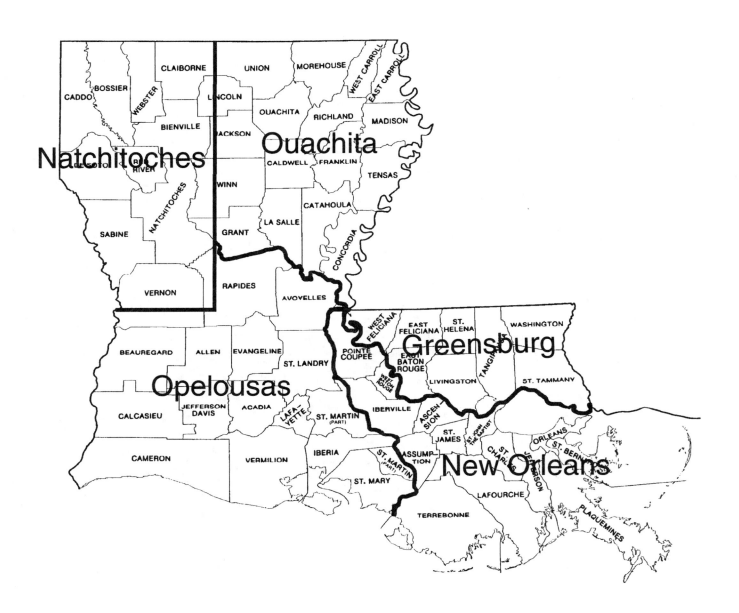

The Natchitoches land office opened 12 October 1838.
The Greensburg land office moved to Baton Rouge 1 January 1844.

Louisiana 3
1848–1866

The Ouachita land office expanded through an Act of 16 January 1848.

Louisiana 4
1866–1878

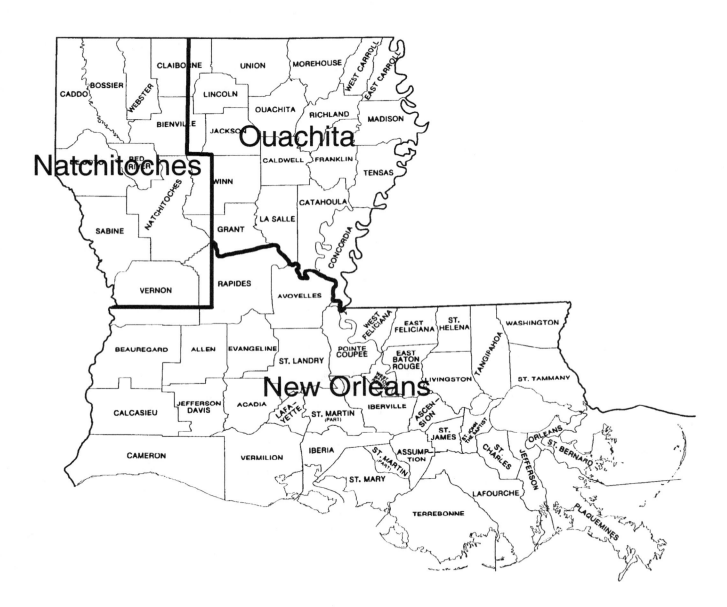

The Baton Rouge land office merged with New Orleans through an executive order of 28
September 1866.

The Opelousas land office merged with New Orleans through an executive order of 28
September 1866.

The Ouachita land office moved to Monroe 23 December 1867.

Louisiana 5
1878–1911

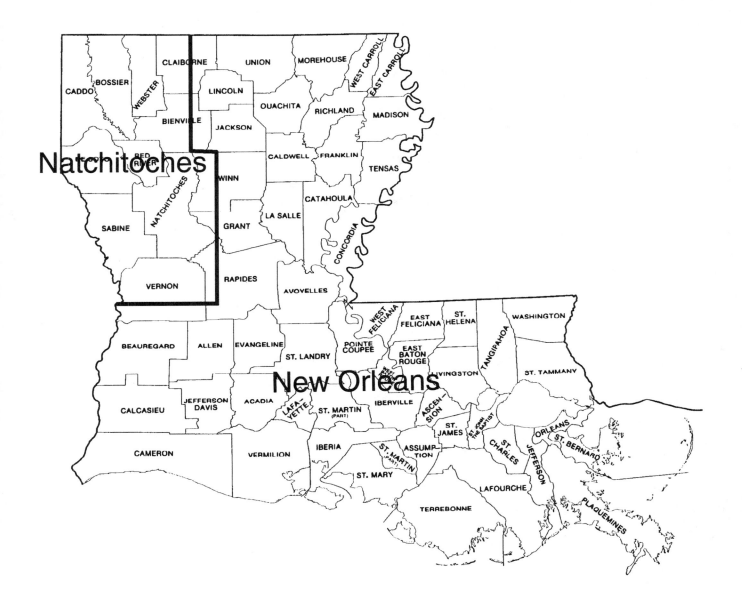

The Monroe land office merged with New Orleans through an executive order of 2 November 1878.

The New Orleans land office moved to Baton Rouge through an executive order of 6 January 1911.

The Natchitoches land office merged with Baton Rouge through an executive order of 6 January 1911.

Michigan 1
1818–1823

The Detroit land office opened through an Act of 26 March 1804, but no entries were made until 7 July 1818.

Michigan 2
1823–1831

The Monroe land office opened 19 July 1823.

Michigan 3
1831–1833

The Monroe land office moved to White Pigeon Prairie 6 July 1831.
The boundaries of all offices were redefined by an Act of 19 February 1831.

Michigan 4
1833–1836

The New Monroe land office opened 8 April 1833.
The White Pigeon Prairie land office moved to Bronson April 1834.

Michigan 5
1836–1848

The Bronson land office moved to Kalamazoo 1 April 1836.
The Ionia land office opened 20 September 1836.
The Genesee land office opened 23 August 1836.

Michigan 6
1848–1854

The Sault Ste. Marie land office opened 1 March 1848.

Michigan 7
1854–1858

The Duncan land office opened 29 May 1854.
The Sault Ste. Marie land office moved to Marquette 14 July 1857.
The Genesee land office moved to East Saginaw 23 March 1857.

Michigan 8
1858–1859

The Duncan land office moved to Traverse City 8 August 1858.
The Detroit land office opened an annex through an Act of 11 May 1858.

Michigan 9
1859–1862

The Kalamazoo land office merged with Ionia through an executive order of 16 June 1859. The Monroe land office merged with Detroit in 1858/59.

Michigan 10
1862–1878

The Traverse City land office for the upper peninsula merged with Marquette through an Act of 16 July 1862.

Michigan 11
1878–1888

The Ionia land office moved to Reed City 1 April 1878.
The Traverse City land office merged with Reed City 1 July 1878.

Michigan 12
1888–1898

The East Saginaw land office moved to Grayling 16 April 1888.
The Detroit land offices merged with Grayling 16 April 1888.
The Reed City land office merged with Grayling 16 April 1888.

Michigan 13
1898–1919

The Grayling land office merged with Marquette through an executive order of
29 April 1898.

Minnesota 1
1849–1852

The Stillwater land office opened 30 June 1849.

Minnesota 2
1852–1854

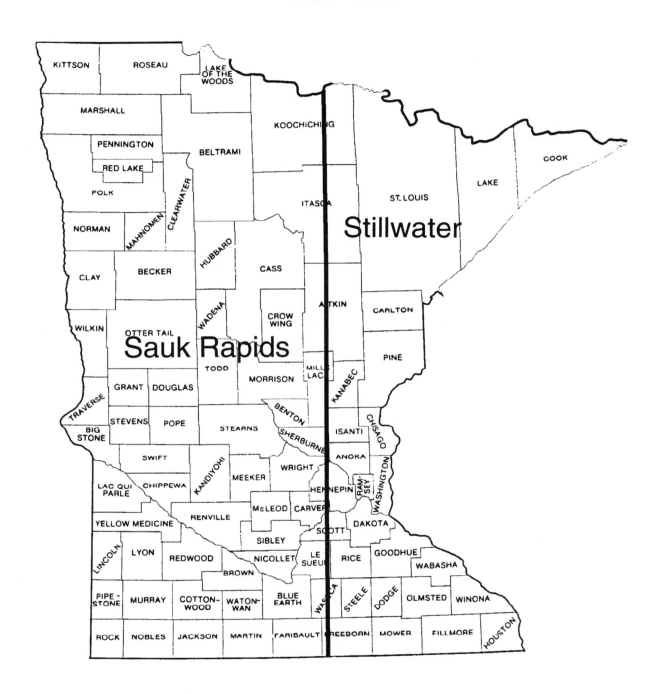

The Sauk Rapids land office opened 2 November 1852.

Minnesota 3
1854–1856

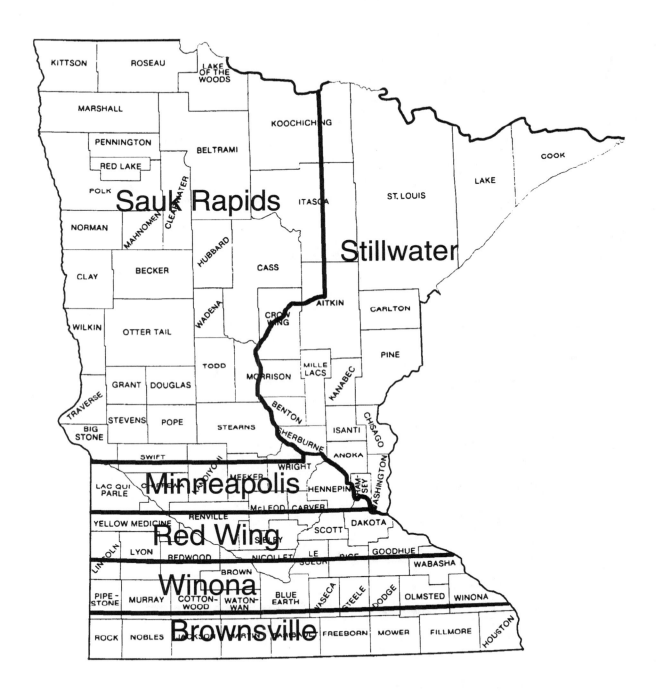

The Minneapolis land office opened 13 June 1854.
The Red Wing land office opened August 1854.
The Winona land office opened 12 April 1854.
The Brownsville land office opened 27 June 1854.

Minnesota 4
1856–1858

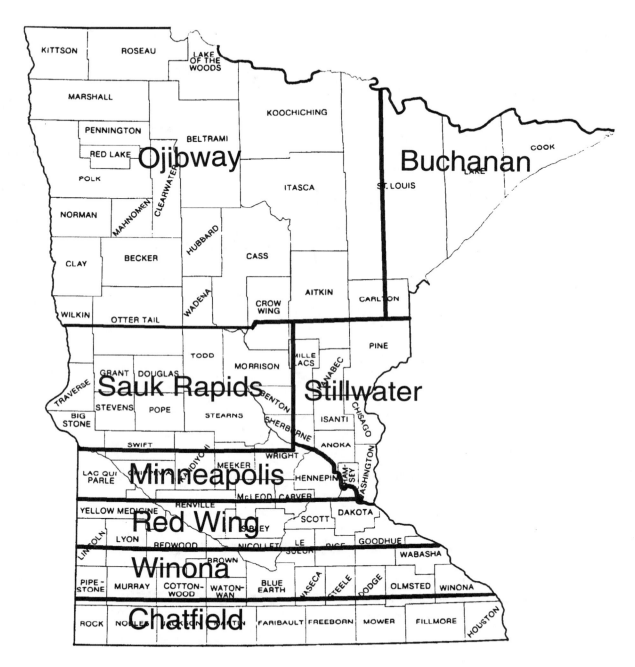

The Ojibway land office opened 29 September 1856.
The Buchanan land office opened 6 October 1856.
The Red Wing land office moved to Henderson 30 April 1857.
The Winona land office moved to Faribault 1 January 1857.
The Brownsville land office moved to Chatfield 12 June 1856.

Minnesota 5
1858–1863

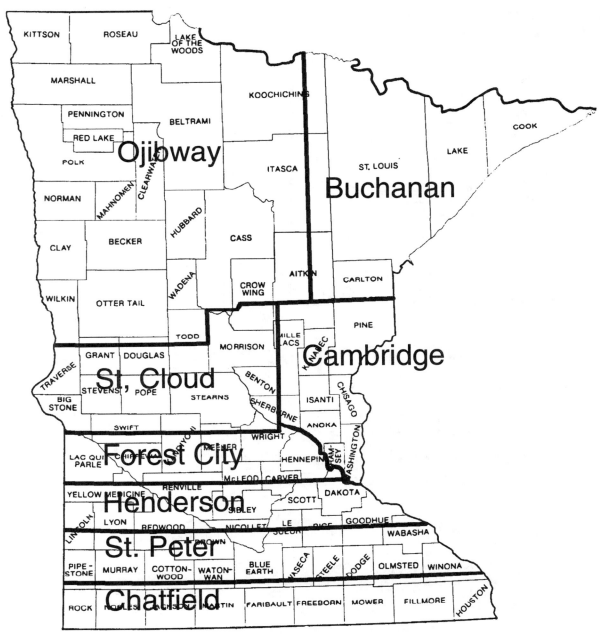

The Ojibway land office moved to Otter Tail City 25 July 1859.

The Buchanan land office moved to Portland 7 July 1859.

The Stillwater land office moved to Cambridge 15 December 1858, to Sunrise City 2 July 1860, then to Taylors Falls 1 October 1861.

The Sauk Rapids land office moved to St. Cloud 19 April 1858.

The Minneapolis land office moved to Forest City 28 March 1858, then back to Minneapolis 1 November 1862.

The Faribault land office moved to St. Peter 23 September 1858.

The Chatfield land office moved to Winnebago City 4 November 1861.

Minnesota 6
1863–1868

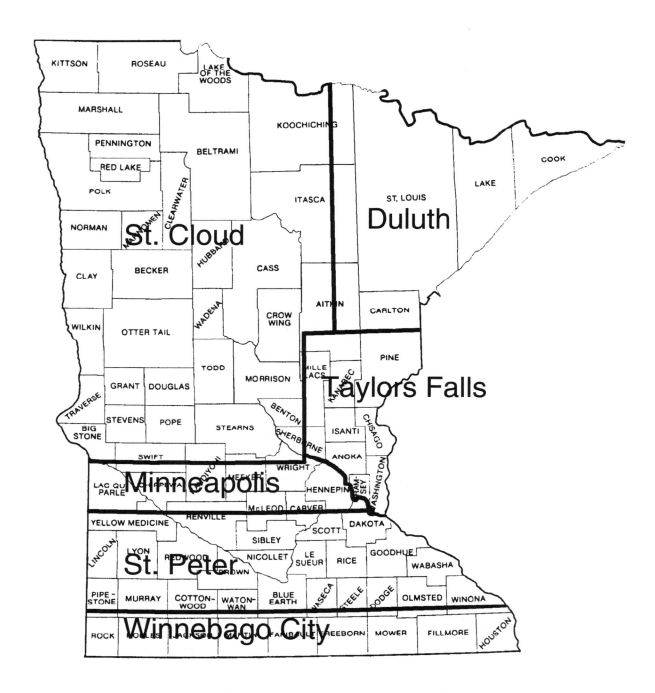

The Otter Tail City land office merged with St. Cloud 17 August 1863.
The Portland land office moved to Duluth 15 January 1863.
The Minneapolis land office moved to Greenleaf 3 July 1866.
The Henderson land office merged with St. Peter 15 May 1863.

Minnesota 7
1868–1871

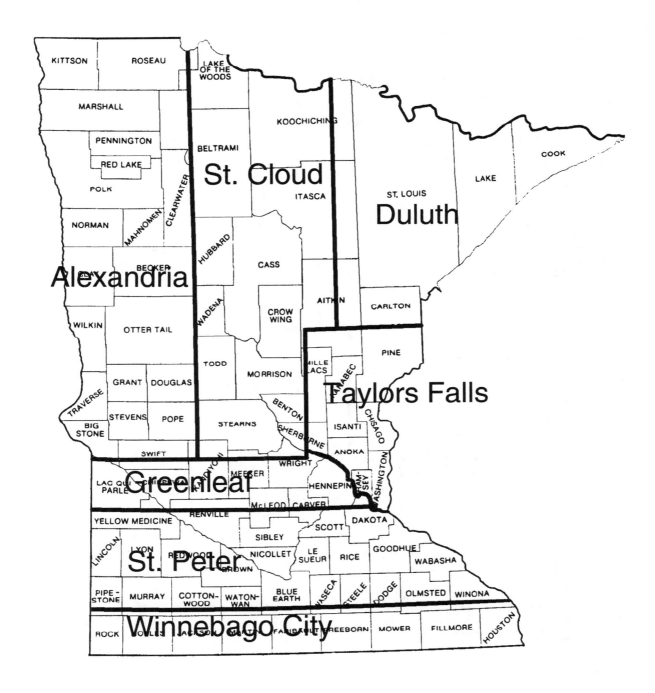

The Alexandria land office opened 4 September 1868.
The Greenleaf land office moved to Litchfield 27 January 1870.
The St. Peter land office moved to New Ulm 17 March 1870.
The Winnebago City land office moved to Jackson 1 September 1869.

Minnesota 8
1871–1872

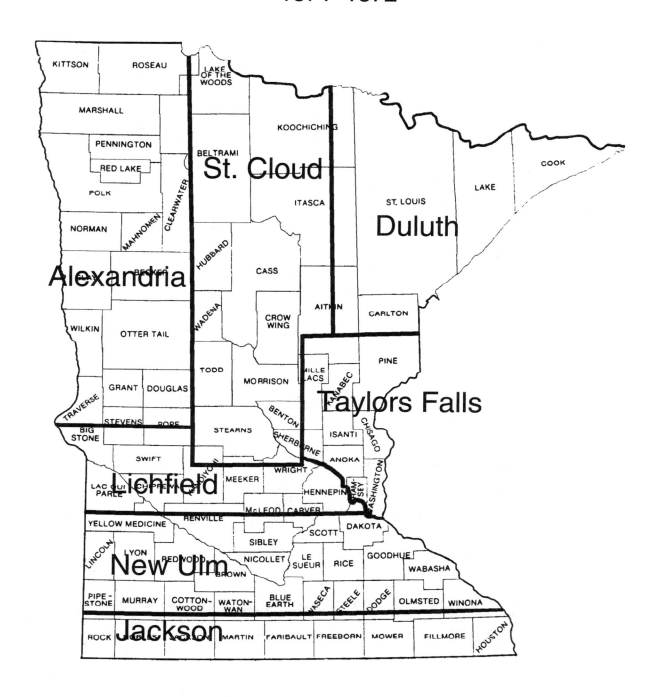

The Litchfield land office expanded through an executive order of 25 August 1871.

Minnesota 9
1872–1889

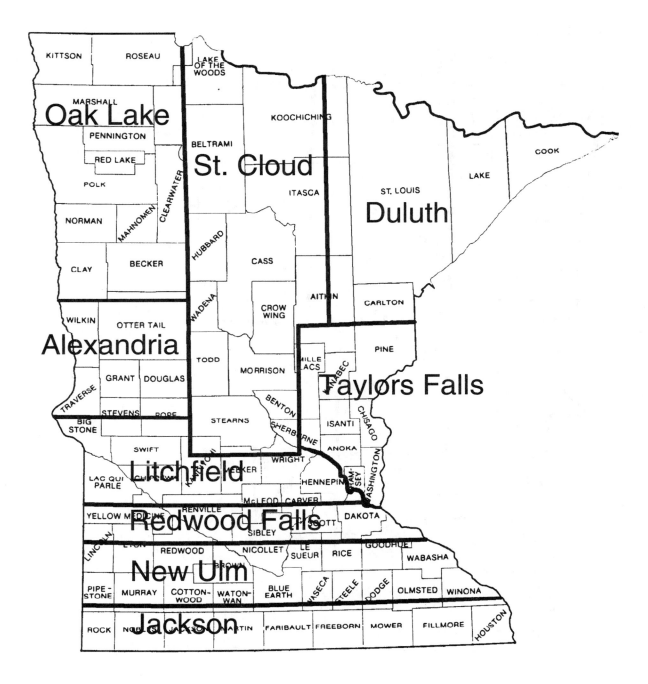

The Oak Lake land office opened through an Act of 12 March 1872, then moved to Detroit 1
   November 1873, then to Crookston 15 July 1878.

The Alexandria land office moved to Fergus Falls 11 December 1876.

The Litchfield land office moved to Benson 19 June 1876.

The Redwood Falls land office opened through an Act of 21 May 1872.

The New Ulm land office moved to Tracy 18 May 1880.

The Jackson land office moved to Worthington 20 April 1874.

Minnesota 10
1889–1891

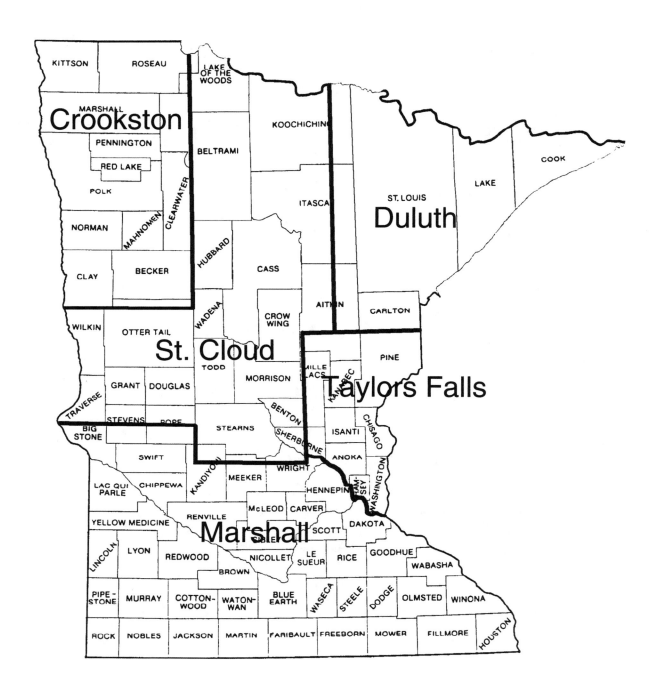

The Fergus Falls land office merged with St. Cloud 19 February 1889.
The Benson land office merged with Tracy 19 February 1889.
The Redwood Falls land office merged with Tracy 19 February 1889.
The Worthington land office merged with Tracy 19 February 1889.
The Tracy land office moved to Marshall 21 February 1889.

Minnesota 11
1891–1893

The Duluth land office expanded through an executive order of 27 February 1891.

Minnesota 12
1893–1896

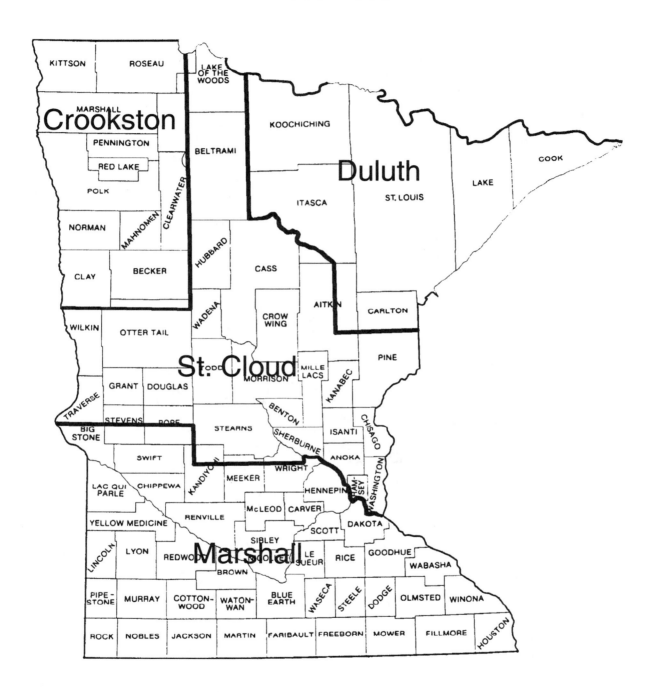

The Taylors Falls land office merged with St. Cloud 11 September 1893.

Minnesota 13
1896–1903

The Crookston land office expanded through an executive order of 16 January 1896.

Minnesota 14
1903–1904

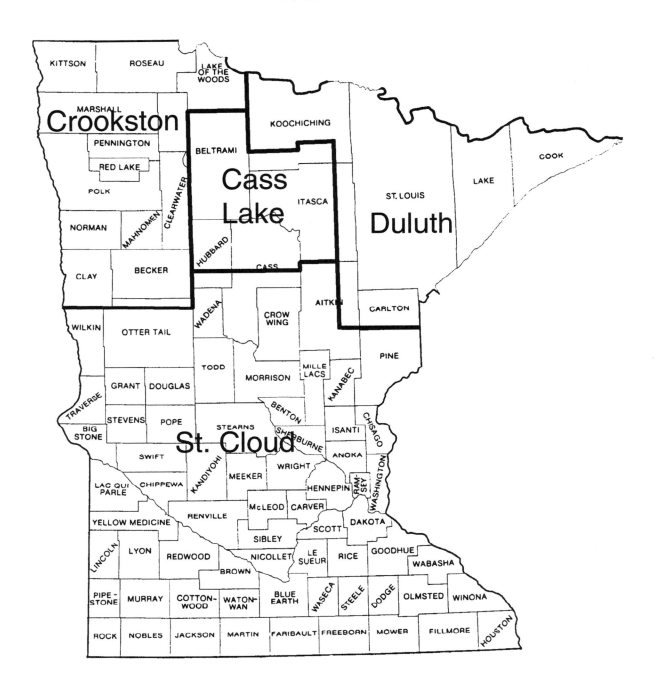

The Marshall land office merged with St. Cloud 1 July 1903.
The Cass lake land office opened 30 June 1903.

Minnesota 15
1904–1906

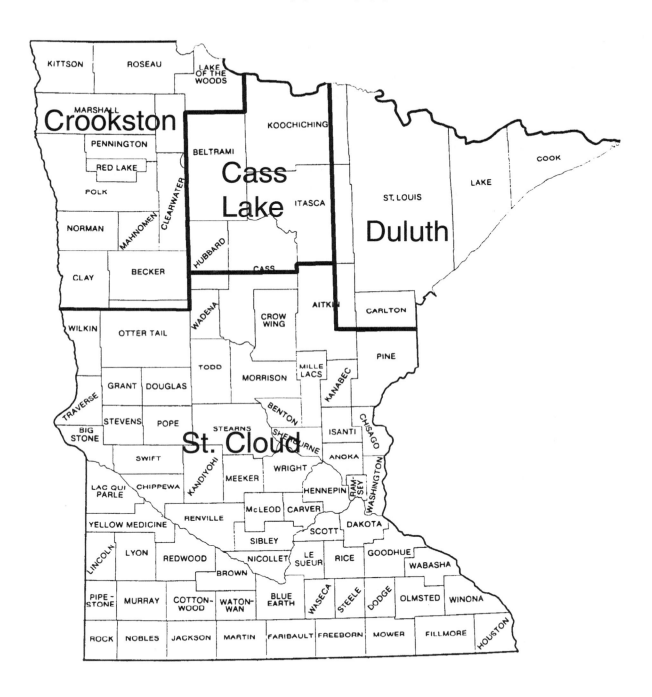

The Cass Lake land office expanded 1 December 1904.

Minnesota 16
1906–1919

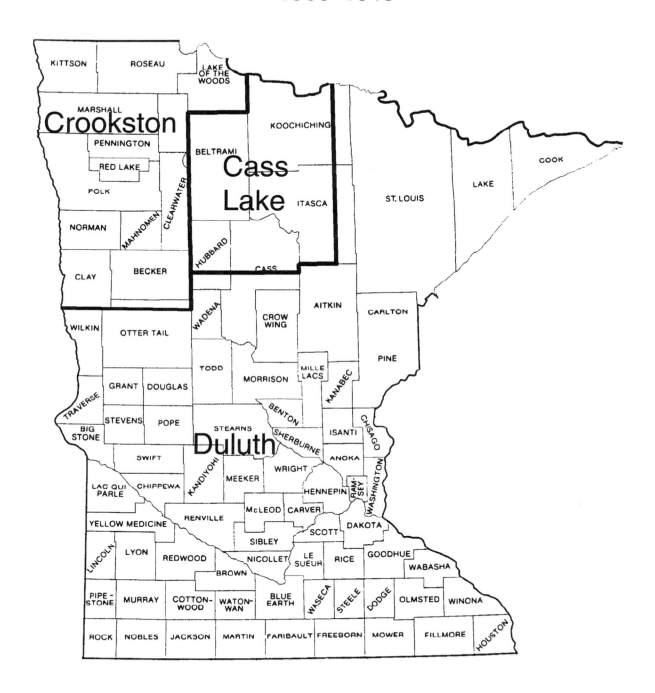

The St. Cloud land office merged with Duluth 17 December 1906.

Mississippi 1
1806–1817

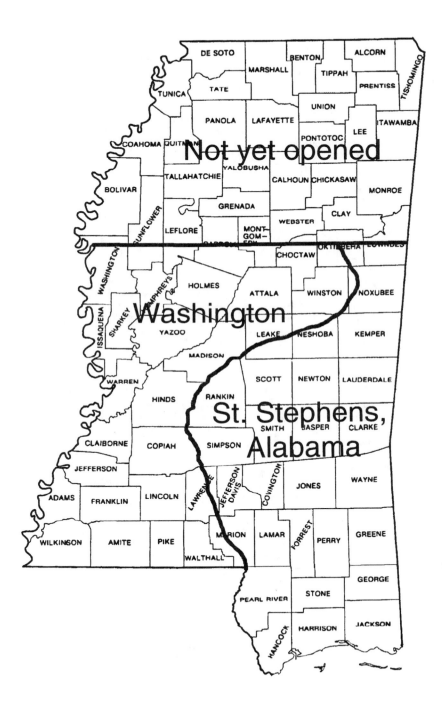

The Washington land office opened 15 November 1806.

The St. Stephens, Alabama, land office opened 26 December 1806. The Mississippi portion of St. Stephens moved to Augusta 25 April 1812, though it was temporarily administered from the Jackson Courthouse.

Mississippi 2
1817–1819

The Madison land office opened through acts of 1815 and 1817.
The Augusta land office continued to be administered from Jackson Courthouse.

Mississippi 3
1819–1827

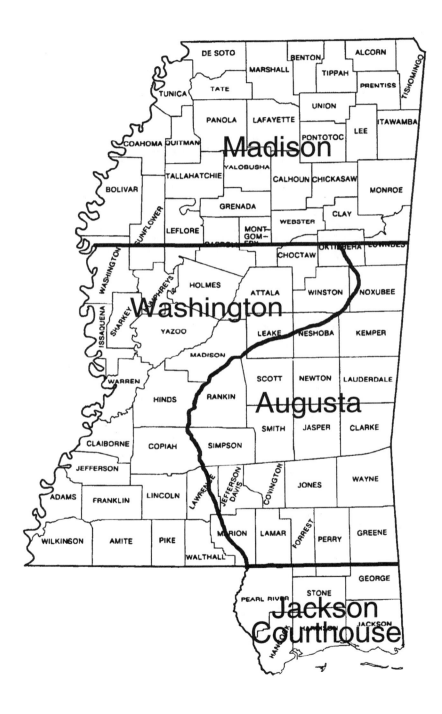

The Jackson Courthouse land office began administering its own jurisdiction 18 May 1819, but it was soon removed to Augusta.

The Augusta land office officially opened March 1820.

Mississippi 4
1827–1833

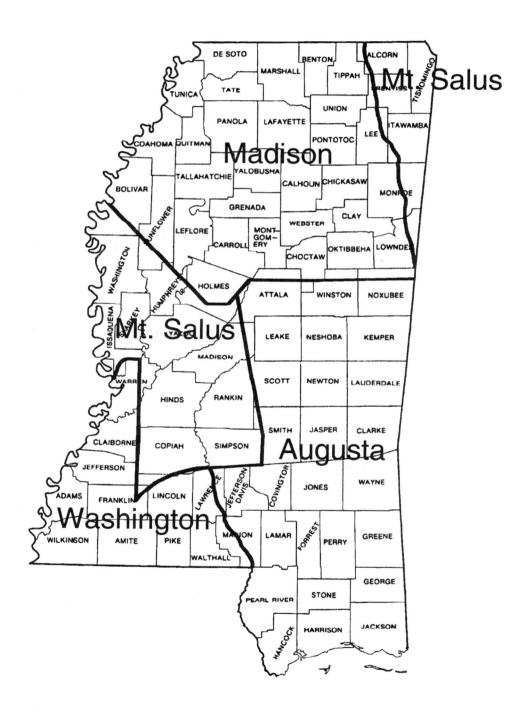

The Mt. Salus land office opened 6 June 1827 and moved to Jackson (not Jackson Courthouse) 22 May 1832. The northeast corner of the state was also administered by Mt. Salus for a brief period.

Mississippi 5
1833–1839

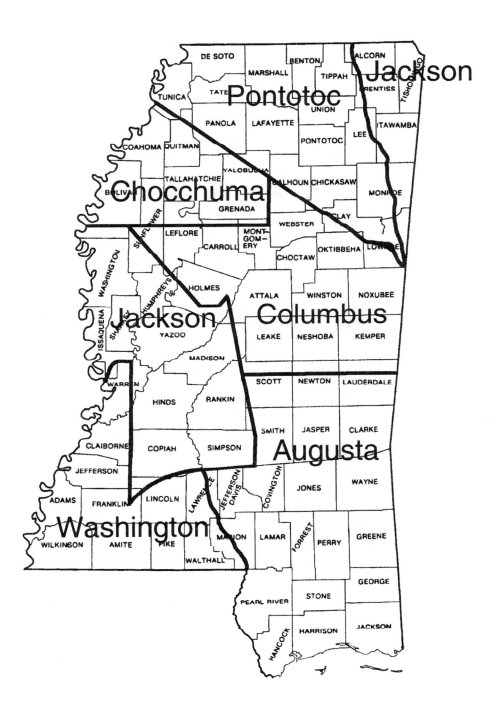

The Chocchuma land office opened 22 October 1833.

The Columbus land office opened 12 July 1833.

The Pontotoc land office was established by a treaty of 20 October 1832, though the first entry
was not made until September 1836.

Mississippi 6
1839–1860

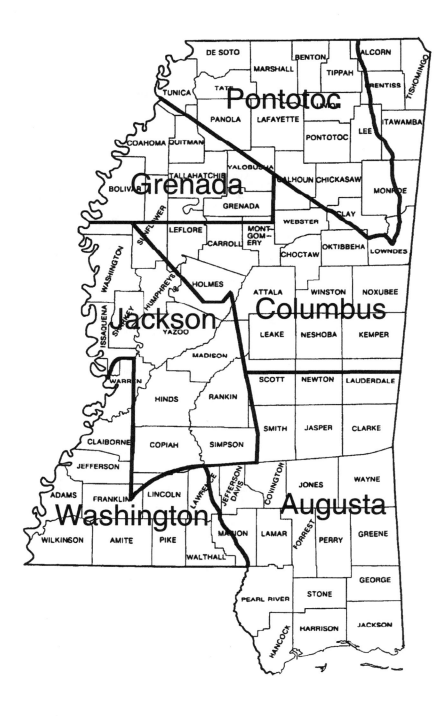

The northeast corner of the state, administered by Jackson, merged with Columbus May 1839.
The Pontotoc land office was officially closed from 1853 to 1861, when it merged with Jackson.
The Chocchuma land office moved to Grenada through an Act of 4 July 1840.

Mississippi 7
1860–1861

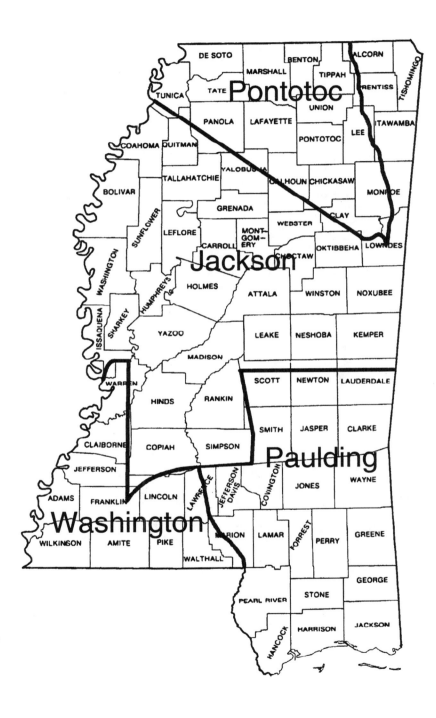

The Augusta land office moved to Paulding 2 January 1860.
The Columbus land office merged with Jackson in the fourth quarter of 1860.
The Grenada land office merged with Jackson 12 September 1860.

Mississippi 8
1861–1866

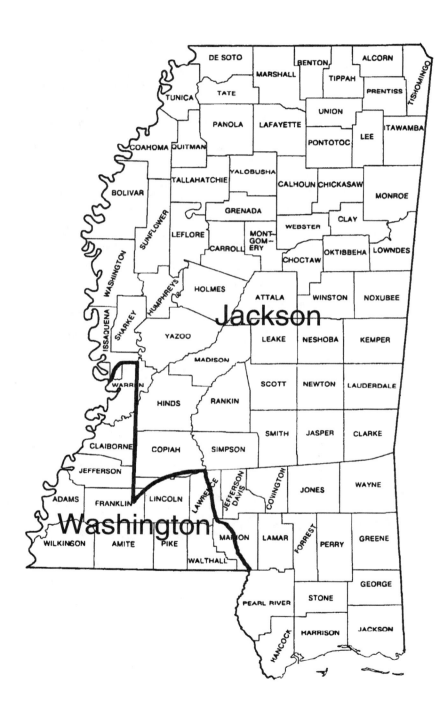

The Paulding land office merged with Jackson in the first quarter of 1861.
The Pontotoc land office, closed since 1853, merged with Jackson in 1861.

Mississippi 9
1866–

The Washington land office merged with Jackson in 1866.

Missouri 1
1818–1824

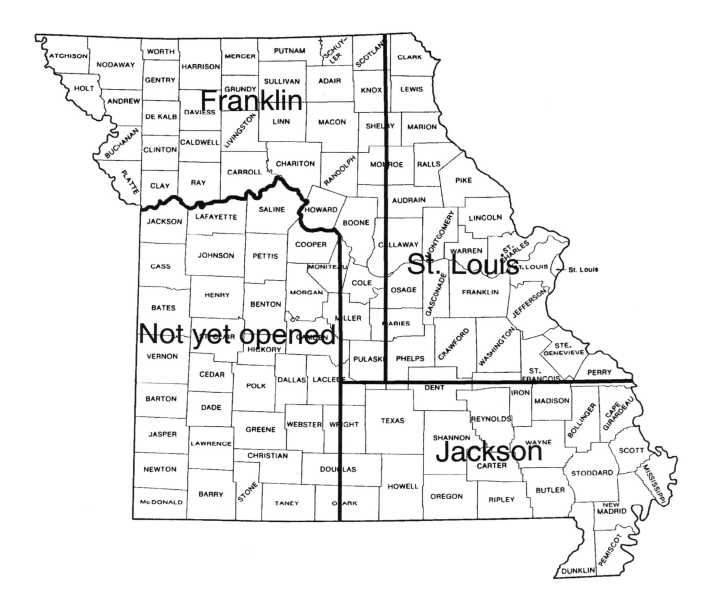

The Franklin land office opened 2 November 1818.

The St. Louis land office opened August 1818.

The Jackson land office opened through an act of 17 February 1818. The first entry is dated 29 May 1821.

Missouri 2
1824–1825

The Lexington land office opened 17 May 1824.

Missouri 3
1825–1826

The Palmyra land office opened 31 January 1825.

Missouri 4
1826–1835

The Jackson land office expanded throgh an Act of 4 May 1826.
The Franklin land office moved to Fayette 5 July 1832.

Missouri 5
1835–1843

The Springfield land office opened 13 June 1835.

Missouri 6
1843–1849

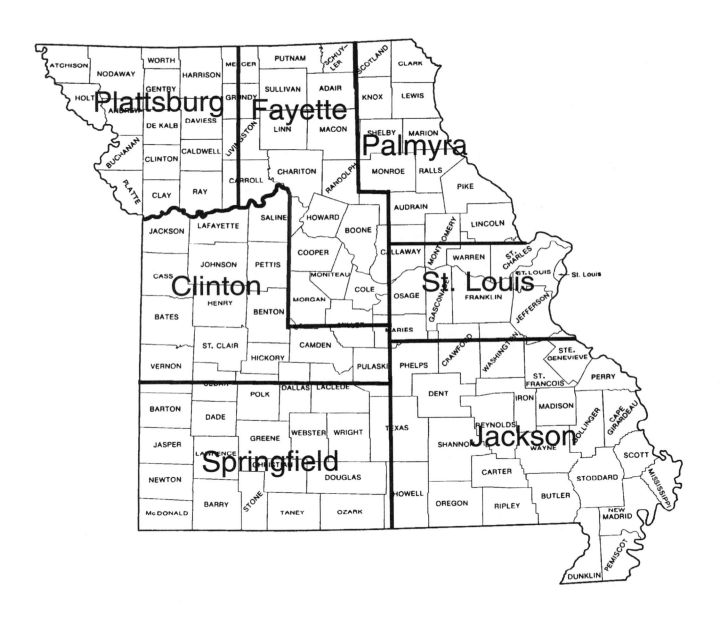

The Plattsburg land office opened 15 May 1843.
The Lexington land office moved to Clinton 3 July 1843.

Missouri 7
1849–1858

The Milan land office opened 24 April 1849.

The Clinton land office moved to Warsaw 18 July 1855.

The Fayette land office moved to Boonville 18 May 1857.

Missouri 8
1858–1859

The Palmyra land office merged with Boonville through an executive order of 24 August 1858.

Missouri 9
1859–1861

The Plattsburg land office merged with Boonville 31 March 1859.
The Milan land office merged with Boonville 31 March 1859.

Missouri 10
1861–1863

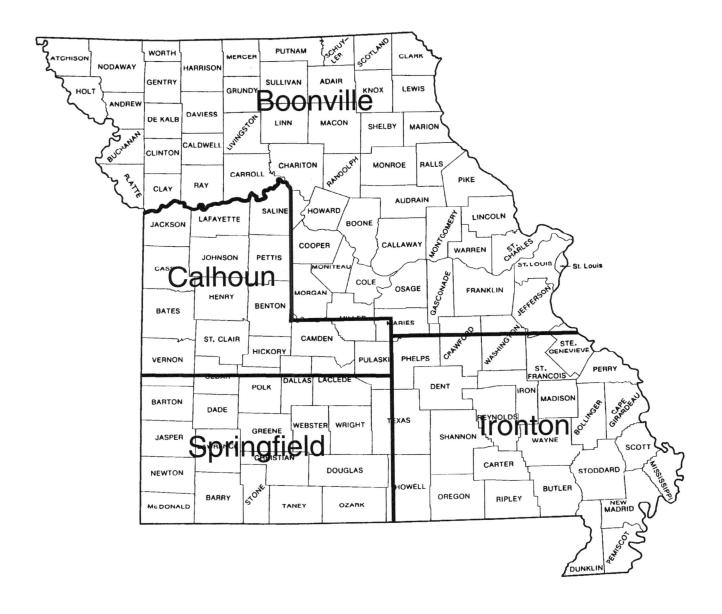

The Warsaw land office moved to Calhoun through an executive order of 26 July 1861.
The St. Louis land office merged with Boonville 1 September 1861.
The Jackson land office moved to Ironton 8 July 1861.

Missouri 11
1863–1866

The Springfield land office merged with Boonville through an executive order of
25 March 1863.

The Calhoun land office merged with Boonville through an executive order of
12 February 1863.

Missouri 12
1866–1905

The Springfield land office was restored through an executive order of 19 May 1866.

Missouri 13
1905–1919

The Boonville land office merged with Springfield 30 June 1905.
The Ironton land office merged with Springfield 30 June 1905.

Montana 1
1867–1874

The Helena land office opened through an Act of 1867.

Montana 2
1874–1880

The Bozeman land office opened 5 October 1874.

Montana 3
1880–1890

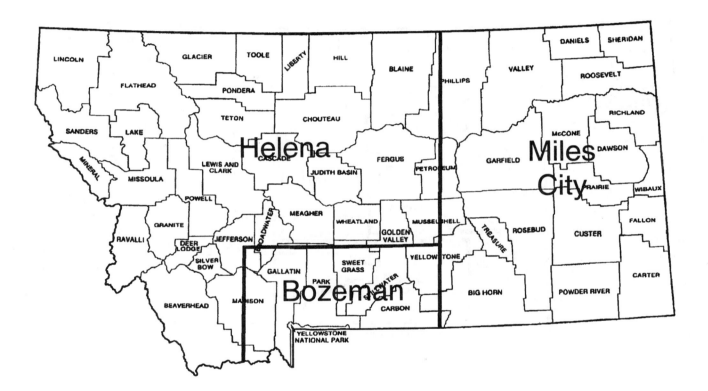

The Miles City land office opened 19 October 1880.

Montana 4
1890–1897

The Lewiston land office opened 26 November 1890.
The Missoula land office opened 20 April 1891.

Montana 5
1897–1902

The Kalispell land office opened 1 July 1897.

Montana 6
1902–1906

The Great Falls land office opened 1 August 1902.

Nebraska 1
1854–1868

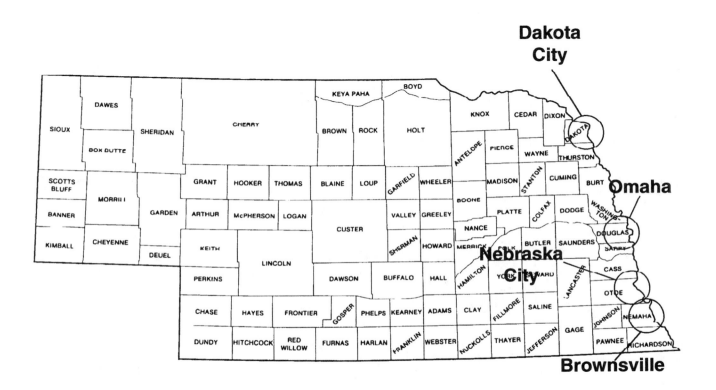

The Omaha City land office opened in 1854.
The Brownsville land office opened in 1857.
The Nebraska City land office opened in 1857.
The Dakota City land office opened in 1857.

Nebraska 2
1868–1872

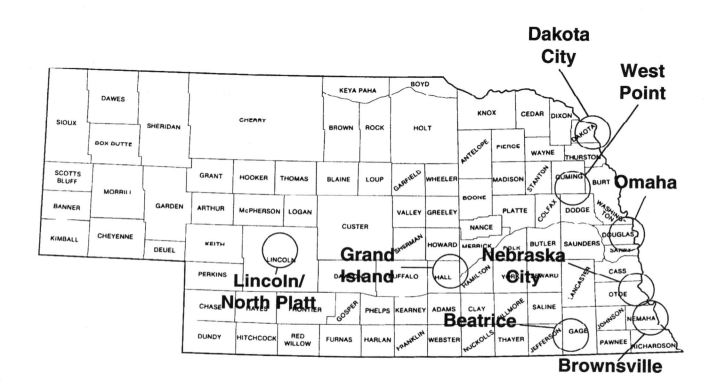

The Beatrice land office opened in 1868.
The Lincoln land office opened in 1868.
The Grand Island land office opened in 1868.
The West Point land office opened in 1869.

Nebraska 3
1872–1881

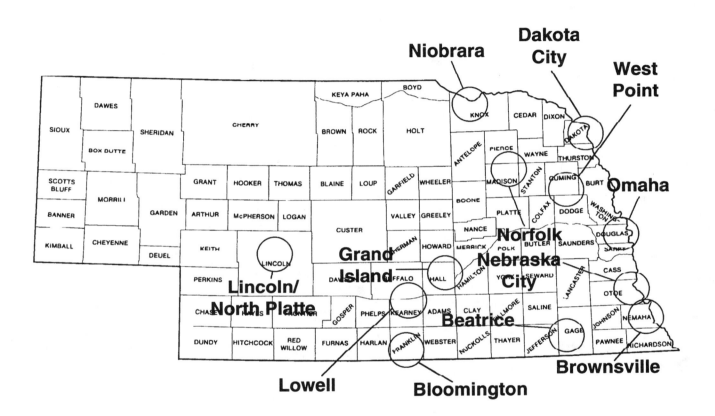

The Lowell land office opened in 1872.
The North Platte land office opened in 1872.
The Norfolk land office opened in 1873.
The Bloomington land office opened in 1874.
The Niobrara land office opened in 1875.

Nebraska 4
1881–1886

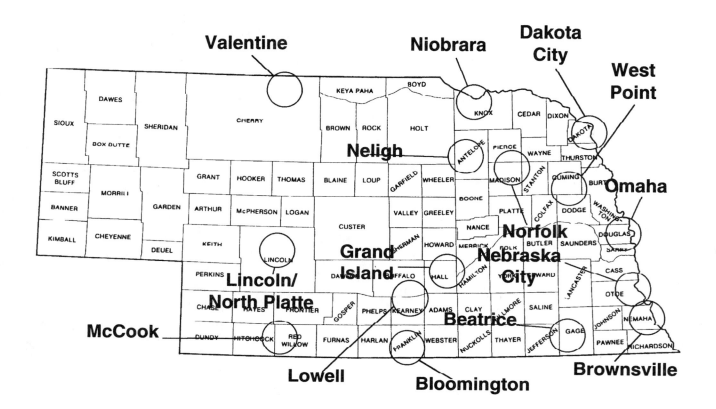

The Neligh land office opened in 1881.
The Valentine land office opened in 1882.
The McCook land office opened in 1882.

Nebraska 5
1886–1890

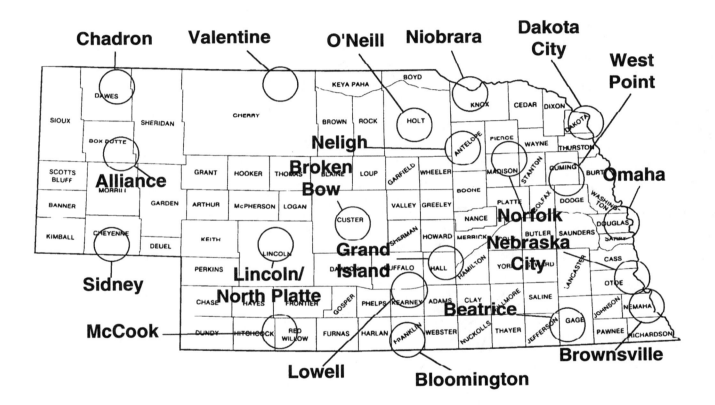

The Sidney land office opened in 1886.
The Chadron land office opened in 1886.
The O'Neill land office opened in 1888.
The Alliance land office opened in 1890.
The Broken Bow land office opened in 1890.

Nevada 1
1862–1867

Carson City

The Carson City land office opened in 1862.

Nevada 2
1867–1872

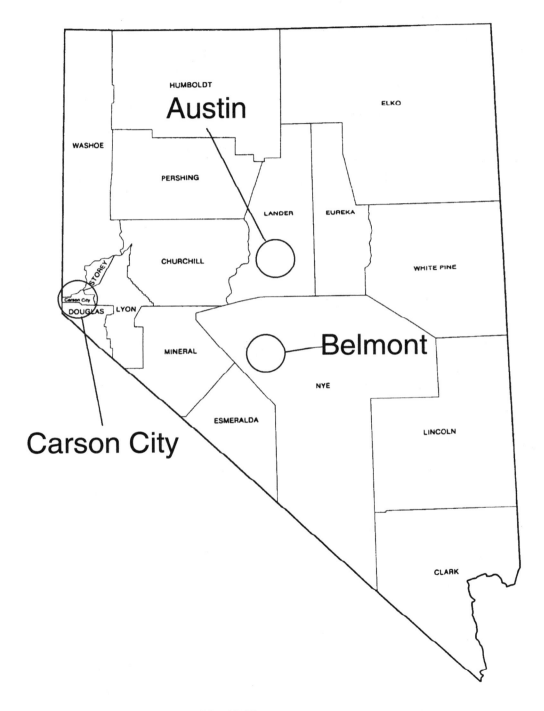

The Austin land office opened in 1867.
The Belmont land office opened in 1868.

Nevada 3
1872–1911

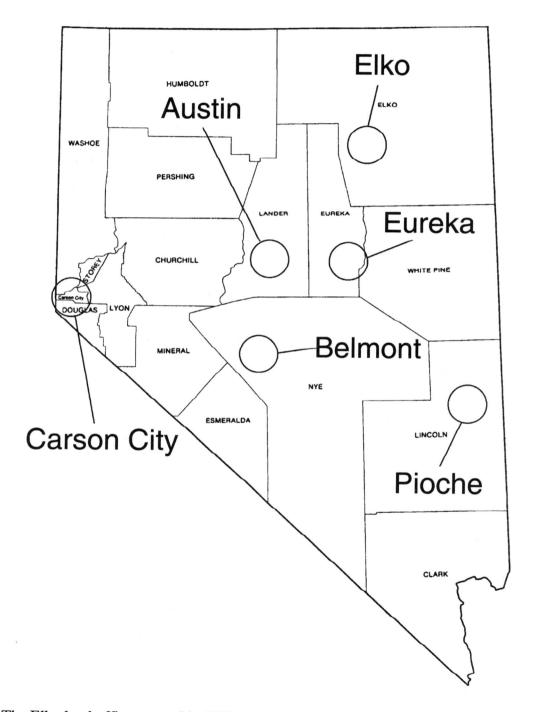

The Elko land office opened in 1872.
The Eureka land office opened in 1873.
The Pioche land office opened in 1874.

New Mexico 1
1858–1875

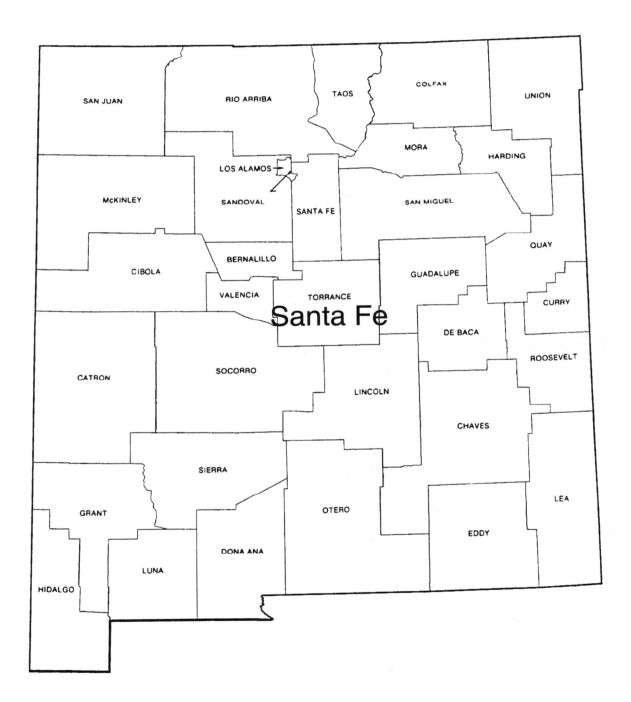

The Santa Fe land office opened in 1858.

New Mexico 2
1875–1889

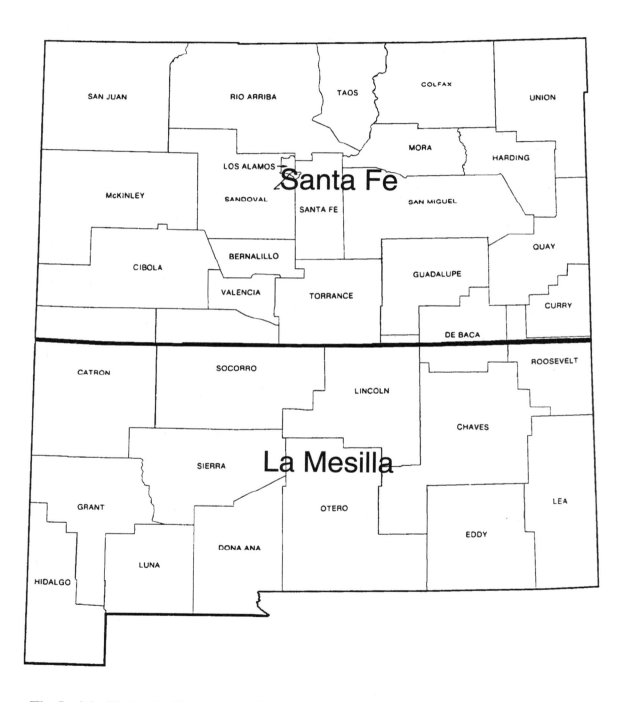

The La Mesilla land office opened through an Act of 9 August 1875, then moved to
Las Cruces 1 May 1883.

New Mexico 3
1889–

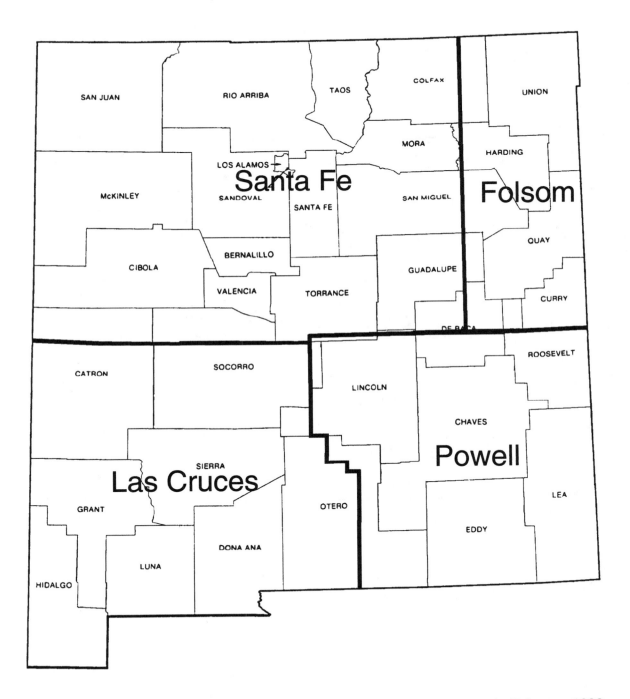

The Folsom land office opened in August 1889, then moved to Clayton in February 1892.
The Rozwell land office opened 9 December 1889.

North Dakota 1
1861–1870

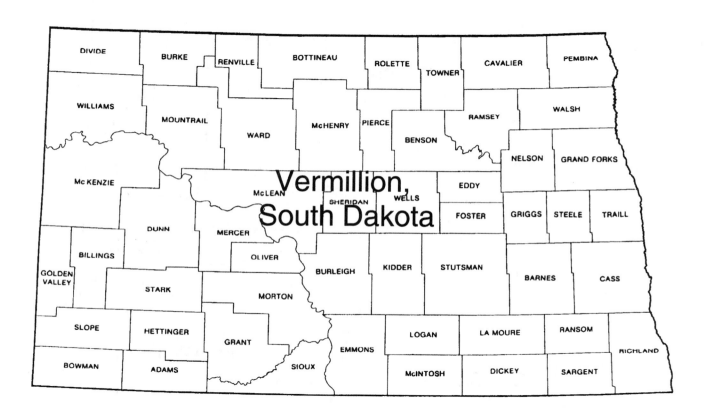

The Vermillion land office, in present-day South Dakota, opened 2 March 1861.

North Dakota 2
1870–1874

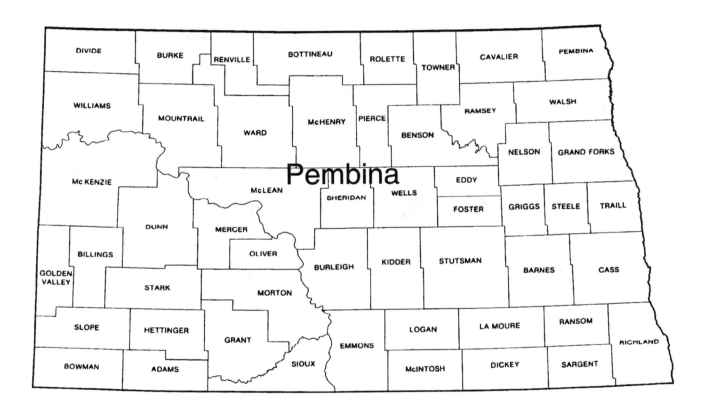

The Pembina land office opened 1 December 1870.

North Dakota 3
1874–1880

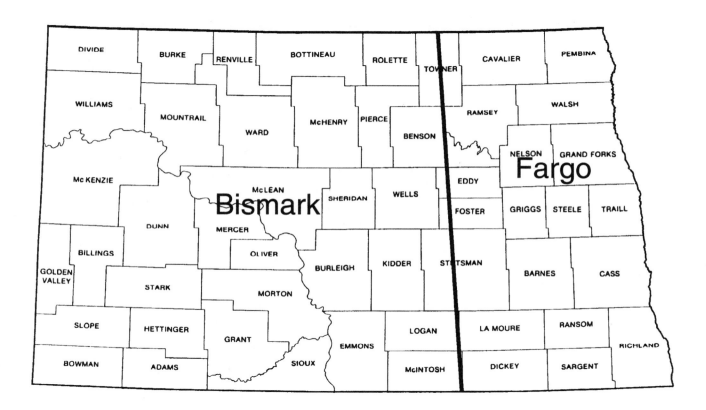

The Bismark land office opened 12 October 1874.
The Fargo land office opened 1 September 1874.

North Dakota 4
1880–1883

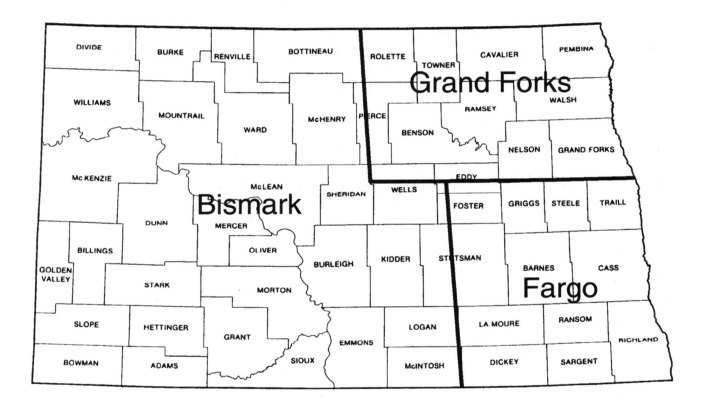

The Grand Foks land office opened 20 April 1880.

The southern-most one and one-half townships in Emmons, McIntosh, Dickey, Sargent,
and Richland counties were moved to the Watertown, South Dakota, land office in April 1879.
Emmons and McIntosh counties then moved to the Aberdeen, South Dakota, land office when
it opened 2 October 1882.

North Dakota 5
1883–1891

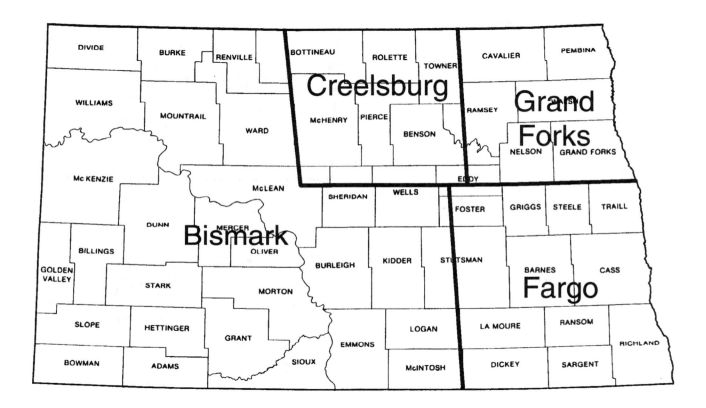

The Creelsburg land office opened 24 August 1883, then moved to Devil's Lake
  17 January 1884.

The southern-most one and one-half townships in Emmons, McIntosh, Dickey, Sargent, and
  Richland counties were moved to the Watertown, South Dakota, land office in April 1879.
  Emmons and McIntosh counties then moved to the Aberdeen, South Dakota, land office
  when it opened 2 October 1882. They moved to their respective North Dakota land offices
  in December 1889.

North Dakota 6
1891–1904

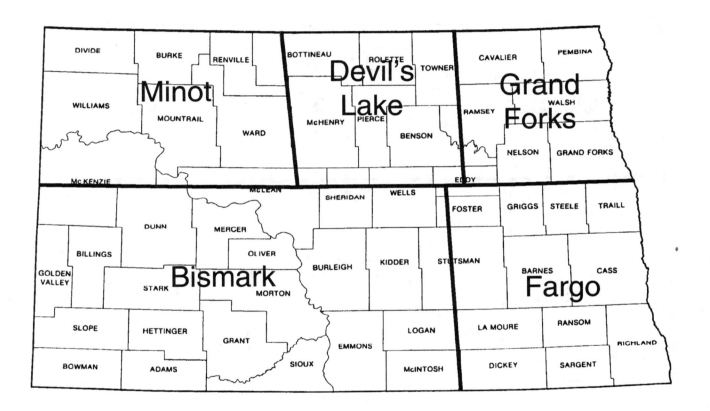

The Minot land office opened 1 October 1891.

North Dakota 7
1904–1906

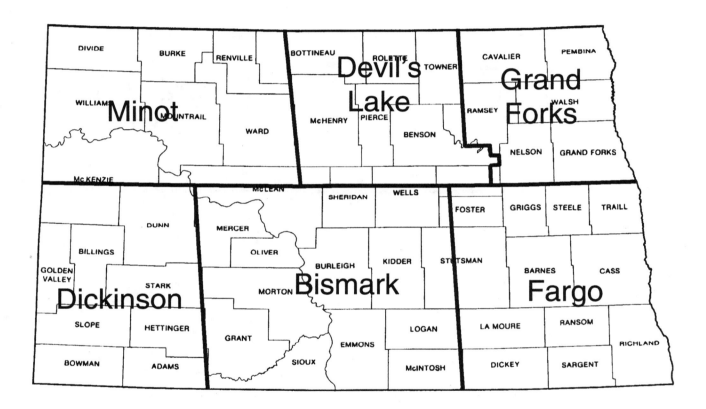

The Dickinson land office opened 21 July 1904.
Portions of the Grand Forks land office merged with Devil's Lake 1 August 1904.

North Dakota 8
1906–1908

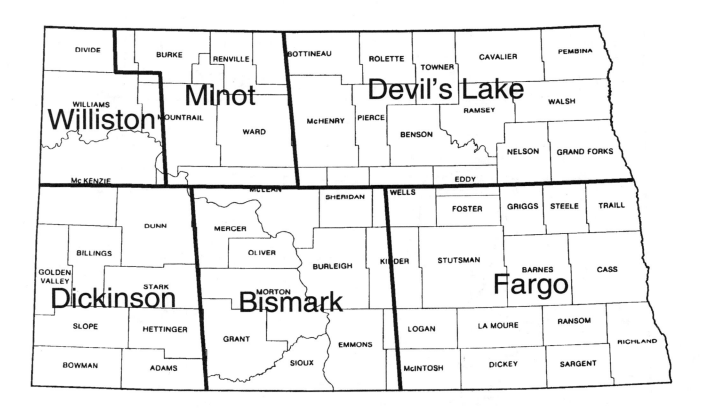

The Williston land office opened 1 August 1906.
The Fargo land office expanded 2 July 1906.

Ohio 1
Pre-Land Office
1784–1792

The Connecticut Western Reseerve opened in 1786.
The First Seven Ranges opened in 1786.
The Virginia Military District opened in 1784.
The Ohio Company's first purchase occurred in 1787.

Ohio 2
Pre-Land Office
1792–1795

The Firelands opened in 1792.

The Ohio Company's second purchase occurred in 1792.

The Symmes Purchase occurred in 1794.

Other small but significant tracts also were generated. For more information, see
  Thomas Aquinas Burke's *Ohio Lands, A Short History.*

Ohio 3
Pre-Land Office
1795–1798

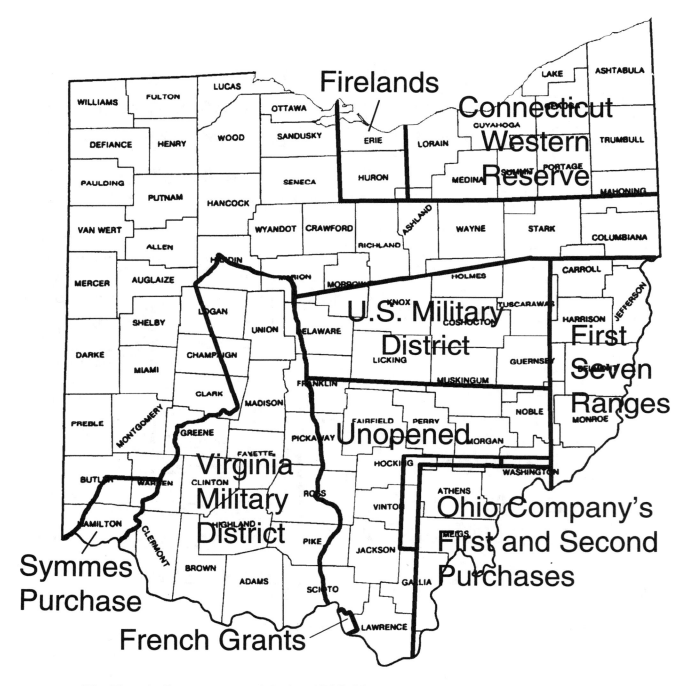

Firelands

Connecticut
Western
Reserve

U.S. Military
District

First
Seven
Ranges

Unopened

Virginia
Military
District

Ohio Company's
First and Second
Purchases

Symmes
Purchase

French Grants

The French Grants occurred during 1795–98.

Other small but significant tracts also were generated. For more information, see
Thomas Aquinas Burke's *Ohio Lands, A Short History.*

Ohio 4
Pre-Land Office
1798–1800

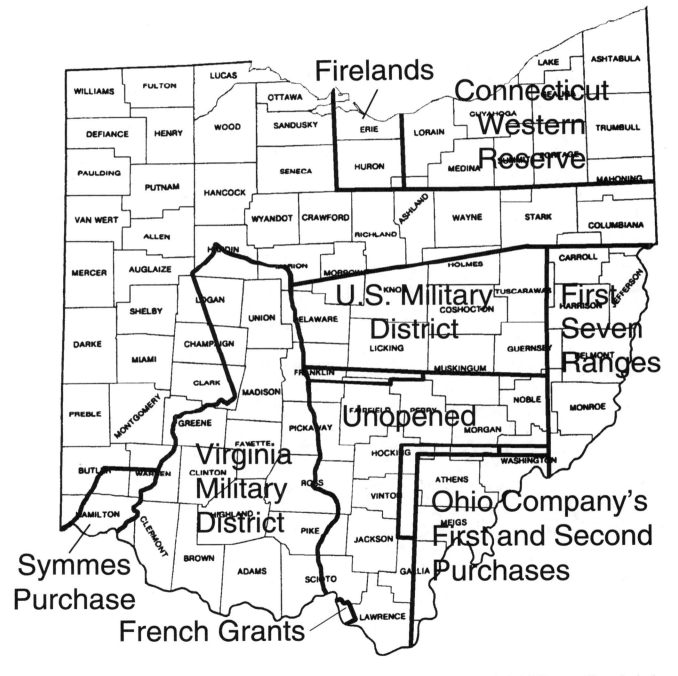

The Refugee Tract opened in 1798 and continued to 1816; it is the small tract directly below the U.S. Military District.

Other small but significant tracts also were generated. For more information, see Thomas Aquinas Burke's *Ohio Lands, A Short History*.

Ohio 5
1800–1804

The Steubenville land office opened 1 July 1800.
The Cincinnati land office opened 6 April 1801.
The Chillicothe land office opened 1 May 1801.
The Marietta land office opened 26 December 1800.

Ohio 6
1804–1808

The U.S. Military District began to be administered by the Zanesville and Chillicothe land
offices through an Act of 3 March 1803.

The Zanesville land office opened in May 1804.

Ohio 7
1808–1820

The Canton land office opened 9 May 1808 and moved to Wooster 1 May 1816.

Ohio 8
1820–1837

The Piqua land office opened 1 July 1820, then moved to Wappakonnetta 2 April 1833, then to Lima 6 July 1835.

The Delaware land office opened 1 July 1820, then moved to Tiffin before 1835, then to Bucyrus 1 May 1835.

Ohio 9
1837–1840

The Marion land office opened 10 April 1837.

Ohio 10
1840–1845

The Wooster land office merged with Lima through an Act of 12 June 1840.
The Bucyrus land office merged with Lima through an Act of 12 June 1840.
The Steubenville land office merged with Chillicothe through an Act of 12 June 1840.
The Marietta land office merged with Chillicothe through an Act of 12 June 1840.
The Zanesville land office merged with Chillicothe through an Act of 12 June 1840.
The Cincinnati land office merged with Chillicothe through an Act of 12 Jun 1840.
The Lima land office moved to Upper Sandusky 2 June 1843.

Ohio 11
1845–1852

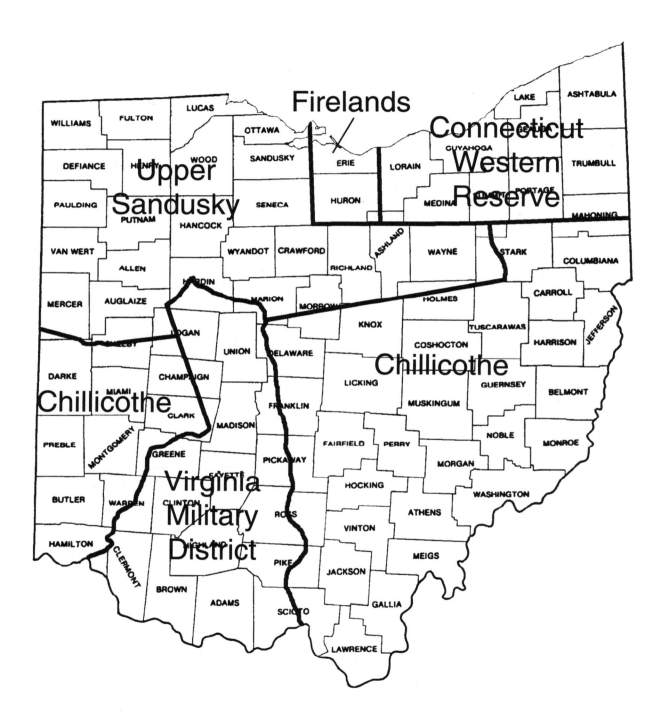

The Upper Sandusky land office moved to Defiance 31 May 1848.

Ohio 12
1852–1855

The Virginia Military District ceded its remaining lands to the U.S. government, being placed under the jurisdiction of Chillicothe in 1852.

Ohio 13
1855–1876

The Defiance land office merged with Chillicothe through an executive order of 15 June 1855.

Oklahoma 1
1889–1893

The Guthrie land office opened in 1889.
The Kingfisher land office opened in 1889.
The Oklahoma City land office opened in 1890.
The Beaver land office opened in 1891.

Oklahoma 2
1893–1897

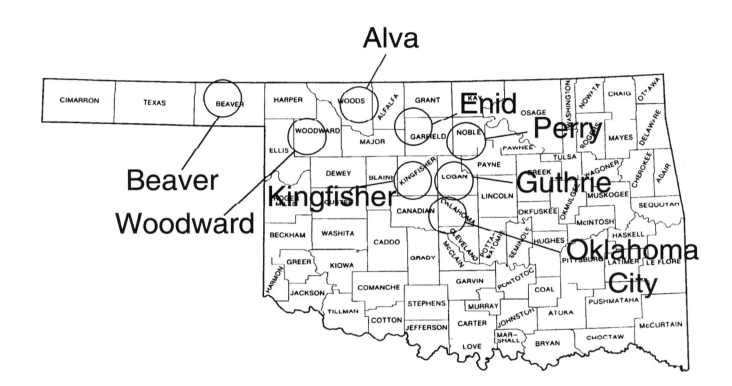

The Alva land office opened in 1893.
The Enid land office opened in 1893.
The Perry land office opened in 1893.
The Woodward land office opened in 1893.

Oklahoma 3
1897–1901

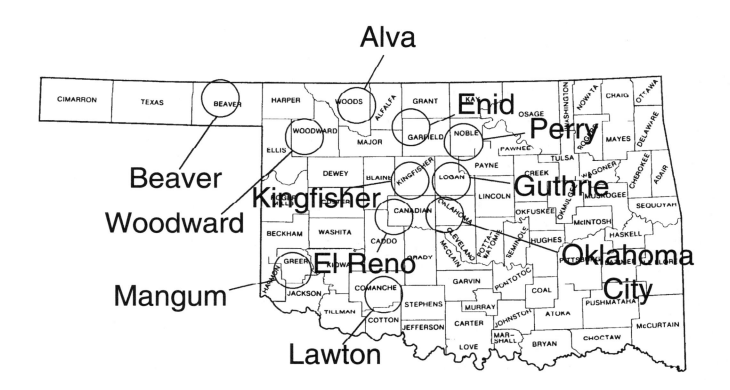

The Mangum land office opened in 1897.
The El Reno land office opened in 1901.
The Lawton land office opened in 1901.

Oregon 1
1854–1866

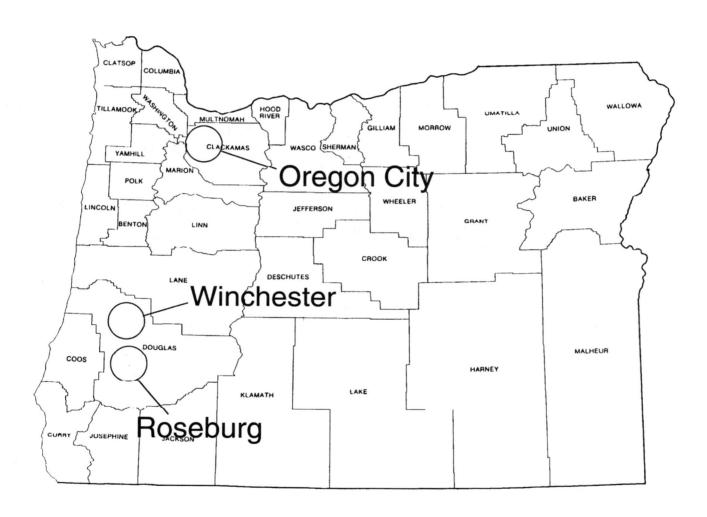

The Oregon City land office opened in 1854.
The Winchester land office opened in 1855.
The Roseburg land office opened in 1855.

Oregon 2
1866–1888

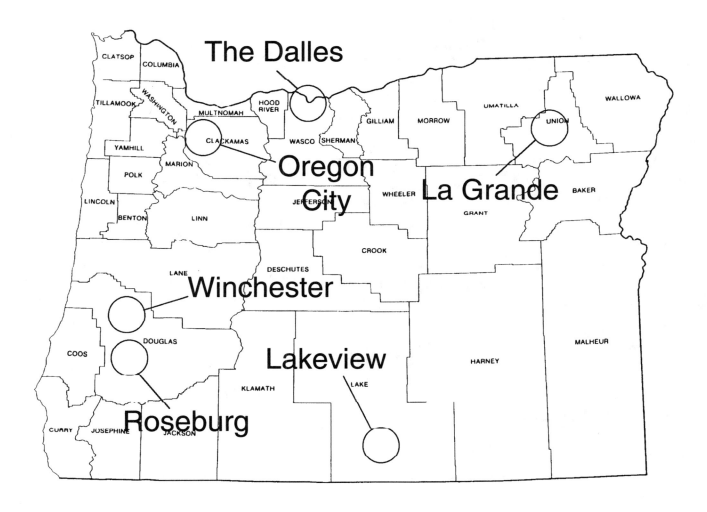

The La Grande land office opened in 1866.
The Linkville land office opened in 1872.
The Dalles land office opened in 1875.
The Lakeview land office opened in 1877.

Oregon 3
1888–1910

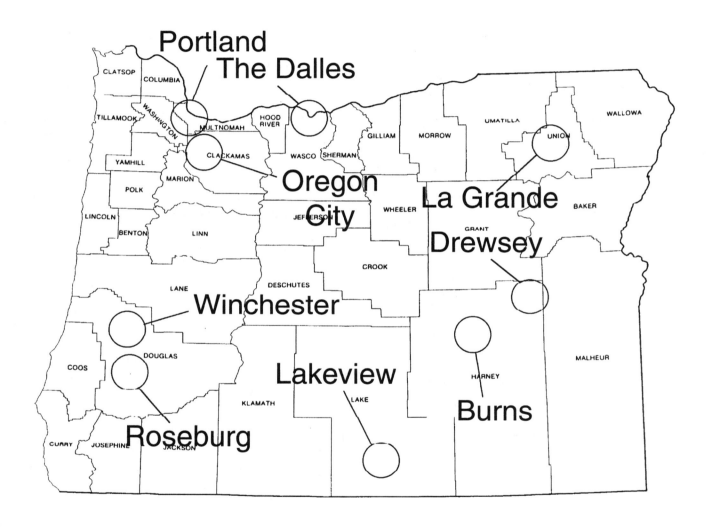

The Burns land office opened in 1888.
The Drewsey land office opened in 1888.
The Portland land office opened in 1905.

South Dakota 1
1861–1870

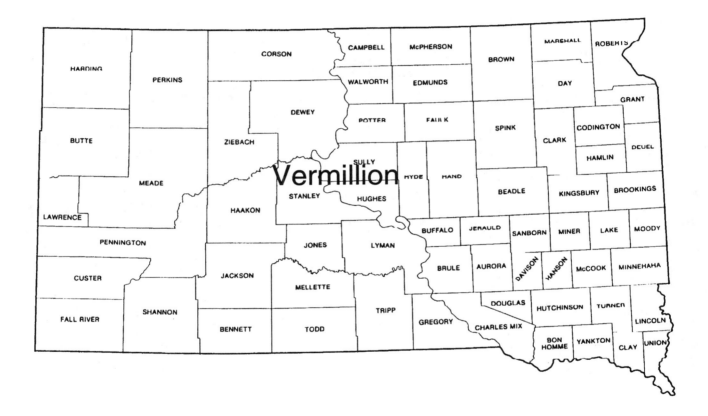

The Vermillion land office opened 2 March 1861.

South Dakota 2
1870–1872

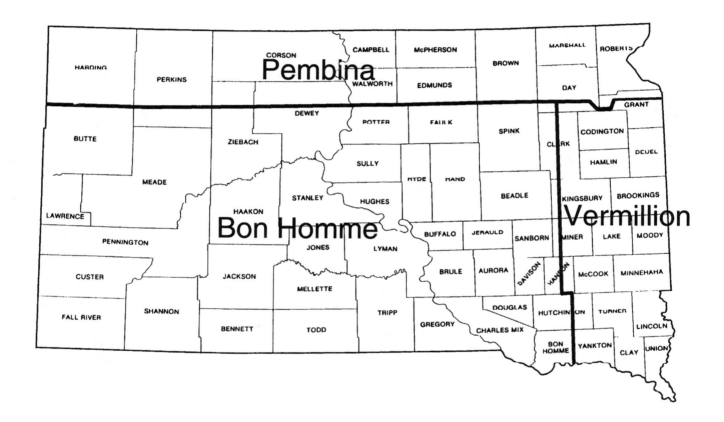

The Pembina land office opened 1 December 1870.
The Springfield land office opened 21 October 1870, then moved to Bon Homme nine
days later.

South Dakota 3
1872–1874

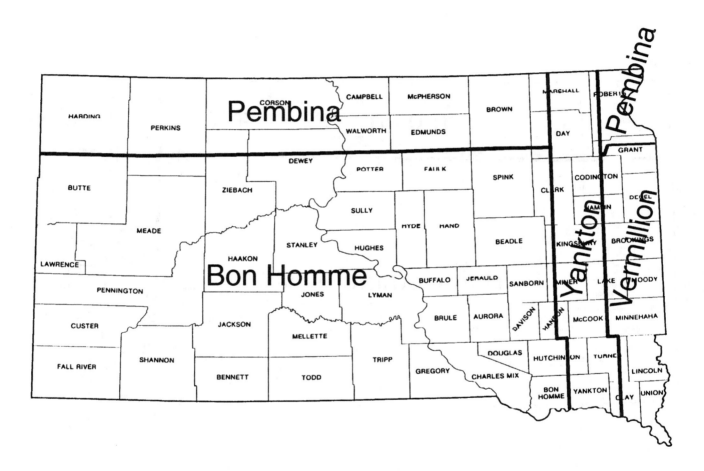

The Yankton land office opened 24 July 1872.
The Vermillion land office moved to Sioux Falls 9 June 1873.

South Dakota 4
1874–1877

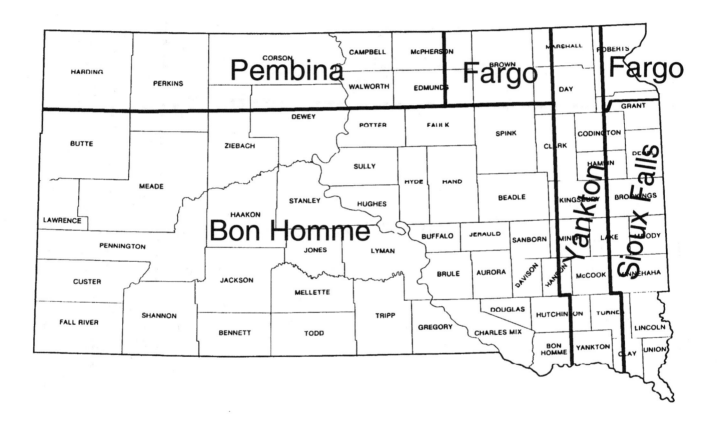

The Fargo, North Dakota, land office opened 1 September 1874.

South Dakota 5
1877–1879

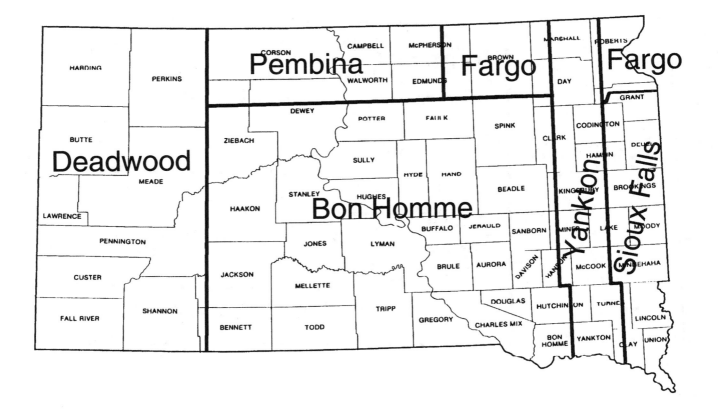

The Sheridan land office opened 22 May 1877, then moved to Deadwood 2 July 1877.

South Dakota 6
1879–1882

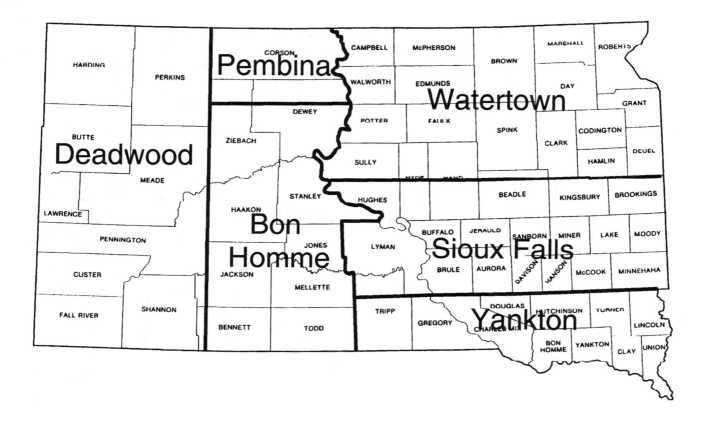

The Watertown land office opened 11 April 1879.

The Sioux Falls land office was redefined through an executive order of 5 April 1879, then moved to MItchell through an executive order of 14 July 1880.

The Yankton land office was redefined through an executive order of 5 April 1879.

South Dakota 7
1882–1890

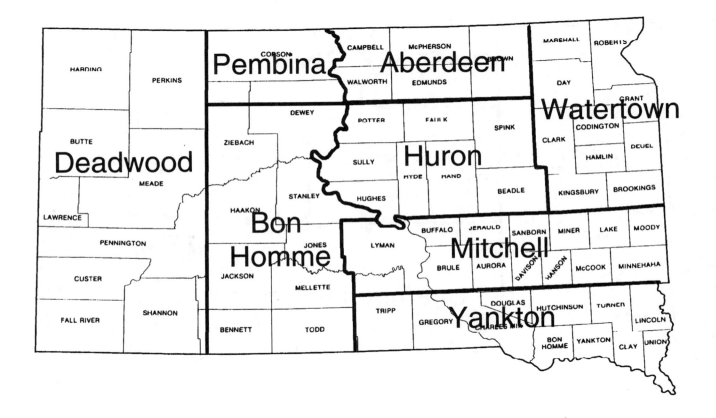

The Deadwood land office moved to Rapid City 29 January 1884.

The Aberdeen land office opened 2 October 1882.

The Huron land office opened 9 October 1882.

The Yankton land office moved to Huron through an executive order of 18 January 1883.

South Dakota 8
1890–1891

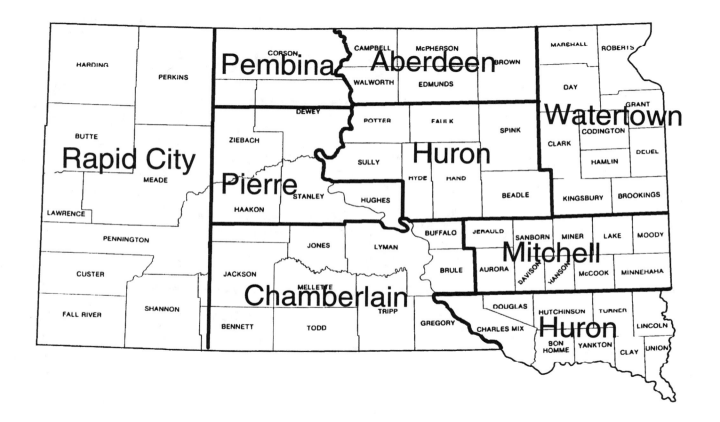

The Pierre land office opened 12 May 1890.
The Bon Homme land office moved to Chamberlain 3 April 1890.

South Dakota 9
1891–1893

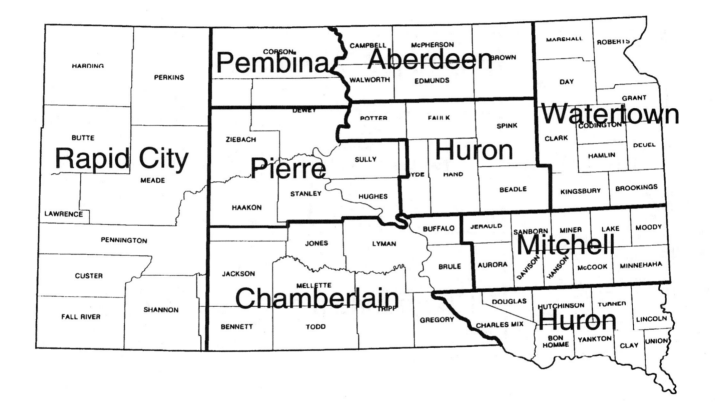

The Pierre land office expanded through an executive order of 23 May 1891.

South Dakota 10
1893–1907

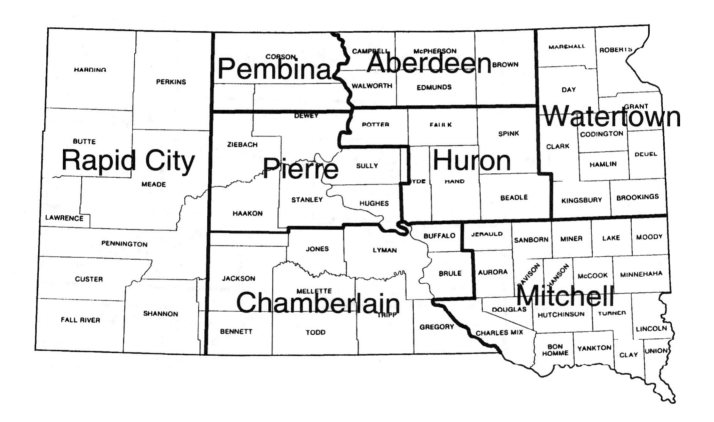

The southern jurisdiction of the Huron land office merged with Mitchell 11 September 1893.

South Dakota 11
1907–1909

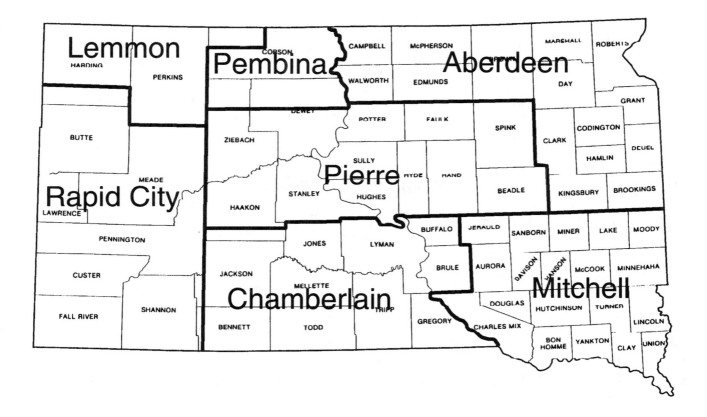

The Watertown land office merged with Aberdeen 1 May 1907.
The Lemmon land office opened 1 August 1908.
The Mitchell land office moved to Gregory 15 March 1909.

Utah 1
1868–1876

The Salt Lake City land office opened in 1868. Some earlier entries were recorded at Denver, Colorado.

Utah 2
1876–1877

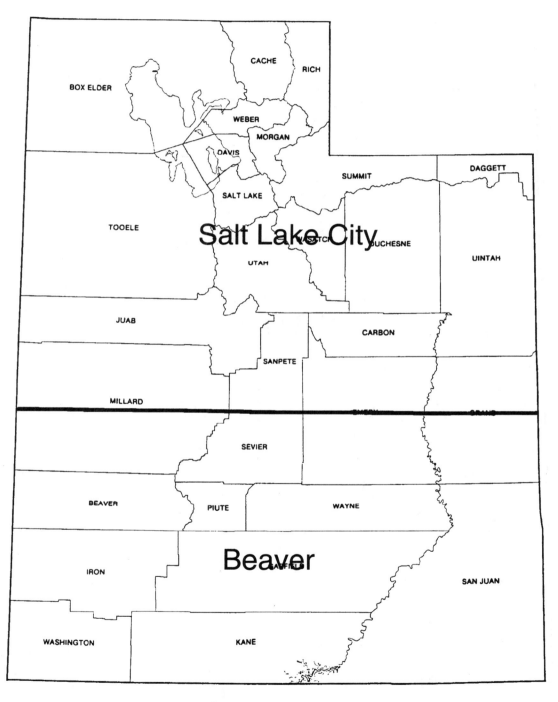

The Beaver land office opened 20 June 1876.

Utah 3
1877–1905

The Beaver land office merged with Salt Lake City August 1877.

Washington 1
1854–1871

The Olympia land office opened in 1854.
The Vancouver land office opened in 1860/61.

Washington 2
1871–1883

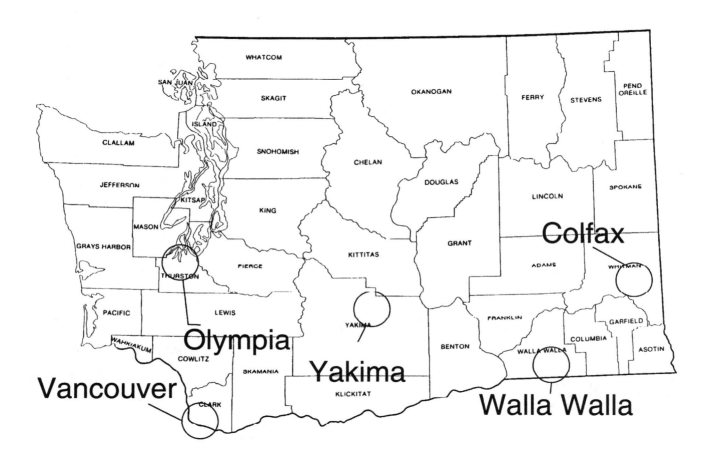

The Walla Walla land office opened in 1871.
The Colfax land office opened in 1876.
The Yakima land office opened in 1880.

Washington 3
1883–1890

The Spokane Falls land office opened in 1883.
The North Yakima land office opened in 1885.
The Seattle land office opened in 1887.
The New Olympia land office opened in 1890.
The Waterville land office opened in 1890.

Wisconsin 1
1834–1836

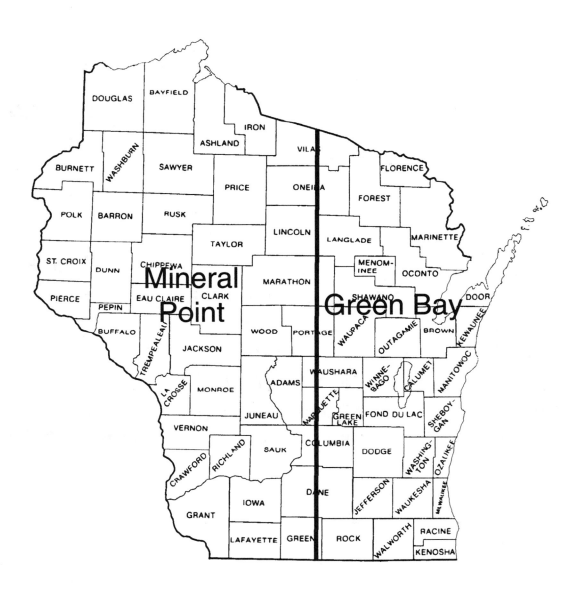

The Mineral Point land office opened 20 October 1834. It and the Green Bay land office were organized through the same act in 1934.

The Green Bay land office opened 3 July 1835.

Wisconsin 2
1836–1848

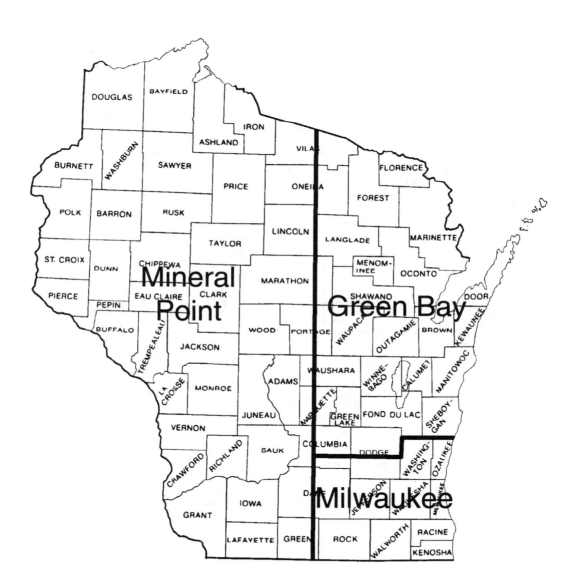

The Milwaukee land office opened 19 September 1836.

The Mineral Point land office moved to Muskoday through an executive order of 26 February 1841, then moved back to Mineral Point 8 May 1843.

Wisconsin 3
1848–1849

The Falls of St. Croix land office opened 7 April 1848.

Wisconsin 4
1849–1853

The Falls of St. Croix land office was redefined through an executive order of 2 March 1849 and was moved to Willow River. It was then moved to Hudson sometime before 1852.

Wisconsin 5
1853–1855

The Stevens Point land office opened 22 April 1853.
The La Crosse land office opened 2 May 1853.
The Green Bay land office moved to Menasha 14 July 1852.

Wisconsin 6
1855–1857

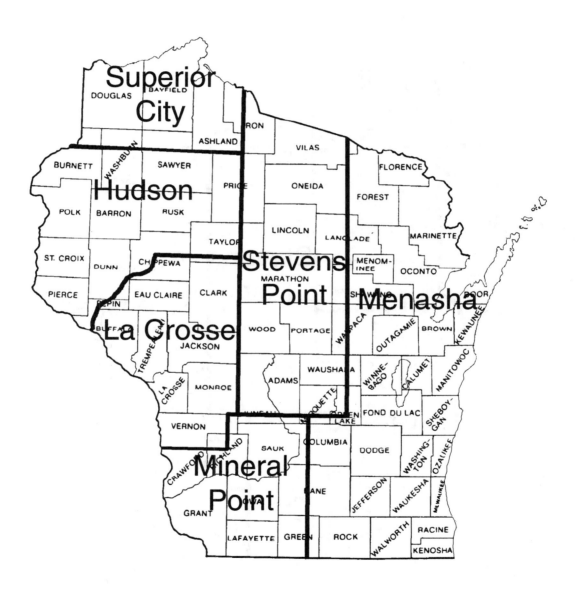

The Superior City land office opened 7 April 1855.
The Milwaukee land office merged with Menasha 12 November 1855.

Wisconsin 7
1857–1889

The Superior City land office moved to Bayfield 5 October 1860, then to Ashland through
   an executive order of 28 September 1886.

The Hudson land office moved to Falls of St. Croix in 1860.

The Eau Claire land office opened 1 July 1857.

The Stevens Point land office moved to Wausau 18 August 1872.

Wisconsin 8
1889–1899

The La Crosse land office merged with Eau Claire through an executive order of 19
   February 1889.

The Falls of St. Croix land office merged with Eau Claire through an executive order
   of 19 February 1889.

Wisconsin 9
1899–1905

The Menasha land office merged with Wausau through an executive order of 11 September 1899.

Wisconsin 10
1905–1919

The Eau Claire land office merged with Wausau 2 October 1905.
The Ashland land office merged with Wausau 2 October 1905.

Wyoming 1
1871–1875

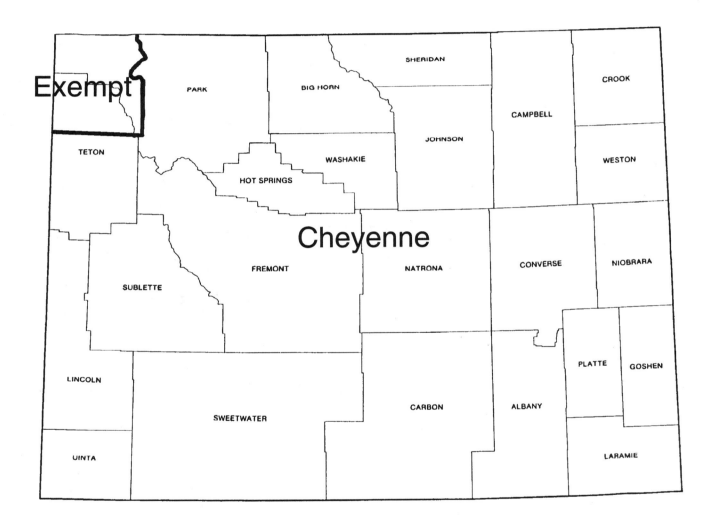

The Cheyenne land office opened in 1871.
Yellowstone, the nation's first national park, was exempt from land sales.

Wyoming 2
1875–1877

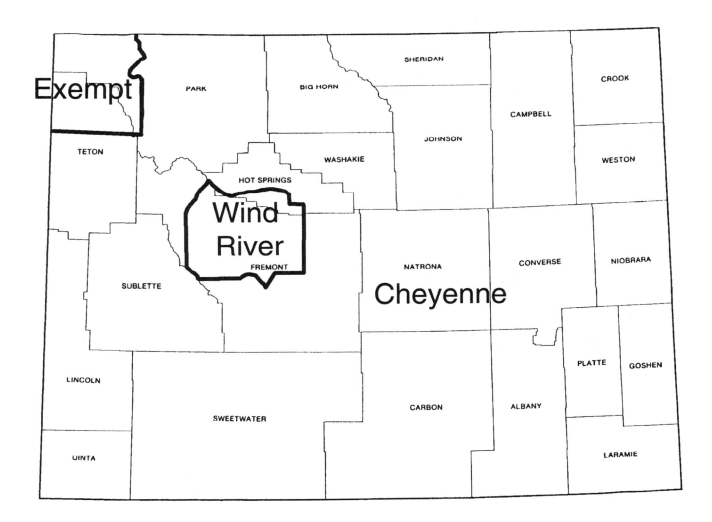

The Wind River land office opened in 1875.

Wyoming 3
1877–1888

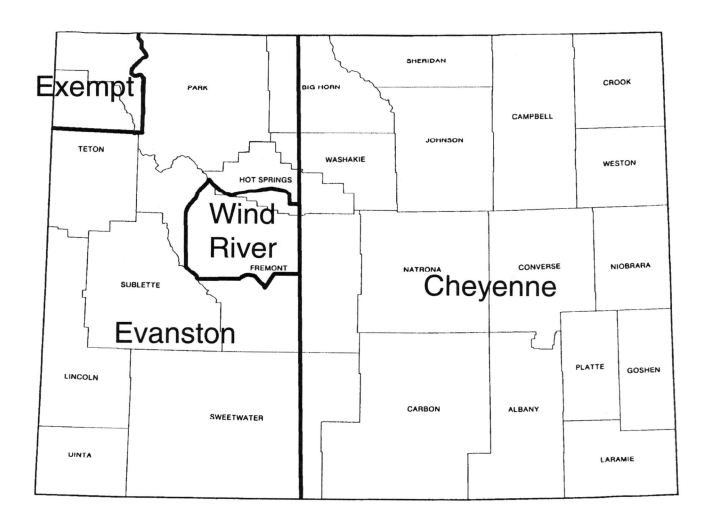

The Evanston land office opened 13 August 1877.

Wyoming 4
1888–1890

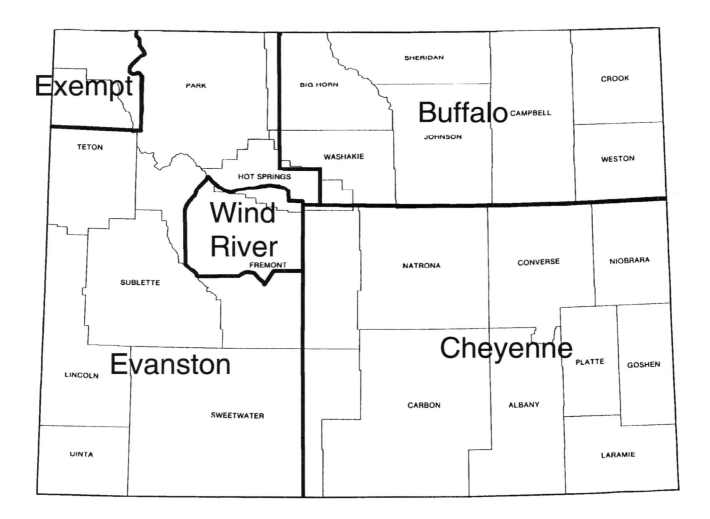

The Buffalo land office opened 1 May 1888.

Index

OTHER RESEARCH AIDS FROM ANCESTRY

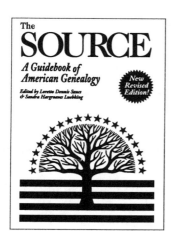

The Source: A Guidebook of American Genealogy (Revised Edition)

Edited by Sandra Hargreaves Luebking and Loretto Dennis Szucs

The Source remains the most complete genealogical reference book available today. New chapters, new editors, new content, updated sources—but the same comfort in using the industry's classic reference work. Each chapter is a book in its own right. This masterful book contains the contributions of an astonishing array of nationally known authors. *The Source* is a complete reference for anyone from the first-time hobbyist to the most experienced genealogical researcher.

$49⁹⁵ Ancestry Research Club $44.95
846 pages, 8½ by 11, hardbound

Ancestry's Red Book: American State, County, and Town Sources

Edited by Alice Eichholz, Ph.D., C.G.

Providing county and town listings within an overall state-by-state organization, *Ancestry's Red Book* is the result of the collective efforts of a host of professional researchers—all experts in their particular fields of research—and state archivists. This book contains information on the holdings of every county in the United States, providing a virtual what's what of genealogical resources in every state and the District of Columbia. *Ancestry's Red Book* also explains how too identify record jurisdictions. For example, jurisdictions in the Midwestern states are typically based in the counties, but in the New England states they are based primarily in the towns. This book sets the standard for resource identification.

$49⁹⁵ Ancestry Research Club $44.95
858 pages, 8¾ by 11, hardbound

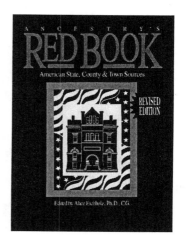

AVAILABLE SUMMER 1997

Printed Sources: A Guide to Published Genealogical Records

Edited by Kory Meyerink, AG, MLS

A major new guidebook that discusses all aspects of published genealogical sources, including CD-ROMs, *Printed Sources* describes nearly all published sources useful to genealogists. It explains how each type of source was created, how to use them, and where to find them. Includes bibliographies and groundbreaking studies of sources that lead to new understandings of their nature, scope, and use. Includes some topics never before discussed in genealogical literature. A comprehensive introduction is followed by twenty chapters discussing virtually every kind of published genealogical source.

$49⁹⁵ Ancestry Research Club $44.95
800 pages, 8½ by 11, hardbound

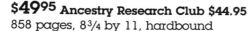

Call 1-800-Ancestry (262-3787) for more information

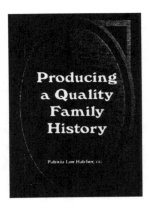

Producing a Quality Family History

By Patricia Law Hatcher

This book focuses on the process of assembling and printing a family history book. The author provides all the information you need for book production decisions—selecting type styles, grammar and punctuation, bibliography format, organization, incorporating photos and illustrations, and more.

$17⁹⁵ Ancestry Research Club $16.15
286 pages, 6 by 9, softbound

Turbo Genealogy: An Introduction to Family History Research in the Information Age

By John and Carolyn Cosgriff

Let *Turbo Genealogy* guide you into the information age. It's a handy guide to research methods for beginning genealogists. Investigative techniques and sources of information are covered, along with invaluable computer software and hardware pointers and up-to-date information on genealogical networking via computers.

$17⁹⁵ Ancestry Research Club $16.15
206 pages, 5½ by 8½, softbound

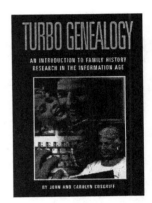

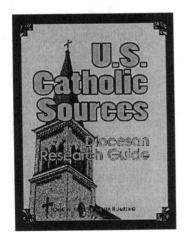

U.S. Catholic Sources: A Diocesan Research Guide

Compiled by Virginia Humling

Church records provide a primary resource for family history. Individuals with U.S. Roman Catholic ancestry will find this guide indispensable. While the parish remains the most fundamental unit for research, diocesan archives often contain copies of diocesan newspapers and records from closed parish churches. For every archdiocese and diocese in the United States, this guide identifies the records available and a contact person for each location. Additional libraries and societies with Catholic records are also included. *U.S. Catholic Sources* helps put Catholic church records to work for you.

$14⁹⁵ Ancestry Research Club $13.45
112 pages, 8½ by 11, softbound

They Came in Ships: A Guide to Finding Your Immigrant Ancestor's Arrival Record (Revised Edition)

By John Phillip Colletta

John Colletta not only tells you what you need to know to begin your search, but also suggests the most likely places to find that information. He explains the records, demonstrating in sample research scenarios how to use the available indexes and alternative resources to find the ship passenger list that lists your ancestor's name. The new edition provides more valuable clues and more useful tips than ever before. An entirely new chapter focuses on the challenge of searching for a ship when your ancestor arrived in a year that is not included in any National Archives index.

$9⁹⁵ Ancestry Research Club $8.95
108 pages, 5½ by 8½, softbound

Chicago and Cook County: A Guide to Research

By Loretto Dennis Szucs

Completely revised and updated, this book is a comprehensive guide to the vastly complex records in this major urban area. Because Chicago served as a springboard for millions of immigrants to the United States, there is a good chance you will find a Chicago ancestor in your family tree. The book covers virtually every genealogical source, from architectural history sources to vital records.

$19⁹⁵ Ancestry Research Club $17.95
528 pages, 5½ by 8½, softbound

Italian Genealogical Records: How to Use Italian Civil, Ecclesiastical, and Other Records in Family History Research

By Trafford Cole

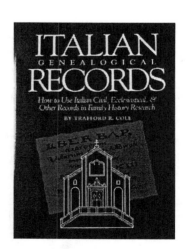

This comprehensive reference book covers Italian records in the extensive detail that only a genealogist of the author's experience could provide. Along with a detailed history of the development of centuries of Italian record keeping, this book will instruct you on the Italian records themselves—civil, ecclesiastical, notary, military, and more. This volume is rich in reproductions of typical records found in repositories throughout Italy, including a complete translation and thorough explanation of each. The author offers advice on how to approach Italian repositories and provides sample letters to help you obtain records through correspondence with a variety of sources.

$34⁹⁵ Ancestry Research Club $31.50
265 pages, 8½ by 11, hardbound

Your English Ancestry: A Guide for North Americans

By Sherry Irvine

Many books provide guidance on English research, but Irvine's is the first to provide a logical research routine for the family historian based in North America. Sherry Irvine not only tells you what records are available and which are most useful, but also provides excellent advice on how to access those records. The book discusses civil registration records, the census, lists and periodicals, church records, wills before and after 1858, civil records, and occupational records. Several appendices, an extensive reference list, and an address list make the book even more useful. This book will make English research easier and more efficient for any North American researcher.

$12⁹⁵ Ancestry Research Club $11.65
168 pages, 5½ by 8½, softbound

Your Scottish Ancestry: A Guide for North Americans

By Sherry Irvine

Your Scottish Ancestry explores the best ways for researchers anywhere in North America to approach Scottish family history research. This book will help you gain an understanding of how much you know now and what you need to know, what records are available and how they may be useful, and where you can find the information. It is a distillation of information about resources in North America and Scotland, combined with summaries and suggestions for thinking through just how you will get at them.

$17⁹⁵ Ancestry Research Club $16.15
267 pages, 5½ by 8½, softbound

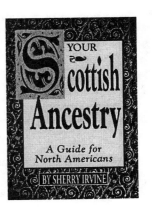

Other Books From Ancestry

Ancestry's Guide to Research: *Case Studies in American Genealogy*   364 pages, 5½ by 8½   **$19.95**

Ancestry's Concise Genealogical Dictionary
259 pages, 5½ by 8½   **$14.95**

Beyond Pedigrees
104 pages, 8½ by 11   **$12.95**

Celebrating the Family: *Steps to Planning a Family Reunion*
64 pages, 8½ by 11   **$9.95**

Writing the Family Narrative
157 pages, 5½ by 8½   **$12.95**

Writing the Family Narrative Workbook
168 pages, 8½ by 11   **$16.95**

Ellis Island: *Gateway to America*
32 pages, 5½ by 8½   **$2.95**

Pitfalls in Genealogical Research
74 pages, 5½ by 8½   **$7.95**

Searching on Location
112 pages, 5½ by 8½   **$8.95**

Plymouth Colony: *Its History and People, 1620-1691*
481 pages, 5½ by 8½   **$19.95**

A Preservation Guide: *Saving the Past and Present for the Future*   48 pages, 5½ by 8½   **$6.95**

From Memories to Manuscript: *The Five-Step Method of Writing Your Life Story* 40 pages, 7½ by 9   **$7.95**

Dear Diary
64 pages, 7½ by 9   **$8.95**

Photographing Your Heritage
128 pages, 5½ by 8½   **$10.95**

Unlocking the Secrets in Old Photographs
202 pages, 5½ by 8½   **$14.95**

Ancestry Magazine

If you're looking for expert guidance to help you succeed in tracing your family history, *Ancestry* is the magazine for you. Each issue of this colorful bimonthly magazine features:

• Articles by authors from around the world. They're full of useful tips, techniques, and little-known genealogical and historical resources

• Columns by eight of the nation's most respected genealogists, many of whom contributed to the popular PBS television series *Ancestors*

• An informative book announcement section to help you make the wisest use of your book-spending dollars

• A technology column, written by experts in the genealogical application of computers, that assists you in getting the maximum benefit from today's technological tools

• A case study, written by readers like you, detailing their solutions to interesting genealogical problems

Whether you are a beginning or advanced genealogist or family historian, *Ancestry* magazine's experts will help you find the best and easiest ways to pursue your family history.

One-year subscription
(6 issues) $21.00

Two-year subscription $38.00

Three-year subscription . . .$54.00

Single Issues $4.95

Genealogical Computing

A Quarterly Journal

Loaded with valuable articles, insightful reviews, and good advice, *Genealogical Computing* is the best quarterly in the field of technology and family history. Its award-winning quality has earned it a special position as the premier journal for computer-assisted research. **GC**'s combination of genealogical expertise and technical know-how keeps you informed on everything from genealogical CD-ROMs to the Internet. Catch regular columns from industry experts such as Art Rubeck, Joan Lowrey, and Candace Doriott. Benefit from our extensive annual directories, handy software tips, and much more! Use **GC** as your personal guide to the computerized pursuit of your ancestry.

One-year subscription
(4 issues) $25.00

Two-year subscription $45.00

Three-year subscription . . .$60.00

Single Issues $8.50

Call 1-800-Ancestry (262-3787) for more information